Seeing Through the Eyes
of the Polish Revolution

Historical Materialism Book Series

The Historical Materialism Book Series is a major publishing initiative of the radical left. The capitalist crisis of the twenty-first century has been met by a resurgence of interest in critical Marxist theory. At the same time, the publishing institutions committed to Marxism have contracted markedly since the high point of the 1970s. The Historical Materialism Book Series is dedicated to addressing this situation by making available important works of Marxist theory. The aim of the series is to publish important theoretical contributions as the basis for vigorous intellectual debate and exchange on the left.

The peer-reviewed series publishes original monographs, translated texts, and reprints of classics across the bounds of academic disciplinary agendas and across the divisions of the left. The series is particularly concerned to encourage the internationalization of Marxist debate and aims to translate significant studies from beyond the English-speaking world.

For a full list of titles in the Historical Materialism Book Series available in paperback from Haymarket Books, visit:
www.haymarketbooks.org/category/hm-series

Seeing Through the Eyes of the Polish Revolution

Solidarity and the Struggle Against Communism in Poland

Jack M. Bloom

Haymarket Books
Chicago, IL

First published in 2013 by Brill Academic Publishers, The Netherlands
© 2013 Koninklijke Brill NV, Leiden, The Netherlands

Published in paperback in 2014 by
Haymarket Books
P.O. Box 180165
Chicago, IL 60618
773-583-7884
www.haymarketbooks.org

ISBN: 978-1-60846-376-3

Trade distribution:
In the US, Consortium Book Sales, www.cbsd.com
In Canada, Publishers Group Canada, www.pgcbooks.ca
In the UK, Turnaround Publisher Services, www.turnaround-psl.com
In Australia, Palgrave Macmillan, www.palgravemacmillan.com.au
In all other countries, Publishers Group Worldwide, www.pgw.com

Cover design by Ragina Johnson.

This book was published with the generous support of
Lannan Foundation and the Wallace Global Fund.

Library of Congress Cataloging-in-Publication data is available.

To Joanna – A Treasure I Was Not Supposed to Find
and
To Anna – The Treasure She Gave Me

Contents

Acknowledgments

Anyone who writes a book usually has a big debt to many people who helped in many ways. In my case, for this book, the debt is more far-reaching than usual, and I will attempt to clarify it here. To begin, I want to thank Indiana University and the Polish Studies Center at IU Bloomington, and the Russian and East European Institute, also at IU Bloomington, for the support they have given me in this project. The Polish Studies Center chose to send me three times on the exchange-programme with Warsaw University. The first, in 1986, was a get-acquainted trip, which made my decision to begin the programme of research that resulted in this book. Jack Bielasiak, who was director of the PSC at the time, was supportive of my efforts to reach beyond my own field of study and to become acquainted with one that was entirely different. This book would not exist but for the aid given me by these institutions, and I am grateful for it.

When I first got the news that I had been chosen for the exchange-programme, I decided that I needed to get some contacts who could help me meet people in Poland. David Finkel vouched for me and put me in contact with Jane Dobija, a Polish-American woman who had gone to Poland because of Solidarity and who had made extensive contacts there. (Jane later became the NPR correspondent for Poland, for a time.) Jane kindly gave me letters of introduction to Wojciech Adamiecki in Warsaw and to Krzysztof Kasprzyk in Kraków, both independent journalists. They, in turn, introduced me to several people – such that by the time I left after five weeks there, I realised that I had good enough contacts to be able to speak with anyone in the opposition whom I chose. It seemed an opportunity from which I could not walk away.

In subsequent visits, both Adamiecki and Kasprzyk helped me continue to make connections. Kasprzyk introduced me to Maciek Szumowski, who took a liking to me; he, in turn, passed me on to Tadeusz Pikulicki, who knew everyone in the opposition in Kraków, and who went out of his way to connect me to these people and to persuade them to talk to me, and who became a good friend of mine. Through this nexus, I not only met the opposition in that city, but also leaders of the reform-movement within the Communist Party, which included Szumowski, Kasprzyk and several others. Kasprzyk later came to the US and stayed with me for a while as he was reconstructing his life. We became good friends.

Adamiecki made connections for me in Wroclaw with Barbara Labuda, who was not in Wrocław when I visited, but who made the crucial connections for me there. Later, I contacted Jan Lityński, who helped me a great deal, and who gave me a crucial connection in Gdańsk to Joanna Wojciechowicz, who connected me with virtually everyone I spoke with there. Adamiecki also gave me a connection with Jarosław Szczepański, who arranged for me to stay in Jastrzębie with Joanna Latoch and her family. She arranged for a translator and set up my interviews. That was a particularly important connection for me as Joanna later became my wife (and translator). Adamiecki furthermore gave me contacts in the US and Canada with key oppositionists who were then in exile. He also helped sustain me when I was in Warsaw. In Warsaw, Witold Morawski provided me with an academic connection to the sociology department at Warsaw University. He also befriended me, encouraged me in my work and read an early version of this manuscript. Similarly, Jadwiga Koralewicz and Edmund Wnuk-Lipiński took an interest in my work and provided me with encouragement and advice.

Beyond those people who were essential to this project were my friends and colleagues who encouraged me. Bert Useem supported the idea of my taking on this entirely new project; his friendship and our debates concerning the world have helped sustain me during a lengthy period. R. Stephen Warner, who I first got to know when we were graduate students at Berkeley, became a good friend for decades. I have thanked him for his help on many projects; he also helped sustain me in this one – and he played a special role in helping my then-fiancée, Joanna, and me get together. When I was in Greece and she in Poland and I could not connect with her, I phoned Steve and asked him to convey a message to her for me (she at first thought it was a hoax).

My thanks go to each of the people whom I interviewed, including those who were not quoted in the text. Many of them granted me large blocks of time, and some of them became my friends, including Wojciech Adamiecki, Krzysztof Kasprzyk, Tadeusz and Elka Pikulicki, Maciek Szumowski and Dorota Terakowska, Ryszard and Zosia Sawicki and Aleksander Krystosiak.

A special thank you to Zdzisław Belina for his hospitality and help arranging an important connection. Traveling with a toddler is not an easy feat, and working can be even harder, therefore a big thank you to Agnieszka Fabiszewska for her care for Anna during the long hours some of the interviews required.

In addition, there are others who helped me in various ways. Thanks to Anne Koehler, who runs the inter-library-loan desk at Indiana University Northwest and who always got me virtually everything I asked of her. I am grateful (there is no other way to put it) to Jackie Coven, one of IUN's wonderful team of technicians; Jackie resolved for me too many word-processing problems to count, as this manuscript began in Word Perfect and later migrated through at least three versions of Word, each creating some difficult-to-handle problems of formatting. She even took my problems home and invited me in as she helped me. And Carol Wood generously shared her knowledge of computers to come to my aid time and again. Mark Uncapher guided me to buy several generations of laptops. It is hard to see how I could have finished this product without their aid. For Brill, this manuscript had to be translated from American-English to British-English and to be formatted in precise ways that their house-style requires. Fortunately for me, my wife Joanna did this job for me, while I fussed with finalising the manuscript. She also did considerable translating for me during my later interviews and found and translated texts for me that contributed to the manuscript.

Parts of Chapter Nine and 'Researching the Polish Revolution' appeared in *The Oral History Review* in 2006, under the title 'The Solidarity Revolution in Poland, 1980–1981' (Volume 33, Number 1, pp. 33–64). A version of Chapter Four appeared originally in Barbara Wejnert's 2002 edited book entitled *Transition to Democracy in Eastern Europe and Russia: Impact on Politics, Economy and Culture*, under the title 'A Line of Blood: How December 1970 prepared Polish Workers for Political Transition in 1989'.

Introduction

In August 1980, Polish workers went on strike, demanding a union independent of the government, with the legal right to strike – something that had never before existed in the Soviet bloc. Their victory presaged a revolutionary upheaval that transformed Polish society and played a central role in the demise of the Soviet Union. They called their union *Solidarność* – Solidarity. It is ironic that a government that claimed to rule in the name of the working class precipitated what may have been the largest workers' opposition movement in history, encompassing most of the nation. At its height, the union had some 10 million members in a nation of 36 million, and it engendered social movements and organisations of farmers, students and others. Beyond the Communist Party leaders and loyalists, people in coveted social positions, professional soldiers and many but not all of the police, almost all Poles identified and sympathised with Solidarity, including a huge section of the Communist Party. (Even some of Solidarity's opponents in the secret police grew to have a grudging respect for what it stood for and the integrity of its activists). But despite the fact that the movement encompassed virtually the entire working class, it has rarely been examined from a class-perspective (with the significant exceptions of Lawrence Goodwyn and Roman Laba).[1] Much more frequent have been claims that this movement was led by intellectuals or by the Catholic Church.

---

1. Goodwyn 1991; Laba 1986 and 1991.

The movement certainly took the *form* of class conflict, with workers fighting against a regime that created what appeared to be a privileged class that monopolised political power and absorbed much of the wealth the workers produced. But inescapably, Poland's economy was forced to bend to the whims of the Soviet Union, thereby often producing shortages even of inferior quality consumer goods, not to mention quality items.[2] Solidarity's adherents felt that the system did not work, was unfair, and did not benefit the vast majority. They greatly desired independence from the Soviet Union. Poles held a deep and abiding sense that they were oppressed by an external imperial power. So, their movement embodied both class and national grievances. During my first visit to Poland, I was told a joke that illustrated just how unwelcome the Soviets were:

> Question: Surrounded by Russians and Germans, whom do you kill first?
> Answer: Germans – business before pleasure.

By 1980, people knew quite well how backward the Soviet bloc's economy and technology were, and how low their standard of living was by comparison with the West – and they resented it. Janusz Pałubicki, the Poznań region's Solidarity leader, described how national oppression shaped people's attitudes toward Solidarity:

> People felt that to be a good Pole you had to belong to Solidarity. If someone
> did not join, he was looked upon as a *beton*[3] *who supported the Soviet Union.*
> *That person was seen as a possible traitor.*

Therefore, even though the conflict *appeared* as a class struggle, people felt they were fighting both for independence and against exploitation, that independence was necessary in order to be able to resolve the injustices they felt they suffered.[4] In a sense, class and national oppression were intertwined and indivisible: as was widely recognised, Poland's class system – and that of the entire Soviet bloc – was imposed and retained by the Soviet Union. Soviet interventions in Hungary in 1956 and Czechoslovakia in 1968 made clear that there was no choice. As in those nations, the Polish regime also existed only because of the presence of the Soviet army, whose military bases were scattered throughout the country, and whose policies were imported wholesale, without regard for Poles' preferences. It all meant that airing class grievances, or challenging the system that created

---

2. I can well recall expressing my frustration about the way the telephones worked to Eugeniusz Szumiejko, then a leader of the Solidarity underground in Wrocław, exclaiming: 'Polish telephones!' For which Szumiejko immediately admonished me, saying: '*Communist* telephones!' This clearly demonstrated how he viewed the issue.
3. Literally, a cement-head. The term referred to hard-line Communists.
4. Ost 2005.

and retained them, implied opposition to Soviet dominance, when such a challenge could be dangerous to the entire Polish nation. This danger, and how to handle it, became a matter of significant disagreement within the opposition that emerged in the 1980s.

How did this movement appear with such strength? Indeed, how had an opposition become possible in Communist Poland? What had changed in the country (and in the world) to enable it to succeed? What were the processes through which it emerged? Who organised it, and who led it? How did it confront the government? What difference did it make to the lives of its participants and to the lives of Poles generally? What was the impact of this movement on the Party and its members? How did the Party/state respond to it? How did its response affect the union's members and the internal life of the union movement? After a difficult 16 months, the authorities finally felt strong enough to declare martial law, to detain thousands of the movement's activists, and to suspend and later outlaw the union. How did the Party come to this position? Having come close to decapitation, how did the opposition survive and rebuild itself? How did it ultimately prevail? Perhaps most importantly, how did people on all sides perceive these events, and how did their perceptions affect their behaviour? This book seeks to answer these questions.

This account of the development of opposition to Communist rule in Poland is distinguished from others in its focus on the experiences and perceptions of the people who participated in these events as presented through *their* voices, as *they* explain here what they saw happen around them, the role they played, and how they understood these events. I travelled around the country, starting in 1986, interviewing people about these matters, and I supplemented these interviews by meeting with people who were in exile. While it was not my original intention to rely so heavily on their own words, I found that I learned a great deal from these people. They were so eloquent that I came to feel that, as much as possible, others should hear their stories directly from them. In this book, then, you will learn of their experiences in their own words. Their accounts – personal, direct and based on their own experiences – are often riveting; they clarify the meaning of broad historical events as they affected the lives, experiences and thoughts of these individuals, and those of the collectivities in which they took part, as well as the conclusions they drew from those experiences. By showing how they reacted to the circumstances that confronted them, we can see how they made history, and why they took the directions they did.

In these interviews, I pursued my subject's life histories, probing to learn how their individual biographies were affected by history, and how they in turn acted to change history. People live their lives in history and they are deeply affected by that history – whether they are aware of it or not. Of course, their lives are filled with contingencies that may appear irrelevant to the broad course of history. But in one way or another, their lives are shaped by and provide reflections of that history. At various times, history makes available greater or lesser opportunities for people to affect what happens around them. When they do so, they become history-makers, whether or not they are so recognised or perceive themselves as such. One of the great values of examining a major social movement like that which produced Solidarity is that it allows us to see people in the process of making history by changing the world around them. We can see what they do and why they do it: what alternatives they see available, and how their actions reflect these perceptions. Such a movement, by challenging the normal ways a society functions, reveals much about broad social trends that is normally hidden.

Moreover, by looking at a large swathe of history – in this case, the entire period of Communist rule in Poland – we can see how historical patterns develop, how historical lessons are drawn and become part of people's lives and their understanding of these lives. We can see how the Solidarity generation – largely the post war generation – was formed and what were its formative experiences.

Who done it?[5]

There has been considerable controversy concerning who (sociologically speaking) organised and led this movement. The first histories of Solidarity argued strongly that the workers were organised and led by intellectuals,[6] especially through an organisation of dissident intellectuals whose Polish acronym was KOR [*Komitet Obrony Robotnika* = Workers' Defence Committee]. KOR was formed in 1976 by long-time dissident intellectuals in Warsaw in response to repression visited upon workers who came out into the streets to protest against price increases, especially for food. Later studies argued that the role of the intellectuals in creating and leading this workers' movement was exaggerated, namely, that the workers had been responsible for the strike that won Solidarity, and for the tactics and strategies that it employed.[7] There has also been debate about the debate.[8]

Jan Lipski, one of the founding members of KOR, and its first historian, argued that KOR played the leading role in Solidarity's formation: 'KOR familiarised workers with the idea of the strike...[and] indicated the possibility of strike

5. This term was first used, as shown here, by Kubik 1994b.
6. Kolakowski 1983; Pelczynski 1988; Touraine 1983; Bromke 1983; Potel 1982; Ash 1985; Lipski 1985; Bernhard 1993.
7. Especially Goodwyn 1991; Laba 1986; and Laba 1991.
8. For example, Tymowski 1991, pp. 157–75; Kubik 1994b; Kuczynski 1988, p. 136.

demands that would go beyond economic issues'.[9] Mieczysław Rakowski, the last General Secretary of the Polish United Workers' Party and the last Communist Prime Minister of Poland, agreed:

> KOR was the organiser of the Free Trade Unions in the second half of the 1970s. I think that without KOR, the opposition in Poland was not possible. In this sense, Jacek Kuroń, Adam Michnik, Karol Modzelewski, and some others played a huge role.[10]

I pressed him further: was he saying that KOR acted like a vanguard party? 'Yes, no doubt. They were pupils of this system, where organising is treated as the most important factor in social and political life, going back to Lenin. Most of them were sons of pre-war Communists'. When I asked him what role he felt that KOR played in creating the workers' opposition, he responded with certainty:

> A huge role, no doubt. KOR was the organiser of the free trade-unions in the second half of the 1970s. People who were members of KOR or co-operated with them were the organisers of this opposition, no doubt. In the end of the 1970s and the beginning of the 1980s, KOR people published a lot of pamphlets and were very active. I think without KOR, the opposition in Poland was not possible.[11]

Many historians and journalists have also viewed KOR as functioning like a Leninist party, leading the workers.[12] Several people with whom I spoke were critical of KOR because they also felt that its members were really Communists.

This viewpoint was challenged, first by David Ost and later by Lawrence Goodwyn and Roman Laba, who argued that the workers led, organised and created *Solidarność* independently of, and at times against, the importuning of the intellectuals.[13] Laba said: 'Solidarity demonstrated that ordinary people such as workers were ... capable of coherent political activity without consciousness-raising or leadership by elites'.[14] He demonstrated that during strikes in 1970 and thereafter, workers originated the central demand of Solidarity: a union independent of the ruling party. At that time, the Party proposed, instead, that they take over the existing unions – in its words, *'to renew'* them. Some workers followed that course, only to find that as the mass movement that had brought them to positions of authority ebbed, repression of the new leaders rendered their efforts

---

9. Lipski 1985, p. 424.
10. Kuroń and Michnik were important intellectual supporters of Solidarity, and Modzelewski, also a well-known dissident intellectual, was a Solidarity leader. All were well-known in their own right both in Poland and abroad.
11. See also Staniszkis 1984, p. 123.
12. See, for example, Goodwyn 1991.
13. Ost 1990; Goodwyn 1991; Laba 1986 and 1997.
14. Laba 1997.

impotent and their persons subject to physical and legal attacks. While questions have been raised about Laba's interpretation,[15] such demands certainly did exist then.

Workers and KOR activists have also debated KOR's centrality to the movement. Leading worker activists in Gdańsk – like Alina Pieńkowska and Anna Walentynowicz – gave KOR considerable credit, while Bogdan Borusewicz, who was active both in KOR and in the Gdańsk Solidarity leadership, was more cautious about KOR's role:

> The *idea* of the occupation of the factories came from the free trade-union... I didn't organise the free trade-unions on the instructions of KOR, but there were those initiatives coming from the *base*... I don't think the results of the latest events were exclusively the work of KOR. It was also based on the immense social discontent that had been growing for years.

Borusewicz did not denigrate KOR's role: 'The peaceful development of the strike – that's due to KOR'.[16]

The truth is more complex than either of these paradigms suggest. Intellectuals and workers eventually came to nourish and aid one another, as a result of a lengthy, inter-generational, experiential process during which each learned some painful lessons, and both ultimately grew stronger from this co-operation. Intellectuals provided media that workers used and helped put groups in touch with one another; their publications also provided a certain amount of protection for the workers (see Chapter Six). But there is little doubt that workers themselves were the creators of Solidarity. (Ost noted that Adam Michnik, one of KOR's, and Poland's, leading intellectuals, stated that 'Solidarity arose, without us and against us, although we always considered it to be [KOR's] child. An illegitimate one, you might say').[17]

KOR emerged, at least in part, out of the experiences that students had in their revolt in 1968 (see Chapter Three), the repression they encountered, and their perceived isolation from the working class, which did not come to their aid at that time. Solidarity arose from the lessons workers drew from their experiences with the worker rebellions that periodically broke the surface in Poland. Each of the worker upheavals was stimulated by failures of the nation's economy: all of them – in 1956, 1970, 1976 and 1980 – were responses to significant food price increases on a population that spent most of its income on food. The inflation resulted from broader failures in the economy that forced the government to

---

15. Bernhard 1991.
16. Anonymous 1980, p. 14.
17. Ost, cited in Tymowski 1990, p. 165.

seek to lower the standard of living of the broad mass of the population (see Chapter One).

The emergence of Solidarity was thus the result of people reacting to, and learning from, these individual economic crises, the political breakdowns they occasioned, and the workers', intellectuals' and government's responses to these events and to one another's actions. A well-known Polish political cartoonist named Andrzej Mleczko produced a cartoon of a skier doing the slalom. Each of the flags he must pass bears a date: 1956, 1968, 1970, 1976 and 1980: the years of social upheavals in Poland. Because of these experiences, by 1980 workers knew what they had to do to succeed.

The development of opposition in Communist Poland

Opposition began almost as soon as the Communist regime was put into power on the shoulders of the Soviet army. Despite her occupation by both the Germans and the Soviets, Poland fielded the fourth largest army in the war against Nazi Germany – an underground army, and soon after the war ended, units of that army pivoted to fight the new unwelcome Communist government. Later, farmers fought to prevent the government from repossessing and collectivising the land they had been granted by that same government after the German army fled. From the start, the Church insisted on maintaining its independence from, and its relevance to, the Polish people and nation. All of these preceded and helped to create a context for the conflicts that emerged and ultimately gave birth to the opposition.

These three earliest struggles against Soviet-imposed Communism helped to lay the foundation for the opposition that created Solidarity. The civil war was first an act of resistance to the regime that was being imposed upon Poland despite the efforts of the AK [*Armia Krajowa* = Home Army], the non-Communist resistance to the German occupation, and of the underground government, based in London, that had functioned throughout the war. The war alerted the population, and the Soviets, to the fact that there was resistance. Many AK partisans were imprisoned or suffered other repression for their resistance to the Communist regime. Many of these warriors remained in contact with one another, and they served as one of the grapevines through which events were analysed and along which information was passed.

The ability of the peasants to retain control of their land – unique in the Soviet empire – became crucial when these same peasants brought food to the strikers occupying the shipyards and other factories in 1980. This gift enabled the workers to out-wait the authorities, who were stalling in an effort to avoid making the concessions that the workers were demanding. Later, Solidarity showed its appreciation to these farmers by helping them create their own Rural Solidarity.

The struggles of the Church for independence of government control were important in several ways. After 1956, the Church won the right to have independent publications and to create the Clubs of Catholic Intellectuals [*Klub Inteligencji Katolickiej* = KIK], where people could come together to freely discuss various issues of concern to them. That was one area where a certain degree of freedom became protected. In the 1960s, the Church fought with the government about how the millennium of both the foundation of the Polish state and of the Polish Church would be celebrated – whether it would be merely a secular or a more inclusive celebration. When Cardinal Karol Wojtyła became Pope, he encouraged independent activity and later he supported Solidarity. While important elements within the Polish Church's hierarchy were not so supportive, strata of priests were more supportive and they pushed back. During martial law, churches became the one place where people could meet, discuss and organise. It is not surprising that in this dark and difficult period, many people came to the Church, even if they were non-believers, as the Church was seen once again as the embodiment of the nation. The murder of an openly oppositionist priest galvanised the opposition and began to turn the tide against the government.

The first major open revolt, in 1956, was carried out in the western city of Poznań by people who had survived World War II and who had been a long-time community, which had developed a cohesiveness that workers in other cities (many of whom were newcomers to the areas in which they lived and worked) still lacked. These workers responded to food-price rises with strikes and a rally that devolved into an attack on the prison that freed the prisoners, and on the Polish United Workers' Party headquarters, as well as a shoot-out with the secret-police. But when they were on the streets, anyone could join in, including provocateurs and people with agendas that diverged from those of the organisers. In response to the revolt, the military was brought in, the government repressed the insurrectionists, and such violence was never repeated in Poland.

Later that year, a broader workers' revolt, centred in Warsaw, succeeded in removing the Communist Party leadership and replacing it with a more popular team, who were at first unwanted by the Soviet rulers. The workers who led that movement stood on the shoulders of the Poznań activists whose revolt had already shaken the government. They had spoken with activists in Poznań and learned the lessons of their defeat: as a result, they remained inside their factories and used them as their base as they sought to maintain an independent presence through the workers' councils which they had created. Through this means, they helped to bring down the government and ease the burden of Soviet control. But in the long run, the new administration co-opted the councils and rendered them ineffective. While never as oppressive or craven toward the Soviet Union as the previous regime had been, the new government still stifled the self-activity of the workers. The lesson was that independent organisation was necessary. Unfortunately, it was a lesson that had to be re-learned (see Chapter Two).

It was another dozen years before Poland's apparently calm surface was again pierced, this time by a student upheaval in 1968. This new flaring of opposition was preceded by a lengthy period of economic stagnation that resulted in few opportunities for advancement for the new generation that was then coming of age. Peaceful demonstrations by Warsaw students were met with violence and an anti-Semitic campaign that blamed the unrest on the Polish Jews who had survived the Holocaust. That shameful episode drove out most of the Jews who remained in Poland and it alienated non-Jews, some of whom likened the government's actions to those of the Nazis. While the emphasis by historians and journalists has been on the *separation* between workers and students in 1968, the divisions between them were not as great as the consensus might suggest. Although many of the students did feel that they had been abandoned by the workers, a large number of workers were moved by and supported the students' actions – a fact not widely recognised, but it was important for its future effects. Later that year, the invasion of Hungary, in which Polish armed forces participated, also deeply shamed many Poles (see Chapter Three).

In December 1970, shipyard workers on the Baltic Coast responded to food price increases with attacks on political targets, including the Communist Party headquarters. The reaction in 1970 was much more brutal than that which the students had faced in 1968: deadly force was used, a disputed number was killed, and many more were injured. Students and intellectuals remained quiet as these events unfolded, thereby emphasising how isolated each of these communities was from public support and from one another. These killings were justified to the rest of the country and to the police and soldiers, who had been brought from elsewhere to fire upon the workers, by the supposed participation in and direction of the protests by Germans, most of whom had been removed from the coastal areas after the war. But over time, the truth about what had happened seeped into the rest of the country (see Chapter Four).

Taken together, the events of 1968 and of 1970 lost the regime the loyalty and support of virtually the whole of the new generation. After that time, very few people who joined the Party, the government or its military and police did so out of ideological agreement. Most did so to advance their own interests.

Those events suggested the importance of overcoming the isolation between workers and intellectuals for anyone who wished to make changes, and of learning the lessons of the past. The coastal workers learned to stay together in their workplaces where they were not so vulnerable, rather than going into the streets to march to government or Party centres. In 1970, they experimented with inter-factory strike committees that united all workers in a region. The result of this catastrophe – as the military and police opened fire on the workers that the government claimed to represent – was that the government fell, as in 1956. It was replaced by one that promised that deadly force would never again be used to settle internal disputes, and that it would improve living standards.

Soon, life did get easier. Yet no-one knew if the promise not to kill those who openly dissented would be kept. So, for the most part, people kept their heads down, although some workers secretly – and very carefully – organised for the next time. Some of these workers sought out participants in the 1956 events to learn their lessons.[18]

Poland was affected by world trends, and in a world recession during the mid-1970s, economic plans again went awry and food prices were again abruptly raised. Once more workers responded by going into the streets, mainly in areas that had not been so troublesome before. As in the past, they encountered repression and reprisal. Although the government cracked down hard, it did keep its promise to refrain from the use of deadly force. That response made open opposition once again a possibility, and people did not wait before acting on that possibility. Before long, experienced intellectual dissidents in Warsaw created KOR to aid those workers and to try to bring the two communities together. Meanwhile, workers continued to organise themselves in isolated groupings, unaware of one another. KOR helped to connect them. (Chapter Five examines the emergence of opposition, some of it open, in the 1970s).

To summarise this discussion about who led Solidarity: to say simply that intellectuals led the workers in 1980 is to give short shrift to the process that characterised this lengthy period. Many of the 1980 shipyard strike leaders, including Lech Wałęsa, had been in positions of secondary leadership in 1970, and they applied the lessons they learned from that time independently. Other workers away from the coast had also learned lessons from 1970; they worried about a repetition of the killings if the shipyard workers remained isolated, and in 1980 they acted to make sure that would not happen. They did so by carrying out occupation strikes and, in some cases, joining the ports in creating inter-factory strike committees that knit together a whole city or region.

Cutting across the worker/intellectual debate has been the argument that the Catholic Church created the conditions for and/or led this movement.[19] Maryjane Osa has argued that the Church's resistance to the Communist regime created the framework within which the opposition emerged. The Church managed to institutionalise its independence, while all other independent movements failed.

18. See Laba 1986, pp. 63–4 for elaboration on this point.
19. Ekiert 1991; Ash 1990; Bernstein and Politi 1996; Kwitny 1997; Osa 1997.

It provided an umbrella for some independent public expression.[20] Osa notes that the Church and the government sparred over how the thousandth anniversary of the founding of the Polish nation, and of the Polish Church, should be celebrated in 1966: whether as a secular or a sacred event. She contends that 'religious authorities prevented the Communists from defining Poland's millennium in strictly secular terms... Church leaders emphasised the primacy of the Catholic faith in the history of the nation'.[21] Through these efforts, she says, the Church nurtured an opposition culture out of which the upheaval that created Solidarity arose. The Church certainly did wage its own battles for independence and its culture wars, and it did protect dissidents, but none of the Solidarity leaders and activists that I interviewed traced their influence back to the Church, although many were grateful for the support it had given them. In Chapter Six, I discuss this issue further.

How Solidarity was won

My research provides a new perception with regard to how Solidarity's right to exist within a legal framework was won. The general understanding has been that the union was born entirely on the Baltic coast, centred in the shipyards in the cities of Gdańsk, Gdynia and Szczecin. That is why Laba and Goodwyn focused exclusively on those areas in their books, as did Neal Ascherson and Timothy Garton Ash when discussing the strikes and the settlement that produced the accords between the Baltic strikers and the government.[22]

There is no doubt that the strikes – both in 1970 and 1980 – originated in that coastal region. In 1980, they forced the government to open negotiations in Gdańsk and Szczecin – an unprecedented accomplishment. However, very little came of those negotiations until the strikes spread to other important industrial areas, notably steel workers in Warsaw, Kraków and Katowice, coal and copper miners in Upper and Lower Silesia and workers in Wrocław – all of which became important Solidarity bases. The government was even forced to open a new set of negotiations in Upper Silesia. It was then that the negotiations on the coast began to bear fruit. Thus, the transformative character of the Solidarity upheaval was broadly based on Poland's industrial working class. (Chapters Seven and Eight show how the strikes began both on the coast and elsewhere, and the role played by workers far from the coast, as well as the shipyard and other coastal workers).

---

20. Osa 1997, p. 351.
21. Osa 1997, p. 355.
22. Ascherson 1982; Garton Ash 1985.

Self-transformation

Anyone who studies or participates in social movements cannot help but find that these movements change the people who are engaged in them, and often alter entire communities and societies. It may take different forms, but as Karl Marx noted,[23] the process of struggle in which social movements engage changes the people who take part in them in important ways. Those people are often forced, or given the opportunity, to undertake activities and responsibilities that they might otherwise never have even imagined, and thus to develop talents and potentials within themselves of which they had previously been unaware. Solidarity activists had to create organisations and make decisions that affected their own lives and the lives of others. They had to cope with the politics of international affairs besides having to be concerned about the Soviet Union (they were well-versed in the disputes between the Democrats and the Republicans in the United States of America). They had to overcome their own fears, both of the state and of public speaking, and to learn how to persuade others of their point of view, through both speech and the written word. They dealt with finances and the planning of strategy and tactics; they responded to state initiatives and to their own members – just to mention some of the more obvious challenges.

As they rose to meet these challenges, people came to regard themselves and one another differently as increased feelings of self-worth and community spread throughout the society. Thus, social relations were significantly altered too, as people treated each other with more respect and displayed greater camaraderie. In many cases, these changes were long-lived: people saw themselves differently – because they *were* now different people. They recognised the changes they had undergone, and they eloquently speak about them in Chapter Nine.

Social movements, collective interaction and political opportunity structure

When social movements challenge the state, each contending side influences and helps to shape the other by the alternative choices of action that their efforts make available or eliminate. A kind of interactive dance proceeds in which each party must respond to the moves of the other.[24] As a result of each collective actor's move, some options may be closed off and others opened for the other side.[25] The dynamics of social movements cannot be understood without recognising this interaction, and the ways it affects each side. The actions, manner,

---

23. Marx 1960.
24. Tilly 1999; Zald and Useem 1987.
25. McAdam, McCarthy and Zald 1988; Zald and Useem 1987.

frames and ideologies of the state, and those of social movements that are making demands on the state, as well as the process of contention, all have their
effect not only on the larger society, but within each of the contending sides.
Their culture, policies, cohesiveness and morale are subject to these influences,
which can have a significant impact on the outcome in the society as a whole.

These collective actors – both the social movements and the state they confront – encompass large numbers of people who have different structural positions, and therefore different interests and possibly different ideologies. They
will often be affected by and respond to new circumstances in different and
sometimes conflicted ways. Thus, disagreements develop within each side, or
pre-existing disagreements become sharpened. The efforts of states, of social
movement organisations or of movement activists may be stymied, stalled or
pushed forward because of the internal turmoil this interaction causes, or they
may proceed because of its absence.

This study shows how dissidents learned from their efforts to confront the
state, how the ruling bodies responded to their efforts, and how these actions
shaped the possibilities oppositionists had available to them – or what social
movement scholars these days refer to as their 'political opportunity structure'.
It illustrates how workers and intellectuals developed their ideas and their strategies in response to those of state actors and their own efforts. These effects
were wide-ranging, in terms of how they affected the internal dynamics of social
movement organisations, and how individuals changed as they participated in
that movement.

In the conflict between Solidarity and the Party/state, each deeply influenced
the other's internal life. The conflict affected not only the relations *between* the
antagonists, but also significantly influenced the *intra*-organisational disputes
that developed during the titanic social struggle that took place at that time.
Chapters Ten, Eleven and Thirteen examine the struggle between Solidarity and
the Communist Party; the disagreements within Solidarity that emerged from
this conflict are discussed in Chapter Eleven, and those within the Party are
examined in Chapter Twelve. Inside Solidarity, major rifts emerged. One faction
wanted to confront and defeat the Party, while the other sought to avoid open
conflict. These disputes weakened the union.

Similarly, the ruling Party contained Solidarity sympathisers, hard-liners and
centrists. The conflict that took place between them is crucial to understanding the course of events. It was not until the hard-liners were able to defeat
the reformers within the Party that they were fully free to go after Solidarity.
That fact underlines something that gradually became clear to me in carrying
out this study. The concept of political opportunity structure (POS) has naturally
become a major theoretical element in the study of social movements. It clarifies
variables that had previously been used to understand how social movements

emerged, such as underlying and precipitating factors. One of the key elements of POS has been the role of the state. Is the state open to reform? Has its control weakened for some reason? Does it repress, attempt to co-opt, or is it willing to accommodate the social movement's demands? These issues were all germane to the options that were available to Solidarity. But in this framework, *the ability of the state itself to act is rarely considered.* What this study shows is that the state may also be subject to the constraints of POS by the social movement that challenges it. Chapter Twelve examines what took place inside the Polish United Workers Party and the state it controlled during this period of conflict between the Solidarity movement and the state in 1980–1, when Solidarity was legal and able to challenge the authority of the Party. The account in that chapter shows that, at least in some circumstances, the state was significantly constrained in its ability to act against Solidarity because of the existence of the reform movement within the Party. That reform movement's strength was based on Solidarity, which in this manner restrained the Party.

Martial law and beyond

The imposition of martial law in December 1981, and the detention of some 10,000 activists, certainly took most of the Solidarity activists by surprise. How were they taken? Who escaped and why? (see Chapter Fourteen). There was some notable resistance, but for the most part it was easily suppressed, with the significant exception of Upper Silesia, especially in the coal mines (see Chapter 15). But even if they were defeated, the experience of Solidarity had broken the fear that people had, and the regime could not repair it, even with the strictures of martial law. People proudly and insistently spoke out. They refused to be cowed; they never abandoned various forms of resistance. There would be no return to the previous normality. Some of the leading activists managed to escape, almost all by accident. How did they begin to reconstruct the opposition? (see Chapter Sixteen). For a few years, however, they were able to make little difference in terms of changing the dynamic. Stalemate set in and persisted until the murder of Father Popiełuszko, a leading opposition-supporting priest. This event tore away any remaining shreds of legitimacy that the regime might have claimed, and it created a wave of revulsion among the Polish population, after which opposition once more burst into the open (Chapter Seventeen). Finally, what precipitated the transition from Communism, and how was it negotiated? (Chapter Eighteen).

Overview of the book

The first chapter examines the political and economic framework within which opposition developed, thereby making clear the grievances that motivated it. Then, I consider the struggle that took place between the Party/state and the opposition in three parts. Part one (Chapters Two to Six) considers the period from the beginnings of Communist rule to 1980, concentrating especially on the critical events that alienated a whole generation at the end of the 1960s, and on the consequent emergence of opposition in the 1970s. The second part (Chapters Seven to Thirteen) begins with the strikes of August 1980, and examines the conflict between Solidarity and the Party up to the declaration of martial law on the night of 12–13 December 1981. The third part (Chapters Fourteen to Eighteen) begins with the imposition of martial law and considers its impact on the opposition. I then look at how that opposition was rebuilt and how it ultimately forced an end to the Communist government.

My approach

This analysis is based primarily on in-depth interviews which I undertook with 150 people, around half of whom are directly quoted in the book. These interviews included Solidarity activists and leaders, intellectual oppositionists (including several people belonging to or affiliated with KOR), people close to the Church, journalists and academics, leaders of the reform movement within the Communist Party and some people from the other side, including an army captain, a former colonel in the secret police, a colonel in the Ministry of the Interior (to whom, as agreed, I have given pseudonyms), and Mieczysław Rakowski, the last leader of the Communist Party/state. These interviews are not – nor were they ever intended to be – a random sample. With a few exceptions as noted, everyone with whom I spoke had no hesitations about my using their names; many of them are well-known in Poland. As I travelled from city to city, I went to the people to whom I was referred by others. I was looking for leaders and leading activists, or those who knew about the events discussed here. Through these interviews, I present the events through the perspectives of the contenders on both sides. I examine what people learnt from their experiences and how they applied what they learnt. The glossary of interviewees explains who these people are. It should be noted that some of them have short descriptions: this is because they were ordinary people who came to play an active role, and were not long-time oppositionists.

I was so impressed with the insights and eloquence of my interviewees that I decided that their words had to see the light of day. As much as possible, I have allowed them to tell their own stories. I found that connecting individual biographies with historical events shone a unique light on both: the connection to history made sense of individuals' lives, and their lives illustrated in the details how history unfolded. By seeing this period through the eyes of the activists on both sides, we can achieve a unique view of how history was made. A wide array of interviews from several parts of the country provides a much broader view than could be found from speaking to one or even several people in one or a few areas. I managed to track down and speak with participants and eye-witnesses to each of the key events before, during and after 1980. Indeed, I know of no other study of this movement in Poland that has covered as broad an array of participants from such diverse geographical backgrounds in relation to such historical events.

After having completed the interviews, I worked with them, at first transcribing them and then reading them over in detail. Next, I began to take parts of the interviews and arranged them together with others covering particular topics: I examined how people came to be dissidents, and how the various upheavals affected their lives and their thinking, so I could compare various perspectives. In doing so, I began to see some patterns emerge that I had not perceived just from participating in or reading the interviews.

A more detailed discussion of how this study was carried out is presented in the appendix 'Researching the Polish Revolution'.

Chapter One
Patronage and Corruption in Communist Poland

The economic and political system from which Solidarity arose was imposed on Poland by the Soviet Union, just as it was imposed on the rest of what became the Soviet bloc in Eastern Europe after World War II. The Soviet Union marched through Poland as it chased the retreating German army; it dismantled many of the factories in Poland; it told the Poles how they should organise their economy; it demanded that they produce military equipment rather than consumer goods; it installed its 'advisors' in key ministries with real power to make decisions; it could and did demand that any person be removed from any position, including the nation's political leaders. The most egregious aspects of this domination concluded with the revolt in 1956, discussed in the next chapter, while the fundamental underlying factors remained until the régime's end.

Nonetheless, to understand how an opposition appeared and ultimately transformed 'People's Poland', one must look beyond a whole litany of understandable grievances, such as the Soviet Union's domination, 'totalitarianism', and the government's official policy of hostility toward the Church. All of these played a role in creating disaffection, but a persistently stagnating economy was an underlying problem that affected the lives and even the dignity of everyone, and thereby undermined long-term allegiance to the system. Economic breakdowns, during which living standards were drastically threatened, precipitated every working-class rebellion that took place under Communist rule in

Poland. These crises occurred in a system that kept most people on the edge of an economic precipice, leaving them little margin for reductions in living standards. The regime de-emphasised consumer goods in order to build up producer goods for a promise of rising living standards in a distant future. But for the *present* it was building a significant industrial capacity. The promises were only ever realised briefly in the first half of the 1970s. Surveys in 1980 – the year of the strikes that created the Solidarity union – showed that Poles felt that their greatest problems were material: their low wage levels and the poor performance of the economy.[1] Moreover, in response to the angry discontent engendered by the continual inability of the economy to perform, the government had regular recourse to its instruments of repression and to retain tight controls over everything: speech, association, organisation, publication, who advanced socially and economically, among other things – all of which created more discontent. This chapter will consider how this system functioned and failed, as well as explain the context within which an opposition arose. The following chapters will then examine this opposition.

I first really began to understand the problem when Jan Uchański, a miner who had once belonged to the Polish United Workers' Party, told me that, contrary to my assumption, the problem was as much *moral* as it was economic. To illustrate this point, he told me about how his son, when aged six, had wanted to go to summer camp and had asked him to arrange it. But Uchański had been unsuccessful. Later, when the son learned that a friend's father had used his connections to secure *his* son a place, Uchański's son reproached his father. Uchański lamented: 'They have so corrupted the society that even children think like this. How will people ever get used to functioning in a normal society?'

Such corruption was a central feature of Communist Poland, and resulted from the sheer scarcity of almost all goods coupled with the efforts people were forced to expend to overcome this scarcity. If desired or necessary goods could not be acquired in a normal way, those who had access to or control over them could offer goods to people in exchange for other goods, services, loyalty or favours. Thus, they had much greater power than was accorded them on any piece of paper. In this way, a not-so-subtle corruption pervaded the nation, damaging not only the economy, but also the character of individuals. Corruption became a means for people to obtain what was otherwise unobtainable. It was a lubricant that enabled people to slide through a frustrating maze that forced them into unending bureaucratic procedures before often denying them the goods they sought. The moral issue Uchański raised was, at the same time, an economic one:

1. Adamski et al., cited in Mason 1985, p. 89.

corruption emerged from the failures of the economy, and it worsened those failures.

There were many irrationalities and ironies in Communist Poland. The Marxian impulse to nationalise the economy had as its motive a desire for equity and rationality. Yet what was produced was the opposite. A third of the production of the steel industry went to provide for the coal industry, and the same percent of coal industry production was for the steel industry, while both took investment funds from consumer goods industries. As a result, adequate housing was unavailable and became an increasingly distant hope. Even the dignity of a sure supply of toilet paper was lacking. Vast amounts were borrowed from the West in the 1970s resulting in an overwhelming debt, which dragged the Polish economy down. A huge steel mill was built just outside of Kraków, whose technology was not only outmoded before it was constructed, but also poisoned the air, land and water of the city and the surrounding region. The acid rain it produced was corroding statues that had endured since the thirteenth century.

During the 1970s, Poland modernised its industry and destroyed many of its older factories. It soon found that it needed machinery and parts that its antiquated equipment had not used. When economic difficulties took hold, the country could not afford the additional purchases, and so a nation that had once been an exporter of matches was now incapable of producing enough to fulfil even its own demand.[2]

Nomenklatura

The *rational* pursuit of self-interest by the privileged elite created these apparent *irrationalities*. The so-called *nomenklatura* referred to a list of names that were considered politically reliable and subject to formal approval by the Communist Party. People were chosen from this list to fill top positions in society, whether in the military, politics, industry, commerce, trade unions or the professions.

Members of this class were able to use their power to attain privileges for themselves. Julia Minc recalled that not long after the war she and her husband, Hilary Minc, third in command of 'People's Poland', had two residences: a villa in Warsaw and a house in Konstancin, an upscale Warsaw suburb. They lived in seclusion, close to other Party leaders and people from the Soviet Embassy: 'There was a big garden, forest all around, and the air was better...Our estate had a club, a canteen and a cook...I had three [dogs] in the kennels there'. Minc said that when they wanted to see a movie, 'We'd ring them up and they'd screen films for us at home'. Minc had a cook and a seamstress, while her husband had

---

2. Szczypiorski 1982, p. 138.

his own tailor. Bolesław Bierut, president of the Polish Republic in those early years, did not have to leave to get a woman: 'They would have been brought to him if he'd wanted'.[3] These were small but significant luxuries in an impoverished post-war Poland.

Members of the *nomenklatura* were a privileged class of people. They had access to special shops which were closed to all others and which stocked otherwise unavailable goods. By the end of the 1940s, they had created for themselves 'luxurious summer resorts, special medical care, and numerous other perquisites … amidst general pauperisation'.[4] Some of these perks included 'annuities, retirement benefits, family supplements, special health-care benefits, access to spas and hunting resorts'.[5]

In the early years, Party activists believed deeply in what they were doing. Their primary purpose was not to benefit from their power. As Minc recalls:

> We didn't have any [friends]. There wasn't time for that … I'd go to bed at three in the morning, get up at eleven and drive to the Press Agency … We all worked hard … Work was our enjoyment. It's a marvellous feeling to be building a new country from the very beginning and it's satisfying to see the results.[6]

This sense persisted into the 1960s. Zbigniew Regucki, chief of staff to Stanisław Kania, the Party's First Secretary during much of the period of legal Solidarity, recalled: 'Under Gomułka … the lifestyle of party activists was pretty humble, for example, one Secretary of the Kraków Committee had a car. He was condemned in public for this as a case of bourgeois lifestyle'.[7]

With the rise to power of Edward Gierek in 1970 the pattern of restraint ended. Thousands of high-level officials were replaced,[8] and many more were added.[9] The new officials were anxious to shed the inhibitions preventing them from taking full advantage of their position. Gierek himself enjoyed luxuries, avoided working long hours and appeared to tolerate abuses and corruption among his associates.[10] By 1980, as David Mason has noted, 'Party members [were] almost twice as likely to be in the top of five income brackets and less than half as likely to be in the lowest'.[11] Gierek nourished Poles' desires for a life richer in material comforts. He said that it was legitimate to prosper, and he argued that increasing inequality would enable some to spend more, thus stimulating the economy

---

3. Torańska 1987, pp. 17–20.
4. Dziewanowski 1977, pp. 171–2; Lewis 1958, p. 9.
5. Smolar 1983, p. 47.
6. Wałęsa 1987, pp. 16–17.
7. Terry 1988, pp. 222–3, n. 4; Malinowski 1984, p. 82; Chęciński 1982, p. 144.
8. Weydenthal 1971, p. 160, n. 183; Lepak 1988, p. 60.
9. Blazynski 1979, pp. 130–1; Bielasiak 1983, p. 17.
10. Pomian 1986, cited in Terry 1988, pp. 222–3, n. 4.
11. Mason 1985, pp. 139–41.

for all. Under Gierek, the Polish people did begin to attain a higher standard of living. Private automobiles became widely available; some good roads were built; imported foods were available in the stores.

The example was taken from the top. Gierek used a state firm to build his house, as did huge numbers of officials at all levels.[12] Highly placed officials built themselves beautiful vacation homes. They lived in opulence, with 'artificial waterfalls, miniature botanical gardens, swimming pools and various athletic facilities'. Their villas' interiors were furnished with pieces 'borrowed' from museums. Their homes were bought at extremely low prices, which were subsidised by charging other people higher prices; or ownership was simply transferred to them by one ruse or another. This embezzlement directly impacted upon the housing market for everyone else, as the resources they devoured meant that fewer apartments were constructed for the rest of the population. Sometimes, construction was undertaken illegally by prisoners or soldiers.[13]

The elites took good care of themselves collectively.[14] In 1972, decrees were passed on pay and retirement benefits payable even to grandchildren, parents and other more distant relatives, with only a short time in office required for eligibility purposes, and to allow officials to continue to receive their salaries for up to two years after they left office.[15] These benefits were extended to Party positions, although there was not even the pretence that they were government employees.[16] Parliament 'granted special allowances and tax exemptions to all party and governmental officials'.[17] Now, even 'political defeat would no longer entail radical material degradation; losing power would not mean losing wealth or privilege'.[18] Former officials were often exempt even from arrest and prosecution.[19]

A wide range of benefits was appropriated by the powerful elite. They had special foods delivered to the door, shops with items sold at very low prices, paid for with zlotys, while everyone else had to pay in hard currency. They acquired cars at low cost and enjoyed easy access to the West, often in subsidised trips, and to western currency.[20] Solidarity leader Ryszard Sawicki said that he 'learned of luxuriously equipped forest preserves which were fenced off and kept out of sight of regular people'. And the public also bore the expense of building the infrastructure of roads, electricity, and so on, which was never supposed to have

---

12. Smolar 1983, p. 49.
13. Czabański 1983, p. 158.
14. Szelenyi 1978; Garton Ash 1985, p. 7.
15. Paczkowski 2003, pp. 364–5.
16. Smolar 1983, pp. 48–9; Laba 1986, pp. 56–7.
17. Misztal and Misztal 1984, p. 171.
18. 1983, p. 49.
19. Czabański 1983, p. 162.
20. Czabański 1983, pp. 158–60.

been in these areas in the first place.[21] A hospital in Warsaw had been ten years in the making and was still not incomplete while a lavish government clinic for the higher *nomenklatura* was quickly erected and furnished with the latest equipment, a large swimming pool and other facilities. Almost one half of the government health fund was spent on this clinic. The cost of a hospital bed at this clinic was over ten times that of one available to normal citizens.[22]

Privileges became more widespread in the supposedly egalitarian Polish society. Local Party headquarters were furnished with beautiful wood and furniture. Newly-created provincial governments greatly extended the patronage. Now, for each of them, new Party headquarters, local council buildings, police quarters and special vacation and medical facilities had to be built and staffed. Maciek Szumowski, editor of the Party newspaper *Gazeta Krakowska*, and a leader of the reform-movement within the Communist Party during the Solidarity period, recalled:

> Gierek's main tactic was corruption. If a writer strengthened Gierek's position by writing positively about the changes that were taking place, he could expect a coupon to buy a car which one could sell and make a profit.

> **Adam Sucharski, a secret-police colonel:** Secretaries and activists in various Party organisations had two faces: officially, he was really engaged; and then, when we were drinking, he would laugh at this whole business and at himself, too. There was a strong fight for a place at the trough.

Zbigniew Bogacz, a coal-mining engineer who played a key role in an underground strike when martial law was declared in 1981: "In the mid- to late-seventies, we noticed people who did not work, yet got money from the mine. They built villas and houses for themselves around lakes. We had a hard time getting vacations, while there were lots of people who worked in the directorship and the Party factory committee who had plenty of time and opportunity to do whatever they wanted."

The police and professional soldiers were the last line of defence for power and privilege, and that defense had to be repeatedly invoked. They found some of these privileges extended to them: access to the special shops, to apartments, extra family allowances.[23]

The *nomenklatura* system was so pervasive that it became routine that when a leader from outside objected to such privilege, he would be brought within the circle of the privileged. It was not difficult to accept the unaccustomed benefits;

---

21. Smolar 1983, p. 49; Malinowski 1984, pp. 83–9.
22. Lipski 1985, pp. 294–5.
23. Majkowski 1985, p. 52.

however, there was a price to pay: he lost the confidence and support of those for whom he spoke, and the latter lost a spokesperson. It took a person of character and experience, and sometimes the careful oversight of his people prepared to fight for his soul, to resist these blandishments. As Aleksander Krystosiak, a Solidarity leader in Szczecin, noted:

> The *nomenklatura* tried to corrupt the members of our governing bodies. For example, in a small town, they opened a new store. Traditionally, before any store was officially opened – suits, furs, food, whatever – the *nomenklatura* went and bought things for a symbolic payment, so no-one could say that they got it for free. This time, the *nomenklatura* invited the chairman of the city trade-union commission as a new *nomenklatura*. The next morning, I got a call asking me to come there. The whole city commission was sitting. He was scared shitless. He lost his position; then he was kicked out of the union.

Spreading out privileges also made the *nomenklatura* more visible to the Polish population, especially in the latter half of the 1970s when the economy was seriously deteriorating. In a series of studies within the city of Łódź, a major textile centre, the sociologist Krystyna Janicka found that between 1967 and 1980 there was a large increase in the percentage of people who saw income differences as a source of conflict (from 52.9 percent to 85 percent).[24] Respondents spoke of a 'red bourgeoisie', a 'ruling elite', the 'proprietors of People's Poland', and suchlike far more frequently in 1980 than in 1965 or 1976.[25] Jan Gajda, one of the strikers in the Gdańsk Shipyard in 1980, recalled:

> [I]njustice was a serious issue. For how could we explain the fact that a worker caught drunk on the premises was reprimanded and deprived of his [bonuses] and other benefits, whereas a dead-drunk manager was on the next day decorated with the Cross of Merit? How could we explain the conduct of the physician who treated a patient with appendicitis as a malingerer, while the man had to be taken the next day, unconscious and with a perforated appendix, by an ambulance?[26]

Managers appeared to have little concern for the difficulties their decisions created for workers, while concerns of equality and social justice virtually disappeared from official rhetoric.[27] Alicja Matuszewska, a leader of the civilian-workers who was employed by the military and who later became Solidarity's national treasurer, noted that 'the workers were treated like rugs. People had no say whatsoever. They stepped on people's dignity'. These were serious failings for

24. Janicka 1986, p. 67, p. 71.
25. Janicka 1986, p. 69.
26. Gajda 1982, pp. 248–9.
27. Malinowski 1984, pp. 64–81.

a regime whose main selling-point was its claim of 'protection from instability, uncertainty and insecurity by a strong welfare state'.[28]

By the late 1970s, nearly everyone was assumed to be corrupt. A poll in Warsaw in 1979 found that only 20 percent of respondents believed that people in official positions had attained their rank on account of their ability.[29] Jan Stępniewski, a Professor of Business at the University of Paris, claimed he was told by French bankers that 'the Polish government workers who negotiated loans were easily corruptible. Very often, all you had to do was to invite them to Paris or to some nice chateau for a week or two of negotiations'.[30] There are allegations that Gierek bought outdated patents in exchange for personal bribes.[31] Kraków Solidarity leader Edward Nowak said: 'There was a notion that whoever didn't steal was stupid. This degradation was one of the causes of the Solidarity upheaval; people didn't want to wade in this dirt anymore'. Janusz Onyszkiewicz, Solidarity's public spokesman, stated: 'There was a sense of moral degradation and decay, and everybody knew it couldn't go on like that'.

Nomenklatura and the economy

The *nomenklatura* shaped the economy according to the dictates of the Soviet Union and its own ideology and self-interest. Poland had suffered the worst devastation of any country in World War II, with six million Polish citizens killed, three million of whom were Jews. National income had fallen to about a third of its pre-war level. Some 65 percent of industrial plants, half of transportation, 60 percent of schools, 62 percent of postal and telephone equipment – all were destroyed. So, too, was 98 percent of Warsaw and significant parts of several other cities, including Gdańsk, as well as nearly half of all arable land and livestock.[32] Moreover, the Soviets dismantled and carted off factories and machinery from the former German territories as war reparations, even though the Germans were forced out and the area was now inhabited by Poles.

Despite these burdens, Poles achieved remarkable success in rebuilding the country and rapidly raising living standards during the reconstruction. In the closing years of the 1940s, gross national product rose by an average of 21 percent per year.[33] More importantly, consumption was rising at a reasonable rate (16.5 percent between 1948–50).[34] But then a programme of large-scale industrialisation,

28. Pravda 1983, pp. 70–9.
29. Mason 1985, p. 142.
30. Stępniewski interview.
31. Wałęsa 1992, p. 248.
32. Ascherson 1982, p. 29; Yakowicz 1979, pp. 13–14; Reynolds 1978, p. 518.
33. Weydenthal 1971, p. 25.
34. Pełczyński 1980a, p. 314.

was imposed via multi-year plans based on the Soviet model, and Poles had to fall into line. The plan centralised and nationalised the economy. Subsequently, everything that was produced was in the plan. If the planners did not provide for something – whether by choice or basic negligence – it was not available.[35] Lechosław Goździk, the Party leader in Warsaw's FSO automobile factory during the mid-1950s, led a major movement to reform the Party in 1956. He said:

> The Politburo decided how many workers were supposed to be employed in production and how many in maintenance, so in a modern factory with new equipment, we had a maintenance department as big as in an old factory. Those people were paid to come to the factory to be bored to death! You had this completely ridiculous situation, where the Politburo decided centrally how many nuts and bolts were supposed to be produced in the five-year plan. And every five-year plan had five one-year plans. The Politburo decided how many bunches of green parsley were supposed to be on the market, and there couldn't be one more bunch without the Politburo having decided on it. It was a situation of complete absurdity.

The plan emphasised capital investment in heavy industry, which inevitably meant that consumer production was slighted.[36] Worse still, there was *selective fulfilment* of the plan, such that capital production was even more heavily emphasised than originally intended.[37] This outcome did not seem to bother Poland's rulers, however, as this tendency continued for decades.[38] Up until 1971, only two of the multi-year economic plans sought to increase personal consumption. The first was between 1946–9, a time when the nation was recovering from the devastation of the war, but was not yet under the fully consolidated power of the Communists. The second period was after the upheaval that forced a change in the government in 1956.[39] Even in the first half of the 1970s, when the emphasis was supposedly on the production of consumer goods, the usual trend reasserted itself, so that over a third of national income was devoted to capital goods. One of the areas most neglected was agriculture, which meant that less production – fewer tractors, less fertiliser, and so on – was designated to it. As a result, food production did not keep pace with population growth, and imports were needed to keep the population fed.[40]

---

35. Zieliński, 1973, p. 13.

36. Feiwel 1971, pp. 99–100; Zieliński 1973, p. 11; Pełczyński 1980, pp. 338–9; Yakowicz 1979, pp. 111–20.

37. Zieliński 1973, p. 4; Lewis 1958, pp. 151–2.

38. Alton 1955, pp. 112–14, pp. 129–31; Majkowski 1985, pp. 56–8, p. 164; Mieczkowski 1975, p. 93, pp. 141–4, p. 156; Sanford 1983, p. 24, p. 32; Zieliński 1973, pp. 35–7; Pełczyński 1973, p. 5; Fallenbuchl 1973, p. 57.

39. Zieliński 1973, p. 43.

40. Paczkowski 2003, pp. 356–7.

The result was an economy of scarcity. The Korean and Cold Wars encouraged the tendency toward heavy industry, which was required by the vast arms industry on which 15 percent of national income was spent in the early 1950s.[41]

Polish trade was structured according to the needs of the Soviet Union and the Soviet bloc, creating a serious drag on the economy.[42] In the early years of the regime, the Soviets dictated who would be the leading figures in government and the army officer corps.[43] Moreover, the Soviets designed much of the economy, including most of the large industrial complexes.[44] The Soviet Union demanded more coal and longer hours for Polish coal-miners, and greater military expenditures from the Polish economy. Poland was also made into a supply base, providing the Soviets with items from the West which Poles subsided. As Jan Stępniewski recollected:

> In the 1970s, Poland was the sixth largest builder of ships in the world. All the mechanical parts of the ships were built in Poland. But the electronic equipment was bought in the West for dollars. The Soviet Union was the main buyer, and it bought with rubles.

The Polish *nomenklatura* served as the transmission belt for the Soviets; it was the condition for the former securing and maintaining their positions.[45] One can only speak of planning in this system with irony. While it is true that plans were made and planners had a great deal of power and authority, in reality there was *anarchy*, as each industry director, plant manager and *individual* sought ways to present himself in the best possible light and to maximise his own personal advantage. As a result, all manner of waste was systematically generated. Zbigniew Pełczyński recounts: 'Orders were evaded, returns falsified, work done badly, equipment and materials treated carelessly, and anything that could be was stolen and sold on the black market'.[46] Each level of planning seemed to function independently of every other, and often against the others, so that real planning simply did not exist. In the early 1970s, Jan Jerschina, a sociologist at Jagiellonian University and a leader of the Party reform-movement, conducted research for the Party First Secretary in his province. In that position, he learned just how the system of planning was undermined by self-interest:

> It was commonly believed that the Party ruled the economic system. But in order to follow systematically what was going on, you would have to have

---

41. Kolankiewicz and Lewis 1988, p. 102.
42. Lewis 1958, pp. 158–9.
43. Roos 1966, pp. 234–5.
44. Kolankiewicz and Lewis 1988.
45. Torańska 1987, pp. 36–7; pp. 46–7; p. 59.
46. Pełczyński 1980, p. 317.

statistics; but there are no statistics. Every report from every factory was written according to a different pattern. The only statistics which are relatively reliable are those which the corporate managers have. They need real information. But apparatchiks can't put together data from factories in the province, so they have no idea what is going on.

Large-scale production and planning were almost ends in themselves, without due regard to the effects they might have on actual production. As a consequence, large amounts of money were channeled into wasteful investments, and feedback from those who saw the problem and advised against these methods made no difference. Helena Łuczywo, who was the editor of Solidarity's underground press, worked in a bank:

> I dealt with investments. At the state farms, they would build huge chicken coops or sheds for cattle. You could see immediately that lots of building materials were being stolen, that the investment was very slow and badly organised, that it didn't make sense to build up such huge things. But that was the kind of investment that was financed by the bank I worked for, no matter what I said.

Heavy industries, which seemed to be preferred by the country's leadership, tended to be monopolistic, with high levels of party and official union membership, and were located in or around large cities. They were politically powerful, and thereby able to demand large shares of national investment. Their well-organised and economically powerful workforces were able to command relatively high wages, so more of the national income was directed to those industries. Lighter industries, which were more consumer-oriented, tended to be concentrated away from the major cities, with female workforces that were less well-organised – all of which made them economically less powerful.[47] The Party admitted that 'various departmental and regional pressure groups had a decisive influence over investment policy'.[48] As a result, by the 1980s, 10 percent of enterprises accounted for 75 percent of the means of production, employed 50 percent of labour, and accounted for 58 percent of industrial production.[49] The insistence of the Party bureaucracy on retaining political control also led it to prefer a centralised economy based on heavy industry. A turn to light industry and consumer-goods production would have meant more reliance on the market and therefore less control from the centre.[50]

---

47. Kolankiewicz and Lewis 1988, p. 115; Jarosińska and Kulpińska 1974, p. 138.
48. *Trybuna Ludu*, cited in Pravda 1983, p. 75.
49. 'Raport: *"Polska 5 Lat po Sierpniu"* Aneks', cited in Kolankiewicz and Lewis 1988, p. 105.
50. Siwiński 1988, p. 26; also Brus 1988, p. 67; Eysymontt 1989, p. 29.

The problem is illustrated in the construction of housing and the infrastructure for providing heat and hot water. According to the plan, apartments were of limited design. For the most part, they were large high-rise blocks with cement walls, which were supposed to allow only nine square metres per person, exclusive of the kitchen and bathroom. Huge apartment blocks were constructed with little concern for the infrastructural needs of the people who would inhabit them. Consequently, there were shortages of shops, places of recreation, schools and other essential services.[51]

Instead of providing heat and hot water on site, gigantic plants were built to heat water for both purposes. The hot water was pumped long distances through large uninsulated underground pipes. Heat was inevitably lost by this method. On average, it took more than a thousand calories at the point of origin to deliver one calorie of heat to a building.[52] Moreover, water leaked out – or poured out when there were breaks in the pipes. As a result, individuals had no control over the amount or availability of hot water and heat. Sometimes, weeks would go by without hot water, at times by design. Occasionally, there was no water at all.

Since the basis on which people were chosen for *nomenklatura* positions was political, the most capable people were frequently overlooked. Even when people with ability were picked, their primary concern was not necessarily finding the best way to produce and deliver goods and services. Instead, they were subject to no outside discipline or authority but that of the appointers – the Party leadership of the country, district, city, industry, and so forth. As Edward Nowak stated:

> The most important thing for a man to be the manager of a factory is that he must be a faithful Party member. Sometimes this system led to circumstances in which people who were put in charge of workers didn't have the slightest idea what they should do, and no organisational abilities.

People were bitterly resentful of the special shops, clinics, private clubs and other ways in which privilege was distributed without merit.[53] It was the source of much of the waste that provoked so much anger. One Solidarity document described the feeling quite clearly:

> The system which ties political to economic power, based on continual party interference in the functioning of enterprises, is the main reason for the present crisis of the Polish economy. The...*nomenklatura* principle rules out any

51. Anasz and Wesołowski 1974, p. 45.
52. Haggin 1992, p. 20.
53. Mason 1985, pp. 143–4.

rational cadre promotion policy, rendering millions of workers who do not belong to any party second class citizens.[54]

A functionary was lost without connections and control of information. During the 1980s, the self-governing councils elected by the workers were supposed to have a say in how money earned by an enterprise was to be invested. According to Henryk Wujec, an adviser to Solidarity, things rarely worked that way because the director's power was bolstered by his connections:

> If the director weren't supported by other men from the ministries and the Party Secretaries, then maybe the factory wouldn't be able to receive necessary materials. It's the unofficial side of our life. You may have money, and you may not have raw materials if you do not have the appropriate connections.

The director's success was thus subject to the whims of others.[55] As a result, people in power could confer largesse upon a particular community if they had personal ties to that community,[56] while clients made sure that their patrons valued them by providing gifts. The sociologist Jacek Tarkowski noted: 'At the top of the power structure, it was customary to give old paintings, expensive rifles, gold jewellery and the like'.[57] The director also had control over information that the workers' councils lacked, as Henryk Wujec has noted:

> Control over information that could provide protection from above is also a resource which the director can use to augment his power over the workers' councils: In practice, it is the director who makes the decisions because he has all the information and he has specialists around him, whereas the workers do not. So they rarely oppose the director's decisions.[58]

Furthermore, there were plenty of opportunities to bribe clerks and draw favours, which further distorted the economy:

> Jan Jerschina: There is a large group of relatively poor clerks in the provinces. It is easy to bribe them: give them some money, arrange a cheaper apartment for them, or provide a signature for cheaper gasoline or a vacation in Bulgaria, and they have them in their pockets.[59]

---

54. Persky and Flam 1982, p. 214.
55. Crane 1988, pp. 15–16; Tarkowski 1983, pp. 504–6.
56. Tarkowski 1981, pp. 175–7, pp. 183–4.
57. 1983, p. 509.
58. Wujec interview.
59. Jerschina interview.

This problem was so great that when the economic crisis hit in 1979 and 1980, the country's leaders had no idea how severe it was nor what resources they had available.[60]

Efforts at reform often failed due to the opposition of powerful interest groups. Gierek's programme, for example, was based on raising living standards to win social support that could not be won with ideology. That goal inevitably meant channelling more national income into consumption. But it was not long before investment priorities once again came to the fore. For all the emphasis on planning, the push for heavy industry made a colossal mess of the plans:

> In 1981, the value of investment projects already begun was 4.4 times the value of total investment spending in the same year. This means that if all investment spending was committed to projects that were already begun, it would have taken more than four years to complete them without any possibility of undertaking new projects (assuming an unchanged investment level).[61]

Huge projects were left unfinished because of shortages of raw materials or equipment, or other bottlenecks.[62] Workers had to make up for the lost production by working harder or longer, usually without extra pay.[63] Because workers were paid by piece-rates rather than by the hour, they paid for the down-time that managerial inefficiency imposed upon them.[64] These problems exerted continuing downward pressure on the standard of living. Alicja Matuszewska recalls:

> Our Solidarity economists figured out that the biggest losses were brought about by the fact that the factories had to stop: 6,000 people couldn't work for three hours because there was no electricity or some other reason. Construction sites would come to a standstill because they had no bricks. Companies that produced machinery had no bolts, no screws, no screwdrivers. Executives would meet, discuss and talk, but they didn't do anything!

Stanisław Matyja, who worked in the giant Cegielski complex in Poznań during the 1950s, remembered one year when, for most of the first quarter, there was no work: people were forced to use their vacation time or get a doctor's note excusing them from work. Then, toward the end of the quarter, 'it was announced to us that we would be working Sundays, holidays and afternoons to meet the plan...Once I had to work 64 hours non-stop'.[65] Lech Wałęsa saw this practice as:

60. Garton Ash 1985, p. 73.
61. Siwiński 1988, pp. 26–7; also Nuti 1982, p. 32; Tarkowski 1981, p. 176 for a discussion of the 'contradiction between macro- and micro-rationality'; Pełczyński 1980, pp. 339–40.
62. Zieliński 1973, p. 41; Kuśnierek 1983, pp. 141–4.
63. Lipski 1985, p. 249.
64. Bernhard 1993, p. 153.
65. Matyja 1981, p. 216.

a great way for management to evade its own responsibilities. Every individual strives to earn as much as he can, but because there's no one around to deliver the necessary materials to the proper work stations, the yard is in perpetual motion, a chaos of comings and goings, with people running around in search of necessary pieces of equipment, even though supply departments have supposedly been established to eliminate this problem.[66]

As a result, by the end of 1970, so much of what Poland produced became simply unused stock that its total value equalled close to half the gross national product for that year.[67] In the 1970s, machinery was purchased from the West before the factories in which it was to be used were even completed. Some of that machinery rusted, became otherwise damaged, or simply became obsolete before it could be put to use.

Workers who bore no responsibility for such situations had to suffer the results; they noticed these effects and were repulsed by them. Seweryn Jaworski, a Solidarity leader in the Warsaw Steel Mill, recalled the situation at his plant:

> A lot of machines were wasted. It could not last forever. My oven produced steel which was one third lighter than other steel. But it was used at only 20 per cent of its capacity because we did not have enough raw materials. In my area, we had a machine, but to complete a job, we needed another one, which we didn't have. So people had to work without the other machine. Here and there we had machines, so you could produce a lot, but there were bottlenecks because in other places we were producing things manually.

Impoverishment

The Polish people were impoverished. There is no doubt as to why: it was part of the plan. I do not contend that they wished people to be poor, but rather that the plan's priorities made such poverty inevitable. The Polish economy grew at reasonable rates in the 1950s, 1960s and 1970s.[68] In the late 1970s, Poland had higher per capita production of coal and cement than the leading Western producers. Investing in heavy industry meant neglecting consumer goods production and thus allowing the standard of living of the population to stagnate.[69] According to official reports, in 1980 only 26 percent of Poland's GDP was consumer goods.[70] Poverty was also a result of the patronage system: the substantial resources that

---

66. Wałęsa 1987, pp. 44–5.
67. Blazynski 1979, p. 3.
68. Wilczyński 1984, p. 78.
69. Majkowski 1985, pp. 163–4; Kuroń 1990, p. 33.
70. Kemp-Welch 1983, p. 81.

it required were literally stolen from the general population.[71] The emphasis was such that virtually all growth was achieved in industry: agricultural production was so neglected that in some periods it actually had a negative growth rate, and most of the rest of the time growth could be simply described as 'miserably low'.[72]

As a result, though the Polish economy progressed, the standard of living did so much more slowly. As the historian Łukasz Kamiński points out, in 1948:

> the average income of a worker was barely 50 percent higher than income of a worker from 1938 in real value... The early 1950s were the time when people quite simply suffered from hunger. In 1951 there is a huge wave of strikes resulting from the fact that in some towns, there was no delivery of meat for three months.[73]

From 1950–70, the standard of living increased only slightly more than half as fast as investment,[74] and actually fell by as much as 36 percent in the first half of the 1950s, before the 1956 revolt temporarily reversed this course.[75] Janina Bauman, a Party member at that time, recalled:

> Despite all the promises, the standard of living dropped and inflation was rising. There were immediate repercussions in our daily life: shortages in basic articles, ever longer queues in the shops, salaries running out before the end of the month... In the winter of 1951–1952... rationing was introduced. Meat became a rarity and only those with an income well above average could afford to eat it often. They bought it at soaring prices on the black market.[76]

In the 1960s, Poland experienced the slowest rate of growth in real wages in all of Eastern Europe.[77] During much of that decade wages virtually stagnated.[78] The cost of food rose fastest; those families making the least were the hardest hit by this trend.[79] In the 1970s, capital flowed outward. Imported machinery from countries outside the Soviet bloc, which had increased in 1972 by 88 percent, and had continued increasing through 1975, dropped in 1976 to a *negative* 3.3 percent,

71. Terry 1988, p. 219.
72. Wilczyński 1984, p. 79; Pełczyński 1980, pp. 318–19.
73. www.niniwa2.cba.pl/komunizm_robotnicy_w_prl_ipn.htm. Translation by Joanna Bloom.
74. Kolankiewicz and Lewis 1988, p. 102.
75. Grzybowski 1956, p. 388; Majkowski 1985, p. 164; Syrop 1976, pp. 43–5; Ascherson 1982, p. 71.
76. Bauman 1988, p. 89.
77. Kolankiewicz and Lewis 1988, p. 141.
78. Feiwel 1971, p. 698.
79. Pełczyński 1973, p. 5.

and continued dropping thereafter. By 1979, Poland was hemorrhaging at a rate of −20.6 percent.[80] In that year, personal income declined by 2.3 percent.[81]

These trends were felt not simply as inconveniences, but as major determinants of the lives of the Polish people. For example, there was a lack of investment in the infrastructure necessary for new housing – such as sewers, water, electricity and roads. There was a huge shortage of building materials, which was aggravated by waste, too few building workers, poor storage and theft (which was exacerbated by the shortages). Consequently, by the 1980s, waiting-lists for apartments would exceed twenty years in many areas of the country. One result was that people who divorced were often forced to live together because they could find nowhere else to live. Young couples had to live with their parents for many years. During the 1960s, many workers had to live in hostels. Lech Wałęsa spoke of this situation:

> At the end of the corridor on each floor there was a kitchen and shower … The hostel provided a metal bed frame with a lumpy mattress, a floor and four gray walls, all in a filthy state and reeking of mildew, a rickety table and two chairs; each missing at least one leg. A man could drink and sleep at the hostel, but he couldn't really live there.[82]

Here is Kamiński's account of the hostels:

> [L]iving conditions are horribly primitive, pallets, horrible food, lack of minimal hygiene. This results in mass alcoholism and rampant sex. That's how the so-called workers' hostels looked. Moral decay, alcoholism, and vandalism. People have absolutely nothing to do besides physical work. It's a desert.[83]

The shortage of housing was by no means the only manifestation of a lack of investment in the consumer economy. A study of the Warsaw Motorcycle Factory in the 1950s found workers lacking basic clothing (like winter coats) and crowded into small apartments with poor facilities: only one percent had hot running water; 46 percent had cold running water; 25 percent had a toilet in the apartment. Over one-third of the Polish workforce in the late 1950s and early 1960s was forced to live at or below the minimum standard of living.[84] In 1970, one family in five earned less than the minimum necessary for subsistence.[85] In the 1970s, over half of working-class families with children lived in one- or

---

80. Mihalyi 1988, p. 449.
81. Nuti 1982, p. 1, p. 21.
82. Wałęsa 1987, p. 47.
83. www.niniwa2.cba.pl/komunizm_robotnicy_w_prl_ipn.htm. Translation by Joanna Bloom.
84. Kuroń and Modzelewski 1967, pp. 12–14; Lewis 1958, pp. 147–8.
85. Kemp-Welch 1983, pp. 196–7, n. 8.

two-room apartments. Virtually no workers had as much as one room per person.[86] New housing did not go to workers not only because they could not afford it, but also because more privileged groups took priority.[87] By 1987, 60 percent were considered poor.[88]

There were visible manifestations of this poverty everywhere. People who have little are generally not treated well. Alicja Matuszewska told me of the working conditions she discovered in 1981 in a factory near Lublin:

> I was shocked. I could not believe that factories like that still existed in Poland. People who worked in the paint shop had handkerchiefs around their noses and mouths as they sprayed poisonous paint on the cars. In the next department, the mechanics who were fixing buses or trams were freezing because they had no heat.

These conditions were not exceptional. In 1980, the Elmor factory in Gdańsk, which produced electrical equipment for the shipyards, was bathed in acid fumes, which attack the nervous and circulatory systems at several times the medically accepted limits. Accidents, even severe ones, were not uncommon. According to official statistics, in 1976 almost a quarter of the workers in Poland operated in unsafe or unhealthy conditions. Safety equipment, protective clothing and official inspections or medical checks on personnel were lacking.[89]

Another place where bad treatment was particularly evident was in healthcare. Poland's healthcare system, for all but the *nomenklatura*, was inadequate. There were terrible shortages of hospital beds and supplies, as well as needles, syringes and drugs. Some hospitals even had to do without running water for much of the time and suffered unacceptable lapses in hygiene.[90] Medical personnel were forced to reuse needles and syringes because of shortages. In the 1980s, I learned from speaking with doctors and nurses that they were taught how to do this in medical schools. As a result, the mortality rate increased in the 1970s.[91]

At certain times, people protested, and these protests temporarily raised their standard of living. In 1970, as in 1956, strikes and demonstrations toppled the government and forced the price increases to be rolled back. Strikes and riots in 1976 halted another attempt to raise the price of food. In the mid-1970s, the nation's debts – reaching billions of dollars – became due for repayment, and the only way to do so was to force down the standard of living. The next such attempt, in 1980, precipitated the Solidarity movement. It is easy to understand

86. Anasz and Wesołowski 1974, p. 65.
87. Malinowski 1984, pp. 16–18.
88. Wnuk-Lipiński cited in Kolankiewicz and Lewis 1988, p. 58.
89. Potel 1982, pp. 7–8.
90. Kennedy 1991, pp. 299–300; Malinowski 1984, pp. 23–4.
91. Lipski 1985, p. 299.

why these workers resisted. Only when martial law was declared did the government finally succeed in maintaining the higher prices. Then, the burden was felt unequally. Pensioners sank into poverty. Youths were especially affected. While the Solidarity generation had flats, cars, televisions, stereos, and so on, those who came of age in the 1980s had none of these things, and, moreover, had no prospect of ever acquiring them. Young people responded in a variety of ways: either engaging in political activity, or emigrating in large numbers, or becoming drug addicts, with narcotics made from opium poppies grown domestically, or succumbing to deep cynicism and alienation.

The Communist regime: expanded opportunities

In the early years, the Communist regime's commitment to industrialisation introduced a great number of new manufacturing jobs and managerial positions. By 1948, there were nearly twice as many workers as there had been ten years earlier in a country whose population had substantially dropped due to the Holocaust and the terrible destruction of the war.[92] The increased workforce meant a vast expansion of opportunities. Many of the new managers and bureaucrats were drawn from the working class, releasing even more positions below.[93] In the 1960s, sixty percent of a sample of 1,541 executives came from blue-collar families.[94] Adam Skwira, a Silesian miner, recalled that prior to 1956 'the manager of the coal mines was taken straight from the shovel'.

Industry grew rapidly, rising from one-third of national income in the late 1940s to three-fifths in 1971.[95] The numbers of new workers grew at the rate of 10 percent per annum between 1947 and 1958. Most of these people were young surplus workers from the countryside.[96] From 1950 to 1965, employment in mining, manufacturing, services and construction almost doubled; by 1979, it had almost tripled.[97] In the first five years after the war, over seven million people migrated from rural areas to the towns and cities. While in 1946 less than a third of the population lived in urban areas, by 1960 this figure had risen to almost half.[98] In 1950, the rural-born already comprised large percentages of the urban population: one-third of Łódź, and a quarter of Warsaw.[99] That trend continued,

---

92. Ascherson 1982, p. 47.
93. Kolankiewicz and Lewis 1988, p. 41; Bromke and Strong 1973, p. 96; Kolankiewicz 1973, pp. 92–3.
94. Matejko 1971, pp. 34–5.
95. Matejko 1973, p. 90.
96. Dawson 1989, p. 77; see also Anasz and Wesołowski 1974, pp. 37–9.
97. Dawson 1989, p. 73.
98. Kolankiewicz and Lewis 1988, p. 26.
99. Kolankiewicz 1973, p. 93.

and in the first half of the 1950s almost two million more people moved from the countryside to urban areas.[100]

In the cities, farmers' children received education, their own apartments, the cultural life of the city, as well as the freedom and anonymity city life brings. Thus, even though real wages fell for industrial workers, former peasants experienced a substantial rise in their standard of living.[101] There can be little doubt that at the time many people experienced these changes as an improvement in their lives. In surveys carried out in 1964 and 1976, Krystyna Janicka found that between seventy and eight-five percent of urban workers had jobs of greater standing than their fathers.[102] Jan Stępniewski recalled how, as a child, he observed the benefits of the new regime:

> My parents worked ten to eleven hours a day as weavers in Łódź, with no sick leave, no vacations, no social security, no benefits. Public education was two to three years; the rest you had to pay for. Under the Communists, my parents worked in the same factories, but in completely different conditions: social security, free medical care, free and required school for all children, vacations, sick leave. They were thrilled. That there was no democracy didn't matter.
>
> Under the influence of our parents' stories about how they lived before the war, we were convinced that there was an indisputable value to the Communist system. My parents underlined the blessing of not being unemployed. My mother's father was killed by lightning when he was watching the landlord's fishing pond. My grandmother was left with five children and no money to raise them. The landlord didn't feel responsible and gave her nothing.
>
> It was a poor country, but there were no beggars. Everyone – old, sick, widows, orphans – all were provided for. They were given apartments, the means to live and to educate themselves, if they wanted to. The police would take a beggar or a homeless person to a shelter. There were kindergartens and pre-schools for all children. Children received milk and food at school. If you didn't act politically incorrectly, you could go as high as you wanted. My mother can barely write her signature, and there I was, a student. So it is not surprising that part of our soul was red.

But it was often not an easy transition. After the war, millions of Germans were expelled from territory that had previously been theirs in western and northern Poland. People moved into the newly-emptied lands from what had been eastern Poland, but was now annexed by the Soviet Union. They were forced by

---

100. Paczkowski 2003, p. 215.
101. Feiwel 1971, pp. 75–6; Garton Ash 1985, p. 7.
102. Janicka 1981, cited in Mason 1985, p. 39.

the Soviets to move or abandon their Polish citizenship. They were bitter about having lost their homes and having been forced to undertake an arduous trek of hundreds of miles. But the areas to which they moved, which included the cities of Danzig, Stettin, Breslau – reborn as Gdańsk, Szczecin and Wrocław, respectively – were much wealthier and more developed than those from which they came: roads, houses, factories and cities offered them opportunities that simply had not existed in their previous locations.[103]

The destruction carried out during the Nazi occupation and the war necessitated rapid reconstruction. Whole cities had been destroyed. More than a fifth of the population had gone, including about half of the intelligentsia – university professors (40 percent), lawyers and doctors (50 percent), writers, architects and other professionals, even high-school teachers (totalling 16,000) – deliberately wiped out by the Nazis and the Soviets.[104] Millions of others were lost to disease following the war.[105] All of these positions had to be quickly restaffed, and new positions developed as the economy expanded. Twelve thousand engineers in 1938 became 130,000 in 1968.[106] In the first half of the 1950s, the number of technical engineers and administrative and clerical employees doubled.[107]

All of this meant increased opportunities for social mobility. By one estimate, in the fifteen years after the war, over sixty-nine thousand manual workers obtained white-collar jobs.[108] Another study revealed that 61 percent of the population had been upwardly mobile.[109] By 1971, an astounding 98.5 percent of the sons of unskilled labourers found their first jobs in a different occupational group than their fathers, and most of these involved upward mobility.[110] As Janina Bauman recounts:

> It was very easy to get a job in the late 1940s. Jobs chased people, age or lack of skills being no bar. For young, intelligent men and women with clean political records and a willingness to learn new skills, the sky was the limit. They could choose almost any job they wished and ... be sure of rapid promotion.[111]

---

103. Dawson 1989, p. 73.
104. Ascherson 1982, p. 69; Kolankiewicz and Lewis 1988, p. 54; Kennedy 1991, p. 239; Reynolds 1978, p. 518.
105. Malara and Rey 1952, p. 153.
106. Bromke 1969, p. 118.
107. Kolankiewicz 1973, p. 97.
108. Kolankiewicz 1973, pp. 97–8.
109. Pohoski, cited in Kolankiewicz and Lewis 1988, p. 22; Anasz and Wesołowski 1974, pp. 46–8.
110. Zagórski 1974, pp. 338–40.
111. Baumann 1988, pp. 60–1.

Teachers were put through shortened training periods to get them into schools that were rapidly expanding.[112] In the 1970s, almost half of the elementary and secondary school teachers did not have an academic degree.[113] Throughout the 1980s, teachers in elementary schools did not require a university degree to begin teaching, although it was advantageous for them to acquire one eventually – for without it teachers were not eligible for tenure.[114]

Those who remained in the countryside also benefitted from the Communist accession to power. The first decree of the new government, proclaimed while the war still raged on Polish soil, promised to take the land away from the pre-war landlords and to distribute it to the peasantry. This policy applied to some six million hectares.[115] Two years later, the government distributed lands in western Poland that had been taken from Germany to peasants. These acts won the new Communist regime considerable support.[116]

The patronage system

Patronage and corruption spread throughout this system and society. Stefan Staszewski, a highly-placed official in the *nomenklatura* during the post-war years, claimed that when he proposed firing someone who was not 'qualified as a journalist':

> He wouldn't reply, but he began to excuse himself, that perhaps he really was a bad journalist; his actual words were: I'm a lousy journalist, but I'm loyal. And thus without knowing it he described, in simple words, the party's personnel policy: no one has to be competent in any post; he merely has to be loyal.[117]

Those accorded the chance to rise were politically reliable. This attitude was read at first from social origins, providing immense benefits to classes who had previously been virtually excluded from all opportunities. The children of workers and peasants were favoured while those of the bourgeoisie and petit-bourgeoisie were overlooked.[118] From 1945 to 1962, 55 percent of university graduates were of worker or peasant origin, compared to just 15 percent in the 1930s.[119] This favouritism sprang from a sincere belief in the ideology. However, it was also an attempt to win over what Communist Party officials regarded as the 'natural

---

112. Kolankiewicz and Lewis 1988, p. 54.
113. Blazynski 1979, p. 134.
114. Kennedy 1991, p. 239.
115. Ascherson 1982, p. 45.
116. Bardach, Leśnodorski and Pietrzak 1985, pp. 559–67; Pełczyński 1980, p. 321.
117. Torańska 1987, p. 187.
118. Markiewicz 1974, p. 243.
119. Kolankiewicz and Lewis 1988, p. 52.

constituency' of the regime. Indeed, there appears to have been a measure of desperation as they sought to increase the number of workers in the Party leadership. Orders would be initiated to advance a specified number of workers into managerial positions:

> from the *Województwo* to every *Powiat* to every larger factory comes a directive: five or six people have to be moved to managerial positions regardless of their competency. This shuffle is done mechanically and often ends when in six months the same people have to be recalled because they cannot manage. The tragedy is that in the meantime, those workers became hated by their peers and so for this reason as well as formalities, they could not return to workers' communities. So later those people are moved to lower administrative positions simply to get rid of them.[120]

But by the end of the 1960s, the children of workers were much less likely to be in academic or technical high schools than the children of other social groups.[121] So the new normal came to be much like the old.

Those early days were also characterised by the three-year-long civil war, which helped engender a sense that the regime was besieged and needed to ensure that its officials offered institutional support.[122] Loyalty became the prime determinant of who would advance. As the system stabilised, more and more people accommodated themselves to it and a class of careerists emerged,[123] as Solidarity leader Edward Nowak bitterly noted:

> I knew a high-ranking Party Secretary who is now [in 1988] a director of a really big enterprise. We both graduated from the same school. He was decidedly the weakest student. I graduated with excellent grades and am now unemployed and have served prison terms.

Even those who were talented and devoted to their occupation had to join the Party to be able to advance. And, having ascended the occupational and status ladders, he began to have his own supply of jobs and other resources to dispense.

Enterprises became the locus not only of production and services, but also of distribution. In part this was because of the inability of the economy to provide what people wanted and needed. To keep their workforces contented, managers provided flats, desired foods and coupons that allowed one to purchase automobiles, washing machines, televisions and other goods. They built vacation dachas,

---

120. www.niniwa2.cba.pl/komunizm_robotnicy_w_prl_ipn.htm. Translation by Joanna Bloom.
121. Kolankiewicz 1973, p. 129.
122. Rakowski 1973, p. 26.
123. Kuroń 1990, p. 33; Misztal and Misztal 1984, pp. 169–70.

health resorts and a variety of other perks for their workers, and they distributed food on holidays. At a time when one might have to wait twenty years or more to acquire a place to live, employers were distributing 55 percent of all housing.[124] The resources of businesses enabled them to price individuals out of the market. These fringe benefits constituted a significant part of the nation's economy and had an important effect within a society of scarcity. Goods tended to be allocated to those who had connections, or to those who were otherwise favoured, rather than to those who had the greatest need or had been waiting the longest, or any other measure of equity.

Prices were not set in response to the market or the costs of production, but rather to further the interests of patrons. Jacek Kuroń, for decades a leading dissident, said:

> When we became part of the government, we discovered that certain factories set prices at whatever level they wished. The factory that produced televisions set prices at a childishly low level. Why? A director received a TV once a quarter, people in lower management twice a year, and the worker probably once a year. From the book-keeper's point of view, they received small amounts that did not mean anything. But later, they were able to sell them on the black market because that was the only place they were available and they could set really high prices.

The unchecked power that such a system created allowed people's lives to be controlled and misshaped in an utterly arbitrary manner, according to the whims of individuals, with the victim being completely unaware not only of what had been done to him or her, but also of the perpetrator's identity. Kuroń recalled that the socialist youth group provided recommendations concerning who should be admitted to the universities. In Poland, as in the rest of Europe, not to attend a university meant that one's career choices were very limited. Kuroń described how he and his friends unintentionally destroyed the career of a fellow student:

> There was a girl, Ela... I met her not such a long time ago, and I asked her what she did. She said to me, 'I am a clerk. I couldn't go to the university because the leader of the District Committee wrote "bigot" in my recommendation'. My conscience was struck by lightning. We are sitting in the school toilet, we are smoking, and we are crabbing about Ela and other new activists. Somebody says, 'we'll have to write in her recommendation that she is a ZMP [*Związek Młodzieży Polskiej* = Polish Youth Union] bigot'. The District Committee gave recommendations to the School Committee and to the leaders

---

124. Smolar 1983, pp. 51–2.

of the School Committee. And surely somebody from our group wrote in her recommendation, 'ZMP bigot'. But after that, somebody crossed ZMP out, because they didn't know what it meant.

Party membership became a prerequisite for a whole range of benefits: to become a manager or even a foreman;[125] to have a better chance to get an education; to get a coupon to buy a car, a refrigerator, a washing machine, a television set. Party-members tended to make more money than others and had the opportunity to work abroad and to earn foreign currency (which, when changed on the black market, was literally worth a fortune in Poland).[126] As Zbigniew Bujak notes: 'When somebody from the factory wanted a flat, he had to join the party'. Lech Wałęsa also recalled:

> The job assignments are handled by foremen, who therefore have power over workers' wages ... If one of the old guard got married, he made more money than usual for a few months ... He'd be the one selected to get the highest-paying jobs.[127]

The habit of corruption that such practices precipitated became deeply ingrained. When Grzegorz Olejnik, a newly-elected member of the Solidarity presidium in Szczecin, was stopped for speeding, he presented the policeman with his papers. Unintentionally included among them was the card denoting his membership in the Solidarity presidium. Upon seeing the card, the policeman returned his documents and let him go, greatly upsetting Olejnik who saw the old habits returning. Awareness of corruption affected even the negotiations that established the Solidarity union. In Silesia, workers insisted upon and won a clause that forbade miners from being used to build private villas.[128]

The corruption was enormously destructive. Jerzy Taylor, the former vice-chancellor of the University of Gdańsk, and his wife, both biologists, informed me in 1986 that they had to choose: either to be professionals or to build a house. If they chose the latter, they could expect to spend two years at the job, full-time, bribing people in order to obtain the necessary supplies: bricks, mortar, electrical wiring, copper tubes, plumbing materials, and so on, and overseeing the work to make sure that they were not being cheated. In an economy of scarcity, bribery became both *necessary*, on account of the shortages, and *possible* because those controlling the materials *themselves* needed so much. Given that choice, the Taylors preferred to spend their time as professionals. Thus, as Jan Uchański worried, the prevailing ethos undermined the economy. The experience of the

---

125. Młodzik interview.
126. Majkowski 1989, p. 101.
127. Wałęsa 1987, p. 45.
128. Czabański 1983, p. 159.

Taylors was not an isolated one, and such moral corruption had a devastating effect on the economy. Throughout the 1980s, the official trade unions used the same methods to get people to join, as did the Communist Youth Organisation.

This system was terribly frustrating for those who tried to live their lives without partaking in corruption. One had to learn to organise one's life in order to survive. But to do so necessarily meant having some means of circumventing the obstacles presented by the bureaucratic structure. The Polish term for these efforts is *lawirować*, and when spoken it is usually accompanied by a hand gesture that evokes a fish, whose body curves as it moves, slaloming to avoid obstacles. One had to find some way to make the system do what one wanted, which necessitated having connections. Jan Uchański worried that the nation had become so concerned with the struggle for everyday needs and desires that his son, and indeed everyone, was being trained that this was how to live, and that they could no longer imagine living a normal life in a normal society. It was as though they were infected with a disease. What had begun as a response to economic chaos was corrupting the very soul of the Polish nation.

Part One

The Emergence of Opposition

Chapter Two
The First Systemic Crisis

> Andrzej Potocki, a leader of the Club of Catholic Intellectuals (KIK): I remember in 1945: in the morning we still had Germans, and in the afternoon the Soviets came in. We were standing in the street talking and a group of Soviet soldiers came into the square. This was liberation! But not a window opened. Not a gate. Nobody came into the street. The square remained as empty as it had been before. I went inside very quickly because I felt so uncomfortable.

Open opposition to the Communist regime began immediately following the end of World War II, as soon as the Communists succeeded the German occupation. At that time, a substantial section of the *Armia Krajowa* [AK = Home Army] turned their guns on the new regime as a civil war broke out that would last for three years. In comparison to other civil wars and the brutality of World War II, it was 'low-level', but it was not insignificant. Stefan Staszewski, an early leader of 'People's Poland', recalled:[1]

> the period of violence, cruelty and lawlessness that Poland experienced in the years 1944–7. Not thousands but tens of thousands were killed then, and the official trials that were organised after 1949 were merely an epilogue to the liquidation of the Home Army, of activists, of independent parties and of independent thought in general.

---

1. Torańska 1987, p. 139.

The decision to make war – first with the Soviets, and later with the Communist government they left behind – was not an ideological one. Rather, it was a response to the actions of the Soviet soldiers who turned their weapons on their former allies. The Soviet army started killing Polish partisans in July 1944. According to the journalist and anti-Communist activist, Rafał Górski, 'by January of 1945, 30,000 members of the underground were arrested. From that number, around 16,000 were sent to the interior of the USSR'.[2] The AK responded essentially in self-defence.

Opposition continued elsewhere not long after the end of that war, as farmers fought the government's efforts to forcibly collectivise their newly-acquired lands. The land was ceded in order to win the farmers' support, and it did so until the government tried to collectivise the land.

A third source of opposition came from the efforts of the Catholic Church to retain its independence from the would-be totalitarian government that came to power. Unlike in other countries in the Soviet bloc, the Church in Poland had never collaborated with the Germans. Indeed, during the period of more than a century when Poland had disappeared as a political entity, having been occupied throughout the nineteenth century and beyond, the Church had stood for the nation, protecting its language, which had been prohibited in schools and in public. As such, the Catholic Church stood unsullied from Poland's long domination by other powers.

Under the Communists, the Church continued to insist upon its independence. In the early days of Communist control, beginning at the end of the 1940s and continuing up until 1956, there was a virtual war between Church and state. Hundreds of priests and several bishops were imprisoned; a few priests were even sentenced to death; seminaries were closed; the number of churches permitted was limited, and many Church lands and buildings were seized by the state. When the Pope excommunicated Catholics who supported the Communists, the latter responded by threatening imprisonment for priests who refused to grant communion to such people. Cardinal Stefan Wyszyński, Poland's Primate, was placed under house arrest. After the events of 1956, this conflict considerably eased as the government backed away. From that time, with each of Poland's crises up to the end of Communist domination, the Church grew increasingly powerful as the government found that it needed the stability provided by the Church.

Nonetheless, despite these conflicts with the new regime, as the journalist Maciek Kozłowski stated: 'Communist ideology in the early fifties was quite popular among the young generation'. Even Pope John Paul II acknowledged that

2. www.rozbrat.org/historia/33-walki-spoleczne-w-polsce/416-opor-spoleczny-w-polsce-w-latach-1944-1989-cz-i. Translation by Joanna Bloom.

'a certain type of unbridled, savage capitalism' provoked a reaction 'that grew and gained the support of many people [who] . . . thought that communism would improve the quality of life'.[3] While the old system had been discredited by the war and economic depression, the material benefits that came with land redistribution, urbanisation and industrialisation helped to win (grudging) acquiescence toward the new regime. As such, some people were prepared to welcome or at the least accept the regime.[4] Wojciech Adamiecki, later an independent journalist and Solidarity supporter, explained how the devastation of World War II seared itself into his being and prepared him for social change:

> After leaving Warsaw, I remember seeing the smoke of the burning city. For a good number of years after the war, I had that picture in my eyes. I remember my father's words: 'Everything up to now is finished'. For many, many years my attitude toward what was going on in Poland was influenced by these pictures. I was a child of this People's Poland – cut off from tradition, educated there, and for some years I supported it. There was a tendency to criticise everything from the old Poland.

Poland was a kind of no-man's land after the Germans fled and before the Russians arrived, as Lechosław Goździk, who was aged 14 when the war ended, recalled of his town Tomaszów:

> The Germans had already left; the Russians hadn't come yet. In Tomaszów, there was a hill over which the German soldiers had to go. It was a very harsh winter in '45 and the horses were tired pulling the wagons. They would fall on that hill, and the Germans would just leave the wagons and the horses behind and take off on foot. So, we would go to those horses and un-hitch them, bring them down to our garden, feed them, get them back on their feet and, when the Russians came, we already had a whole herd of horses. But, of course, the Russians took them. From those wagons, we took machine guns, pistols, munitions, grenades. Our mother was terrified to move around because our whole house had turned into an arsenal. We had weapons everywhere – an armoury.

> People felt they had the freedom to take what they could – whatever wasn't tied to the ground. I remember like today: people were walking back and forth with clocks, bookcases, whatever you could think of. I remember my father coming home and telling my uncle that they had to go protect the factory. This weaponry that we had collected at the time became really useful. Altogether there was my father, my two uncles and two of their friends and me and my

3. Gawroński 1993, p. 18.
4. Ascherson 1982, pp. 43, 64.

brother. We all got machine guns and we went to protect the factory. When people took fabric from the factory, we just stood by and watched because we understood that people needed fabric so they could make clothing. At the time, the company used steam engines to move the machines, not electricity like today. All those machines used transmission belts. When people went for those belts, because they were leather, my father said we could not allow that because that would stop the factory. So, we fired in the air and people just took off. Then other workers joined in, and we gave them weapons and from then on, the factory was guarded until the Russians came – so Polish workers were already in control of the factory. A week after the Russians entered, the factory was opened again and started producing again. My father became the general director of the factory, and he was there for many years.

However, disillusionment with the new Communist state began early. Goździk joined Poland's Communist Party that took power. He started out as a strong supporter of the government, but his idealism did not last long:

The peasants were required to sell their grain to the government. Since they did not have as much as was demanded from them, groups were organised to go out to the villages and rob the peasants of the grain that they kept for planting. I was in one of those groups. According to the ideology, people who had over fourteen hectares were *kulaks*.[5] A *kulak* was a blood-sucking beast who exploited the lowest class in the village. With that image in mind, we went to a farmer who had more than thirty hectares. He had a hut that barely stood together, covered with straw. My first thought was 'People's Poland has only existed for five years and they have already managed to camouflage their wealth so well'. But the real psychological shock came when we went in and saw the people who lived there. I said to the farmer's wife, 'Grandma, we came here to get the grain'. A little girl turned to me and said, 'This is not grandma. She is my mother'. She wasn't even forty and she looked like she was closer to seventy! That's what life in the village and poverty did to her. These people told us we were worse than the Nazis. When the Nazis came to collect the required produce, they always left enough so that they could barely survive and have grain to sow next year. We took everything. The government was merciless: if the peasants were unable to produce as much grain as they were assigned, they would be arrested and put in prisons.

For some others, if there were any illusions, they were quickly dispelled. It should not be surprising, given the enormous destruction that Poland suffered during World War II – not only the physical liquidation of vast numbers of people, but

---

5. A hectare is about 2.5 acres.

also the damage to cities, plants, machinery, roads, and so on – that the working class itself should have been severely disrupted. In the mining region of Upper Silesia, the disruption was both immense and criminal. According to an investigation carried out in Katowice, some ten thousand Polish miners were forcibly rounded up and deported to the Soviet Union because it needed miners – skilled labourers.

In many if not most cities there was (and needed to be) a vast influx of people from eastern Poland – which had been annexed to the Soviet Union – and from the countryside. All of this meant that these people neither knew nor trusted one another. They had no shared traditions. As a result, they were not in a good position to resist whatever the government should demand of them. Polish historian Stanisław Jankowiak explained the situation as follows:

> The years '47 and '48 are a breaking point where an influx of people . . . begins. They're pulled from the villages, moved into factories, and turned into workers. The old workers are very reserved towards them for many reasons, like the fact that their technical abilities are low. They are not partners but the unqualified mass. In such mixed crews communication and understanding is very hard since these people entered a foreign community where they are a minority. They are aware that it is not a welcoming community, [but one] that perceives them as a kind of intruder with poorer qualifications for work.

The Communist regime encountered most resistance in the few cities – such as Łódź and Poznań – where there had been very little influx from the outside and where the working-class had made it through the war together. Polish historian Łukasz Kamiński recalled:

> In the years 1945–8, it can be clearly seen wherever there are old communities where migration did not happen and stability of social structures among the workers is significant, that's where there are more strikes. The most strikes happened in Łódź because statistically speaking people had over ten years seniority in one factory. The strikes explode there by the end of March 1945.[6]

In 1951, mine workers struck by staying underground in the Kazimierz Juliusz Mine, as well as others in Zagłębie in Upper-Silesia. Edward Gierek stated that he was sent into the mines in order to persuade the miners to cease the strikes, in return for which he was promised that he would become First Secretary for the region in Katowice. He and Marian Czerwiński were sent underground to negotiate with the miners. Czerwiński spoke first and was shouted down by the miners. Then, as Gierek recounted:

---

6. www.niniwa2.cba.pl/komunizm_robotnicy_w_prl_ipn.htm. Translation by Joanna Bloom.

I spoke, but I was immediately interrupted: 'What do you want, son-of-a-bitch? Into the shaft with him'. Then I yelled with the loudest voice I could: 'Who do you want to shove into the shaft, ME? There is enough blood of my forefathers spilled here. Here died my grandfather, father, relatives, and now you want to toss me into the shaft!' Then it became quiet, so I yelled again: 'My name is Gierek, there are my relatives here, they can vouch that I'm telling the truth'. When they did not interrupt me again, I spoke more at ease: 'You think that only you can organise strikes? I also organised, and I got kicked in the arse for it ... but I organised them against forced migrants,[7] against capitalists, but for your strike we will all have to pay'. I spoke in the Zagłębie dialect, I was determined, nervous, and I guess I must have come across as authentic, because they began listening, asking questions, and after a few hours of persuasion and discussions, they agreed to come up.[8]

According to an article that appeared in *Gazeta Wyborcza*, Poland's largest newspaper, other mines also surrendered after that:

Then came the time for punishment ... It was a truly Soviet 'holy Mass'. In the mines which had gone striking, public mass meetings of the Party were called, and the participants of the strikes were publicly stripped of their Party membership as their cards were taken away. They were publicly humiliated, branded, and forced to leave their beloved communities.[9]

Tadeusz Tomaszewski, who worked in the mine at the time, told me that afterwards the secret police 'came after these people, and they were arrested, either at work or in the middle of the night'. The directions given by the government are summarised below:

1. All strike leaders to be tracked down and arrested to remove from public eye, let UB handle the issue and cooperate with their investigation;
2. Dilute the mine crews with new workers recruited from other parts of Poland and the re-settlers from the East.
3. Miners in charge of explosives to be strictly watched while they train their replacements from among men considered loyal and reliable.

---

7. Gierek used the term 'Przesiedleńcy', which referred to Poles who had lived in Eastern Poland and had been forced by the Soviets to abandon their properties and move into the new and revised Polish borders which no longer included large chunks of lands that became part of Lithuania, Ukraine and Belarus, which at that time were all part of the Soviet Union. In return, Poland gained lands in the west and north, which included: parts of eastern Prussia, large chunks of Wielkopolska and Silesia.

8. Rolicki 1990, p. 27. Translation by Joanna Bloom.

9. www.wyborcza.pl/1,75517,863825.html#ixzz1nyglghko. Translation by Joana Bloom.

4. In any mine whenever possible elevate men considered loyal and reliable to mid-management and higher. Advancing Silesians should be avoided if possible since they are not reliable and their loyalties to Poland are unclear.

5. In the interest of keeping up coal production, the creation of incentives for the men recruited from outside of Silesia should be considered a priority. It is acceptable to use housing currently occupied by the Silesians to achieve this goal.

6. Use of Silesian dialect to be discouraged in the mines and banned from schools.[10]

In other words, a reign of terror was waged among those who remained, and native Silesians were subject to significant discrimination. They were branded as 'Germans' and therefore untrustworthy. Based on their experience, the Silesians were hostile to the Communist government and they voted against it when the opportunity arose. To limit their influence, outsiders were recruited with promises of good jobs and apartments, while apartments elsewhere were extremely hard to come by. As point five above indicates, the government was prepared to remove the Silesians from their homes for the benefit of newcomers. Now, not only were native Silesians terrorised, but the cohesion they had fostered was destroyed. It took a considerable amount of time for workers in this area to act against the authorities again, and this is one of the main reasons why Upper-Silesia remained quiescent before the 1980 upheaval that produced Solidarity.[11]

While these examples are indicative of a growing disillusionment or even hostility towards the new regime, they did not, however, translate into active opposition to the government. Indeed, how could they? In a theme that repeatedly surfaced in my interviews, *there was no choice*. Moreover, people genuinely hoped that the promises of the new government would be realised. As Goździk noted:

> We were proud of every building, of every street, of the old town that we rebuilt. We donated our time. It was a time when pretty much everyone was choking with joy on for Communism. The idea was that there would be general well-being in the country.

I heard this sentiment expressed by several people whose memories could take them back to those days.

Discontent did not first crystallise into overt popular resistance until post-war Poland's first systemic crisis in 1956. Stalin had died a few years earlier, and in 1956 the new Soviet leader, Nikita Khrushchev, revealed and denounced

---

10. Woźniczka 2010, pp. 146–9.
11. Dziurok 2001. Translation by Joanna Bloom.

many of Stalin's crimes. Polish leader Bolesław Bierut, who had visited Moscow to attend the Party Congress where Khrushchev famously blasted Stalin's practices, died mysteriously, thereby beginning a struggle for leadership within the Polish Party and setting the stage for the crisis. Within no time, the Polish Party became factionalised, as some sought to preserve the policies and organisational practices that had developed under Stalin's insistence, while others fought for some democratisation and increased freedoms.[12]

The year 1956 evokes the revolutionary uprising in Hungary and its brutal suppression by Soviet troops (joined by Polish troops), an episode to which Khrushchev devoted a chapter of his memoir.[13] It is less widely recounted in the West that the upheaval started in Poland, in the city of Poznań, located some ninety kilometres due east of Berlin. While other cities in western Poland – such as Szczecin and Wrocław – had been largely German, Poznań had a longstanding Polish majority. It was an industrial city, not seriously damaged during the war, with a substantial workforce whose members knew one another and had a tradition of organised struggle that had not been undermined by a large influx of outsiders.

Poznań's grievances

A new tax law significantly cut into earnings: some five thousand workers each lost approximately two months' salary.[14] Stanisław Matyja, who worked in the railroad car factory in the vast Cegielski complex and became the protest leader in 1956, said that until then, 'working hard, I made 100–150 percent of the norm. Now I would not have been able to make even seventy percent'.[15] Stanisław Machnicki, a machinist who worked in the factory, recalled: 'This unfair tax made the glass of bitterness overflow. People were ready to explode'.

The announcement of an open meeting in March 1956 drew crowds of angry people, all of whom, Matyja reported, 'vehemently demanded explanations to all kinds of problems, but got none'. As a result, 'We came to one conclusion: we have to demand, always demand'.[16] Matyja had seen the books and learned that the director had taken a huge salary for himself. Work stoppages began in mid-June and the workers demanded to see representatives from Warsaw. The next day, a government commission arrived but 'did not answer the questions we showered them with', said Matyja, who warned that: 'If we did not receive

---

12. Paczkowski 2003, pp. 270–3.
13. Khrushchev 1970, pp. 456–73.
14. Ziemkowski 1981, pp. 60–1.
15. Matyja 1981, pp. 215–16. Translation by Joanna Bloom.
16. Matyja 1981, p. 218.

an answer by the next day, we would go to the streets'.[17] The commission suggested that the workers select representatives to go to Warsaw to discuss their concerns. These representatives were joined by Party and management representatives.[18] During the trip, Machnicki, who was one of the delegates, said the discussions about the forthcoming meeting in Warsaw were conducted in an atmosphere in which they were pressured not to 'spit in the water we drank'. In Warsaw, said Matyja, 'among us sat a few strangers who did not speak but who obviously had "bones" [guns] under their jackets'. They agreed upon several items and the government representatives promised to travel to Poznań the next day to present the agreement to the workers. The meeting ended, the delegation split up and its members found their own ways home.[19]

The next day, 27 June, at the W-3 plant in Cegielski, the meeting did not go well. Matyja recalled: 'When the minister began talking ... it turned out that he was saying the complete opposite of what was agreed upon in Warsaw. My voice breaking, I ... said ... that ... we had ... made a completely different deal'. The workers were ready to hang the minister. Matyja walked him out of the meeting to protect him.[20]

Strike

The next morning, workers from the night-shift refused to change back into civilian clothes. When Matyja arrived, his workmates 'came running to me yelling that ... the people were ... waiting for me ... When I entered the hall, I heard a great "hooray!" and the whole mass of people moved toward ... W-4'.[21] An estimated eighty percent of the workers left the factory.[22]

Workers in several other companies knew of the impending walkout. When the siren signal came, they joined the protest.[23] The director of the tram depot tried to stop the departing workers. Matyja said that 'They put him into the oil pit and dumped a barrel of dirty oil on him'. When they came to the clothing factory, the women workers there cried that 'they were locked up and could not leave. This infuriated the already angry crowd which chanted: "We want bread! We want freedom! We want religion!" Gates were forced open and ... the seamstresses came out with us'.[24]

---

17. Matyja 1981, p. 220; Ziemkowski 1981, p. 63.
18. Matyja 1981, p. 220; Ziemkowski 1981, p. 65.
19. Ziemkowski 1981, p. 66; Matyja 1981, p. 221.
20. Matyja 1981, p. 222.
21. Matyja 1981, p. 223.
22. Ziemkowski 1981, p. 68.
23. Matyja 1981, p. 223; Ziemkowski 1981, p. 68.
24. Matyja 1981, p. 224.

As they marched, couriers went to other factories and whole crews joined in, including in some cases as many as half or more of the Party members. So did people on the streets, including high school and university students. People yelled in support from the windows as the workers passed by. Crowd estimates ranged from one hundred thousand to two hundred thousand – in other words, between one-quarter and one-half of the city's population.[25] According to Matyja, 'All was very orderly; not even the grass was stepped on'.[26] They marched to Freedom Square, and then on to the Party building. Jerzy Grabus, a student at the Polytechnic University in Poznań, said he 'crashed into the event in the city centre. The square was filled. It was a very quiet crowd. The main thing they did was sing patriotic and religious songs'. When Machnicki arrived, the crowd was 'so thick that there was no room to move. A Party secretary from the Provincial Committee was yelling at people, getting them so angry that they would have lynched him'.

Insurrection

The slogans demanding bread and lower prices soon gave way to more political expressions: 'Away with the Bolsheviks!' 'Down with Communism!' Party cards were collected and burned.[27] When officials tried to stop the demonstrators from invading the Party building, the crowd beat them up. As Matyja observed, the 'windows opened and shouts came out: "Look, how they live!" Tableware ... hams, vodka and other delicacies were shown. The people became inflamed'.[28] Soon, a white flag of surrender hung from the Castle.[29] Then, recalled Jerzy Grabus, a 'few trucks filled with police tried to go through the crowd, but they could not move. There were shouts that they should get out of the truck and they did'. This episode appeared to give heart to the demonstrators, some of whom shouted: 'The militia are with us!'[30] They were neither feared nor hated. No-one disarmed them. But the same good will was not offered to the police commandant. When he spoke to the crowd someone struck him in the face.[31]

The organisers of the protest were losing control. Soon, the huge crowd began to go in different directions as rumours diffused through it, including one that claimed the Cegielski representatives who had gone to Warsaw had been arrested –

25. Majkowski 1985, p. 75; Kemp-Welch 1983, pp. 3–4; Goodwyn 1991, pp. 64–6; Ziemkowski 1981, p. 73. Matyja 1981, p. 225.
26. Matyja 1981, p. 224.
27. Machcewicz 1996, p. 16.
28. Matyja 1981, p. 225.
29. Ziemkowski 1981, p. 73.
30. Matyja 1981, p. 224.
31. Ziemkowski 1981, p. 74.

which was untrue.[32] Aleksandra Banasiak, a young nurse on her day off, was on her way to the railway station to meet her father, who was coming to visit her, when rumours of these arrests circulated: 'Word was passed from one person to another to go to the jail and get "our people out", and the crowd started moving toward the prison', which it soon stormed.

> **Jerzy Grabus:** I joined them. We got there and shouted to the guards to open the gate. They refused. It happened that they were replacing the electric poles, which were conveniently laying right there. We used them as battering rams. The gate opened very suddenly, and the whole crowd just burst into the prison. All the prisoners were released. The rest was chaos.

When Banasiak arrived, the prisoners were already free:

> They greeted us with hugs and kisses, and thanked us for liberating them. The crowds were throwing documents and furniture out of the windows onto the streets, and people were trampling upon them. Destroying the prison gave people a sense of strength: they were destroying the power of the police.

Another group set out to topple the powerful radio transmitter that was used to jam the broadcasts of the BBC, Voice of America and Radio Free Europe. Meanwhile, Matyja recalled:

> A group...showed up and announced that they were going to [the secret police headquarters] because the [Cegielski] delegation was imprisoned there. I grabbed the [leader] by the front of the coat but I did not convince him, even though I told him I was one of the representatives who was not locked up after all.[33]

Matyja saw things spinning out of control: 'The...demonstrators became a wild element. Shouts. Singing. People were very excited'. He felt there was no more he could do: 'I decided that my role...as...a leader of the crowd had come to an end'. He left the demonstration and headed back to the factory.[34] On his way, Matyja saw a tram being overturned; then a few tanks arrived. Surrounded by the crowd, the soldiers emerged from the tanks and left them: 'I saw a group of civilians man the first tank and drive it to [the secret-police headquarters]',[35] to which another part of the crowd went, accompanied by the chant: 'Let's go for the spider web!'[36]

---

32. Ibid.
33. Matyja 1981, p. 226.
34. Ibid.
35. Ibid.
36. Ziemkowski 1981, p. 74.

War

The move on the headquarters of the *Urząd Bezpieczeństwa* [UB was the office of security, the secret police] was deadly serious, and was apparently encouraged by (false) rumours that battles were also raging in the cities of Łódź, Katowice, Gdańsk, Szczecin, Warsaw and Bydgoszcz.[37] Józef Rybak, a worker who joined the attack, said:

> The secret-police officers understood that if the crowd got in, there wouldn't be much left of them, so, they defended themselves with everything they had. First, they used water. The people responded with bricks and stones torn out of the street, throwing them at the windows. That's when they began to shoot.

The secret-police headquarters was just down the street from the hospital where Aleksandra Banasiak worked:

> Someone saw me walking into the hospital. They asked me if I could get some of the purified gasoline we used. I went in, got a big basket, collected one- and two-litre bottles of gasoline, and gave them to young men who wanted to burn down the secret police building.

From her living quarters on the third floor of the hospital, she could see the street below:

> I heard shots fired and people screaming for help. I got into my nurse's uniform and went out into the street. By then, it was about 11am. I stayed out until late into the night, helping people get to the hospital. As I was doing this, bullets were whistling past my ears.

The crowd overturned trams and trucks for barricades. Local troops were brought in, but they were reluctant to fire on the townspeople,[38] and in some cases tanks were abandoned and troops disarmed.[39] Groups stormed police stations, from which weapons were taken. Once the offensive capabilities of the city's six police stations had been emptied, they started attacking stations in the suburbs. Thus, a continual supply of arms was being delivered to the crowds outside the headquarters, intensifying the battle. Shots were fired from basements, attics, roofs and courtyards.[40] Banasiak stated:

> There were lots and lots of wounded. Just in our hospital, in a very short period of time, we brought in sixty-five. There weren't enough beds, so they were lying on the floor, on mattresses, on blankets.

---

37. Machcewicz 1996, pp. 18–19.
38. Goodwyn 1991, pp. 67–8.
39. Ziemkowski 1981, p. 79.
40. Ibid.

The fact that people were being shot did not stop the crowd; instead, this seemed to enrage it. A *UB* report claimed the following: 'We met several people . . . who carried a torn national flag smeared with blood. They called people to avenge the workers murdered by the *UB*'.[41]

Jerzy Grabus hastened to where the shots were being fired. Across the street from the UB building was a parking lot, which provided sanctuary from which people were shooting at the secret-police headquarters. Grabus soon acquired a gun from an injured man and joined the fray:

> I was shooting at the building. After a while, the secret police had me pegged and I couldn't move. Bullets passed within a couple of centimetres of my head. A part of my sleeve stuck out and it got shot. I yelled to my helper, who was about 17, to get me some rounds. He started throwing bullets to me, one-by-one. They landed right near me, but I still had to reach out to get them. I used the butt of my gun to pull them to me, and as I did, they were shooting at it. He had a big packet in his hand, so I told him to throw it to me. The kid stood up and started walking towards me. He made a step forward from behind the post, and as soon as he did, he got a bullet right in the forehead. He fell without even a moan. He lay next to me, and there was nothing I could do for him.

Grabus escaped from the garage. Later, he continued:

> In the middle of the shooting came a tractor, pulling two wagons filled with cement. He jumped out and ran. We disconnected one of the wagons. The street there went downhill, so it was easy to push it. The wagon then started rolling down from its own impetus. It slammed into a lamppost which was close to the building, and stopped there. I looked behind me. I was the only one left. All the others had gone. I couldn't move. The shooting was incredible. But, since I was under the wagon and I was very close to the windows, I could see that some of the officers were actually sticking out of the window to shoot. I withdrew and hid behind the wagon, waiting for an opportunity to get away. The group saw what was going on, and they called me to come. They started throwing Molotov cocktails and shooting harder, so I would have a chance to get out. I pressed the gun to my chest and ran as fast as I could. I got behind the wall, collapsed on the ground. 'I'm alive!' I was lucky.

Tanks were still being surrendered to the crowd.[42] Some soldiers fired at the UB headquarters. When a UB agent was discovered, a crowd of more than a hundred people beat him: kicking him, hitting him on the head with stones, burning his

---

41. Machcewicz 1996, p. 19.
42. Ziemkowski 1981, p. 81.

face with cigarettes. By the time he was taken into an ambulance, he would be in his death throes.[43]

By the late afternoon, soldiers from other parts of the country were moving in with force. Even then, people did not surrender easily. Some thirty tanks were 'severely damaged or destroyed' before the day was over. Snipers continued shooting until the early hours of 30 June.[44] Banasiak recalled:

> The army repossessed the tanks; to do it, they had to pull people out of them. I saw one worker come out with his hands up, waving a piece of white cloth to signal he was surrendering. A soldier stuck a bayonet into his stomach: *his guts came out.* I witnessed a group of kids huddled together with a soldier pointing a machine gun at them. He was going to shoot, so I ran over: 'Are you a Pole? You are going to shoot children?' They told me that they had an order to shoot any gathering of more than two people who stood together – regardless.[45]

Gradually, the soldiers took back the streets.

A reign of terror

With the situation increasingly coming under control, the elation that had previously reigned dissipated and was replaced by terror. As Banasiak remembered:

> They shot at everything that moved. There was a nurse recording the people who were coming in. She had to leave for a moment. As she left, a shot hit her chair. She would have been dead.

The police sought the names of those who had participated in the fighting.

> **Banasiak:** People did not want to go into the hospital, where there would be a record. If a wound was not too serious, I would just bandage them and they would go home. The secret police were already in the emergency room, writing down the names of the wounded.

The next day, Matyja was arrested, beaten and held for 16 days, whereupon he was abruptly released and told to report for work first thing the next morning. He later learned that he had been released so quickly because his workmates had given an ultimatum: free him or they would come for him.[46] But almost two years later, after things had calmed down, Matyja was fired. He was blacklisted for years. Jerzy Grabus also suffered ten years of blacklisting. The police greatly

---

43. Ziemkowski 1981, p. 82, p. 84.
44. Machcewicz 1996, p. 20.
45. See also Ziemkowski 1981, pp. 80–1.
46. Matyja 1981, p. 231.

enlarged many photographs of the events. When they arrested someone, they demanded that he identify people in the photographs. In this way, they picked up more and more people. Józef Rybak was arrested two days after the uprising; he was interrogated and beaten for hours – his injuries included a broken eardrum.

The harrowing experiences of Grabus and Rybak were not isolated incidents. There were many casualties resulting from the suppression of this insurrection. One report estimated 74 dead and 575 'severely injured'.[47] This toll was greater than all the others that followed, at least in terms of official estimates.

Although Poland was to experience several more serious upheavals, there would never be a repeat of the armed conflict in Poznań, which remained quiet during much of the subsequent disturbances in Poland. The government did its best to keep information about these events from spreading. When the news became known, Alicja Matuszewska recalled: 'the propaganda claimed that it was Germans who had stood against the Polish government'. Months later, in July at a Party plenum, they decided that the workers had been correct in their efforts, but that 'hooligan elements hostile to the system ... had joined it and exploited a justified workers' protest'[48] – in the hackneyed and stilted phraseology used at the time.

'October Revolution'

Regardless of how they chose to speak about it, the disturbances in Poznań had a huge impact upon the ruling Party, putting great pressure on the existing leadership and encouraging dissident elements within. The latter took heart from the fact that earlier that year, in April, news of Soviet leader Nikita Khrushchev's speech to the Twentieth Party Congress of the Soviet Union, detailing Stalin's crimes, was leaked by the Polish delegation. Lechosław Goździk, who was a workers' leader in the FSO automobile plant in Warsaw at the time, described the speech's impact as 'a tremor that sent shock waves throughout the society'. He and his colleagues had spent a good deal of time discussing it:

> All of a sudden, you had all these cracks. People started discussing what to do so it would never happen again. We realised that not all the crimes could be blamed on Stalin because there had to be a *system* and there had to be people willing to follow him. Our idea was that the Party should not be the servant of the functionaries, but of the people.

---

47. Sanford 1986, p. 60.
48. Torańska 1987, p. 176.

They soon began considering how some of their ideas might be implemented:

> I wanted to create a workers' council chosen by direct and secret elections. The council would make plans, figure out finances and choose the management. If the workers' council chose the director, he would know that he was dependent on it, and not on the Central Committee. We knew people's abilities.

This movement spread through what Goździk referred to as the 'grapevine' that arose from the failures of the economy:

> You had to barter for everything because the only thing the system produced in abundance was a constant deficit. That is how these people got to know each other. They exchanged information, so they knew what a given factory could give them.

By late summer, Goździk was regularly addressing public meetings in Warsaw and several other cities. He also broadened his contacts to students who had organised themselves into a Union of Revolutionary Youth, with chapters in Warsaw, Kraków, Poznań, Łódź and Gdańsk. Through this organisation, the students met and worked with workers. Karol Modzelewski, one of the leaders of this movement, recalled:

> The Union of Revolutionary Youth was a national organisation of radical students and young workers, with about 20,000 members and chapters all over the country. I was responsible for contact with workers in the car plant, the most important point of contact in Warsaw. Two or three of us went each day to the factory to organise a discussion with the workers.
>
> Goździk: People came from Warsaw University, from the Warsaw Polytechnic, from the Military Technical Academy. They had daily contact with us; we informed them of what we were doing, and they would tell us what was going on at their campuses.

This activity helped to advance a deepening split within the Party. At the Eighth Party Plenum in October, Władysław Gomułka replaced First Secretary Edward Ochab, returning to the office he had held before having been purged as Stalinism surged through the Soviet Union's satellites. The workers' council movement played a significant role in this faction fight:

> Goździk: We had groups of people who went from factory to factory, telling about courts that sentenced people to death without trial, about executions in the middle of the night, about people who disappeared and never came back. The last week before the plenum, people were so worried about a provocation that men slept at work on wooden grates right by their work stands. At some point, we learned that they were preparing mass arrests, so anyone who we

could possibly expect to be arrested stayed with us. We had about 100 such people. To arrest them, they would have had to storm us.

The movement into the factories was, of course, exactly the opposite of what had happened in Poznań, where the workers had marched *out* of the factories to the city centre, where provocateurs and people with alternative agendas had misdirected the protesters. The difference was not accidental. Goździk had spoken with Matyja and others about what had gone wrong in June:

> When the organisers led people out of Cegielski, they had no expectation that it would turn into this bloody event. Once you are out on the street, you get all kinds of characters joining in, who take over. We were really afraid that it would happen to us because at the time, the anti-Soviet feelings had reached their peak and we were afraid that people would go out into the streets. We warned people never to think about doing that. On the basis of Poznań, we told them that it could turn into a monster that no-one could control.

This network was centred in the FSO plant: 'Calls came from all over Poland, 24 hours a day. We had people sitting by the phones, serving as an information service'. The fear that brought about these factory occupations was well-placed: Soviet tank-units stationed in Poland were advancing toward Warsaw from several different directions, while Soviet troops moved to the Polish border. As Goździk claimed: 'We told the plenary that tanks were on the way to Warsaw. Party leader Ochab told Soviet Marshal and then-Polish-Defense Minister Rokossowski to stop them'. Polish troops took up defensive positions, prepared to go to war if necessary, and some workers were armed to defend against the Soviet troops.[49] One group of Polish troops was also advancing toward the capital; workers were sent out to meet them, and to agitate among them: they stopped the advance. It was evident that a real battle could ensue.[50] Rokossovski warned the Soviet leadership that 'the Polish army would fight to defend Gomułka'.[51] When Gomułka assured the Soviets that he would be a reliable ally, and promised a 'Polish road to socialism', they departed.

The workers' council movement

These developments made Gomułka very popular. People gathered in mass meetings to support him and to prevent any Soviet efforts to block his accession to

---

49. Ascherson 1982, p. 73.
50. Pełczyński 1980a, p. 355; Ascherson 1982, p. 73.
51. Talbot 1971, p. 461, n. 3.

power. Work virtually came to a halt.[52] When it was over and Gomułka appeared in public, he was cheered by huge crowds – in Warsaw there were between three-to four hundred thousand[53] people present to revel in his triumph. For the first (and last) time, the Communist government came to have truly popular support and the potential to significantly broaden its base.[54]

Faced with a cheering crowd numbering in the hundreds of thousands, in addition to the Hungarian uprising,[55] Gomułka's response essentially was to tell people to go home and be quiet; he would dutifully lead them. But of the huge crowd, tens of thousands did not leave; they remained and chanted the name of Cardinal Wyszyński who, at that time, was still under house arrest.[56] This did not bode well for major change.

The Polish workers refused to leave their workplaces; they were staking a claim to legitimate authority. Goździk said: 'We believed that we were the ruling class. So, we were demanding that we be allowed to rule'. Large numbers of *nomenklatura* were forced to resign in the face of the crowd's demands.[57] Many political prisoners and people who had been forced to work in the mines were freed. The trials that had begun in Poznań ceased, and all prisoners arrested from the June upheaval were released (some twenty-eight thousand).[58] Alicja Matuszewska recalled: 'Poles went into the homes of Russian advisors and told them to pack up and get out, and they took them to the train stations, where they sat on their luggage waiting for the train! [laughs]'.[59]

The standard of living improved as more resources were put into meeting the needs of consumers. Private merchants were also allowed limited freedom. Speech became much more unrestrained in this period. The secret police were reorganised, renamed and had their powers curbed. Universities abolished compulsory courses in Marxism-Leninism.[60] A purge of *apparatchiks* dismissed many of the officials most strongly associated with the Stalinist period. Similar changes occurred within many other organisations: unions, youth and professional organisations all changed their leaders and became more independent of the state.

This atmosphere gave much encouragement to Goździk and the workers' council movement. Early in 1957, a leadership was elected by secret ballot, despite pressure from the Party to have people openly raise their hands. Very soon, reported Goździk, the movement began to alter the manner in which

52. Syrop 1976, pp. 133–43.
53. Pełczyński 1980a, p. 359.
54. Nowak 1981, p. 49.
55. Torańska 1987, p. 180.
56. Ibid.
57. Pełczyński 1980a, pp. 359–60.
58. Kennedy 1991, p. 25.
59. Pełczyński 1980a, p. 360.
60. Pełczyński 1980a, p. 361.

things were done in the factories: 'We began to decide how many long-johns, how many uniforms, how many supplies to order. Soon, we had the right to choose the company director'.

The reach of this movement was wide: it included not just factories in Warsaw, but also had connections with the largest companies in Poznań, Wrocław and Kraków, as well as having ties in Gdańsk and Szczecin. It continued to grow after the October Party Plenum. Limits set on the workers councils' authority inevitably began to give way.

> We wanted to produce more cars than the plan ordered. There were many factories which cooperated with ours, so the director of our company and our workers' council went around to all these factories, agitating and trying to convince the workers there to produce more than the plan allowed, which created chaos in the central plan.

Clearly, this movement was a threat to Party control, magnified by the efforts to democratise the Party. As Goździk put it:

> The party structure was normally vertical: from the top down. But now the factory party secretaries met, exchanged information, and made decisions together. We understood that we were creating a new type of party. We believed that political life in this country had to be open, and we wanted to create structures that would allow this to happen. But this situation was extremely ill-received by this vertical structure.

The split within the Party, which had been revealed following Stalin's death and wrenched further apart by the events in Poznań, made it more difficult for the party-leaders to crack down.

Reaction

This bottom-up movement was a clear threat to the new leadership. Gomułka wanted independence from Moscow's dictates, and he recognised that the government had to make some concessions to the people, but he had no use for independent activity that could potentially threaten him in the future.[61] The workers' councils reflected an entirely different conception of how society should be organised, and where power should be lodged in Communist Poland, than was embodied in the Soviet model. So it is not surprising that, when the chance came, Gomułka began to suppress them. Janina Bauman, a Party member who was later driven out of Poland for being Jewish, reflected on this situation:[62]

---

61. Bielasiak 1983, p. 12; Ascherson 1982, p. 78; Goodwyn 1991, p. 75.
62. Bauman 1988, p. 163.

> Party policy fell back into its own tracks. Many of those who had fought for change in 1956 were now accused of . . . holding anti-Marxist views. Some were purged from the party, others were threatened . . . Any . . . who claimed that the Stalinist legacy was still deeply rooted in our society were denounced as aides to the capitalist West, vilified and harassed.

The student-run newspaper, *Po Prostu*, which had agitated for significant change, was banned and its supporters were physically attacked as they protested.[63] Other newspapers were told they had to adhere to the line.[64] By the end of the 1950s, the accommodation between Church and state began to fall apart, and some priests were arrested.[65] Goździk, who had been a hero for a while, was now reviled. While the workers' councils were never abolished, they lost their independence.

A measure of the change can be seen in the contrast between a speech Gomułka gave at the Party plenum in October, shortly after he had come back to power, and one he gave in June the following year to the workers at the Cegielski complex whose actions had begun the upheaval. 'Poznań's workers', he affirmed in October, had 'protested the bad which was widely spread in our social system and which had touched them painfully'. He laid the blame for those events on 'us, the party leadership and the government'.[66] In June 1957, however, his tone was remarkably different. Gomułka suggested an equivalence between the workers and the secret-police. He now spoke about what had happened a year earlier as a 'serious crime', saying the workers had 'lifted their arm against [the people's government]'. He warned that he would not be merciful if such an act were repeated. Rather, it was time 'to cover [this] tragedy with a mournful curtain of silence'.[67] By the early 1960s, Gomułka had gradually stifled all forms of independent organisation, save the Church, which encountered increasing hostility.

The impact of 1956

Despite Gomułka's reversion to the old order, the upheavals and the régime – change that took place that year had a lasting impact. The old-style Stalinism ended. The power of the secret police was permanently diminished, and Poland became less directly dominated by the Soviet Union. The Catholic Church had its autonomy somewhat restored and the regime abandoned forced collectivisation of agriculture. More freedom was permitted in expression, organisation and

---

63. Chęciński 1982, p. 125; Ascherson 1982, p. 81.
64. Pełczyński 1980b, pp. 368–9.
65. Pełczyński 1980b, pp. 373–4.
66. Maciejewski 1981, pp. 15–16.
67. Maciejewski 1981, pp. 17–18. Rakowski undated, p. 10.

academia. These were concessions that the party-leaders felt they were forced to make.[68] Yet none of it was permitted to interfere with the fundamentals of the state.[69]

This experience was discussed in many parts of Poland over the years, and lessons were drawn from it. Never again did anyone resort to arms to confront the state. When Gomułka was later driven from office by another massive worker upheaval, his successor could not count on the same trust that Gomułka had enjoyed in 1956. Nonetheless, some of the mistakes that were made in 1956 were repeated: most importantly, in 1970 and 1976 workers again went out into the streets where state repression could effectively be (and, indeed, was) used against them.

No organised opposition existed in Poland until the late 1970s. Nor was there really any oppositional current. Karol Modzelewski said of that time: 'The umbilical cord with the ideology of communism was not yet cut'. The regime was still young and had not yet been completely discredited. There was dissent. Policies were disliked. There grew to be a deep aversion to the common use of propaganda and lies. But, for many reasons, none of this sentiment translated into any kind of organised activity, primarily because people had little hope or expectation that they could accomplish anything. The *raison d'état* unfailingly invoked was the Soviet Army that occupied Poland. These feelings of discontent were privately held and had no public or collective representation. Whoever did oppose knew only of himself. To act openly in such a situation was to commit a form of suicide, if not to one's life, then most certainly to one's career or livelihood. Few were prepared to follow that course of action. Only after the wrenching experiences of the end of the 1960s would opposition become something to contemplate seriously.

---

68. Torańska 1987, p. 59.
69. Wasilewski and Wnuk-Lipiński 1995, pp. 671–2.

Chapter Three
'Living Parallel to the System': The Solidarity Generation

Helena Łuczywo: There is a huge lecture hall at Warsaw University that fits thousands. Public meetings about the history of Poland and the Soviet Union filled the hall. These meetings prepared the 1968 protests. I very well remember one of those meetings. In 1967, Adam Michnik talked about the extermination of the nation by Stalin. I hadn't known anything about it. I still remember it even now – the way he talked about it and what he said, and my feelings and emotions, and how I hated Communism for what it did to those people.

Zbigniew Bogacz: The first and basic idea of Communism was to set people against one another, including the intelligentsia and the workers.

The emergence of an opposition in Poland rested especially on the events that took place in 1968 and 1970, nearly a generation after the upheaval in Poznań. More than a decade after Gomułka's return to power, open dissent re-emerged. In the late 1960s and early 1970s, the people of the Solidarity generation were young workers and students. They were still being formed, both individually and collectively. The crucial event in the development of each was the experience they shared of the brutal repression of their protests by the regime. In fewer than three years – from early 1968 when student protests were repressed, to the end of 1970 when workers underwent bloody confrontations with the government – they became profoundly alienated.

The 1968 student protests proved influential. Mariusz Muskat was at that time a student at Jagiellonian University in Kraków: 'The police entered the university and beat students there, even women and professors. We saw *fascism*: the government used anti-Semitism, which drew our attention to the affinity between these two systems'.

In 1970, workers were treated even more harshly than the students. When shipyard workers on the Baltic Sea demonstrated against sharp hikes in food prices, they faced bullets. Afterwards, people were terrorised. Sławomir Majewski, later a Solidarity activist in Gdańsk, was one of those whose allegiance was lost to the régime as a result of these events:

> In 1970 I was fifteen and a half. I was one of the participants who set the Party Committee in Gdansk on fire. I spontaneously joined the crowd. Then, I was in the shipyards for two days. I saw the massacres. This was the 'people's government' who murdered people.

Even the priests of that generation had a similar formative experience, according to Professor Andrzej Stelmachowski, who was closely connected to the Clubs of Catholic Intellectuals:

> The most radical priests are those who were in seminaries in the 1960s and early 1970s. Why? Because then the government tried to pressure the young seminarians. In what way? They were obliged to do military service in special companies where they were trained and treated very harshly, where officers tried to indoctrinate them. Sometimes they were persecuted, and so were their families. If the father was an officer or held another sensitive position, he would be immediately fired from his job once his son entered the seminary. So, weaker persons left the seminaries, while those who remained were stronger, and more in opposition. This generation is the most radical among the priests.

Father Zalewski was one such seminarian. He served in the parish that included workers of the huge Lenin steel plant in the Kraków suburb of Nowa Huta. Zalewski had a long history of association with dissidents, although he avows that he did not think of himself 'as an oppositionist', because that would mean 'taking part in the political life of the country'. He said that his ideas stemmed instead 'from Christian motivation'. But what he described sounds very much like the kind of political conflict to which Professor Stelmachowski referred:

> I was in the army from 1975 to 1977. Seminary students from all over Poland were gathered in one place, and apart from working, we had political lectures where we were told 'how well Poland was developing'. This was a very formative period, since it was during these years that I learned the basic feeling

of solidarity with those subjected to pressure. We conducted hunger strikes, which was unheard of in the military. For this, we were frequently subject to arrests and threatened with punishment or imprisonment. The result was opposite to the one intended, since most of the priests were more radical after serving their time. By the time I left the army, the seeds of opposition were already planted in me.

People of this generation were well-suited for the task they undertook, as they had borne neither the miseries of the war nor the terror of the Stalinist period. To become an organised opposition, rather than just dissidents, they had to recognise that their values were incompatible with the regime and to gain a sense of empowerment that would enable them to challenge its apparently overwhelming power, as well as the recognition that they were not alone in feeling discontented. Moreover, they had to recognise what changes were necessary for them to attain their goals. They needed to know whom they could trust. These next years provided the crucial formative experience, after which nothing would be the same for most members of this generation.

The first break

By the late 1960s, disappointment at the failed promise of Gomułka's government had long set in. The years of political and economic stagnation were felt both in the standard of living, whose downward turn provided the context for the upheavals at the end of the decade,[1] and in the lack of economic opportunities for youth.[2] The ambitious people who, after the war, had poured into the cities and occupied the positions made available by an expanding economy were still there, meaning that the prospects for young people were limited. Students felt that those in positions of authority were often incompetent and that their horizons were being narrowed.[3] In 1971, several complained that 'there were too many of the "old guard" who should have retired long ago'.[4]

Krzysztof Kasprzyk, a student in Kraków at the time, and later a leader of the Party reform-movement and of the Journalists Union in Kraków, remembered how the Gomułka regime appeared in the late 1960s: 'Terrible stagnation, iron grip on propaganda, a lack of any perspectives'. And whereas, after the war, people who came from rural areas had been pleased to attain professional

---

1. Staniszkis 1984, p. 254.
2. Pełczyński 1980c, p. 385; Pełczyński 1980b, pp. 378–9; Paczkowski 2003, p. 300.
3. Bromke 1971, pp. 483–4.
4. Błażyński 1979, p. 172.

opportunities, their children often had higher aspirations. The sociologist Jan
Jerschina said:

> The first generation who got higher education in the forties and fifties simply
> appreciated that they had such a wonderful thing. Being a son or daughter of
> illiterate parents, he was a doctor, a lawyer, a manager. It was great! But his
> sons, his daughters, were not as happy as daddy was. Daddy was a doctor; and
> now his son wanted to be a *real* doctor, a *real* engineer. The system didn't
> permit it. A doctor was told: in one hour, you have to see twenty patients,
> make a diagnosis and write out a prescription. An engineer was told that
> to make housing cheaper, the kitchens should have no windows, and the
> apartment should have no more than nine square metres per person.

Mariusz Muskat presented a striking view of how his thought-processes developed in these circumstances:

> In the early 1960s, in secondary school, we were told that we lived in a demo-
> cratic country which did what was best for the workers. Later, we visited a fac-
> tory and we saw that the workers were half slaves; we saw a medieval system
> in the prisons.

General discontent found its reflection within the apparatus. Many of the
nomenklatura balked at the asceticism Gomułka demanded. The ageing leader
responded to criticism and discontent increasingly with an iron fist. Popular dissatisfaction began to manifest itself, at least among intellectuals, by the middle
of the decade. There were those within the *nomenklatura* who hoped to capita-
lise on the discontent in order to replace Gomułka. Maciek Szumowski recalled
that, beginning with the events of 1968 and thereafter until Gomułka was ousted,
he was encouraged in his capacity as a journalist to portray the failings of the
régime:

> 1968 to 1970 was a transitional period, when Gomułka was losing ground.
> At that time, I was filming documentaries against some of the Party appara-
> tus which were actually welcomed by those in the hierarchy who wanted to
> replace Gomułka. That was the way to prepare it. It was a very short period of
> time that I experienced when I had practically no restraints imposed on my
> reporting.

The 'Prague Spring' experiment of 'socialism with a human face', which began
in Czechoslovakia in January 1968, was carefully observed in Poland, as it represented what reformers hoped to create there.[5] Krzysztof Kasprzyk remembered
those days: 'When the Prague Spring started, my generation saw the total split

---

5. Bromke 1981a, p. 27; Weydenthal 1971, pp. 192–3.

between the people's expectations and what the régime was doing'. One of the students' slogans was: 'Poland is waiting for her Dubcek' – referring to the leader of the reform movement in Czechoslovakia.

In March 1968, an issue emerged that brought thousands of student protesters and their supporters out into the streets. It began in Warsaw, where a play called *Dziady* ['Forefathers Eve'], which concerned Czarist oppression in the 1830s, was being produced. The large audiences responded to the anti-Czarist, anti-Russian allusions as anti-Soviet, and greeted them with loud applause. The government then announced that the play would be closed within three days. Jan Lityński, a long-time dissident, recalled that when they heard that the performances had been cancelled, and that they had been given a definite date and time to organise for it: 'we immediately decided it was a fantastic tool for us to be defending Polish independence'. They drew upon an already developing network to organise the demonstration. As Lityński noted: 'We organised the demonstration through our contacts. I knew practically everybody who took part in any meeting and said something against the government'.

The students filled the theatre. 'There were three- to four-hundred people outside, and the hall was full of people sitting, standing, so it was like a rally'. When the play was over, they left the theatre and then revealed their signs. They began to march from the theatre to the town centre. 'It meant that we would go right past the party-headquarters', said Lityński. The police cornered them and arrested some one-hundred and fifty people. The students later circulated a petition containing about three thousand signatures demanding that the play continue and that the censorship be lifted. Two of their leaders were expelled from the university, prompting some four thousand students to demonstrate in opposition to the expulsions. The police attacked them and badly beat a number of the protesters. An elected strike committee was arrested, which brought the students into the streets once more.

Word of these events spread quickly, and soon students all across the country began protesting. There was almost no major city with a university that did not experience some of this turmoil, the impact of which was felt even in smaller towns.[6] Krzysztof Kasprzyk was then a student in Kraków:

> We had a nearly-week-long sit-in in my college. At the peak of these demonstrations, we marched to the old market. We were brutally attacked by the police with water cannon and tear gas. I escaped with three- to four-hundred others. The police entered the university and beat people; we shouted: 'Gestapo!' We were united in hatred toward the regime.

---

6. Weydenthal 1971, pp. 121–4; Banaś 1979, pp. 126–30.

It was not only university students who were caught up in these events. Bogdan Borusewicz, who later played a central role in the Gdańsk opposition and in Solidarity, then attended secondary school. He created and distributed leaflets supporting the students, for which he was sentenced to three years in prison. Tadeusz Jedynak, later a miner leader of Solidarity, attended high school in the city of Płock, not far from Warsaw. In response to these events, he and some of his fellow students refused to attend school for a week: 'All we knew was that there were demonstrations in Warsaw; we didn't know anything about their reasons. We joined them because we knew they were directed against the Communists'.

Workers and 1968

It is commonly believed that workers were uninterested in or antagonistic to these protests. This view came about in part because some workers (mostly Party members) had been armed with clubs by the Party leadership and set against the students. Intellectuals bemoaned their isolation from the workers, while Party officials encouraged it, and most journalists and historians have affirmed it.[7] But there was no way to hermetically seal off the workers from the students. While the students were generally separated from the *working class* as an organised entity, many individual workers observed what happened and were moved by what they saw. Several of them were brought into contact with the students by haphazard and idiosyncratic connections. Some had relatives who were students, including their children or siblings; others encountered their leaflets; others still saw the police beating the students.

They were often disgusted by the attacks on the students and provided some clear demonstrations of public support for their cause. Jan Lityński recalled: 'The streets were full of support for us'. Some of the workers cooperated with the students.[8] This experience was important to the workers' development and sensibilities; its significance to them has usually been missed. Stanisław Handzlik, who was later a leader of Solidarity, worked in the Lenin Steel Mill outside of

---

7. Tadeusz Jedynak said: 'It must be stressed here that the attitude of a Polish worker to an intellectual before 1976 was very negative. That was the result of the communist propaganda. Workers were told by the official propaganda that they had to work so hard to support intellectuals, who did nothing. There were also difficult relationships between workers and their superiors. Superiors were seen by workers as representatives of the Polish intelligentsia, and these relationships were very bad. They were so bad that, when it came to the [Solidarity] agreement in Jastrzębie in 1980, they included a point about improvement of the relationship between workers and engineers'.

8. Interviews with Lech Wałęsa and Franciszek Zorza, cited in Majkowski 1985, p. 172.

Kraków: 'I identified with the students. They appealed to my conscience. I knew that their ideals were for the whole society'.

Some students worked in the Gdańsk shipyard as part of their training. In the locker room, after a demonstration, someone noticed 'a trainee whose back had been clubbed black and blue'.[9] They were outraged by it: 'We paraded him, shirtless, through the shipyard, chanting: Are we going to let them beat up our children, the children of workers and peasants?' Later that day, in a Gdańsk suburb, workers brought coiled steel springs, which they used to launch projectiles at the police during street skirmishes. Wałęsa said of that day: 'The riot hadn't been stirred up by intellectuals, but by workers who had taken the side of the students'. Later, when a meeting was held in the shipyard to condemn the student demonstrations, workers who had refused to participate stormed in and broke it up.[10] Mieczysław Gil, a Party member in 1968, also worked in the Lenin Steel Mill situated in the *Nowa Huta* suburb outside of Kraków. He recalled his experience, as did others. All of them were moved by what they saw in favour the students:

> 1968 was the first time I had a conflict with the Party authorities and the regime. My sister was a student of political science in Kraków, so I had contact with the students. I hated this approach of using force against them, since I knew they were right by reading the leaflets. Occasionally, I also carried leaflets from my sister and secretly distributed them in the workers' hostels. At a meeting of the party executive, my attitude was unequivocally condemned. The next day, I was suspended.

> **Zbigniew Bogacz:** We were set up against the students in March, 1968. The propaganda pictured them as youth who 'fought against workers' management, and workers had to defend against them'. It was the last time they succeeded in using workers against the intelligentsia.

> **Aleksander Krystosiak:** My opinion about the students was absolutely positive. They wanted freedom for the country. All these nice declarations that 'we want more free air to breathe' – what it was really all about was kicking out the Communists and shaking off the Russians sitting on our backs.

Anti-Semitism

The government carried out a huge propaganda campaign against the students. Kasprzyk recalled: 'Newspapers ran phony letters, signed by the "despairing

---

9. Wałęsa 1987, p. 53.
10. Wałęsa 1987, p. 54.

mother of a student in the second year of philosophy" (or economics, law, or whatever), demanding that the local authorities make order so her "beloved son" could return to study'. In addition, the government orchestrated huge meetings to support its policies. Alicja Matuszewska said:

> In the shipyard, they would get 12,000 people in one place. No one could leave. And then the Party Secretary would read the statement and demand a vote to condemn the students. Everyone had to sign.

To discredit the demonstrators, the government claimed that they were the children of highly-placed Jewish officials who had been responsible for the terror of the Stalinist period, which was said to have been a *Jewish* product and not the natural outgrowth of the regime.[11] The voices below provide examples of the view expressed at the time:

> **Helena Łuczywo:** The general line was that the protest was fomented by the children of Jewish Stalinists who wanted to get back to power. These kids were called 'banana kids' because bananas were a symbol of luxury in Poland at that time. It was the most disgusting populism, strengthening and creating the most appalling stereotypes: that Stalinism was 'something alien to Poles, imposed by the Jews'.

> **Aleksander Krystosiak:** If you turned on the faucet and the water didn't flow, it was 'because the Jews drank it all'.

Even in normal times, Poland's closed political system made it possible for people to use alleged *ideological* differences to settle their *personal* scores. Małgorzata Celejewska, later the treasurer of Solidarity in Gdańsk, noted: 'There was always someone in the Party who wanted to get someone else and would do it through the Party'. In this highly-charged period, just being Jewish could provide a weapon to one's adversaries. As Jan Jerschina recounted:

> A faculty member here decided in 1968 that it was the time to go for promotion to full professor. He wrote an article that said that because I am Jewish I should not teach Marxism at Jagiellonian University. Someone in the sociology department called me and said, 'Take a leave "to improve your heart", and disappear for a while. We will say that we can't dismiss you because you are on leave'. (We have a rule that you cannot fire a man on leave to improve his health). So I did.

Not everyone was so lucky. Some twenty thousand Jewish survivors were driven from their jobs and forced to flee the country. One of them was Janina Bauman, who wrote of how her family had to endure losing their jobs, being followed and

---

11. See Banaś 1979, pp. 133–61; also Paczkowski 2003, pp. 329–31.

spied on, receiving late-night hate calls, having their phones tapped and their children harassed at school and attacked outside of school – all because they were Jewish.[12]

Suppressing the Prague Spring

In August 1968, when the Warsaw Pact armies (including that of Poland) invaded Czechoslovakia to put an end to the Prague Spring, students in Warsaw distributed leaflets protesting the invasion.[13] For many people, it was a shameful experience. Eugeniusz Szumiejko was a student at the time: 'It was a big shock for me. I remember that even devoted communists had tears in their eyes when they learned about it'. Józef Pinior, later a leader of Solidarity in Kraków, recalled:

> I was 13. That year I remember first of all the aggression against Czechoslovakia. I lived near the border. The sight of the Russian army heading toward the border made a strong impression on me.

Tadeusz Jedynak stated: 'I have a close friend who served in the parachute troops and who was sent to Czechoslovakia. When he came back, he told me everything, and it certainly influenced my political views'. Krzysztof Kasprzyk recalled:

> There was a very tough propaganda sell in Poland then, telling people that it was our 'international duty to help our brothers in Czechoslovakia, to fight the counter-revolutionaries', and so on. This was after the trauma of March '68, after the open anti-Semitism in the media. So nobody believed what the propaganda said. There was total stagnation. Hanging in the air was the feeling that 'something must happen; it can't go on like this'. We felt the Gomułka régime was over.

Even Colonel Adam Sucharski, who served in Poland's secret-police at that time, said 'Polish participation in the pacification of Czechoslovakia was disgusting to me'.

Just as intended, the Czech invasion telegraphed a powerful message to would-be Polish reformers: change was not on the agenda and attempts to bring it about could be met with terrible repression.[14] It certainly had its intended effect on some people, as the two voices below testify. Janusz Całka noted: 'For me, the invasion of Czechoslovakia, more than the student strikes, was proof that all attempts to get rid of the dependence on imperial Russia were in vain'. Meanwhile, Helena Łuczywo recalled:

---

12. Bauman 1988, pp. 192–202.
13. Bromke 1978, p. 745.
14. See Banaś 1979, p. 148.

Crushing the Prague Spring meant for me that there was no hope for any change in Poland. I believed that the Communists could not be overthrown because of the Soviet power, and it could not be reformed. So it was better to try to be useful in some way besides politics.

The impact of 1968

The events of 1968 drew a sharp line between a significant stratum of students and the government. Students were beaten, arrested and interrogated. Some were jailed, expelled from their universities, drafted into the army, blacklisted from their professions and cast out from their ambitions. It was a terribly traumatic experience. These young people were the first generation that had grown up under Communism, and many had borne its ideals. In 1968, they sought reforms rather than an end to the system. Karol Modzelewski, who was close to some of the student activists, felt that the 'motivation of this revolt was the hiatus between the system and its ideology'.

The experience changed people; it made clear that they must embark upon another path, even though few if any had an idea as to what that might be or how it might be found. In both deeds and words, the state had shown that the students' demands were unacceptable; there would be no reform.[15] It was clear that their ideals and hopes could not be realised within that system, and that no quarter would be conceded: they had been treated as enemies. They drew conclusions from this treatment. Adam Michnik, one of the organisers of the 1968 demonstrations in Warsaw, who was expelled from Warsaw University for his actions, stated: 'It took March, '68 before I saw with my own eyes, that the régime was ready to trample the most basic human values'.[16] Bronisław Geremek was a member of the Party in 1968:

I felt that all political activity should be inside the party. In fact, party membership is a kind of citizenship right that allows you to act. Nineteen sixty

---

15. Weydenthal 1971, pp. 130–5.
16. Michnik 1993, p. 124. This sentiment did not mean that Michnik and his co-thinkers had abandoned their socialist views. In his book, *The Church and the Left*, he urged the 'secular Left', of which he considered himself a participant, to 'defend its socialist ideals in the face of an anti-patriotic totalitarian power shouting socialist slogans'; Michnik 1993, p. 210. Michnik later provided some definition of what he meant by 'socialism': 'the continual movement toward the self-determination of labour, a movement for the liberation of labour, a movement based on the ideas of freedom and tolerance, human rights and national rights, a just distribution of the national income and an equal start in life for all'; Michnik 1993, p. 239. The conclusion drawn by Michnik, Blumsztajn and many others following their experiences of 1968 was that the regime had lost all legitimate claim to be considered part of the Left.

eight allowed me to understand that it was an illusion, and that finally to be inside the party meant to support the regime.

Faced with the demonstration of brutality and callousness to public feelings, many of the students finally abandoned their allegiance to Polish Communism. Here was a fundamental break by a significant section of the new generation. The impact was to be felt in different ways by many individuals. Seweryn Blumsztajn, a long-time dissident activist:

> What happened wasn't only the question of the brutal intervention by the police, but the scale of events. It became a mass movement of students in all of Poland. Some said that in a totalitarian system a mass demonstration was unthinkable, but it exploded. After you survive a revolution, you believe that it is possible. Whether or not we thought that we could create some kind of mass movement around us, or were able to break this system, we had already left it.

This step is absolutely crucial in the development of a social movement of opposition. If one is critical of one's society but rarely has an opportunity to share the feeling, and sees no public manifestation of it, it is hard to imagine that there are others who feel the same way. But the significant upheaval that emerged all around the country opened up new possibilities. What was once a mere fantasy had now become a real possibility, which affected the ways in which people acted and the risks they might take. People came out of that experience changed – and many of them had determined that they were against the regime. Blumsztajn and others illustrate the impact that those events had on them at the time:

> We started to act like free people. If you wanted to live in such a way, you had to give up any kind of career. So we crossed the barrier of being dissidents. *We became people who lived freely in a totalitarian society.* That was not yet opposition. After leaving prison, those who could, finished their studies; we worked in factories or whatever. But we lived parallel to the system.

> **Jan Lityński:** For our generation, there had been no truth in public life. For our history lessons, we were supposed to recite out of the book. It was not important if it was true or not. March created a generation that demanded that in public life there should be truth.

> **Bogdan Borusewicz:** March 1968 influenced me very much. I went to prison as a boy and I left it as a man. Prison assured me that *I* was right, not the *government.*

> **Franciszek Zorza, a worker in Gdańsk:** The beginning of my oppositionist activity dates from 1968 ... At that time I went out into the streets of Gdańsk, as many others did, to express my solidarity with students ... I had

an opportunity to learn . . . how the police treated opposition groups. We were driven from one place to another by tear gas and police truncheons. That was a turning point for me.[17]

Stanisław Handzlik: When you are in opposition, at first you don't know if you are right or not. People are not so open, and you don't really know what they think. So you start to think that perhaps there is something wrong with you. And when there comes an upheaval like the student protest, you get one of those leaflets put into your hand, you find out that you are not isolated, that there are other people who think the same way, and it boosts your morale. There are more such angry, crazy ones. And then you start looking for such people.

Many of the students who participated in the events of 1968 were terrorised. The first lesson they drew was that change was not possible, given the brutal character of the Soviet system, as Helena Łuczywo articulated:

I believed that the communists could not be overthrown because of the Soviet power and it could not be reformed because of what happened in Czechoslovakia, so it was better to try to do something useful and reasonable for oneself and for one's family and for other people. I decided to be totally non-political at that time.

Some of that generation became permanently alienated from the regime and hostile to the stifling control of the state and its agents' lies.

Still, they had seen the possibility of collective action – that it was possible to confront the power of the state, and ultimately that was also an important lesson that they drew from this experience, though it was not evident for several years. As Seweryn Blumsztajn noted, that was not yet opposition, but it marked a crucial step along the way. Most of those who later worked in the dissident intellectual milieu that sprang up in the late 1970s had experienced the events of 1968. Blumsztajn recalled:

Particular moments may create the consciousness of a generation, and 1968 did for mine. KOR was created by the generation of '68. In the late 1970s, I was the editor of the KOR *Information Bulletin*. I needed a lot of flats – to print it, to glue it and to make it a normal monthly. And 90 percent of the flats I used were in districts where my generation lived.

Helena Łuczywo, who later became the editor and publisher of KOR's periodical, *Robotnik*, despite having been driven into apathy, agreed with Blumsztajn:

---

17. Majkowski 1985, p. 179.

Sociological research revealed that the intelligentsia who were involved in Solidarity in 1980 were people whose experience was somehow rooted in 1968. When you knew those people, or you read about them, most of them said that in 1968 this or that happened to them and that was how they somehow arrived at Solidarity twelve years later. For workers, it was young people whose experience was shaped by 1976.

The events of 1968 weakened Gomułka and strengthened his rivals.[18] The intensity of factional struggle within the Party increased.[19] When in 1970 Gomułka created a far more serious breach, he had little effective base of support and was easily toppled.

---

18. Bromke 1978, pp. 746–8; Weydenthal 1971, pp. 139–43; Wasilewski and Wnuk-Lipiński 1995, p. 672.
19. Bromke 1981a, p. 25, p. 29; 1981b, p. 37; Wasilewski and Wnuk-Lipiński 1995, p. 672.

Chapter Four
A Line of Blood

The events of 1968 weakened Gomułka. Opposition to his rule was growing within the bureaucracy, even as discontent simmered below and the economy stagnated. Colonel Adam Sucharski:

> There was no doubt that Gomułka had to leave. Quietly, even lower-level Party secretaries spoke of factions in the Central Committee. The leading players and the wider circle of activists, including the secret police and the first secretaries of the basic Party organisations, the managers of various departments in the city council, the directors of larger companies, knew that something was wrong in the Central Committee.

Gomułka's proposals to deal with economic stagnation meant that sacrifices had to be borne again by the already burdened workers in the form of longer hours and harder work.[1] Expenditure for safer working conditions, sanitary installations and social facilities in factories virtually ceased. Housing construction lagged and the waiting times for apartments grew. Increasingly, the responsibility for crucial social infrastructure – such as schools, roads and housing – was shifted from the state towards communities and individuals.[2] Poland had disastrous harvests in 1969 and 1970, while imports of grain for livestock were severely curtailed, forcing a cut in the animal population, which meant that meat prices were substantially raised.[3] As

---

1. Blazynski 1979, p. 4.
2. Pełczyński 1980d, pp. 401–2; Laba 1991, pp. 16–17.
3. Blazynski 1979, p. 4.

Krzysztof Kasprzyk noted to me, 'meat at that time began to play the crucial role as the strategic "political" grocery'.

On 12 December 1970, large price increases took effect,[4] including foods coveted for the holidays. In Poland, an average of 58 percent of salaries went towards food; the price rises brought this figure closer to seventy percent, and created a precipitous drop in real wages just before Christmas, which is normally a time of significant expenditure and vast food spreads.[5] Since the standard of living had remained stagnant for a decade, this move threatened much of the hard-won gains of the post-war period. Especially hard hit were lower-paid workers, who spent an even greater share of their earnings on food. Some workers faced 'a spectre of hunger'.[6] While prices were lowered for some manufactured goods – for instance, televisions and stereos – these were luxuries that many workers could still not afford.[7] The prices of other consumer goods, such as clothing, went up substantially.[8] When word of these prices spread, initially at Party meetings, Wałęsa reported that a woman complained that times had been easier under Hitler, and that she did not know how she would manage with three children.[9] Yet Gomułka did not permit any questioning of his policy. Edward Gierek, Gomułka's successor, recalled that:

> At the meetings of the Politburo, to which I went reluctantly in the last years, Gomułka was capable of screaming and insulting his most important co-workers...At the last meeting of the Politburo before the unfortunate December price rises...Jędrychowski [the Foreign Minister] brought him to blind fury with his question: 'Were the social results of the price rises thought through thoroughly?' This question...ignited a half hour tirade on the subject of trying to teach him Marxism.[10]

In the shipyards on the Baltic seaports, the anger sparked by this move was underlain by conflicts between labour and management. There had been talk of closing the ship-building industry,[11] and during the late 1960s the norms were regularly raised, requiring workers to produce more. Then, in an attempt to complete a ship quickly, the management forced some workers to work as long as 36 hours. A human error had allowed fuel to leak and ultimately to explode, trapping some twenty-two men in the ship's hold where they were burned

---

4. Blazynski 1979, p. 7.
5. Majkowski 1985, p. 75.
6. Zbigniew Szczypiński, cited in Laba 1991, p. 19.
7. Singer 1981, p. 157.
8. Blazynski 1979, p. 7.
9. Wałęsa 1987, p. 60.
10. Rolicki 1990.
11. Singer 1981, pp. 165–6; Laba 1991, pp. 16–17.

alive.[12] Conflict over these issues occurred routinely.[13] Workers noted that Party members received favouritism in obtaining housing, land and financing. Wałęsa recalled that the workers 'were fed up with this kind of special privilege... [T]hey knew they were paying for it with their own blood'.[14] The abrupt price-rises ignited the glowing embers of discontent that remained and provided workers the opportunity to give voice to their accumulated hostility.[15]

The workers were not only motivated by economic adversity. They felt aggrieved by the arrogance of the authorities, and they resented the disproportionate benefits that flowed to the *nomenklatura*. Workers were becoming better-educated, more sophisticated and self-confident; consequently, they were, as George Blazynski wrote, 'more interested in taking a share in running the country'. Like the students almost three years earlier, they resented the daily diet of lies they were fed from the media, and they too found their opportunities for upward-mobility constricted: promotions to white-collar occupations had virtually ceased, while the income discrepancies between workers and management had increased substantially.

Workers responded to their cost-increases with work stoppages and demonstrations throughout the country.[16] In Gdańsk and Szczecin, shipyard workers attacked and burned Party headquarters, while in Gdynia and Elbląg, the headquarters were stoned by workers. One Gdańsk participant's description illustrates the intense hostility felt by the workers:

> We began burning buildings that were owned by the Party and the police. We made Molotov cocktails, and even had a contest to see who could throw them higher, into the second or third floor. When they had practically begun to burn alive, they asked us if they could come out. We told them yes, if they would take off their uniforms. So they came out in their underpants. Police who wouldn't take off their uniforms were beaten up, and people practically tore off their uniforms. Some of the police, especially officers, were taken ... as hostages.[17]

While there were no gunfights, as in Poznań in 1956, the workers did assault public buildings, and in doing so became vulnerable. The police deployed provocateurs to discredit the demonstrators. Małgorzata Celejewska:

---

12. Wałęsa 1987, pp. 51–2.
13. Wałęsa 1987, p. 56.
14. Wałęsa 1987, p. 57.
15. Rakowski 1973, pp. 30–1.
16. Weydenthal 1981, p. 195.
17. Polish TV, 17 December 1990.

People looted stores. We later learned that they were secret-police agents. The shipyard workers told me that they tried to stop them, but they got brutally beaten up by the police and the stores got broken into anyway. Later, the government had the basis to accuse the crowd of being 'hooligans'.

The crowd's behaviour supplied the régime's justification 'to meet violence with violence'.[18] The police and the army shot and killed workers in Gdańsk, Gdynia and Szczecin. The army fired upon people as they arrived to work at the train-station in Gdynia, a city adjacent to Gdańsk. Workers were shot without warning as they exited the commuter-trains onto the platform. The shots kept coming, even as more trains arrived, disgorging more workers. With nowhere to flee, possibly hundreds were killed, with many others injured. More workers were killed and wounded in the city centre. Those arrested were forced to run gauntlets between two lines of police with truncheons.[19] In Szczecin, workers drew up demands, which included the revolutionary idea of independent unions. The strike spread to other factories in the city. In a few days, there were 94 workplaces on strike; effectively, it was a general strike. The Warski Shipyard became the base out of which the workers ran the city.[20] In the public interest, they established that 'food stores, food-delivery firms, bakeries, and clinics were not to strike'. A workers' militia patrolled the streets. Censorship broke down in the city, and newspaper and broadcast journalists simply stated what was happening. As the strike in the city was ending, it began to spread to the entire province surrounding it.[21] There were other clashes as well: in Elbląg, one worker was killed and three were wounded.[22]

There is considerable evidence that injuries and deaths were widespread. I have in my possession the records of hundreds of injuries brought to just one emergency room in a single hospital in Szczecin. Andrzej Jarmakowski, then a high school student, recalled that one parish priest in Gdańsk found over three-hundred wounded 'just from that one parish'.[23] Małgorzata Celejewska, who had contacts in one hospital, remembered being told that 'in the emergency room,

---

18. As Roman Laba wrote: 'By now General Jaruzelski had ordered mobilisation of the army; and in addition to sending 25,000 soldiers in to the coastal cities, divisions were massed in the Kraków, Poznań, Wrocław and Warsaw regions. Others remained on full alert in the central region. Military sources later reported that the army directly engaged in more than 100 operations involving 61,000 soldiers, 1,700 tanks, 1,750 transporters, air transport, a large number of helicopters and several dozen warships'; [1991, pp. 70–1.]
19. Singer 1981, pp. 164–71.
20. Warski was the largest and most important shipyard in Szczecin.
21. Laba 1991, p. 69, pp. 74–6; Green 1977, p. 71.
22. Blazynski 1979, p. 20, p. 22.
23. Interview with Jarmakowski.

they just pinned numbers on people. In one hour they brought in 1,300 wounded people! Nothing could be done for some of them'.

> **Alicja Matuszewska:** The police would arrive at night to the families of the dead; they would allow one person from a family to go with them to identify the body. In one case, the body was without shoes and socks, and dirty from mud and sand. They did not allow him to be washed or dressed. They were just wrapped in sheets and taken to the cemetery, where they were buried in common graves. The newspapers said that 27 people were killed. His body was number 217. That says something about how many people were really killed.

In Gdynia especially, it all had the appearance of a set-up. Workers came to the train station the morning after Vice-Prime Minister and Politburo member, Stanisław Kociołek, had appeared on late-night television and called for them to return to work.[24] The view that the killings were intentional was widely held. Mieczysław Rakowski, who was at that time a member of the Party Central Committee, acknowledged that the killings in Gdańsk and Szczecin were intentional:

> When public buildings are attacked, and the demonstrators are unwilling to move, what can the army and the police do? The tragedy is that there were grounds for such a demonstration. But when attacks occur, you are not far from such 'accidents'.

The government found that the soldiers they brought in to enforce the repression were reluctant to turn their guns against their fellow Poles, especially when strikers appealed to them not to do so.[25] Some units appear to have fallen apart, while others resisted orders to shoot.[26] In Gdańsk, several soldiers from adjacent Gdynia gave their gas-masks to the striking workers, and some threw their rifles into the harbour waters.[27] The garrison headquartered in Szczecin rebelled against orders.[28] As a result, as Tadeusz Pławiński noted: 'During the night, they brought in soldiers from outside the area. On nearly every corner in the city there was a tank and lots of soldiers'. Tadeusz Jedynak was in the army at the time. He recalled the following: 'We were driven around Warsaw in locked trucks; we couldn't get out, but we could see tanks in the streets, almost no people and police patrols. We were frightened'. When Captain Edmund Wejner was told to shoot to kill, he refused: 'I was told that there were pickpockets, thieves, and so

24. Blazynski 1979, pp. 17–18.
25. Laba 1991, pp. 72–3.
26. Laba 1991, pp. 33–5.
27. Laba 1991, p. 34.
28. Laba 1991, pp. 61–2.

on, out on the streets and they were using live ammunition. It was not true'.[29] But they insisted:

> 'You have to return and make order on the street. You may use grenades, can-
> nons, guns, tear gas and water guns'. I told the officers that the people ... were
> workers and their demands were right and I didn't want to go back ... Colonel
> Urbańczyk ... said that if I didn't do it, they would put me in jail and court-
> martial me.[30]

Gomułka appealed to the Soviets to intervene on his behalf. But two years after invading Czechoslovakia, they refused. The government told its soldiers that they would be fighting Germans who wished to return the city to German rule.[31] Tadeusz Pławiński said of the soldiers brought to the coast:

> They were eighteen to nineteen years old and they didn't really understand.
> They had been given a wake-up call and jumped out. Most thought they were
> just going out for a few hours and would come back. In December it was cold
> and they didn't even take warm clothes. Then they landed a few hundred kilo-
> metres away to fight with 'Germans'. That was the story that I personally heard
> from the soldiers.

A soldier brought to Gdańsk for this conflict explained how it appeared to him:[32]

> We came to Gdańsk at midnight, and we didn't know what was going on ... They
> took us to ... a military camp and allowed us ... one hour of sleep. Then they
> took us to the shipyard. Around 9am, they gave us real bullets ... and told us
> we could shoot anyone who tried to attack us ... They told us they were CIA
> agents. We were terrified and didn't think about what we were doing. We just
> shot ... Soldiers began to make contact with the demonstrators. Because of
> that, the police made a cordon between us so we couldn't communicate.

Chilling as these details may be, they do not convey the full impact of the events upon the individuals who lived through them. What follows are eyewitness accounts that give a real sense of what happened in three major ports: Gdańsk, Gdynia and Szczecin. These cities were the core of the strike that established Solidarity in 1980. Each of the reports is particular due to the unique experiences of the speaker. Małgorzata Celejewska and Alicja Matuszewska were observers of the action; Aleksander Krystosiak was a member of the strike committee

---

29. There were many instances of discipline breaking down as the soldiers found it impossible to fire upon their fellow workers; see Laba 1991, pp. 33–4.

30. Polish TV broadcast.

31. See also Laba 1991, p. 34.

32. The soldier was interviewed on Polish television on 17 December 1990.

in Szczecin. Different people stress distinct aspects of the whole, but they all reflect the more universal experiences of many people. No-one experienced or saw all that happened. Invariably, when people started discussing the events of December 1970, they cast a powerful emotional spell, even on paper.

Gdańsk

Małgorzata Celejewska: On Saturday, December 12, party-members were told to come to a meeting after work. There, a Secretary from the Gdansk Committee told us that there would be a fifty to sixty percent price-hike on food and other products. People got really upset because they could not live with that price-hike. The meeting became a shouting match.

On Monday, there was no real work done. Then, around noon, workers came from the Gdańsk shipyard, calling us to go to the provincial Party committee. They had sent a delegation to the First Secretary of the shipyard, which had not returned. A co-worker and I decided to go see what was happening. We were told that the workers had gone toward the radio station and seized a car with loudspeakers. It became a public stump: everyone could speak his mind. They called for a public meeting at 7pm at the Gdańsk Polytechnic University. After speeches, thousands of us headed for Party headquarters. As we approached, we saw that there was fighting in front of the Party headquarters that we learned had already been going on for two or three hours. People tore bricks and stones from the street and caught tear gas grenades and threw them back at the police. A group of young men carrying stones and tear gas cans rode a tram into the police and bombarded them. As I stood there, a policeman shot a tear gas canister into the crowd that flew just inches from my face. That was enough. I got out of there and went as far out of my way as possible to avoid any crowds, but there were people and tear gas everywhere – even where I lived, about seven kilometres away, you could smell it.

Tuesday morning there was no work – just discussions about our right to demonstrate and strike. Around noon, they sent us home. Workers from the Gdańsk Shipyard and the North Shipyard once again went to the provincial Party headquarters. That day, they set fire to the Party building. I learned that a tank had crushed someone in front of the Party headquarters after the workers had attacked the Party building and burned it.

On Wednesday, when I came to work, I was told by someone that a worker had been killed at the railway station. The workers had soaked a handkerchief in his blood and taken an oath of revenge over his dead body.

Celejewska noted that the workers decided to continue the strike by staying on the premises because it would be safer than to go out into the city:

> People were already working on demands to the Party Secretary and the ship-yard management. So, people were more peaceful, but more determined about what to do. By Wednesday evening, we decided to have an occupation strike. People were told to stay by their workstations to protect them. My boss told me to go home because 'it could be really dangerous'. But they just wanted to get rid of people. Then they could close departments and say there was no strike there. So to go home would have meant I did not support the strike, and when you live in a community like that, that is impossible. And I did support the strike. When you go on an occupation strike, you stay as long as the strike goes on. People open up, and that created new ties between us.

> There were also Party people – this evil, red spirit – floating around. Someone barged into our department, claiming that German army divers were coming to storm the shipyard from the sea. It was bullshit and people who were smart and politically educated understood what it was, but for some people, it was scary. And that was the whole idea: to create a feeling of panic among the workers. That night, police cars with loudspeakers demanded that we come out, or else. We heard tanks coming; the police and the army surrounded the shipyard. Around 4am, it was decided to leave, though some of us felt very strongly that it was the wrong decision. Tanks and police were all around the shipyard and in front of the gates. Only later, we learned that they had used bullets against the workers at the Gdańsk Shipyard.

The decision to leave was difficult, said Wałęsa: 'Most saw [it] as a betrayal, though they also understood that it would probably prevent the loss of more lives. Twenty thousand of us ... left the yard through lines of soldiers and militiamen'.

Gdynia

Alicja Matuszewska: We knew what was happening in Gdańsk. The distances were too small to prevent it from spreading. [The two cities are adjacent to one another]. The day after the Gdańsk strike started, workers walked to the mayor's office in Gdynia to announce that they were preparing to strike; they would come back for an answer the next day. I wanted to be there, so I told my boss that I wanted a few days off.

Tanks were everywhere around the city. That night, by my building, two tanks shone their headlights right into my windows, so it was like daylight. That was the sixteenth. The workers were really scared. They didn't know what to do. Exactly at six o'clock in the morning I was awakened by machine-gun fire. My husband tore into the apartment and said, 'Get up! They are shooting the workers by the Paris Commune Shipyard!' I had two kids at home. I woke them up and told them, 'Your grandma is coming. Stay home and don't move'. And I left.

Kociołek's appeal to go back to work was made late at night, so there was no-one to consult: they just came to work at the train-station by the Paris Commune Shipyard. People who were arriving did not know what had happened by the gate to the Gdańsk Shipyard. When the trains arrived, the workers disembarked and walked up to the overpass to get to the Paris Commune Shipyard. Many people were killed because the soldiers started shooting indiscriminately. That was what woke me up. Four workers were killed then; others were wounded.

The people surrounded the whole area in front of the mayor's office, waiting for the shipyard workers. I stood across the street. A friend who lived on the second-floor called us upstairs, where I had a great view of what was going on. On one side, I could see the train station, and on the other side I could see what was going on at the mayor's office. We ran back and forth to see what was happening. A horrible scream came from the other side, so we ran to that window. The shipyard workers were coming in an organised column. They had the body of a murdered worker on a door from the train. He was young. He was wearing a brown work-jacket, pants and boots. Someone threw a bouquet of flowers at his feet. A military doctor came out, went over to the worker, checked the pulse on his hand and on his neck and waved that he was dead.

Then all hell broke loose. The people ran to the soldiers: 'They are murderers! They are like the *Gestapo*! They are shooting us! Don't be like them'. The soldiers didn't know what to do. They didn't shoot, but the police did. Ambulances came. They put sheets over the faces and threw them into the ambulances, so we knew they were taking away dead bodies. The shooting lasted several hours. Now hundreds of people ran to their windows, opened them and screamed 'Murderers!' The police looked up with glazed eyes. They acted like wild savages! More police came, with more tear gas. They shot, and people backed away. On the street, they were hunting kids – thirteen, fourteen years old – to see if their hands were dirty from handling stones. They caught a lot of them.

By four o'clock, we decided to go back home. We scurried from one building entrance to another, afraid to walk openly because shots could still be heard.

When people dispersed, the police chased them, looked for where they were hiding, and shot at them. When I finally got back home, it was after dark. The police announced a curfew. Close to the train station, there was a big workers' hostel, where workers who came from other parts of Poland stayed. It was surrounded by the police, so they went into the forest, and stayed until midnight. Then they decided to return. When they did, the police arrived a few minutes later and massacred them.

They did horrible things. They would tear into the prison and get a shipyard-worker, mess up his hair, put a piece of metal pipe in his hand and then take mug shots of him to prove that he was one of the 'hooligans'. My mother's friend had a son who was a fire fighter in the army. When the shooting began, there was a hospital close to the fire department that had a shortage of workers. So the army sent its fire fighters to the hospital to work. Two days later, this man told me what he saw. He was 20 years old, pale, and his hands were shaking. He could not collect himself. He said they just collected corpses! No one was alive.

For several months I could not stop thinking about it. That year, people did not put up Christmas trees. There was nothing to celebrate.

Szczecin

Aleksander Krystosiak: When people decided to strike, each department immediately chose its strike committee. The department strike committees met and elected the factory strike committee. Why were they organised so quickly? The beginning of a strike is chaos. Once the strike committee was elected, it created order. Why these people and not others? The potential leaders were known to the workers. In every department, there were always a few people who were more active than others and more politically educated. These people knew how to read between the lines. There were a very small number of them, and they were in diapers in terms of organisation, but they were known. Still, until they were elected, they kept quiet so they couldn't be picked as the organisers of the strike.

The demands of the strike crystallised on the first day. Why? Spontaneity doesn't last long; emotions wear out. To make the strike last, the strike committee had to make sure that people understood what they were fighting for. The day after the strike began, we published a strike newspaper. The strike committee announced that it was taking over. It immediately created a guard to watch over the factory. It ordered no alcohol in the shipyard. The workers policed each other. If they found that someone had a beer or whatever, they would take it away and break it on the pavement. The strike committee also immediately demanded a ban on selling alcohol in the city.

There weren't any rules about how to conduct a sit-in strike. People were free to do whatever they wanted. At the beginning, some left; others stayed. Later, the strike committee gave passes. Even though the factories were surrounded by tanks and the military, the people who went home got fed, slept and rested, and were allowed to re-enter. The whole time, there were calls to go back to work: the military hoped that maybe they would.

The strike committee in Warski proclaimed itself an *interfactory* strike committee. Edmund Bałuka, the strike leader, had said that the only way to win was by unifying, that only in numbers was there strength. If they tried to deal with their demands factory-by-factory, they would be squashed like cockroaches, one-by-one. Only if they gathered together could they win something. Each factory which joined the strike sent two delegates. This body elected a presidium which made most of the decisions. The structure worked like a transmission belt: the interfactory strike committee [*Miedzyzakładowy Komitet Strajkowy* = MKS] gave orders to the factory strike committees; they gave orders to department strike committees, which gave orders to the workers.

The strike committee demanded that the government come talk to us. The government tried to wait us out, hoping we would go away. The committee insisted that phones be put in the cafeteria immediately so the delegates could connect with their factories. They also demanded that these phones be connected directly to the city lines and not to a relay plant, so no-one could listen to what was going on. Why were these phones so necessary? Because when the government representatives came to talk, the committee had to know what was happening in the other factories. As soon as a demand was negotiated, the representatives would run as fast as they could to the phone to tell their people.

People realised that the real power lay in the hands of the Party, so they went there. A few thousand went, joined by workers from a nearby factory. As they walked to the Party building, people on the streets joined the demonstration. The workers were very disciplined and well-organised. As the crowd walked down the street, if someone tried to break a shop window or something like that, he was immediately kicked out by the workers. They didn't need the police for that.

The crowd was attacked by the police with truncheons and batons. In self-defence, they broke apart benches and fences and tore up the pavement. There was hand-to-hand fighting. They pushed the police back and reached the Party building. When people entered, they saw all the wealth: TV sets everywhere, incredible furniture, expensive carpets. They went to the cafeteria and saw things that had not been available since before the war: smoked eye of tenderloin, salmon, smoked eel, caviar. This cafeteria was available to the workers of the Party headquarters building and the officials in the provincial committee. Not only could they get those things, but the prices were so ridiculous that it was really free. After people saw the cafeteria, they demanded liquidation of the special stores available to high Party officials and police and army officers, where they could buy things unavailable to anyone else. While in the Party headquarters they had only food, these stores had everything: furniture, carpets, foreign shoes, pants, silk. People unloaded their anger on the building. There was no robbing; simply destroying: they dumped the TVs out the windows and burned the building down. People then stormed the police-headquarters. Even then, they distinguished between the secret-police agents and the criminal police. The secret police were hated, but the criminal police had some respect. They protected society and individuals.

While everything was burning, the military surrounded the Party building with tanks. The soldiers didn't shoot; they just took position. Young workers would climb on the tank and shove things into gun holes. (I remember one of the workers shouting to people to get off one of the tanks and not to burn it because his son was inside!) By now, the workers had unloaded their rage and returned to the shipyard; the crowd dispersed. By the next day, all official government buildings were protected by tanks and heavy arms. My shipyard, Parnica, was also surrounded. There were no Germans around Szczecin, so the propaganda they used in Gdańsk would not work. Here, it was organised by 'criminals, thieves, socially marginal people and the CIA'. The government's anger turned against the Warski Shipyard because those workers had initiated the march. It was surrounded by heavy military equipment and so many armed servicemen that it seemed that they were gathered against the army of an enemy country. When the massacre took place, it was the government's revenge. People were gathered in a crowd around the main gate to the Warski shipyard, in a corner, with brick walls on two sides. All of a sudden, without even an order being given, the army fired on the crowd trapped in that corner. The attack was completely unprovoked. People fell, dead and wounded. I can't say how many because the military immediately moved in. The funerals were at night, and no family members were allowed to go. The victims were put in nameless graves. Some of the grave diggers and the people who did the funerals were brave enough to scribble the names of the victims somewhere. Later, we were able to get 17 names and to find their graves. But there may have been more.

The impact of December 1970

The protests of 1968 paled in comparison to these events. The official figures apparently underestimate the numbers of the dead.[33] The actions taken by the government to suppress workers' discontent destroyed the last shred of the régime's ideological legitimacy. If confrontation with the authorities in 1968 had alienated much of that generation of students, the events of 1970 drew a line of blood. The killings were deeply engraved into people's consciousness. They formed the reference point when opposition activity began more than half a decade later. Some of the first stirrings in the late 1970s were to memorialise those murdered, and in 1980 huge monuments were built in Gdańsk and other cities to commemorate the fallen workers. The monuments survived the imposition of martial law (which had attempted to obliterate Solidarity) because the authorities dared not destroy them. At the first opportunity after the Communist régime fell, the twentieth anniversary of the event, Polish television ran a week of reminiscences by participants.

The first response to these massacres was a sense of defeat and terror. The regime appeared unmovable and willing to resort to any means in order to maintain its power. The terror did not end with the killings. Małgorzata Celejewska:

> There was a curfew imposed from 6pm to 5am. The military moved at night, and it was a scary picture: a company of tanks moving, so the buildings shook as they went by. There was no way you could sleep through it. I woke up Przemek, who was six at the time, and brought him to the window. I wanted him to see the military passing by at night, like thieves. There was an officer with a gun in his hand, sitting on a tank with a sharp light shining on the buildings, checking every window. As the light moved, this guy had his gun pointed at the windows. People moved away because you never knew if he would shoot or not.

The terror persisted when she and others returned to work:

> Tanks were all over the shipyard. A guy with a crazed expression on his face came to me and put a gun to my chest. It was quite terrifying, and there was no way out, so we just had to back out and go home and face the tanks again as we were walking by.
>
> **Aleksander Krystosiak:** There was incredible despair. People were really in deep mourning. Many people considered giving up and going back to work. But people said 'No. We have to continue so these people won't have been killed in vain'. The strike continued, but there was a sense of defeat. We got

---

33. See Kubik 1994, p. 22, n. 18.

most of what we wanted on paper, except for rescinding the price-rises, but they never followed through.

Bogdan Borusewicz: I knew what had happened, and I saw how people were affected by it. March 1968 affected only me, and December 1970 affected everybody. I walked down the street, I saw tanks and patrols. I felt helpless that there was no group, no organisation in which we could meet together and assess everything.

This sense of isolation was widespread. As Wałęsa recalled:[34]

a complete lack of solidarity between the different sections of the population, in Gdańsk itself and even in many workers' homes. There was a crushing sense of loneliness, fear, and uncertainty about the prospects of our movement... Nor was there any sign of international solidarity.

But terror was not the only feeling present among the population. There was also a deep and abiding anger at the idea that justice had been mutilated. The police became targets. It was not simply revenge; they also served to put their targets on notice that their actions bore a cost to themselves. Alicja Matuszewska:

People knew where they lived. They would go to their homes and light a candle in front of them. Several families left the seashore as a result, and that was so well-known that in 1981, when they arrested us, we said: Just remember what happened in 1970!

Tadeusz Pławiński: People hated the police so badly that in my area a number of them were killed. One was found with a piece of paper that said: 'For my brother'. When they sat down in the inter-city trains, everyone would get up and leave. A lot of police quit.

The killing was isolated to the coastal cities and much of Poland was at first unaware of it. People heard from official sources that the troublemakers were Germans, hooligans and thieves. Information about what had actually happened gradually seeped out. Colonel Sucharski reported that he had many informers among the railway workers who 'travel, and with them travels information. They told horrifying stories about the killings'. People learned from friends who were visiting the coast, or who lived there. Marian Krzaklewski, president of Solidarity in the 1990s, recalled: 'I got on a train that was coming from Szczecin [in northwestern Poland] and going to Przemyśl [in south-eastern Poland]. A sailor there was crying and shaking, and telling stories about people being shot and the city burning'. Winicjusz Gurecki, later a Solidarity activist, stated:

---

34. Wałęsa 1987, p. 81.

I worked in a restaurant in Świnoujście. It was a small town, so among my clientele were policemen, and some of them I knew. I asked one who served on the coast in 1970: 'Where were you in 1970?' And he said, 'I was in the tri-city area'. So I said, 'Tell me the truth. How many people were killed there?' He was drunk, but even so, when I asked him that, he looked at me more consciously, as if being awakened. There was tragedy in his eyes, and he said, 'You tell me how many people can be killed after shooting a machine gun into a crowd for two hours'.

Workers on the coast had these lessons deeply burned into their psyches. These lessons were crucial to the workers' victory in 1980. Małgorzata Celejewska recalled: 'People acted impulsively. They went into the streets to demonstrate their anger, but they realised that to get anything, they had to stay in the work-places'. As word of what had happened spread, workers away from the coast also learned some of these lessons:

> **Zbigniew Bogacz, who lived and worked in Upper Silesia:** In 1970, people went into the streets from Lower Silesia. They achieved nothing, and the pro-paganda used the fact that they went on the streets against them. So, they realised that it was necessary to stay inside.

> **Władysław Frasyniuk in Wroclaw:** The murders in Gdańsk showed us that only organised forms of protest had a chance of success. It was most evident in 1980. That is why we did not leave the factories.

> **Tadeusz Jedynak:** The events of 1968 and 1970 were a short period of very intensive political education. After those two years I knew what to think about Communism.

Aleksander Krystosiak recalled that when the workers demanded an indepen-dent union, the government had responded: 'Elect your own people [to the exist-ing unions] and put them in charge!' After the killings, the workers had little choice. But, in Krystosiak's view, at that point, they still did not fully appreciate the significant difference between these alternatives: 'People didn't understand that even if they did put their best people in charge of the old unions, they would be destroyed'. Their experience in 1970 drove home this lesson. In some places, workers took up the government proposal and elected their people to the trade-union bodies. But once the movement ebbed, the government repressed the strike leaders. One was found dead in his apartment from gas inhalation; another awoke after having been beaten in his apartment to find the gas turned on. He was arrested soon afterwards, promptly charged with rape, and fired.[35]

---

35. Ost 1990, p. 56.

Krystosiak recalled that they went after Edmund Bałuka, who worked in the shipyards in Szczecin and was a leader there:

> Bałuka was elected the leader of the regional trade-union branch. The government realised that with him, it would be really an independent trade union. So, he had to be taken down somehow. Previously, he had tried to go to sea. A man like him, bright and defiant, couldn't get a job like that. But now they offered him a position as a sailor. Bałuka understood that the people who elected him would not be able to protect him, so he accepted the position. When the ship moored in South America, a secret-police agent came to Bałuka, gun in hand, and told him to get off the ship and disappear. He had no choice. Later on, the Communist press threw mud on him, saying that he had 'betrayed the trust of the workers who had elected him', and that he 'took the first chance to defect to the West and didn't care about the workers'.[36]

Others recalled similar stories:

> **Małgorzata Celejewska:** There was a guy who had been on the strike committee and who was elected to the workers' council. They murdered him about a year after the events. He was standing with his friend in the evening at the train station. The train came, his friends got on, but he didn't. They looked around for him and he was not there. So, they decided that they would get off at the next station and go back, which they did. As they came there, it turned out that there had been an accident: Janusz had been killed on the track. The newspaper claimed that he was drunk. But he was not. People got scared after that 'accident'. I was really shaken by it.[37]

> **Lech Wałęsa:** Gradually the management got rid of those who had been most active in the strike. I was always being given the worst work, and I was never allowed any kind of promotion.[38]

Gdańsk activist Joanna Duda-Gwiazda recounted the following:

> After 1970, efforts were made to elect authentic Factory Councils, to make unions independent. However, these bodies were soon fitted into existing

---

36. After being active in exile circles for years, Bałuka returned illegally to Poland in April 1981 and was an activist in Solidarity. When martial law was declared, Bałuka was one of those interned. He was tried on charges of forming an illegal organisation, slandering Poland abroad and publishing an opposition paper. He was sentenced to five years in prison; Niklewicz 1983, pp. 16–17.
37. See Laba 1991, p. 92, for other cases of workers who played leading roles in 1970 and who were found murdered, lost their jobs or suffered other forms of repression.
38. Wałęsa 1987, p. 85.

structures and all these attempts were soon foiled: the system absorbed them without any difficulty. That's why we chose the road of full independence.[39]

As Duda-Gwiazda said, when workers were confronted with the same choices in 1980, they had learned lessons from the bitter defeat they suffered a decade earlier and as a result they were unwilling to compromise on their demand for an independent union. This time they were able to make their demand stick, because they enjoyed both local and national support from workers. Krystosiak recalled that Bałuka 'was the one who stood on the stump and through a bull-horn thundered to all the rest of the workers that the only way to win was to unify'. By 1980 this maxim of unification was widely understood. As Krystosiak noted: 'In 1980, the shipyard workers asked other workers to join us'. This idea of common interests had become broadly assimilated. By 1980, many workers all over the country had come to understand that only their unity, their *solidarity*, could protect them. Zbigniew Bogacz:

> After December 1970, the situation radicalised, and then it was more possible to move the workers. We didn't believe the propaganda, which claimed that it was just hooligans and organised groups of thieves, when thousands of people went into the streets. We felt there was no hope of radical change if the workers did not have some kind of power. If we acted as a handful, we wouldn't be able to do anything. So we had to organise. People realised that just one workplace going on strike wasn't enough, and the best would be if all the regions joined. People on the seashore asked, 'How will Silesia react?'

December 1970 also produced a layer of secondary leadership, trained in the events of 1970, who would play an important role in 1980. Among them were Lech Wałęsa and Anna Walentynowicz (in Gdańsk), and Aleksander Krystosiak and Marian Jurczyk (both of whom led Solidarity in Szczecin). Wałęsa recalled that he 'had December 1970 strongly etched in my heart and memory. I prayed after those events that I would be given a chance once more to fight the battle'.[40]

The line of blood these events drew between the workers and the Communist regime changed things forever. Through the killings, the regime lost standing as a moral entity. Never again would the government attempt to appeal to its population in moral or ideological terms.[41] After December 1970 there was little sign that anyone really believed in Marxist ideology. The people on the coast – indeed, the whole country – never forgot these events. Gomułka, who had come to power in 1956 on the hopes of so many people, had now lost his last base of support and was unceremoniously dumped within a few days of the killings.

---

39. Jakowczyk 1982, p. 8.
40. Paczkowski and Byrne 2007, p. xiii.
41. Blazynski 1979, p. 34.

His replacement was Edward Gierek, the Party head from Silesia.[42] Gierek's accession to power created a wave of enthusiasm, albeit minor in comparison to that enjoyed by Gomułka in 1956. To achieve an enthusiastic response, Gierek had to promise that he would improve the material basis of people's lives. He asked his countrymen to judge him by his competence, and specifically by the effect of his policies on their standard of living. *His administration would live or die by this standard.* When that failed, there would be precious little to fall back on.

---

42. Bielasiak 1983, p. 15.

Chapter Five
An Opposition Emerges

> **Zbigniew Bogacz:** Gierek's rise to power meant that we lived better, but we paid close attention to all the construction projects – like the grand opening of the Piast mine. We put asphalt on the road; there were TV, radio crews, all the pompous ceremonies. The day after the celebration, we had to dig up the asphalt because we had yet to put the wiring down, and it was supposed to go under the road. It was all done for Gierek and Jaroszewicz. We laughed, but it was money and people's hard work. People from all over Poland said it was the same.

A decade after the 1970 massacres, it was Gierek's turn to be ejected from power by the workers. Their insistence on an independent union effectively constituted a revolutionary challenge to the regime . How did they get there? What happened to these workers during this decade? What conclusions did they draw? How were their experiences combined to create a broader understanding of December 1970 and to learn how to build an opposition?

The allegiance of a generation was lost to the régime, perhaps irrevocably, by the experiences of 1968 and 1970. Reform appeared impossible. So, what now? Gierek sought to alleviate the economic problems by increasing productivity, both through capital investment and by lengthening and intensifying the working day. In January, the Party initiated a series of meetings for workers to volunteer to work harder, beginning in Gierek's power base in Upper Silesia, among the relatively well-paid miners. These pledges were publicised all over the country in the print and electronic media. The national television news literally faked such a meeting in the Warski Shipyard in Szczecin by splicing together shots from three years earlier with banners in support of the new programme.[1] The next day, due to the outrage caused by the bogus report, a new strike began at the Warski Shipyard – it quickly became a co-ordinated general strike of the whole city. While they did not achieve their objective of forcing back the price-increases, Gierek was forced to travel to the shipyard to plead his case to the workers. The meeting – to which Gierek and several members of his government were required to request permission to enter – went on for nine hours, right through the night, and was contentious.

Gierek insisted that he had nothing to do with faking the meeting. He stressed his own working-class background: 'I am only a worker like you. I even have a pension from France and from Belgium, because I worked there 18 years. I don't have any relatives in high places'. He blamed Gomułka for all that had happened: 'It was impossible to say the slightest thing to him . . . We warned Gomułka often; we told him that the price of foodstuffs should not be raised'. Gierek spoke of the bleak economic situation Gomułka had left, arguing that the price-increases could not be rescinded, contending that: 'The only solution . . . is that you work harder and still harder – so that our economy produces its maximum'. Then he appealed to the workers: 'So . . . I say to you: Help us! Help me!' For the next several hours, speaker after speaker complained of the killings, their working conditions, the class divisions encouraged by the government, which doled out wages in hugely unequal proportions. Like the students of 1968, they protested against the proliferation of lies throughout the mass media. But the workers appeared to accept Gierek's request, and a resounding chorus of 'We will help!' met his pleas.

This was the first of almost two hundred appearances, speeches and appeals by Gierek to the workers, both in person and on television during 1971. These appeals gained him considerable support.[2] To gain acceptance, Gierek made concessions. Thus, when he was asked for a permit to build a new church in an area where it had previously been denied, he immediately approved.[3] Discontent similar to that in Szczecin simmered for weeks in Gdańsk, where the main shipyard formed a strike on 24 January, and, as a result, they were also granted a meeting with Gierek that produced a similar outcome to that in Szczecin.[4]

---

1. Laba 1991, pp. 79–80; Kubik 1994, p. 32.
2. Dziewanowski 1977, p. 318; Wałęsa 1987, p. 78.
3. Wałęsa 1987, p. 77.
4. Wałęsa 1987, p. 79; Szczesiak 1982, pp. 31–2.

Most people hoped for the best. Gierek promised a new course, and as they had so recently learned, people had no choice. Władysław Frasyniuk said: 'It is hard to accept anything or not in this country, Gierek was the First Secretary, and nobody could influence that. Most thought he was more enlightened than Gomułka, so we expected more from him'. It is not surprising that people would wish him well.

Ultimately, on 15 February the government rolled back prices in response to continuing strikes, including that of predominantly women textile workers in the city of Łódź who stayed out until the government backed down. To ease the substantial unrest that remained, wages were increased overall by an estimated total of some five percent.[5] The perhaps paradoxical result was that despite the mass killings, people emerged from the 1970 experience with a certain feeling of power: they had brought down Gomułka and forced the rescission of his price-rises. The workers were aware of what they had won. Małgorzata Celejewska: 'That felt to me personally a victory, and a lot of people felt the same way because Gierek had to swallow his own words. The general feeling was that the rebellion had given us something'. Aleksander Krystosiak: 'Most workers felt that Gomułka's fall and Gierek's rise to power was their victory. It was only later that they learned that someone new on top didn't change anything for them, and it wasn't a victory at all'.

Gierek still had to persuade the Polish people. He began by vowing to end privation. For that purpose, he turned to the West, from which he borrowed money to purchase consumer goods and to make capital investments. He thereby produced a rapidly increasing standard of living in the first half of the 1970s.[6] In his first year, real wages rose by over five percent and consumer goods production by seven percent. By 1973, Poland had the third-fastest growth rate in the world,[7] and by 1975 the standard of living had increased by over fifty percent since 1970.[8] Life became easier and political tensions diminished for a time, as Poles grew more confident about their futures. Gierek won himself some room for manoeuvre, which was reflected in public-opinion polls: in 1974, 60 percent of people felt the previous year had gone well, with this percentage rising to 81 percent in 1975.[9] Solidarity activists-to-be were among them:

> **Krzysztof Młodzik**: The shops were full of goods. I began to think that the events of December were just a mistake and we could forget about them and start anew.

---

5. Paczkowski 2003, p. 352.
6. Bromke 1981b, p. 4; Green 1977, pp. 80–1.
7. Ascherson 1982, pp. 107–8.
8. Paczkowski 2003, p. 355.
9. See Mason 1985, p. 16.

Adam Skwira: Very quickly the working conditions in my coal mine changed: mechanisation began. Our work was not as hard as it had been before.

Edward Nowak: People travelled a lot; they visited their relatives in the West; they bought expensive, new, Western cars. Every family dressed nicely and had a TV, a radio. The improvement was visible in every direction.

These steps produced a wave of new recruits to the Party, which aimed to include more workers.[10] While it was a much smaller wave than Gomułka's previously, it was nevertheless real. There appeared to be a new and less rigid regime. Dorota Terakowska recalled: 'The new Kraków Party Secretary allowed more press freedom; many new people joined the Party in the hope that they could make a difference'. They saw Gierek's rise as a signal that the Party was prepared to move in new directions.

Visits to the West helped to shape the expectations of Poles and later heightened their dissatisfaction when Poland's economy began to falter. Mieczysław Rakowski:[11]

> Between 1957 and 1989, more than ten thousand young sociologists, economists, historians and journalists went to study in the US, France, West Germany and Great Britain. A fair number of those who studied in the West joined the anti-regime opposition.

Although Gierek publicly distanced himself from the massacres in December, according to Adam Sucharski, all the police from his province who had served in Szczecin in December 1970 'received special treatment afterwards: financial rewards, medals, promotions'. I asked Sucharski about this apparent contradiction. He responded as follows: 'This was the split between the top and the bottom: the top did whatever it wanted and the bottom did what it wanted'. Did the top have any problems with what the bottom was doing?

> They were beautifying the top so it would look nice, while down on the bottom we were shovelling dirt. They would say, 'Our security services are not interested in such-and-such a problem', while we would get an order to work on this same problem day and night. Somehow, I do not remember any signs of discontent for what you could call overzealousness.

Building an opposition

How did this world appear to Aleksander Krystosiak, who 'wanted in 1970 what happened in 1980', and who felt the battle had been lost? Certainly, it was a defeat,

---

10. Bielasiak 1983, p. 21.
11. From a lecture given at Indiana University in Bloomington on 10 March 1998.

but the conflict was by no means over. Krystosiak, who had served as a member of the strike steering committee in the Szczecin shipyards in 1970, backed off, as others had also, to await better opportunities. He and a group of friends developed into a nucleus of opposition. After the strikes in 1970 and 1971:

> In my factory, eight of us who were close friends became the organisers of the strike in 1980. We discussed the events of the past again and again, trying to come up with solutions. Through those discussions, we learned how to speak with the workers, how to understand them, how to communicate things without saying them openly, how to read workers' feelings just by looking and listening.

Krystosiak had spent seven years in prison for having served in the AK, and so was perhaps more self-conscious about his activity than most. Yet even he had no clear idea about where he was going at first: 'The process of creating a feeling of solidarity among people was slow. We had a cigarette break and we talked. We had a lunch break and we talked'.

It was not a one-way street. Their fellow-workers, who had also experienced the events of 1970, were eager to participate in these discussions: 'We had extraordinarily good students. They picked up things that we didn't even talk about openly; they drew their own conclusions without us'. Krystosiak was aided in his efforts by his experiences in prison:

> I was in prison with the smartest intellectuals. That's where I studied law seriously: Roman law, the Hammurabi Code, German law, Napoleon, all that. It put me a step ahead of the grey mass of the workers. I knew all the laws concerning work safety. Whenever there was an accident, they would come to me. I would know what to dig out, how to dig it out, how to use it, so that workers who got hurt could get money.

Because the activity of Krystosiak's group had no public manifestation, few outsiders were aware of it. Karl Marx referred to this process with the metaphor of a mole silently digging its tunnels, undermining the society, unnoticed until the ground finally collapsed. Krystosiak described it as 'ant-like work':

> to explain again and again to every worker why he worked long, hard hours and still couldn't live like a human being. It was important to educate the workers how to read between the lines in the news. If a journalist was critical of an anti-Communist organisation that had been created somewhere, instead of getting upset, the worker should be happy that he could learn about the organisation that the Communists felt threatened enough to write about.

But to educate their fellow workers, Krystosiak and his colleagues had to earn their trust:

It was critical for people to learn who could be trusted. I wouldn't have been able to do such 'whispered propaganda' earlier. Because if I had, I would have landed in prison faster than I could imagine. Later, when people realised what the Communists were doing to them, it was possible to influence them.

The problem was to motivate them to act.[12] As Władysław Frasyniuk, the Solidarity leader from Wrocław, phrased it: 'to make people believe that something was possible and to get them to work for something farther off into the future'. At times Krystosiak and his collaborators felt they had to stretch the truth for this purpose:

We had to get the workers to feel that they weren't alone, so we would claim that somewhere in Poland there was an independent, underground organisation. We would tell that to, say, two people in the factory. By the end of the workday, the whole factory and the whole port knew about it. Not only did they see that they had the right to be angry, but that there were others who were not only angry but were doing something about it.

By the middle of the decade, they began to encounter others who were involved in similar work, so they no longer had to make things up: people's tracks were beginning to converge as isolated dissidents were finding and aiding one another:

We saturated the shipyard with illegal papers and books. We might have only two copies of an underground paper for a thousand workers, but all read it! Once, when I got a copy of the KOR *Information Bulletin*, I had to read it and return it the next morning. My wife and my daughter sat up all night and copied 75 pages by hand. Then I got someone to type it. To use a typewriter was a big risk. You had to have permission to have one. Every typewriter was registered with the police and they had samples of its type. Someone else got access to the mimeograph machines – they were locked up and really watched. Then, I got a few hundred copies made and passed them around. At first, we passively took whatever publications we got; second-, third-, fourth-hand. Later, we contacted distributors who knew where the papers came from and who published them. Through them, we tried to influence the content of the publications.

As the group progressed, more individuals were willing to take risks, and the scale of activity grew:

---

12. This problem was systematically raised by Mancur Olson, who argued that most people would not get involved in social movements because of the dangers of repression and their preference to allow others to take the risks when, if they were successful, everyone would enjoy the benefits that were won: see Olson 1977.

> To get underground papers into the factory, someone who had legal papers
> went in front of the guy who carried the illegal papers. They would pull him
> into a room, and go through those papers page-by-page. And while they were
> doing that, our guy would go through!

It is not difficult to imagine the feelings of contempt toward the authorities
that successes with this tactic would engender. Such feelings, if smugness were
avoided, could certainly raise morale.

Over the years, Krystosiak and his friends came to know their fellow workers:

> People did not hide their true feelings from me, as they would if some profes-
> sor came to take a poll. *I* knew how they felt, but the *government* had no idea
> what was going on. In 1980, there were 42 of us in our group. If we had not
> known the workers, how could we – 42 people – put the whole factory on
> strike? We knew they were ready. If a judge asked me: 'How did you know?
> Who told you that they would go on strike?' Well, no one. But through the
> years I learned to read people's mood.

Reading people's mood correctly was a vital skill because of the dangers of
repression:

> The secret police were really active then. Some people were jailed for seven
> days, two weeks or thirty days. I know someone sentenced for 'illegal posses-
> sion of a gun', which was never looked for and never found. Imagine a sys-
> tematic search of your house once a week. The searches were nerve-wracking
> because I never knew if my house was completely clean, that something wasn't
> lying around, stuck somewhere – in a book or whatever. That could be the
> basis for arrest because the 1970s were pretty tough in terms of dealing with
> the 'enemies of People's Poland'. We were very cautious about bringing people
> into our group. Only very few of those who wanted to join made it.

Krystosiak felt that the police waged psychological warfare against the emerging opposition: 'You got arrested. Someone else did. But *he* didn't, and he is the
leader. It was psychological death'.

Nonetheless, Krystosiak felt that Gierek's repression 'wasn't really serious, but
it was unnerving and unpleasant'. Perhaps for that reason, the group continued
to grow and to become more active. As Krystosiak recalled, in 1975:

> I was urged to run for safety inspector in the workers' council election. 'In
> that position, you will have the opportunity to travel around the factory and
> to talk to other people legally'. So, I became the inspector. My people made
> sure that I was elected. That position was connected to the trade unions. The
> secret police had to get the permission of the regional trade-union commit-
> tee to arrest me. Of course, it wasn't pleasant for them if one of theirs got

arrested. That position helped, but only because people knew why and how I was elected; otherwise I would have been seen as a traitor. I'll give you an example of how it worked: our workers were sent to fix a ship that was being unloaded. One of our people suddenly called the shipyard director and said, 'The working conditions here are incredible. Send Krystosiak'. What I went to see was not the working conditions but two sailors who wanted to talk to me. By then, our ideas had already crystallised.

Anticipating future conflict with the government, they specifically sought contacts with the shipyard workers in Gdańsk, where similar efforts were underway. Activists in both cities sought to involve workers in struggles for reforms, which they felt would ineluctably lead them to broader opposition. Joanna Duda-Gwiazda, one of the organisers of the Free Trade Unions in Gdańsk, explained their approach to journalist Jacqueline Hayden: [13]

> The immediate aim was the creation of a free, independent trade-union... Our success in small areas drew people's attention to the possibility of greater demands. Even though we did not believe that the system could be reformed... we were aware that many people thought that reform was still possible. Taking part in trade-union activity... allowed us to demand improvements without supporting the system.

They felt that this approach would be successful in securing better standards of living. As Gwiazda's husband Andrzej, who later challenged Wałęsa for the presidency of Solidarity, clarified:

> Our official line was that if the system was able to ensure human rights and proper living standards, then our role would end. We knew, of course, that if we did not abolish the system, it would abolish us... We knew that our activity was dangerous.

The third systemic crisis

The development of these groups greatly depended on what was happening within the wider society. By the mid-1970s, it became clear that Gierek's economic programme was falling apart. Oil price-hikes in 1973 occasioned an international wave of inflation in 1974 that became a world recession in 1975 (and brought about Poland's first decline in real gross domestic product since World War II)[14] which ended Gierek's plan to repay the borrowed dollars by competing in the world market. The economic squeeze meant that Poland could sel-

---

13. Hayden 1994, p. 22.
14. Flam 1994, p. 29.

dom continue to import consumer-goods (especially food), which now had to be *exported* to service the debt. As a result, the prices of food and a variety of other consumer items increased. One estimate held that around fifty percent of families suffered a decline in real wages.

Workers who produced for the export market were now pressed to work especially hard. In 1978, a new pay system was introduced in several areas that provided over half the workers' pay for work on Saturdays, Sundays and holidays, thus forcing these workers into longer working weeks, with fewer breaks, too. Some managers cheated workers out of their pay to make themselves appear more efficient. Neglect of the public health system was compounded as occupational health and safety standards were relaxed, resulting in more accidents, increased damages to workers' health and avoidable deaths.[15] All of these developments were part of the general policy of passing on costs to the working population. Zbigniew Bogacz described how the policy had an impact on coal-miners who worked especially long shifts of up to eleven hours on Saturdays and most Sundays in 1978 and 1979:

> The mines were expected to produce about 200 million tonnes of coal a year. The mine worked every day of the year, with three shifts working and one off. You got a day off in the middle of the week, but your wife worked and your children were in school, so what was the point? They attracted people from all over Poland by offering them apartments.[16] They kept building apartments and nothing else [meaning few schools, stores, cinemas, restaurants or other places of entertainment]. People continually had to work overtime and with intensity,[17] with no relaxation from 1975 on. Miners, who were overtired and overworked, didn't realise what was going on. Take myself: I felt I was making a lot of money, and I didn't even realise I worked every day – it was just work, work and nothing else. You can't live like that. Anger grows in you.[18]

As the push for more productivity intensified, serious accidents increased. As Bogacz noted:

> The machinery was used continually, with no time for repairs or maintenance. There was a series of catastrophes in the mine because people were

---

15. Bernhard 1993, pp. 153–5.
16. The terrible shortage of apartments and of food and other commodities elsewhere, combined with the relative abundance in Silesia, lured many people to work in the mines. Krzysztof Zakrzewski was one of them: 'Silesia was America to us. Flats were guaranteed in a very short period of time. For the first time, I could buy a piece of sausage without standing in line. I bought some meat with my first paycheque and took it back to Toruń in a bag. I put the bag on the table before my mother. She cried. "My son, how many nights did you stand in line?"'
17. Bernhard 1993, p. 155.
18. Bernhard 1993, pp. 155–7.

overworked and tired. Deaths by accident went up to 200 a year, with 100,000 people injured. The first big disaster was a gas leak; it was a danger-zone and they should not have worked there. For 200 pounds of coal, 34 people were killed. I decided it was murder. Then, the mine could be closed for a week and it was okay, but earlier they wouldn't even give one day off.

Several studies have indicated that by the late 1970s, nearly everyone except the most privileged felt worse off. As discontent grew, the regime escalated its 'propaganda of success', which trumpeted how well the Party's programme was working,[19] but this merely deepened people's cynicism and led them to intensify their search for other sources of information.[20]

Gierek's popularity plummeted as his promises proved to be false and shortages appeared in an economy that had been free of them for half a decade. Edward Nowak felt that change: 'The main cause of Solidarity was the discrepancy between the hopes that were stimulated throughout the 1970s, and the impossibility of actually fulfilling these hopes'. George Blazynski described a disturbing vision of how Gierek responded to his declining popularity with the rigid formality that had previously characterised Gomułka, thereby protecting him from reality:

> When I visited two factories... I was told that... they had painted only one side of the machines when Gomułka paid a visit because his itinerary was so carefully prepared. When Gierek came, they had to paint all the machines because they did not know where he would go. By 1976, they again only painted one side. Gierek's visits had become more formalised.[21]

In this situation, Gierek's underlings sought increasingly to please him, regardless of the waste, as they carried out elaborate efforts to create the *appearance* of efficiency. (Recall the remarks by Zbigniew Bogacz at the opening of this chapter.) Anna Walentynowicz spoke of a similar meeting with Gierek in the Gdansk shipyard in 1978:

> For... two days the main dining-hall had been prepared for him. They brought in new tables, armchairs, carpets. More than that... they painted the grass... in front of the canteen, using green wall-paint... There was a panel... of living flowers... about two metres wide and one metre high... a solid wall of red and white carnations... I found out the visit had cost a million zlotys, and this in the middle of the... crisis.[22]

---

19. Blazynski 1979, pp. 305–6.
20. Koralewicz 1987, pp. 4, 6, 8
21. Blazynski 1979, p. 315.
22. Interview with Anna Walentynowicz, conducted by Ewa Barker in Gdansk, September 1980. Received via personal communication.

Adam Sucharski: Gierek liked to be praised. He would not allow criticism of him or the Central Committee. As a result, they had no idea what was going on. I would send a telex to Warsaw and they would return it to me, saying 'You have to change it because Gierek will not take it as it is'.

Mieczysław Rakowski, Poland's last Communist Prime Minister, said of Gierek:

He had been accepted by Helmut Schmidt [the Chancellor of West Germany], by Giscard d'Estaing [the President of France]; the workers applauded him, and the people who surrounded him only praised him. Every leader is surrounded by opportunists, careerists. Every day, they come to you and tell you, 'Comrade Rakowski, you are fantastic, excellent'. This is the biggest danger for a leader. He began to believe that he really was the best man.

Since the government was unprepared for economic setbacks, it had reason to be nervous about a restive working class. Gierek held off from making inevitable choices as long as he could, but in 1976 the government finally announced a sharp rise in food prices.[23] It was an admission that the programme had failed. Anticipating trouble, the government ordered military units and security police to patrol the streets of Gdańsk, while several people considered politically dangerous were arrested.

Workers responded with strikes in three-quarters of the country's largest factories.[24] In the city of Radom, workers attacked Party leaders, built barricades, burned their Party cards, broke into and ransacked the Party building of virtually everything, from furniture and curtains to Party files, before setting the building alight and preventing fire trucks from reaching it. Later, they turned on government and police buildings, set ablaze police cars and looted stores (although there is evidence that some of the looting may have been by provocateurs). In the Warsaw suburb of Ursus, workers physically assaulted Party leaders; later, they blocked the railway line, stopped trains and took food from them. In Gdańsk, Gdynia and Płock, there were demonstrations and hostile encounters with party-leaders.[25] Strikes took place in several other cities.[26] In each of these cases, workers demanded that the government withdraw the price increases, which it finally did.[27] Faced with this rebellious response, Gierek did not repeat the murderous repression of 1970. That did not mean there were no deaths: the official death toll was two; rumours circulated that it was 17. As in 1970, the dead were hastily and secretly buried at night.[28] While the military was not used to

---

23. Green 1977, p. 97.
24. Blazynski 1979, p. 258; Bernhard 1993, p. 47.
25. Bernhard 1987, pp. 384–6.
26. Ibid.
27. Green 1977, pp. 100–2; Bernhard 1987, pp. 370–86; Bernhard 1993, p. 51, pp. 56–7.
28. Bernhard 1993, p. 69.

suppress the discontented workers, a massive police and propaganda apparatus had been prepared to smother the protests. There are credible reports of the police having killed at least three other people afterwards.[29]

If deadly force was not widely used in response to this rebellion, severe repression was deployed. Several thousand lost their jobs or wages; about 2,500 were detained. Many were sentenced or fined.[30] In Ursus, secret police circulated in the crowd, 'marking outspoken workers and those who seemed to be leaders with a special phosphorescent paint that could be detected under ultraviolet light'. People were beaten on the streets; some were unconscious as a consequence; others were arrested and later beaten. Later, those who were identified or suspected were sent along the 'health path' – the militia's cruel term for a gauntlet. Others were beaten.[31] Many of these people were innocent.

> **Jacek Kuroń:** After 1970, the government created huge police forces to control demonstrations. Tanks and machine guns are very inefficient in putting down street rebellions; police with shields, nightsticks, water cannon and plastic bullets are much more effective. They filmed the demonstrations from helicopters; at night, they arrested those in the pictures. People went to prison; they were tortured. In Radom, the police searched building by building, gate by gate, apartment by apartment. Whenever they found something new, and you did not have a receipt showing that you bought it, they took it and you. They had a huge parade of police in Radom to end this two-week operation. It was the occupying force of the victors. The day after, mass meetings took place at big stadiums in every city, where workers from all around were brought in to condemn the demonstrators in Radom. Those who did not land in prison lost their jobs and they could not get jobs anywhere.

In Gdańsk and Szczecin, attendees at these rallies were hand-picked and brought in from elsewhere by bus.[32] A policy of collective guilt was applied, as articulated by Tadeusz Karwicki: 'Each of us, as inhabitants of Radom, is morally responsible for the recent events and their causes'.[33] Funds for health services, culture and other areas were reduced in Radom.[34]

---

29. Bernhard 1987, pp. 373–81; Bernhard 1993, p. 69.
30. Paczkowski 2003, p. 379.
31. Bernhard 1993, pp. 51–2; Bernhard 1987, pp. 372–3, 379–81.
32. Bernhard 1993, pp. 65–6.
33. Bernhard 1993, p. 65.
34. Bakuniak and Nowak 1987, pp. 409–10.

A populace unbowed

Crucially, this systematic repression and terror did not succeed. For many people, these events were a turning-point in their lives. Some sought independent jobs or went abroad. For others, increasingly, *a sense of opposition was born.* Wojtek Adamiecki told me that at that time he felt part of a real opposition for the first time. Leszek Budrewicz, then an eighth-grader in Wrocław, was drawn to activism then; soon after he joined the newly organised Student Solidarity Committee (SKS). Mariusz Muskat, barred from working in his profession as a sociologist because of his activism in 1968, was moonlighting from his job as a railway clerk, conducting interviews for the Polish Academy of Science. During the 1970s, he completed around a thousand interviews. He found 1976 to be a turning point in people's attitudes. Sławomir Majewski:

> The factory management summoned the workers to denounce the demonstrations in Radom and Ursus. Since I was vice-president of the Communist youth organisation in the factory, I called a meeting where I said that the *gestapo* had acted and that no decent worker could condemn those workers. I recalled 1970 and told them about the lies and falsehoods. The next day, the Party leadership accused me of instigating and supporting hooliganism in Radom, of saying things which should be forgotten about December 1970, and of calling the people's police '*gestapo*', and of making accusations of corruption, which were 'not correct'. They suspended me, but I tore up my Party card and threw it in their faces.

With the threat of a strike in the Gdańsk shipyard looming large over the government's head, and with demonstrations and attacks on Party headquarters much more widespread than in 1970, the price-rises were quickly retracted.[35] The workers had established an effective veto concerning price-rises. And opposition was now safer: they would not kill you.

People attributed the government's relatively mild reaction to external pressures, which they felt restrained Gierek.[36] Janusz Onyszkiewicz: 'The regime tried to build its position inside the country by keeping a good image in the West. For that, it could not have political prisoners'. His critics within the Party thought he should have taken a much harder line.[37] But Colonel Sucharski felt that 'liberalisation was unavoidable':

35. Bernhard 1993, p. 60.
36. This policy was opposed and bitterly contested by hard-liners and this was a major source of opposition to Gierek within the Party; see Staniszkis 1984, pp. 177–9.
37. Lepak 1988, p. 180; see also Matejko 1982, p. 112.

The society was changing. They were getting more education, more culture. Poland had opened up to the West, so you had Polish cultural centres from the West bringing stuff in, influencing the society. You could not go to people with a stick. You had to conform to the way society changed if you wanted to exist in it.

Within narrowly confined limits, dissent was allowed in Gierek's Poland. If dissent was punished, it was done without great severity.[38] Journalist Andrzej Krzysztof Wróblewski made the caveat that this policy was only valid for 'as long as [Gierek] didn't think it [dissent] would challenge the system'.[39] Colonel Sucharski admitted that even the secret police did not really understand what was going on:

> Until 1980, I would say that the general opinion in the secret services was that socialism in Poland was so powerful that no matter what happened we would be able to choke it down. We had this feeling because we were misinformed ourselves. They indoctrinated us. They said that we had such superior moral power in the society that we had nothing to fear, that those groups of oppositionists were small and insignificant. They would tell us that every normal society has waves of discontent and if those waves were permitted, then the discontent would disappear.

People perceived that the repression was not as harsh as in 1970, and whether people were right or wrong in their perceptions, one thing is certain: *they felt freer to act*. Thus, 1976 was a turning point that significantly weakened Gierek. It shattered the base of public support he had won by reminding people of 1970, while the repression did not instil fear in people. Zbigniew Bogacz: 'We realised that if the Communists were so strong they wouldn't have had to back off of the price rises'.

Alicja Matuszewska: In 1976, the price-rises were called off, the brutal repression of 1968 and 1970 was not repeated; and in neither of those cases did Russia get involved. People talked about it a lot. They felt that they could act more freely.

Adam Skwira recounted: 'Many realised that if they opposed the government together, they could get something. I had great hope because the barrier of horror was broken'. Skwira's expression of hope in the face of repression surprised me, and I pressed him further about it: 'Yes. We knew about the repression, but we were no longer afraid'. Bogdan Borusewicz: 'The repression was not especially tough – just 48 hours [detention]'.

---

38. Green 1977, pp. 82–4.
39. See also Staniszkis 1984, p. 166.

Thus, the events of 1976 played an important role in preparing for 1980. They gave people a sense that *the regime might be vulnerable*. Sławomir Majewski, who had witnessed the events at the Gdańsk shipyard in 1970 and who had been active in 1976, recalled that: *'The mixture of 1970 and 1976 turned me into an oppositionist'*. These matters were discussed and lessons were drawn within the nascent groups.

Meanwhile, the secret police were put under the control of the provincial Party apparatus, and their actions became increasingly constrained, a demoralising step for them:

> **Adam Sucharski**: We got instructions written as though someone outside would be looking at them, and soon our work became filled with obstacles. It seemed that the Party wanted to weaken us. We were not to enter the factories as an organised police force, even in civilian clothing. We were forbidden from recruiting Party members as informers without permission from the First Secretary of the Provincial Committee. We could no longer call a person in for a talk. It became harder to detain someone. They reduced our ability to place bugs in phones and in rooms. During strikes, we were only able to cover the main gate, preventing outsiders from coming in. Letters, or whatever got sent out, had to be signed by the provincial police chief; our supervisor was no longer sufficient.

The secret police began to discover increasing hostility to their work on the part of Party leaders:

> As we were doing our job, we learned that this Party Secretary sympathised with Solidarity; that one did something wrong; another one built a dacha. And we had to report these things to the provincial Party Secretary. Those reports showed that half of his people were against him and the other half were unfit – and we were the bad guys because we knew it. It got to the point where we stopped informing the First Secretary about these matters.

They felt misused by politicians:

> Whenever there was a successful action, it was the smart First Secretary who did it. Whenever something went wrong, 'it was the secret police who screwed up again'. While we had been better paid than the militia, now they got a raise that equalised pay.

Moreover, they met with further resistance from below. As Sucharski noted: 'Our operational activity became harder because the society developed a stiffer neck and it was harder to convince people to co-operate with us'. One reason for this was that since Gierek had rolled back some of the controls, there was less that the secret police could offer to potential collaborators: 'The border opened up and international travel became easier. People got their passports without any favours'.

Public-opinion surveys at the time showed that workers were growing more oppositional. Large percentages favoured illegal methods to resolve conflicts, including strikes, absenteeism, slowdowns and even industrial sabotage. Very few saw the existing channels as effective for their interests. And their goals were also overtly political: they wanted free speech and equal access to schooling.[40]

The social standing of Silesians

During the 1976 protests, the quiescence of Upper Silesia – the industrial and mining base from which Gierek had come to power – stood out. Gierek's rise was in part recognition of the region's power. The workers' inaction there was partly due to Silesia's favourable treatment in comparison to the rest of the country, so its inhabitants had less reason to protest. But it was also a result of the terror they had suffered in the late 1940s and early 1950s, and of the government's policy of dividing Silesian workers by bringing in outsiders who knew nothing of the region's conflicts and who often received benefits that were unavailable to native Silesians (as discussed in Chapter Two).

These outsiders had moved to Upper Silesia because of its relative abundance, a tribute both to Gierek's skills as the region's boss and to the real necessity of attracting many people to work the coal mines that provided energy and foreign currency, as well as a means to divide the region. Few Poles outside the region were aware of the demographic shift. For them, everyone who lived in the region was a 'native Silesian' and subject to the prejudice and stereotypes aimed at this group (with their different accents and dialect). At the same time, the native Silesians resented the newcomers who had first access to the new apartments and the better mining jobs which brought many other privileges along with them.

Poles noticed the region's silence during 1976 (as in 1956 and 1970). As Aleksander Krystosiak noted: 'Silesians were seen as pampered, stupid miners who would blindly follow the Party line'. Many people from that region were brought to a realisation of their status by the way they were treated outside of Silesia. Zbigniew Bogacz recalled:

> When we went to other regions, our cars were damaged or destroyed; we were treated with hostility. Train carriages came from the seashore to Silesia carrying nasty graffiti about Silesians. There was a saying at that time: 'stupid like a Silesian'. Only when these people got so much shit did their eyes open and

---

40. Bernhard 1993, p. 152.

they felt ashamed of their actions or non-actions. We knew that because of the backup the miners gave to Gierek and Jaroszewicz in '76, they had lost in the eyes of the rest of the society.

This realisation would prove to be important for events in 1980 and in 1981.

An opposition emerges

Some independent groups (like Krystosiak's) began to cohere even before 1976. After that time, they came much faster. They were mostly informal and isolated from one another. Few people knew about the activities or existence of others. But they were part of the ferment that was occurring, as these informal associations emerged around the country. Some of these associations sought out similar groups, while others took a more conspiratorial approach and often remained ignorant of one another. Many people with whom I spoke had been in or around one of these groups. The phenomenon was widespread at the time.

How did they come together? Sociologist Stefan Nowak found that people did not identify with social institutions or officially-sanctioned organisations. He concluded that the 'social structure of Polish society in the subjective vision of its members would . . . appear to be a "federation" of primary groups united in a national community'. Poles had a close identification with self, family, friends, classmates and workmates – seen as primary associations – before their identification leapt to the nation, ignoring the proliferation of unions, professional associations, voluntary associations, and enterprises. In this sense, they were atomised. Not surprisingly, when independent associations did begin to develop, they arose through primary group relationships – relatives, close friends and workmates who could be trusted, with whom one could feel safe. Aleksander Krystosiak stated: 'It was very subtle. It worked through family ties: cousins, brothers, sisters, friends – people we knew and trusted. Here, the experience of 1970–1 came in handy'.

Pre-existing groups were generally not available to be 'taken over' and used against the ruling party. Rather, they had to create their own organisations. These groups were self-selective in their membership, which often accidentally cohered as groups of friends grew into organisations. Recruitment paths varied, as did the motivation for participation and the degree of commitment. Self-interest was not usually the crucial consideration;[41] participation was sometimes provoked by police repression, which surprised its victims who may have been unaware that organising independently was forbidden:

---

41. On the 'free rider' problem for social movements, see Olson 1977.

Leszek Maleszka: We began in 1975 as a group of Polish sociology students at Jagiellonian University who wanted to start editing our own literary periodical. Our views were mainly apolitical. There is always a first step made by people who become opposition activists. *My first step was being detained and questioned by the secret police for six hours, after a search of my house.* It was a very unpleasant experience, and changed my attitude radically from a passive one to active opposition. This must have been in January or February of 1976. *It was as if by chance we were becoming oppositionists.*

Bogdan Borusewicz: In 1975, one of my friends had criticised the government in letters to his wife and friends. He was arrested. We tried to organise a protest. Our contacts with other people broadened through this activity. There was already a group of young people who met together in a Jesuit church. We discussed, we read books, we got money for the arrested man. These people later created the Young Poland Movement.[42]

Anna Walentynowicz: Every time they arrested us we would come back with renewed determination, and we worked with twice the energy than before, arranging the next meeting, putting together the next issue of *Robotnik*.[43]

While the existing literature has frequently discussed the organising of Polish dissident intellectuals among themselves, I am speaking here of working people. As Aleksander Krystosiak recalled, a 'lot of groups became visible in 1980. When the strikes broke out, you could immediately see where the groups were, who they were. They came to join us, to help us to organise. Their members could be trusted'.

Krzysztof Zakrzewski worked in a textile-mill in the city of Toruń: 'We started to come together during cigarette breaks at work. We exchanged views about all the wrong things happening in our factory'.

Workers organised to aid those subject to repression, in their own defence and in disgust at what they saw. Since 1968 students had generally avoided political activity. Opinion polls published in 1972 illustrated this reality.[44] Yet students too began to organise themselves. These groups' purposes were wide-ranging. Some simply discussed, while others engaged in various forms of activity such as publishing, collecting money and agitation. Some of them were institutionally based and thus somewhat protected – for example, the Clubs of Catholic Intelligentsia (KIK), which were under the umbrella of the Catholic Church and

---

42. Young Poland provided a large number of activists, some of whom played a significant role during the strike that established the right to an independent union. They later worked closely with Solidarity.

43. Unpublished interview with Anna Walentynowicz, conducted by Ewa Barker in Gdansk, September 1980. Received via personal communication.

44. Blazynski 1979, p. 174, p. 176.

dated back to 1956. But once developed, these groups were available for political purposes. Over time they began discussing how to make political changes. Bogdan Lis explained how his workmates in a factory in Gdańsk came together cautiously in this new environment, while Józef Pleszak explained how Upper Silesia was drawn into opposition activity:

> **Bogdan Lis:** At first, only friends got together at parties; we discovered that we had similar opinions and we started to meet more often to discuss. In this way, in 1978 and 1979, the group of activists for free trade unions was created.

> **Józef Pleszak:** I started meeting with a group in 1976 in response to the events in Ursus and Radom. When three people from our group went to Warsaw, they were invited to a secret meeting and asked to collect money here in Silesia. They thought they were going to a birthday party, but one of the real purposes of the meeting was to involve Silesia in the secret operation.

While generally social movement analysts have found existing patterns of social organisation to form the basis of social movements,[45] in Communist Poland and the Soviet bloc, official organisations were not available for transformation and independent organisations were not permitted. (KOR did call upon workers to go into the trade unions and call upon them to change, but most activists knew that was a chimerical route). Leaders emerged because friends, workmates and relatives knew each other, as well as who could be trusted. Józef Pleszak helps us imagine the atmosphere within which groups were coming into existence and becoming aware of and making contact with one another, on the basis of primary associations:

> By 1977–8, sometimes there were ten to twenty of us and later fifty. Our meetings had to be secret. We gathered in private flats. We knew each other and who could be counted on. Each of us was allowed to bring in a new person. We had various contacts in Warsaw, Radom, Wrocław. We met those contacts especially in the churches because it was officially prohibited.

After 1976 this network grew significantly as people's contacts – both within and outside of their regions – flourished. Such contacts made it much easier for organisations to work together. Connections were also made between cities. It was especially important that not only *groups*, but *individuals* became familiar with one another. By 1980, *many people knew whom they could trust.* That made co-ordinating activity more feasible. In July 1980, as strikes were taking place around Poland, workers in Gdańsk and elsewhere began meeting to make preparations.

---

45. See Orum 1972, p. 50; McAdam 1986; Barnes and Kaase 1979; Von Eschen, Kirk and Pinard 1971; Walsh and Warland 1983.

> **Bogdan Lis:** There were many meetings and discussions about what would happen in Gdańsk if this wave of strikes should come. What should be the demands? What could be won and what not? In Elmor and several other factories, the factory council was in the hands of people from the free trade unions, so I organised a meeting between different factories to estimate the situation. It was a conspiratorial meeting so it was only eight to ten people, one from each factory. Its purpose was to organise co-operation.

This effort proved fruitful. Lis's factory struck within one day of the strike in the Gdańsk shipyard. The workers elected a leadership and posed demands that were similar to those in the shipyard. Yet this network was fragile and could easily be broken apart. As Pleszak noted: 'The end of '79 and the beginning of '80, there was a break in the supply of underground literature because one of the people with whom we were in touch died. Only in May 1980 did we make some further contacts and get more'. None of the groups was particularly large. Prior to the 1980 strikes, all of the groups could count their followers in the tens or fewer – recall that Krystosiak's group began with eight people and included only 42 by 1980. Not all such groups played an oppositional role. Ryszard Sawicki cautioned: 'I took part in such group meetings all the time. We talked about things, but there was no obligation to do anything'. But several of the people with whom I spoke had been in such groups, and while many of them did not become a part of the opposition, a large number of those people who did become part of the opposition were from these groups.

During the 1970s the workers became increasingly sophisticated in conspiracy. They learned not to give information when they were detained because within 48 hours the police would have to release them.[46] Underground publications informed people how to behave when questioned by the police.[47] Workers learned to send out couriers to announce to other workplaces when they were striking, while the secret police learned to intercept those couriers. The police took this lesson a step further to attempt to isolate particular departments within a given factory by taking over loudspeakers and disconnecting telephones. But of course, the success of such moves depended upon their ability to intervene quickly once the workers started to act. The police also investigated key individuals and prepared to isolate them when they learned that a strike was being planned.[48] Adam Sucharski:

> We would produce leaflets with false information – like a date for the strike which was different than what was actually planned. Or we would start a

---

46. See Goodwyn 1991 and Laba 1991.
47. Lipski 1985, pp. 65–6.
48. Sucharski interview.

diversion in some other part of the town. Once, where we knew that there was going to be a mass meeting, we were able to misinform them to the point that the demonstration was split into three groups that went to three different places.

But despite this destructive activity, it does not seem like the secret police were able to seriously change the course of events.

Approaching the fourth systemic crisis

In the period leading up to the 1980 strikes, individuals were developing reputations in their workplaces and beyond. In Radom, a group of workers and intellectuals formed a committee around the underground journal *Robotnik*, produced by KOR (see Chapter Six). Meanwhile, in Upper Silesia two workers proclaimed a Founding Committee for Free Trade Unions.[49] Ryszard Sawicki helped lead a strike in the Rudna copper mine in Lower Silesia. Strikes were forbidden and even when carried out were usually not called by the name.

> **Sawicki**: Three shifts went underground. After 24 hours, the management agreed to all our demands, which were presented by being shouted behind somebody's back. There was no strike committee, no written demands, no negotiations. It was the first strike that we knew of that was won. In our region, everyone knew about it: the mines, the steel mills.

Sawicki was shouting the demands. Zbigniew Bujak and his friends in the Ursus tractor-plant became well-known:

> After many weeks of discussions, we knew that we would do something together. KOR gave us the answer to the question, 'What to do?' The appeal said to go to the official trade unions, join them and talk about the situation in the factory. So we did. We tried to fight for concrete things for our work groups: for a mercury laboratory connected to our workplace, equipped with good machines; to change the system of wages. This continued until the summer of 1980. Management scheduled Party meetings in various departments where they wanted to fire us. They repeated our names, so we became famous in the factory. At a big meeting, one of the Party members stood up and said, 'Look, comrades, they are so well-known that I don't think we can fire them'. Two to three weeks later, it was August and the strikes in Gdańsk began. Then people came to our department and asked, 'Where are those three famous men? We would like to contact them'.

---

49. Stefancic 1992, p. 49.

At the Elmor plant in Gdańsk, Gwiazda, Bogdan Lis and others took over the official trade union.[50] Alicja Matuszewska attended a regional meeting of trade unionists in May 1980. At the meeting, the Party Secretary charged that many civilians working for the military were social misfits. Their term was 'socially marginal'. Matuszewska recalled:

> For several minutes there was silence. I said, 'I am surprised to hear about people who are socially marginal, because before a civilian is allowed to work for the military, the secret-police check him back to the third generation. We all know of the scandals committed by military leaders. The chief financial officer of navy headquarters embezzled a lot of money and went to prison. An official of the naval air force sold airplane fuel illegally. We know that officers have built themselves houses with wood from military warehouses'. The delegates stood up and applauded me. My name became known from Bydgoszcz to Kołobrzeg.

In 1976, Bogdan Borusewicz and others wanted to remind people of what had taken place in December 1970. On 1 November, All Saints' Day – when Poles traditionally go to visit their dead in the cemeteries and leave candles and flowers – Borusewicz and others 'put up a sign to remember those killed'. This effort went mostly unnoticed. But next year:

> I felt that Gierek couldn't disperse a demonstration to commemorate what happened in 1970 because that was what put him in power, so we organised one on 16 December. At 4:30, when the workers left the shipyard, we went to gate number two with flowers and a wreath. About four hundred workers joined us. The news spread very quickly in the shipyards. By 1979, there were already two thousand people at the demonstration, most of them from the shipyards.

Lech Wałęsa was fired from his job at the Gdańsk shipyard for his political activities. Florian Wiśniewski, a skilled worker at the Elmor plant, recalled that 'Wałęsa had an incredible facility for establishing contacts and what he said about the role of the free trade unions seemed to convince his listeners'. Wałęsa spent three months in 1979 travelling to workplaces looking for jobs. To each one he visited, he brought underground literature. The Committees for Free Trade Unions, which flourished on the coast, helped to organise public lectures and to bring more people into organised activity. They openly agitated for and promoted the idea that workers needed independent organisations for their own self-defence. In Gdańsk, several people who would later become national leaders of Solidarity were involved in this organisation. Begun by Andrzej Gwiazda and

---

50. Hayden 1994, p. 47.

Joanna Duda-Gwiazda on 1 May 1978, it came to include Wałęsa, Walentynowicz and Lis.[51]

In Szczecin, Krystosiak worked with the Free Trade Unions. All of them were leading figures in the strikes and the Solidarity trade union. These groups apparently had a real impact upon the thinking of many people, and they helped dissidents to connect with one another. Krystosiak recalled:

> In 1980, in the factories where we had these few members, all the workers dumped their membership cards from the old trade unions and made lists for the new unions. The influence of these ideas was just incredible. At first, the membership of the Free Trade Unions was small: five to ten per factory. These were the nuclei of what was to become the opposition. In some factories, they started with five and by 1980 there were still five. But in my factory, it really spread around and there were 200 by 1980. That was the largest group. Each time at payday, there was about six thousand zlotys for the Free Trade Unions. It happened because the workers in my shipyard were the best educated politically. They got more of the underground press than others and they really understood.

Lech Kaczyński, a Gdańsk lawyer and later Poland's President, was deeply involved with the Free Trade Union. He explained how it worked:

> I lectured on labour law, but in reality about politics. Borusewicz gave lectures on history and contemporary events; Gwiazda about methods of union activity. The lectures were given to workers of the Lenin shipyard, and from the port. Many came from Elektromontaż, where Wałęsa worked. They were mainly young workers. The people changed, but there was a total of about one-hundred who attended overall, sometimes as few as three, while others attracted as many as forty. Friends told each other about them. The lectures began in August 1978. We tried to deal with workers' problems. Leaflets were distributed in the churches after Mass, and in the streets on occasions like May Day or the proposed changes in the norms of work, or Gierek's visit to the Gdańsk shipyards. Some were made in the tens of thousands of copies. They would say not to work overtime, to oppose changes in the norms of work, how to divide the earnings among the workers.

The Free Trade Unions in Gdańsk set up their own local paper, *Robotnik Wybrzeża* ['The Seashore Worker'] in late 1978. It was a spinoff of KOR's paper, *Robotnik* ['The Worker'].[52] Kaczyński recalled that while *Robotnik* was a newspaper *for* workers, written *by* intellectuals, *Robotnik Wybrzeża* was a newspaper not only

---

51. Szczesiak 1982, p. 37.
52. See the section on KOR in the next chapter.

for workers, but also written *by* workers. It was fairly strong in the shipyard because the workers were unafraid.

By 1980 the Committee for Free Trade Unions in Gdańsk reached many places. In *Elektromontaż*, where Lech Wałęsa had worked and been fired, the president of the workers' council was defeated because of the power of the Free Trade Union. At *Tekmet*, workers called to an election of the workers' council turned the meeting into a protest. At *Elmor*, the committee came to dominate the workers' council.

As 1980 approached, the foundation for real opposition was developing. In the Gdańsk region, the oppositionists regularly met in secret while the police attempted to break them up.[53] In Silesia, Zbigniew Bogacz recalled, 'all that: people being overworked and finding that the authorities didn't care about their lives, opened their eyes, and they finally realised that something was wrong with the system. Rage was growing in them'. Adam Sucharski felt that the government helped this movement to be perceived as an opposition as part of its effort to normalise expressions of discontent:

> The top ordered us to refer to them as an opposition. Suddenly, 'work stoppages' became 'strikes'; 'enemies of the system, anti-Communists and regime haters became 'opposition groups'; 'hooligans' became 'political demonstrators'. Nothing had changed, but it sounded different.

Colonel Karol Miller, in the Ministry of the Interior, stated that 'Gierek decided that the existence of opposition would be "healthy", it would be "competition"'.

In retrospect, it is possible to piece together what appeared at the time to be unrelated developments. An opposition was growing, people were perfecting their skills. By the late 1970s, underground printing operations, for example, were becoming increasingly sophisticated. Adam Sucharski knew of such an operation which put out high-quality printing; it took the secret police in his province three years to find out where the print shop was.

The authorities demoralised

One of the most important characteristics for both sides was the fact that, in light of mass corruption and increasingly empty ideological justifications, the opposition could occupy the high moral ground, and it did so. The opposition believed their cause to be just; moreover, there was growing demoralisation within the Party and the secret police. The leadership and its programme increasingly became objects of derision as more and more information about the

---

53. Wałęsa 1987, p. 104.

extent of corruption was released.[54] By the latter half of the 1970s, the morale of the authorities plummeted.[55] Mieczysław Gil, a steelworker and Party member in the Lenin Steel Mill plant near Kraków, felt that 'the Party was disintegrating as an organisation'. Krzysztof Kasprzyk, a physics student who was becoming increasingly involved in journalism, spoke of what he saw happening inside the Party in the late 1970s:

> I realised that there was no real chance for significant change, so I gradually became disillusioned. I asked myself if I had to stay within the Party. Our editorial policy was paralysed. We were pressured to go with the propaganda of success. The *apparatchiks* at our Party meetings tried to convince us that [Gierek's] policy would pay off, that life in the country was better. But I had another perspective, much sharper because of my work in the media. I could see how all this propaganda was created and transmitted from the top to the bottom, how arbitrary they were in shaping their policies. By 1976, all the social energy from the 1971 was gone. Only the propaganda of success remained. The housing problem grew every year. We knew that a lot of western products were introduced to the market, but who at my level would expect that things were going so badly? That all these imported goods, all this Heinz Ketchup that we used to buy in the stores would create the national debt a few years later.

Kasprzyk thought that the internal decay of the Party became evident when it was confronted with the events of 1976:

> My party cell had about twenty-five people. About ten of these were old bastards who looked at us as immature greenhorns. Gierek had reconstructed the whole Gomułka machine; there was no possibility of open discussion. I had a lot of talks with friends, who said, 'Why are you so militant? What do you want to achieve? You had better sit quietly. Don't you see that it is all hopeless?' There was a lot of conformism and feelings of resignation and helplessness. Very few people left the Party at that time. And all who did, in '76 or '77, became oppositionists. From today's perspective, I should have left the Party at that time, no doubt about it. But then I would not have been given a chance to participate in the Party reform-movement of 1980–1. I knew that to leave the Party would ruin my chances as a journalist. I would not be allowed to publish anymore.

To Kasprzyk and to opposition activists and Party reformers, it appeared that as the economic situation worsened, cynicism grew. There was no recognition from

---

54. Szczypiorski 1982, p. 111.
55. Ascherson 1982, p. 135.

above that anything new was happening, nor could anyone raise the issue from the ranks. As Kasprzyk recalled:

> I brought it up at a meeting, but nothing happened. Many members of our party were simply not interested. People didn't want to be involved in politics because they knew it might end their career, or they might not get a passport to go to a western country. I was part of it because I was responsible for my family. My wife did not work; she took care of our daughter at home. They were totally dependent on me, and I considered this.

Faced with the growing opposition movement, the Party leadership appeared to be in denial:

> Only the official interpretation was given. There was no real discussion, no exchange of opinions at all. They said that the problems of the worsening economy were temporary, that the government was making an 'economic manoeuvre' right then. I had big difficulties with work. I was very critical; I had a status as an *enfant terrible* in my Party cell. They wanted to fire me; I didn't publish much then because I didn't want to be castrated.

Adam Sucharski remembered that the secret police were impressed with the opposition: 'We got to know them and we respected them. Some of the things the opposition was saying and doing, we actually applauded'. Such sentiments would create difficulties for a branch of the service whose job was to destroy the very people they respected, and many of these operatives could not escape the ensuing demoralisation. As Sucharski said: 'We had several cases where younger officers of lower rank asked to quit the job for ideological and moral reasons. Several of them were moved to the regular police, and some were allowed to quit'.

Chapter Six
Independent Organisations and Opposition

Independent organisations play a significant role in helping to spark, organise and promote oppositional social movements.[1] In Poland, two organisations played a crucial part in aiding this movement. The growing workers' movement was given support and some direction by, firstly, the emergence of a new independent organisation, namely the Workers' Defence Committee [*Komitet Obrony Robotnika* = KOR], formed in 1976, and, secondly, by the only independent organisation that had survived throughout the period of Soviet domination, namely the Catholic Church. Each provided an umbrella of protection from government repression. As mentioned in Chapter Five, KOR helped to spread information about opposition activities among intellectuals and workers, and it encouraged and helped to connect the incipient oppositional groups. The Catholic Church provided much inspiration, especially after the election of Kraków's Cardinal, Karol Wojtyła, as Pope John Paul II. The Pope encouraged a spirit of independence and resistance, but the Church's role in creating and sustaining opposition was mixed. As I argued in the introduction, neither of these organisations created or led Solidarity.

---

1. This insight provides the basis of resource mobilisation theory; for example, see Oberschall 1973 and Morris 1984.

The Workers' Defence Committee (KOR)

KOR was created by Warsaw intellectuals who were among the regime's leading dissidents. Its original purpose was to aid workers who suffered repression from the 1976 protests, including legal difficulties, health problems, and an inability to support their families. Several of KOR's founders have stated that their motivation was essentially moral: to defend the persecuted workers. But there is no doubt that the emergence of open opposition and defiance of the government came about as a result not only of moral repugnance, but also because the government crackdown had not used deadly force, as it had done in 1970. That made it possible for these dissidents to act without fear of being murdered.[2] KOR activists collected money to help pay bills, secured competent lawyers and attended court sessions to ensure that legal cases were either properly disposed of, or, failing that, adequately publicised so that the world knew what was happening. KOR kept in touch with the workers' families and made sure that they were supported. It distributed over three million zlotys (a considerable amount of money at the time).[3] Once these workers had been released, the organisation turned to assist anyone deprived of rights and unable to defend themselves. The organisation publicly set itself the following four objectives:

1. To fight reprisals against people on political, religious and racial grounds and to render them appropriate help.
2. To fight abuse of the law and help the sufferers.
3. To demand the institutional safeguarding of civic rights and freedom.
4. To support and protect any social initiative undertaken to achieve these aims.[4]

KOR's goals included encouraging others to organise independently.[5] KOR encouraged workers to stand up to the police. In the Ursus tractor works – where workers had suffered repression as a result of their protests in 1976 – the organisation urged their fellow workers to demand the reinstatement of those who had been fired, and suggested they call for a special parliamentary commission to investigate the repression they had endured. Letters to that effect were sent, mostly from intellectuals (who were less likely to be subject to repression).[6] As one of the organisation's

---

2. Based on a discussion with Jan Lityński.
3. Rupnik 1979, pp. 84–5.
4. 1983, 'The Dissolution of KOR: The Disbandment Statement', *Uncensored Poland News Bulletin* (hereafter UPNB), 6: 18.
5. Bernhard 1993, p. 88.
6. Lipski 1985, pp. 98–106.

founders, Adam Michnik, noted: 'The vital question for us was not "how to reform the regime", but how to defend ourselves against it'.[7]

The KOR *Information Bulletin* made a painstaking effort to document and to publicise repression. In turn, as KOR developed a reputation for veracity, people came to rely on it for a glimpse of the truth, while foreign reporters found in it an important source of information that would be otherwise unavailable. The resultant publicity put pressure on the regime to improve its human rights practices and extended KOR's domestic reach and public standing; stories generated by the organisation were broadcast back into the country, alongside information about their source. KOR's influence grew over time. While KOR never had a mass base, it developed a network based largely around veterans of the events of 1968. Seweryn Blumsztajn, who edited the *Information Bulletin*, said that KOR was 'created by the generation of '68. People of that generation identified themselves with workers'.

KOR members publicly stated their names, addresses and phone numbers on their leaflets and publications. Being open about their identities subjected them to repression, but it also made it much more feasible for people to find and work with them. It encouraged others to be active and gained them much respect. This was notably different from workers' groups, as the latter acted secretly. This difference is reflected in how the two social strata were treated, with intellectuals being significantly less subjected to repression. Still, Wałęsa recalled:

> At this time I came across an issue of *Robotnik Wybrzeża* (The Seashore Worker) which contained a declaration announcing the creation of the Free Trade Union. The editors gave their names and addresses, in black and white: I could scarcely believe that it wasn't a hoax.[8]

KOR's relief work put its members in contact with workers.

KOR was able to protect its activists and provide an umbrella for others through its ability to publicise, especially through its contacts with the international press. This was among KOR's most important contributions because it 'lowered the barrier of fear', as Jacek Kuroń and several others phrased it: 'People began to see that they weren't alone'. Zbigniew Bujak, in Ursus, was one of the activists whom KOR was able to help protect: 'The factory Party cell held a meeting where they voted to fire us. But someone said, "They have contacts with KOR. This case is very famous and Radio Free Europe will talk about them if we fire them"'. Some workers had their spirits raised by the simple fact that an open opposition existed. As Tadeusz Jedynak noted: 'Until 1980, the mere fact of KOR's

---

7. Michnik 1982, p. 94.
8. Wałęsa 1987, p. 99.

existence was crucial; we realised that there were people who were fighting for our rights'.

KOR began in Warsaw and later spread. Bogdan Borusewicz, in Gdańsk, told me how he became connected: 'Quite by accident, I met the KOR group from Warsaw when I went to the court in Radom. I joined KOR in December. Then I went to meetings in Warsaw; I distributed the underground press; I went to the factories and distributed leaflets'. It was not long before Borusewicz came to the attention of student activists in Gdańsk: 'Once my name and address became known, people from outside came to me, including students from the Technical Institute of Gdańsk, and a new group was created in the student dormitory'. Borusewicz and his co-workers began to have contact with workers from whom they learned that while the scale was smaller than in Radom and Ursus, the protests and the repression of 1976 had been widespread:

> We learned that in 1976 there had been a strike in the shipyards in Gdańsk and about eighteen people were fired. There were strikes in other factories where people got fired. I went to their homes to meet these people. It was my first contact with the workers.

These contacts opened up new perspectives for Borusewicz and his colleagues, and this gave them access to a new world of possibilities:

> Anna Walentynowicz came to us after a mass for the victims. Later on, I got a letter from Andrzej Gwiazda. Alina Pieńkowska got my address from *Robotnik*.[9] This network grew continually. It included Wałęsa. Through me, it was connected to KOR. It was no longer just students, but also people who worked in the factories. Wałęsa and Walentynowicz had been active in the shipyards in December 1970. Gwiazda and his wife had been active with the student-network. So we had the entire experience of December 1970.

Through its publications KOR also helped workers realise that they were not alone. Aleksander Krystosiak recalled:

> All these underground papers and books and the *Information Bulletin* created turmoil and gave ideas to people. KOR created the mind food for free elections and meetings. Then there were underground lectures and meetings, the Flying University. The workers got the idea of how to achieve their goals.[10]

---

9. These three came to be leaders of Solidarity in Gdansk. Walentynowicz and Pieńkowska played an important role in the strike that established Solidarity in 1980. Gwiazda ran against Wałęsa for the presidency of the Solidarity trade union in 1981.

10. Goodwyn disputes this contention, arguing that KOR did not prepare the consciousness of the workers for the upheaval, although it did contribute to the understanding of other sectors of the society (especially the Church) as to what the workers wanted; see Goodwyn 1991, p. 200. It is certainly true that the workers were experientially in

KOR began publishing the newspaper *Robotnik* ['*The Worker*'] in 1977. Jan Lityński, one of the paper's founders and later a leading Solidarity adviser, told me it originally had three purposes: 'To trigger workers' commissions; to provide information, and to organise a network; and to break down the barriers between workers and intellectuals'. But during the paper's first couple of years, it was not clear that it was having any impact. Henryk Wujec, another of the paper's founders recalled that in the early years *Robotnik* 'by no means had a leading role':

> We were much more active among the intelligentsia because at first there weren't many workers willing to join in. But, in time, contacts with workplaces grew and then the free trade unions began to be formed, and in the long-run this work produced important results.[11]

> **Helena Łuczywo, *Robotnik's* editor:** I couldn't tell if the work made sense or not because there was little response to what we were doing. Lots of copies weren't distributed; some workers would take them because they wanted to look important, to brag that they were able to distribute, say, 2,000 copies. But later on, we would find out that they didn't because the police would search their apartment and find the copies. You began to suspect that, really, you were just doing it for yourself, as can happen when you do clandestine jobs. It's very easy to create fake constructs, a whole make-believe world. Many people are involved; they feel important, but in fact they do it for themselves. That's what I tended to suspect from time to time. I remember the last period before August 1980 was very difficult to bear.

Łuczywo continued to note that it later became clear that the paper was, indeed, having a real impact:

> At some point, we had a sense of our circulation because I was able to enforce my idea that *Robotnik* be sold. Then it was verified how many people read it. The greatest circulation, in the summer of 1980, was up to 80,000. The average circulation was fifty to sixty thousand. Some copies were read by more than one person. When I went to the [Gdańsk] shipyard in 1980, it was a very moving experience. A young man from a sports equipment factory near Warsaw said that when he found a copy of *Robotnik* in a telephone booth, he knew he found something. Then I really felt that what we had been doing paid off. It was only in August 1980 that I really knew that.

---

advance of the KOR group, and their experiences told them to go beyond what KOR was advising: to go into and attempt to take over the established unions – though KOR people viewed that as an educational step that would take the workers beyond it. They were, in many cases, already beyond it.

11. Wujec 1985, p. 38.

> **Jacek Kuroń:** It was only after we started to publish *Robotnik* that real activists started to come to us: future Solidarity activists. It wasn't that *we* went to *them*; *they* came to *us*. They needed those two years to watch us and see. Wałęsa, Anna Walentynowicz, Alina Pieńkowska – all in Gdańsk; Bujak in Warsaw, Zadruziński in Grudziądz, Zadrożny in Lublin – came to us in groups, all in the spring of '78.

Everyone agreed that papers were shared, so there were many more readers than the number of copies printed. Moreover, these papers were locally copied and distributed, making it difficult to estimate the true extent of their circulation. *Robotnik* was widely shared and made use of the existing networks.

KOR also had an impact inside the Communist Party. Maciek Szumowski recalled:

> There appears something that had been previously unheard of: an opposition – puny, but still open opposition. Gierek cannot squelch it, so his policy toward KOR is harassment: detaining people for 48 hours, releasing them. The very fact that KOR existed contributed to the idea that Gierek did not have a firm grasp on the situation.

Within the next few years a proliferation of groups emerged, in part because of KOR's efforts and inspiration as a precedent. These included the Student Solidarity Committee (SKS) and the Founding Committees for Free Trade Unions on the Baltic Coast. KOR's Intervention Bureau helped people who had problems with the government, and developed the first real contacts with workers; it also began to knit the opposition together, as people learned that there were other dissidents who were fighting the government.[12] Later came the 'flying university', which sponsored informal and uncensored public lectures on a range of topics, including history and politics. Soon there was a rich heterogeneous oppositional culture, comprised of independent leftists and right-wingers, Catholics, nationalists and others less easily categorised. By the end of the decade it was becoming possible to survive economically and even to have a career as a writer, printer or editor outside of the 'official' society.

Many workers with whom I spoke respected and appreciated KOR. In the coastal cities, a recurring statement was that the 'Free Trade Unions were a child of KOR'. The organisation certainly helped to create the atmosphere that encouraged these informal groups to come into existence. In some important cases, people connected with KOR played a key role in pulling together the Free Trade Unions and some other elements of the opposition. KOR's ability to publicise was extremely important in the summer of 1980 as the strike wave increased. It

---

12. Interview with Lech Kaczyński who served on the Intervention Bureau.

brought news of the strikes taking place in various locations and made people aware of the demands being raised. Consequently, demands escalated as one group piggy-backed on another.

Aleksander Krystosiak, who initiated the 1980 strikes in Szczecin, recalled that he and his fellow organisers made sure that workers saw these underground publications – not so much because of the specifics in the papers, but more so because they could offer hope. Hope could inspire the workers to fight.

Through KOR's publications the intellectuals (and later some of the workers who began to contribute to and distribute them) made programmatic and organisational suggestions. Jan Lityński was a leading intellectual dissident and Solidarity adviser, as well as one of the creators of *Robotnik*. Lityński acknowledged that the guidance given by intellectuals was not necessarily taken up by the workers, since the latter had their own ideas based on their experiences:

> We said in the first issue of *Robotnik* that it was necessary to create workers' self-help organisations. We meant trade unions, but we tried to avoid the name because we thought (mistakenly) that it was far from the workers and was only connected with the official trade unions, which always took the side of the authorities.

Krystosiak did not feel that the intellectuals were leading him and his fellow workers, but rather that they provided what he called 'mind food', which helped the workers to think through the problems they faced and to decide what to do about them. While workers did not necessarily accept what the intellectuals suggested, they were perfectly willing to listen. That is why, when the 1980 strikes began, intellectuals were often invited to be advisers. But as others have noted, they did not set policy.[13]

This movement was bigger than the horizons of those who saw things through the lens of the Leninist Party. KOR was neither responsible for the creation of most of the groups, nor did it provide them with direct leadership in terms of goals, tactics or strategy. Łuczywo gave a modest indication of KOR's influence:

> The most representative list of people was in the 1979 *Charter of Workers' Rights*, signed by about one hundred people. That was what we had after two years of publishing *Robotnik*. So it was not really impressive. And some of the names were not real, as it turned out later on.

Most of the workers' groups were independently formed. And, while many workers were glad to have intellectuals on their side, it was not KOR or other

---

13. David Ost has argued that after the fall of Communism, intellectuals did play a crucial leadership role, which, in his view, misled the workers by deflecting them from class politics; see Ost 2006.

intellectuals but the *workers* who established the agenda in 1980 and refused to compromise it.[14] KOR activists and their collaborators have acknowledged the limitations of their contribution.

But recognising the limited role played by the intellectuals does not change the fact that KOR made crucial contributions. By announcing itself, it raised the possibility of others doing the same; meanwhile, by providing information on the repression of others, and by suggesting ways to handle repression and specific grievances, it offered 'food for thought' and vital information. KOR especially facilitated the ability of these groups to function and to contact one another. As people learned of the travails and efforts of others – through both the KOR *Bulletins* and *Robotnik* – they became aware that the universe of the discontented was considerably larger than anything of which they could have personal knowledge.[15]

The Church and the Polish Pope

The role of the Catholic Church has also been debated. Some have argued that the Church was the inspiration for Solidarity,[16] while others have denigrated its role.[17] Jonathan Kwitny gave Pope John Paul II primary credit for the emergence of Solidarity, while Maryjane Osa emphasised the Church's institutional role in contesting the Communist state as the protector of the Polish nation (especially against the domination of the Soviet Union). I will discuss the Pope's role below. First, as noted in the introduction, Osa argued that through the space that the Church won in 1956, and in its contestation with the government over the celebration of a millennium of Polish history, the Church created the symbolic framework through which opposition was developed by emphasising the Church's connection and identification with the nation. The millennium

---

14. For strong presentations of this view, which runs counter to that of most of their predecessors, see Ost 1990, Goodwyn 1991 and Laba 1991.

15. See Anderson 1991, especially Chapter Two, for a discussion of how especially print-capitalism helped to create a national consciousness in much the same way as the smaller underground press had helped to create a consciousness of an opposition. Once attained, this consciousness helped to alter the socially-constructed knowledge of the political world within which they lived, and with it the subjectively-perceived possibilities for action. As the image of the opposition grew, so too it is likely that people became somewhat bolder, or at least more able to envision attempting something in the future. Admittedly, this is a speculative view, but evidence for this tendency abounds in this chapter. Difficult though it may be to prove outright, it is nonetheless a factor that should not be discounted.

16. Ekiert 1991; Garton Ash 1990; Bernstein and Politi 1996; Kwitny 1997; Osa 1997, pp. 339–65.

17. See especially Goodwyn 1991.

celebration was for a thousand years of Polish history *and* of the Polish Church.[18] The conflict between the Church and state, Osa contends, 'asserted a collective identity antithetical to that promoted by the state'.[19]

Moreover, while Osa does not state this, there was a significant stratum of oppositionist priests in pre-Solidarity Poland, as discussed in Chapter Three. They were the men who had been in the seminaries during the 1960s and early 1970s, and were part of the same generation as the workers who created and led Solidarity. Some of these priests supported and encouraged the strikes that established Solidarity. And prior to the late 1970s, the Church was sometimes the only organised resistance to the Party/state.

But the Church's role in this movement was actually mixed, even though most workers viewed the Church as an ally and often as Poland's moral voice. While some priests and some members of the Catholic hierarchy supported the union – as did Pope John Paul II from afar – there were many who openly opposed it. The Church's allegiance was always to its own mission, and if that was seen to conflict with Solidarity's needs, there was no question which would be sacrificed. Church supporters and spokespersons, when asked about this matter, emphasised that the Church was *not* a political institution, but rather sought to minister to all sides. And they often acknowledged that the Church was not identified with any side and had to look out for its own interests. The Church's official reaction to the strikes of August 1980 was not generally welcoming. Poland's Primate encouraged the strikers to go back to work, for those who paid attention to such things, in a patronising fashion:

> You, dear mothers, you know how sometimes your daughters who want to be smartly dressed ask so much of you: Dear mother, give me this, and that, and yet another thing. And you, too, you do not satisfy these needs at once. It is sometimes also the case in public life that we have to wait. Do not forget that we are a nation which is still rebuilding its prosperity ... We know that in the great toil of reconstruction of Poland much has been done in the Fatherland, but much more still remains to be done, and we must multiply the efforts of work ... in order to bring about the proper order.[20]

Some priests aided Solidarity and protested at Wyszyński's less than enthusiastic support of the strikers, with one priest stating that 'all the faithful, and I personally, are surprised at the passive attitude of the Polish Episcopate towards these

---

18. Osa 1997, pp. 354–62.
19. Osa 1997, p. 356.
20. Wyszyński, cited in Paczkowski and Byrne 2007, p. 54.

fundamental matters [facing] the Polish nation'.[21] However, it is farfetched to perceive the Church as the seedbed of Solidarity.

To achieve a fuller view of the Church's role, one must recognise that just as there were priests who openly encouraged and supported the opposition, and others who quietly comforted and supported those who were repressed, especially after martial law was declared, there were also those who administered to the authorities and those who actively collaborated with the government and the secret police. Colonel Adam Sucharski, who led the 'Fourth Department' in his province and was charged with overseeing the Church, detailed some of the ways in which priests were compromised and corrupt. Some were bribed (for instance, helping them obtain driver's licenses or passports) or blackmailed (for example, concealing a lover, especially a child). As Sucharski noted, 'in 95 percent of those cases, the priests would agree to co-operate because they were afraid that word would get out to the religious community and to the bishops':

> Very often, we used, for example, the criminal past of the person. For example, if he had once stolen something and had served time. In Poland, once you served time, you had a clean slate; you did not have to tell anyone about it. So, we would go after them and we would say, 'if you don't co-operate with us, we'll tell the people with whom you work'. In Poland, having a driver's licence was a privilege. So, under any pretext, we would stop them and take their licence away, and the restrictions were very harsh: you could not drive for two to three years. We would say, 'You can have your driver's licence back, but you have to co-operate with us'.

According to Sucharski, in his province:

> We had about one hundred and fifty priests altogether, and we had about twenty secret informers. Besides that, about thirty percent of the priests had some kind of contact with our services that had more of a social character to it: sitting, drinking coffee or alcohol, meeting on special occasions. I want to emphasise that of those 150 priests, there were only twenty or fewer who told us categorically that they did not want any contact with us, that we could assault them and they would still not talk with us.

Moreover, when foreign aid for the opposition was channelled through the Church, it made its way down to individual parish priests who were then to distribute it to those who needed it. But according to Sucharski:

> When Western charities sent goods here, a priest got a truck full of goods: cheese, butter, whatever. The first thing he did was call me up and say, 'Come

---

21. Cited in Paczkowski and Byrne 2007, p. 55.

on over. I have things I can share with you'. So, we loaded up the service car with as much as it could take of the better goods: cheeses, hams. I had all those goods so available and in such amounts that I was able to share them with my colleagues, friends. My mother remembers to this day that I brought a can of American oil for her.

Such statements may not be credible, given their source. When I sought ways to verify them, Sucharski informed me that before the end of Communist-rule they had been ordered to destroy almost all of this information. I managed to locate a judge who was then the chairperson of the commission in Sucharski's province that was investigating crimes against the Polish nation carried out by the Communists. While he refused to meet with me or allow me to use his name, he stated that 'it's common knowledge that the clergy co-operated with the security services'. He estimated that 20 percent of the clergy in certain provinces co-operated with the secret services.

A decade later, on 7 January 2007, Stanisław Wiegus, the newly-appointed Archbishop of Warsaw, resigned his position at what was supposed to have been his installation ceremony, after it was revealed that he had collaborated with the secret police during the period of Communist rule. The next day, the Reverend Janusz Bielański, rector of the Wawel Cathedral in Krakow – where Polish royalty was entombed – resigned for the same reason. Shortly thereafter, one of the country's newspapers printed excerpts from secret-police documents implicating a dozen high-ranking Church officials (including a bishop) in this collaboration.

In 2005 it was revealed that one priest, who had been sent to the Vatican during John Paul II's reign, had been providing the secret-police with information about the Church. Meanwhile, another priest, Father Tadeusz Isakowicz-Zaleski, who had learned that the secret police had a large file on him, had researched and was preparing to reveal the identity of 39 priests who had collaborated in Kraków, including three who were then serving as bishops. (Father Zaleski was very disturbed to learn that among those who had informed on him to the secret police were two other priests.)[22] As a result, the Polish Church itself called for an investigation of all of its bishops to see who else had ties with the reviled secret police.[23]

Of course, this information was not known until long after the end of Communist rule in Poland. Before and during the 1980s people fiercely stood up for and identified with the Church. In the 1970s and 1980s religious participation became more widespread than ever, and even people who were known atheists

22. Hundley 2007.
23. Smith 2007a; 2007b.

took part in religious ceremonies and rituals. By participating in the Church and its activities, they were affirming their identification with the Polish nation and against the regime. In that sense, religious participation was also a political act; even according to Osa, the motivation for participation was political and not 'strictly religious'.[24]

Osa argued, as did many spokespersons for the Church, that Solidarity's eschewal of violent tactics was a result of the influence of the Church (a position that Borusewicz ascribed to KOR's influence):

> It was ... an effect of prior pastoral mobilisation and the adoption (and adaptation) by mobilised workers of Great Novena rhetoric, symbols and tactics. The Great Novena of the Millennium was a sustained and complex nine-year program, leading to the Church's celebration, in 1966, of one thousand years of Polish Catholicism.[25]

That effort, Osa noted, was the framework under which the Church struggled with the state over how to celebrate and to interpret the culmination of a thousand years of history.

There is no doubt that the Church played an important *indirect* role in promoting opposition. In 1978, Kraków's Cardinal, Karol Wojtyła, was elected Pope John Paul II. The assumption of a Pole to the papal throne gave the Church a new stature within the country and weakened the government's ability to act against it. Jan Lipski, a KOR founder and later its historian, recalled: 'When the Pope was elected there was this huge wave of enthusiasm and joy in Poland; even some Party leaders stated that they were caught up in the wave of pride'. Rakowski explained to me: 'When Wojtyła was elected Pope, the whole nation, including Party members were proud: a Pole became "the deputy of God on Earth"'.

The Pope was an independent and alternative source of authority for the Polish people. The new sense of dignity that he engendered, and the sense of entitlement to justice that accompanies dignity, could have political ramifications. That this development was a serious threat to the Party was evident. When the government suggested that it might refuse to permit a papal visit in 1979, Archbishop Poggi, in charge of Eastern Europe for the Vatican, warned Gierek: 'Have you ... weighed what preventing the Polish Pope's visit would mean? It would cause a great outrage. The pope wouldn't swallow this denial. He would speak out against it'.[26]

When the government censored his speeches in print, the Pope would broadcast his sermons and masses on radio frequencies designed to reach his fellow

24. Osa 1997, p. 357.
25. Osa 1997, p. 354.
26. Kwitny, 1997, p. 307

countrymen.[27] This development was taking place at a time when religion had become politicised: since the Party opposed the Church, some purposely chose to be associated with the Church as a political expression. Even some known atheists did so, affirming that in this way they wished to identify with the nation.

I asked Rakowski if the Party leadership understood the threat that this Pope posed to them. He responded that Gierek did not understand it at all.[28] As Krzysztof Kasprzyk saw it, *the Party was at a total loss*, like a deer caught in a car's headlights:

> The election of the Pope was a strike right between the eyes to the Party, which was in a completely new situation, totally unprepared and isolated from the life of the country. It was an alternative way of thinking, and a real gift to the people of Poland by history. I remember meetings at that time with Party officials who had nothing to say about how to cope with the country's problems. The economic situation was already much worse than in 1974–5. But in the media, you would not find any of these concerns because the propaganda of success was still strong.

But whether or not Gierek understood the situation, what choice did he have? In response to Leonid Brezhnev's suggestion of refusing the pontiff's entry to the country, Gierek claims to have responded: 'How could I not receive a Polish Pope?'[29] A vital organisation would have instigated a serious discussion. But no-one from the Party came, as Kasprzyk recalled: 'The internal life of the Party was dead by that time. Party officials were very unconvincing, very orthodox'. Kasprzyk was in a good position to see how the Party line played out:

> I was offered a job as one of the managers of the press centre for international foreign journalists covering the Pope's visit. I could see how the whole visit was prepared by the state, and how the propaganda machine worked on presenting its image of the Pope's visit. It was amazing to see the secret documents concerning how to cover the Pope's visit: directions about how to operate the cameras so that big crowds would not be shown on TV, but only elderly people, nuns and priests in the first rows.

Instructions were issued to the press explaining what it should print: on the first day of the Pope's visit, the daily press would publish 'only the photograph of the Pope, his biography, an item on the beginning of the visit and a PAP [Polish

27. Kwitny 1997, pp. 307–8.
28. Bernstein and Politi claim that Interior Minister Kania, Defense Minister General Jaruzelski and, indeed, the whole Politburo did understand some of the dangers that this Pope could pose to the Party, and to the Soviet system as a whole; see Bernstein and Politi 1996, pp. 172–5. For some support for this view, see Szulc 1995, pp. 286–92.
29. Rolicki 1990.

Press Agency] commentary'. There was similar detail for the Party press, week-lies of various sorts and radio and television coverage.[30]

From the very start of the Pope's visit, it became clear that he was challenging the division of Europe since World War II. He claimed to be the people's spokesman.[31] Gierek looked on fearfully as the Pope addressed an estimated million people in downtown Warsaw. Gierek worried of a potential uprising of unprecedented magnitude.[32] As Jaruzelski recalled: 'We were afraid that this was . . . an escalation' in the Church's assault on the status quo.[33] In the view of journalist Andrzej Krzysztof Wróblewski, 'They feared hundreds of thousands of people gathering in one place and the sense of togetherness that would come from filling the entire square where that mass took place. What happens if, instead of people going home, they go to the Central Committee?'

The government attempted to limit attendance at the papal masses by restricting the cities to which John Paul II could visit, but the Church organised convoys from all over the country.[34] Attendance thus became not only a religious and national event, but also a *political* one. Some estimates suggest that as many as thirteen million (or approximately one-third of the population) attended these masses.[35] The political character of these events was enhanced by the Pope's overt message. Kasprzyk noted that 'He inspired people. He spoke about the necessity to preserve human and national dignity – to fight for it'. In Kraków, the Pope insisted that human dignity did not permit workers to be demeaned and made mere means of production. In Częstochowa, Poland's religious centre, he appealed to 'the people of Silesia', since he was denied permission to travel there: 'If you shout loud enough, the pope will hear you and will reply, "God reward you"'.[36] Besides his open-air Masses, the Pope held private meetings with various groups, including Silesian miners. This event helped integrate the Silesians with other Poles.

Somewhat independent of the Pope's message, his visit had a *sociological* impact that helped to change the atmosphere within which the opposition existed. The huge masses of people, stretched out as far as anyone could see, made a powerful impression. In this *indirect* sense, the Church significantly aided the opposition. Janusz Onyszkiewicz:

---

30. 1983, 'The Behavior of Mass Media During the Visit', *UPNB*, 11: 14–15.
31. Kwitny 1997, p. 326.
32. Kwitny 1997, p. 325.
33. Bernstein and Politi 1996, pp. 219–20. Their sources are books by the principals and Rolicki.
34. Bernstein and Politi 1996, p. 222.
35. Weigel 1999, p. 320.
36. Bernstein and Politi 1996, pp. 222–3.

Before the Pope's visit, people used to talk all the time in terms of 'we' and 'they'. Everybody knew what 'they' was: the ruling group, the Party, the whole establishment. 'We' was not so clear. 'We' were the others, but people felt fairly atomised and somehow 'we' was practically family. With the Pope's visit, people saw themselves, and they realised that 'we' was not just myself, my family and my five friends, but millions, basically the whole nation. And 'they' were a very tiny, isolated group. So we really felt that we had power.

What was the impact of this experience? How were people affected by it? Such moments can be transformative, both to individuals and collectives. When large numbers of people suddenly see themselves together, they recognise – just as Staszek Handzlik did in 1968 – that they are not isolated after all. New possibilities can be imagined as people finally come to perceive their power. Tadeusz Jedynak, who later became a member of Solidarity's National Commission:

> It was the first time that I saw such huge masses of people in one place. Strangers expressed their hopes for the future. People concentrated on one issue: their feeling that the days of Gierek, and maybe of the whole Communist system in Poland, were almost over.

It is easy to underestimate the impact of this experience. There were no tangible changes or organisational developments, and there was no direct link with the strikes of 1980. Nonetheless, the experience of having been among those masses of people who came together to see the Pope, had an important effect on the individuals who were there. Jan Lityński said that the Pope's visit changed everything. Adam Michnik, one of Poland's leading intellectual oppositionists, said:[37]

> Something very strange happened here. The same people who are so frustrated in everyday life, so angry and aggressive when queuing for goods, suddenly transformed themselves into a buoyant collective of dignified citizens. Discovering dignity within themselves, they became aware of their own power and strength. The police vanished from the main streets of Warsaw; as a result, exemplary order prevailed all around. A society deprived for so long of its rights suddenly recovered its ability to take care of itself.

Such moments have been important at other times in history. A crowd gathers and actions that had previously appeared impossible to contemplate now move into the realm of the possible in the minds of the participants. The perception from the gatherings at the Pope's visit, namely that the regime was isolated, surely had an influence on people's calculations of their possibilities of success in a confrontation with the regime. Tadeusz Jedynak said that the Pope's visit

---

37. Michnik 1993, p. 223.

'created hope and a sense of strength. We workers could feel that something was going on, that things were going to change for the better. We had much more hope than before'.

Colonel Adam Sucharski felt that the government 'took a servile position toward the clergy, who got everything they wanted':

> special trains to Czestochowa or wherever the Pope was. Factories were closed for a day or two so people could go see the Pope. It was impossible to think about doing it any other way because the enthusiasm in the country was such that everyone, Catholic or not, was very excited about the Pope.

Deepening the impression of the millions, who could see each other's faces and sense the shared attitudes at the outdoor papal masses, was their self-organised and orderly behaviour. Janusz Onyszkiewicz reported that 'People realised that they were not atomised, not isolated, that rather the ruling group was isolated in this nation'.

The Pope made other direct efforts to intervene in Poland and the Soviet bloc. Jonathan Kwitny reported that in the fall of 1979, John Paul II created an underground Church information service that smuggled all the Pope's speeches into Poland, as well as a Church-produced bulletin. Money was also raised from expatriate Poles to purchase books for the 'flying university', and to pay professors who lost their positions because they had participated in this activity.[38]

Kasprzyk felt that the Pope's visit encouraged oppositionists and made their efforts easier: 'By late 1979, a couple of months after the Pope's visit: suddenly, there was open criticism in the Party; substantial circulation of underground publications'. Meanwhile, the Party's leaders still had no strategy to respond to the growing challenge to their authority. Kasprzyk once more:

> The Party was dead ideologically; it could not offer anything. No attempt to deal with the question of ideological rivalry, or fight for the minds of the young generation. They didn't openly admit that there was a problem. I attended several media meetings at the headquarters of the Party Central Committee then. There was no room for any open discussion, for any hesitation, any doubts. No room to discuss what was going on within the intelligentsia, for instance, or how the Church affected people. Only official directives, produced by the propaganda department. The situation was terrible.

Yet despite the moribund character of the Party/state leadership, Kasprzyk noted that down below there was considerable ferment:

---

38. Kwitny 1997, pp. 343–4.

With the Pope's visit, I felt the end of a certain phase of socialism in Poland. You must remember that since 1976 there had been vibrations in the air: that something must happen, that it was just unbearable – especially this terrible propaganda that clashed so much with the reality of daily life, which was worsening. I remember the meetings of my Party cell of some twenty people: they were much more vital with an exchange of ideas, and a lot more unrest than in '77 or '78. I wouldn't say this was just the impact of the Pope's visit, but the climate in the country had changed tremendously. And between our expectations as editors of a daily newspaper, what the readers used to say to us and the demands from the top – the propaganda, policy-shaping direction and so on – we were quite alienated. And we had a lot of very critical meetings, but nothing really came out of them.

Approaching the fourth systemic crisis

Many Party members were very dissatisfied with the existing state of affairs. Neal Ascherson reported that in 1979:

> In factories, the party meetings often turned into unruly protests that concentrated on the chaotic food supply, the growth of corrupt privilege in public life, the infuriating effect of official 'success propaganda' on working-class families and the lack of effective workers' representation in the plants.[39]

These protests prefigured the battle that developed within the Party when it was faced with the challenge of a huge social movement that was both independent of and opposed to the Party. It is clear that as the country headed into crisis, the Party was also in crisis and the leadership had no programme to deal with either of these crises. Its inability to cope resulted from a lengthy process. Neal Ascherson:

> There was a gradual decline in the quality of the people at the top ... Twenty years of faction-fighting, always at the expense of the original minds and individualists carried out a negative selection. The leading personalities by 1980 were limited, pragmatic men, often with a background in the peasant youth movement or in local Party bureaucracy, whose talent was for survival rather than innovation.[40]

At a Party conference held in the spring of 1980, just a few months before the strikes, the only change that took place was the replacement of Premier

---

39. Ascherson 1982, pp. 126–7.
40. Ascherson 1982, p. 136.

Jaroszewicz. Beyond this change, it was business as usual. It is worth noting that if it appears to *us* – as outsiders looking in – that the Party was unable to act effectively, it was certainly much more evident to people in the opposition at the time. That perception strengthened their resolve as the confrontation approached.

Part Two

The Solidarity Revolution

Chapter Seven
The Solidarity Explosion

Aleksander Krystosiak: In the middle of the summer, when it's really hot, you see a huge black cloud coming over from behind the forest. It is quiet; there is no wind, nothing. But you know that in just minutes it will pour. There will be hail, thunder, lightning, everything. That's how it was among the factory-workers. You could feel the tension before the storm.

Piotr Polmański: August was a turning point in the history of Poland because barriers of fear that existed in people's minds were destroyed.

Mieczysław Rakowski: The economic situation became worse – for me, it was clear that this Gierek era was coming to the end.

In 1979, the Polish economy entered its first post-war recession, a decline that deepened in the next year. By the end of 1980, national income had declined a total of 7.7 percent. Every sector was affected – industry, mining, agriculture – with some becoming drastically reduced.[1] Poles felt especially bitter about the shortages because of the widely-held belief that much of Poland's wealth was being shipped to Russia to support the Olympics, which Moscow was hosting that year. Ryszard Sawicki, who led the copper miners during the period of legal Solidarity, recalled:

---

1. Garton Ash 1985, pp. 104–5.

People naturally reacted to the robbery that was taking place in broad daylight. At that time, in Poland you couldn't get anything: not a nail, not a bucket of paint. Everything went to the Soviet Union.

On the eve of the mass strike wave of the summer of 1980, it is unlikely that an active opposition numbered more than a few thousand. Jan Waszkiewicz, a professor in Wrocław who later served on the Solidarity National Committee, gave some sense of its reach: 'By Easter 1980, we could hold a meeting of the whole Wrocław opposition in one not very big flat: about eighty people'. The government estimated the opposition throughout the country to consist of some twelve thousand people.[2] Underground publications may have reached a few hundred thousand. Nonetheless, it was increasingly felt that something would have to give. Seweryn Jaworski in the Warsaw Steel Mill and Aleksander Krystosiak shared their perceptions of the time:

> **Jaworski:** By the spring of 1980, rationing had begun. With the economy crashing and shortages of everything, a lot of people started talking about the waste in their workplaces. I felt this tension since the spring, and I think everyone felt that way.
>
> **Aleksander Krystosiak:** You could see the workers turning against the managers and Party officials. They would show their anger, and their psychological quality toward *each other* changed: they were more helpful to each other. It wasn't a question of *knowing*. Each factory worked. But we got together with groups from other factories more often, and our meetings were more political: we talked about what to do and how to do it. We turned all of our activity toward keeping up the tension among the workers, and you could feel that the workers were restless. I couldn't say to the workers in our factory that something was wrong when they came to work and saw that everyone did what he was supposed to. So we talked to them not about *our* place, but somewhere else. *This* factory was really tense ... another shipyard. We told them that in that *other* shipyard they were talking about *our* shipyard being ready and wanting to do something. The main point was to get the workers upset, so when they got up in the morning they would think about how to organise themselves to do something.

That spring, Krystosiak's group carefully tracked people's sentiments when they met:

> We discussed what the workers were talking about, why they were saying this or that, what upset them. *We* were getting ready to do something because *the*

---

2. Wałęsa 1987, p. 116.

people were getting ready to act. Practically from spring, we can talk about slow-downs. They were doing as little as possible, and if they could get away with doing nothing, they did.

On 1 July 1980, the government yet again raised prices and almost immediately strikes were formed. The authorities quickly offered wage-increases to those who made trouble, in an effort to localise discontent. But the strikes spread. In July alone, some three hundred thousand workers in 100 factories struck.[3] Word of the strikes spread largely through the news apparatus established by KOR (thereby demonstrating again its importance to the workers' movement), as well as foreign shortwave broadcasts.[4] These strikes showed that the underground network was functioning well. Helena Łuczywo:

> When the strikes broke out in July of 1980, it turned out that we [*Robotnik*] had a fantastically efficient network. When they disconnected a telephone, we would find a new one, and we would somehow be able to let people know. They would call and say 'at this plant we went on strike, our demands are this and we are doing this'. Then we would try to check it out. Also, we had our own informants whom we trusted because we knew them. We had to give true information, because if once or twice we were wrong, we would stop being considered reliable.

Łuczywo insisted that:

> If it hadn't been for us, the news about the strikes would have been suppressed, and they would not have spread. The official Polish media said nothing about the strikes. But people listened to Radio Free Europe and to the BBC, and everyday we were their source of information. After some time, the official media had to admit that something was happening.

The rolling strike wave indicated that there were widely shared feelings of discontent. The workers were learning from one another's experiences: their demands grew as they piggy-backed from one to another, picking up others' demands and

---

3. Sanford 1983, p. 49.
4. There has been controversy over this issue. Several historians and journalists have claimed that this source of information was very important. Goodwyn has argued that their emphasis has been overblown; see Goodwyn 1991. Florian Wiśniewski, who was on the Gdańsk MKS negotiating committee, certainly felt it was an important source: 'We were spat on and lies were spread all over Poland through this unfortunate censorship. Only the world's press helped us to get through'; cited in Kemp-Welch 1983, p. 94. Clearly, this avenue did help to spread word of the strikes. Józef Kuczma, from the Paris Commune Shipyard in Gdynia, remembered the following: 'Polish Radio states that yesterday and today there were short work stoppages in some plants in the Gdańsk conurbation. [From] Radio Free Europe ... and BBC ... we learn quite different news'; Kuczma 1982, p. 259. But as Goodwyn has effectively argued, the foreign press played no role in *organising* the spreading movement.

adding to them in order to cover their own grievances. The strike wave attained a new level of intensity when workers in the city of Lublin stopped city transport and demanded work-free Saturdays, an end to press censorship, the same family allowances granted to the police, and unions that 'would not take orders from above'.[5] That strike expanded into a city-wide general strike in mid-July.[6] Later, rumours claimed that the workers stopped a train that was going to the Soviet Union, welded the wheels to the tracks and searched it. They found hams apparently stuffed into cans marked as paint, which seemed to confirm Poles' worst fears that their hard work and resources were being taken from them by the giant in the East.

Still, the shipyards remained quiet, despite efforts in Gdańsk to start a strike in July. Anna Walentynowicz recalled: 'We thought there was little prospect [of provoking a strike]. Shipyard workers were still too frightened'.[7] Those workers were watching and gauging events. In Szczecin, Aleksander Krystosiak and his colleagues began to prepare for action:

> When the Lublin strikes ended in July, we began working on educating the workers for the future. We told them that they should do an occupation-strike and elect a strike committee immediately. Our main point was that the people in Lublin did not understand the importance of unity: that to achieve anything people had to get together. Welding the trains to the track would not stop them from going to the Soviet Union. For that, you had to organise a general strike, with everyone in Poland standing up to the government and saying 'No!'
>
> The workers felt that something was getting ready to burst. So, we decided to talk people into believing that the time was ripe, so ripe that it was within our reach. We were certain that the same thing was happening in Gdańsk and Gdynia. We had contact with factories in Warsaw, Lublin, Kielce, mostly through family-members who worked in big factories. We asked them to tell their workmates that in other factories, like ours, people were getting angry and something was about to happen, and they should get ready in case other factories started. It was an absolutely conscious and agreed-upon move to try to agitate people into some action.

---

5. Kemp-Welch 1983, p. 16; Ascherson 1982, p. 131.
6. MacDonald 1981, p. 9.
7. Kemp-Welch 1983, p. 17.

The Solidarity strikes

Gdańsk

In Gdańsk, the government had begun a crackdown on 'troublemakers'.

> **Bogdan Borusewicz:** In 1979, the factory directors started firing workers. That autumn, three young workers from the North Shipyard were dismissed. Andrzej Kołodziej was fired for distributing leaflets. In spring 1980, Wałęsa tried to organise a strike, but it didn't come off. He was fired, along with five others. Still, the strikes in July raised the atmosphere of dissent in the factories. Workers in the shipyards were under stress, so a situation was created in which you could move from working within a small group to influencing large groups of people. There were more copies of *Robotnik* going around; and there were meetings. Then, they fired Anna Walentynowicz.

A crane operator in the Lenin Shipyard in Gdansk, Walentynowicz was also a member of the Free Trade Union and a long-time activist with a history of fighting for workers' demands.[8] She had been in the shipyard for thirty years and had received the bronze, silver and gold crosses of merit. She was just five months short of retirement.[9] This particularly egregious dismissal seemed to be a warning that activity like hers would be punished severely. But the injustice provoked more anger than fear. Word of this spread and, as Borusewicz reported, 'throughout the shipyards it was repeated' that they should strike. The day after Walentynowicz's dismissal, Borusewicz and his colleagues 'estimated that the atmosphere made it possible':[10]

> I told people in the shipyards that they should defend her and themselves.[11] I explained to them that they had to be determined. If the leaders hesitated, no strike could be organised. I organised a meeting devoted to the details of how to organise the strike. Soon there were several of these meetings.

It was by no means clear that they would succeed in organising a strike. Jerzy Borowczak, one of the strike organisers, noted: 'Even we didn't believe that we would succeed. We gave ourselves a 50 percent chance of success'.[12] Despite the growth of oppositional sentiment, for the most part people kept their thoughts

---

8. MacShane 1981, p. 14.
9. Kemp-Welch 1983, p. 17; Goodwyn 1991, pp. 157–8; Persky 1981, p. 9.
10. See Hayden 1994, p. 20.
11. The leaflet read: 'Stand up for crane operator Anna Walentynowicz. If you don't, many of you may find yourselves in a similar situation'; Persky 1981, p. 10.
12. Persky and Flam 1982, p. 73.

about these matters to themselves and their associates. Journalist Jacqueline Hayden, who sat in on the meeting the night before the strike began in the Gdańsk shipyard, recounted: 'There was no indication that something cataclysmic was going to happen as I sat in Anna's flat on the night before the strike began'.[13] Borusewicz said:

> Of 15,000 workers in the shipyards, few knew when the strike was to begin. We prepared over ten thousand leaflets to be distributed as people went to work to get them to gather in one place. The leaflets spoke about Walentynowicz, but it was only to be spoken, not written: 'We will strike'. We decided that we needed Wałęsa to come to the shipyards because these people were not sure they could organise the strike.

Andrzej Jarmakowski, an activist in the Young Poland group, was asked by Borusewicz to print the leaflets. Jarmakowski recalled: 'The next morning, we went to the shipyard to see what was going on. To our surprise, in a short time, a crowd of around five thousand started marching to the Director's building'. The plan was to organise protests on two sides of the huge shipyard, and for them to march to the centre to join one another, picking up workers in other departments as they proceeded. On Thursday 14 August, Borowczak tried to start the strike in the small department in which he worked. People there were nervous.[14]

> Borowczak: 'Why doesn't a larger department begin the strike?' someone asked...People started to return to their machines and turn them on. I went up to them, saying, 'Let's go to [departments] K-3 and K-4. They've both stopped'. It was a shot in the dark because I wasn't certain that anything had happened yet, but I wanted to get them to follow me.

> Borusewicz: Soon the whole shipyard knew that something was happening. One section went around calling out to people to join them as they went. By the time they came to the director's office, their ranks had swelled by several thousand. The shipyard was not working.

Evading his police minders, Wałęsa slipped into the shipyard and took his place at the head of the strike. After haggling for the morning, around midday the director accepted three demands, which, according to Borusewicz, were:

> to raise wages by 1,500 to 2,000 zlotys per month [wages then averaged 5,500 zlotys][15] to build a monument to the workers from December 1970; and to

---

13. Hayden 1994, p. 23.
14. Strike Bulletin, p. 31; Persky and Flam 1982, p. 75.
15. MacShane 1981, p. 17.

rehire Walentynowicz. The first two were put forward just to get the third, which was the easiest to fulfil, and which he finally accepted. If he had publicly agreed to take her back in the morning, the strike would have ended. But by midday, people had seen that they had power and they wanted more.

This *perception* of workers' power broke the hold of fear. The intoxicating experience emboldened people. Borusewicz continued:

> By then, the strike was so strong that these demands which we thought could not be granted concerning the monument and the wage-increases became possible. So the strike continued. In the evening, the Strike Committee was founded. On the first day of the strike, the North Shipyards and the Repair Shipyards also struck to support us.

The strikes were occupation strikes. Anna Walentynowicz, whose firing provoked the strike in the Gdańsk Shipyard in August 1980, said that the 'experience [of 1970] helped us greatly. No one went out into the street. The gates were locked and there was no possibility of a provocation.[16]

Still, the police made some attempts to provoke. Walentynowicz:[17]

> We found out that [the police] wanted to put us to sleep by spraying a drug from an airplane and then break in and overpower us ... So we were prepared for an actual battle with the police. We redoubled our perimeter guards; all the cranes along the waterfront were turned around, lights were put on and additional floodlights installed. We reinforced the guards at the gates and impressed upon them the need to be doubly vigilant, and somehow they didn't dare try it. No-one slept a wink that night.

A workers' militia soon began to police the shipyard. Alojzy Szablewski, who later led the Solidarity union in the shipyard: 'The strike committee ordered that there be no vodka in the shipyard. We opened the lockers, took the bottles and threw them on the stones'.

Negotiations were publicly broadcasted over the shipyard loudspeaker system. Shipyard director Klemens Gniech noted that the workers' negotiating committee did not represent all the departments in the shipyard. He proposed that each department elect delegates. In several sections, the Party had some strength and his supporters were elected. They made up about one-third of the committee, making it less militant.[18] Nonetheless, the next day, the city of Gdańsk began to close down as other workplaces joined the strike. Soon transport came to a

16. Ewa Barker, unpublished interview, September 1980.
17. Ibid.
18. Borusewicz interview.

halt. The conspiratorial activity that had preceded the strike was now paying off. People knew what to do. Bogdan Lis:

> I organised a meeting where we proposed 18 of the 21 demands of the strike. This meeting ended about 3am, and later in the morning I went to my factory. In my section, I also organised a meeting, and delegates from other sections came to it. In about a half-hour, almost the whole factory went on strike. Elections were held in all sections of the factory and delegates to the strike committee were elected. The strike committee took one of the rooms in the director's office. We presented demands to the director. We took over the transmitter for the factory and the central telephone lines.

Within a few days, the shipyard-workers won a raise of 1,500 zlotys, a promise of increased family allowances, reinstatement of Walentynowicz and Wałęsa, a guarantee of safety to the strikers, and the right to build a monument to those who were killed in 1970. The committee voted to accept the settlement, and on the afternoon of Saturday 18 August, Wałęsa declared the strike over.[19] But there were many who felt that it was too early to settle the spreading strike. Here, the pre-strike planning paid off. As Lis stated: 'It was important that we had already had these discussions. It helped during the crisis when, after three days, the shipyards wanted to end the strikes'. Workers now joining the strike from other workplaces berated the shipyard workers for settling their own grievances and leaving everyone else to face the government alone. Henryka Krzywonos, who led the bus and tram drivers, cried in despair: 'Buses can't face tanks!'[20] Borusewicz remembered:

> Representatives of the other striking factories came to the shipyards and shouted, 'You betrayed us! They will simply destroy us!' So, they decided to continue their strike in solidarity with the other factories in town. Wałęsa went to the microphone to announce it but the microphone was already cut off. Three women ran to the gate and stood on some tyres. They and others began to shout: 'We must have a solidarity strike!' The shipyard workers were already out of their work clothes, and in their street clothes, and were going home. There were only one thousand left, perhaps fewer.

Meanwhile, Joanna and Andrzej Gwiazda seized a truck and went first to *Elmor*, their workplace, and then to other workplaces, telling them to join the inter-factory strike committee.[21]

---

19. Kemp-Welch 1983, pp. 18–19; Goodwyn 1991, pp. 158–66.
20. Garton Ash 1985, p. 41.
21. Hayden 1994, p. 25.

The strike was now reconstituted as a solidarity strike, without Gniech's supporters. This time the first demand was for the right to constitute a union independent of the Party and state, a demand in which they were soon joined by strikers in Szczecin, who had also created an inter-factory strike committee.

As a result of the reduced numbers in the shipyard, Saturday night was the time of the strike's greatest vulnerability. Borowczak: 'The management spread gossip saying that workers were being kept forcibly...and they began to threaten that the police and secret police would come'.[22] Borusewicz: 'That was the most difficult night; we feared we would be attacked'. Once they survived the night, it was evident that the strike would continue. A Sunday Mass brought the strikers together and enabled them to see their strength; it united them with their fellow-believers outside the factory gates, and it positioned them with a powerful symbol of Polish nationhood.[23]

> **Borusewicz:** We went to many priests and asked them to celebrate a mass in the shipyards. Most of them refused. In the end, we found two priests. In Gdynia, Father Jacek agreed to celebrate a mass, and in Gdansk, Father Jankowski. (But first, Jankowski made out his will).

During much of the strike, the Church hierarchy generally kept its distance from the strikers. The Polish Primate, Cardinal Wyszyński, urged the workers to return to work.[24]

The organisational form of the Inter-Factory Strike Committee [*Miedzy-zakładowy Komitet Strajkowy* – MKS], invented by the workers in Szczecin in 1970, was now resurrected.[25] On Monday, the strikers were joined by the shipyard workers who had left on Friday, as well as by delegates from other workplaces in the city.[26] The movement grew quickly. By 22 August there were over four hundred enterprises represented in the MKS. A week later, it was over five hundred. Soon the MKS began negotiating the demands of each enterprise, as well as the 21 points generally agreed upon. It began to act as an alternative source of power within the city: it gave permission for various food-related and other necessary enterprises in the city to continue functioning during the strike. Anna Walentynowicz:

> We issued permits for food shops to reopen. Delivery trucks still operated, so did the bakeries. The canning factory stayed at work so the fish would not be wasted. The factory making tins had to work as well, as did the transport.

---

22. Persky and Flam 1982, p. 77.
23. Ibid.
24. Weigel 1999, p. 402.
25. Garton Ash 1985, p. 42; Kemp-Welch 1983, pp. 19–20; Goodwyn 1991, pp. 166–7.
26. Goodwyn 1991, pp. 174–5.

Those working wore red and white arm-bands and flags were flown outside the shops.[27]

Soon, the strike was spreading to other cities and to more enterprises within the cities where strikes had already been constituted.

Gdynia

In neighbouring Gdynia, news of the strike in the Gdański Shipyard arrived on foot and by bus, just as it had done in 1970. Andrzej Kołodziej, who had just started working in the Paris Commune Shipyard the day the strike began in the Lenin Shipyard in Gdańsk,[28] spent that first night with the strikers and then returned in the morning. Tadeusz Pławiński, who later became the strike leader, was vacationing when the strike began. He recalled the following of Kołodziej: 'That morning, he got a number of people, locked the director in his office, and put a guard on him. Then he began to organise a strike committee.[29] It was mostly people like himself: young, inexperienced, but brave'.[30] In explaining the youth of the strike committee, one of the participants noted: 'They had the least to lose. (We kept remembering what happened to the organisers of the 1970 strikes)'.[31]

When Pławiński returned to the striking shipyard from his vacation, he had to ask permission to enter: 'People coming from vacation had to be confirmed. If someone went home and decided to come back, he was kicked out. I personally kicked out a number of people later on'. Pławiński saw a troublesome situation: 'Kołodziej had been without sleep at least since Friday. The directors slept in their offices. Everyone slept in the shipyard but him. He was unable to do anything because he was just falling asleep'.

They attempted to improve the situation by creating a strike committee with delegates chosen in department meetings. Pławiński recalled that finding volunteers was not always easy:

> If you are chosen and it ends in the wrong way, you are done for. You might not find a job for the rest of your life, or you might turn up dead. Nobody knew what would happen. I worked in the electrical department. I had become known because of my verbal fights with the management. Someone mentioned my name as a good guy to be the departmental delegate to the strike

---

27. Barker 1981, p. 19.
28. Goodwyn 1991, pp. 162–3; Kuczma 1982, p. 256; Persky 1981, p. 6, p. 21.
29. Persky 1981, pp. 67–8.
30. Barker 1981, p. 117.
31. Ibid.

committee. I didn't refuse, but I thought of my baby daughter, who had just been born in November 1979.

Pławiński soon found himself in an important if vulnerable position:

> I became chief of propaganda. From the commie point of view, that is the most dangerous position. They figure that you are really pulling all the strings, like *their* propaganda people do. So, I knew I was in trouble.

People were given tasks: maintaining essential machinery, guarding the shipyard, and checking the walls to make sure no provocations were made outside. Kołodziej and others were sent as representatives to the inter-factory strike committee (MKS) in Gdańsk,[32] where Kołodziej soon became vice-chair of the MKS. Pławiński:

> We had strict rules, a good guard system, military-like duties. There were probably five thousand people there all the time, and you had to feed them somehow. We got food from bakeries.

Pławiński said that maintaining the strike in the Paris Commune Shipyard in Gdynia made it more difficult to attack the Gdańsk Shipyard.

> They dropped pamphlets from planes and helicopters, telling people that the Gdańsk shipyard workers had left. Kołodziej told people that it was all a lie. He locked the shipyard from the inside and didn't allow anyone to leave. I think that if the Gdynia shipyard had left, it would have been over, finished. They would have used the police and army.[33]

The police established blockades around the shipyards in a futile effort to prevent people from bringing in food and other supplies. Couriers to and from the shipyards were seized and detained. For this purpose, roadblocks were established on major roads. Nonetheless, some police informed the strikers of their sympathy for the strikers' cause.[34]

---

32. Goodwyn 1991.
33. If Pławiński is right about the consequence of maintaining the strike in the Paris Commune shipyard (people in Gdańsk agreed with him), it shines an interesting light on the possible role of the individual in history under exceptional circumstances. By Kołodziej's sheer will-power and audacity, he held together the shipyard in Gdynia, which was the salvation of the strike in the Gdańsk shipyard, the core of the strike-movement and of what came to be Solidarity. The significance of this feat is heightened when one recalls the enormous pressure that these workers endured at that time. No-one was more aware of the state's capabilities. In the Paris Commune Shipyard, for example, one striker recalled: 'Nervous strain was felt by strikers already during the first days of the strike: on Saturday evening I witnessed three fits of epilepsy'; Pawelec 1982, p. 274.
34. Potel 1982, p. 30; Goodwyn 1991.

Szczecin

Once the strike began in Gdańsk, Krystosiak and his colleagues in the Parnica shipyard felt that it was time to act:

> The forty-two of us got together and discussed what to do. We met outside, on the grass near a castle, and organised it so it would look like a picnic and not a political meeting. We had blankets, vodka, chicken, cards – everything. We decided to start the strike on Monday. We wanted to organise it so that in case it didn't work out, we wouldn't land in prison. We were ninety percent sure that once we ignited something, the workers would follow. But there was that ten percent of 'what if?'

Their plan was very similar to what took place in Gdańsk:

> We took the smallest, most average-looking man in our group, who worked in the biggest department of the shipyard. He went to the pipe and engine department to tell just two people that his department was on strike. At the same time, another guy who worked in the electrical department went to the body-welding department and told them that the pipe and engine department had stopped. The carpentry department was informed about the strike of those two departments. We picked people who were the hardest to remember so they wouldn't get arrested for starting the strike. They were told that as soon as they gave their message, they should disappear. We already had our demands. We knew the workers were ready for some action and that the news would spread with the speed of lightning. My idea was that these departments would go to each other, through the main traffic area to see what was going on there. They would collect all the workers who were in-between. So the workers of these two huge departments met somewhere in the middle.

The plan proceeded as expected:

> When the strike started, we kept low to the ground. We were very concerned to make sure that it looked spontaneous.[35] We weren't in any hurry to become the strike committee. One of our guys caught the vice-chairman of the old trade union, grabbed him by his arse, put him on a stump and told him to tell people to elect a strike committee. So he looked really scared and said, 'People, choose a strike committee'. At that point, the people started giving out names,

---

35. One gauge of their success in covering their tracks can be seen in the account of the strike given by Neal Ascherson: 'On Monday, 25 August, a large, formless crowd *simply coagulated* by the gate telling each other that they must do something to show support for the Gdańsk comrades'; Ascherson 1982, p. 169. Generally, when there are claims that people came together for some kind of collective action, those assertions come from observers who are ignorant of the planning and efforts to produce that action.

and mine was the first one. So, I became the chairman of the strike committee. That person from the old trade unions vanished. As soon as we were elected, we set about to organise ourselves. We installed guards to check entrances and exits to the factory. I immediately seized the big factory motor boat for the use of the strike committee. We relieved the management and the unions of their duties and told them they were obliged to accept directives from the strike committee like the rest. We took over the factory grocery store because people would need food. We began at 6am. By 10am, everything was organised.

But a strike in one small shipyard was an invitation to repression. The strike had to spread:

> Once my shipyard was taken care of, I got into the motor-boat and went to the Warski Shipyard. Once I was inside, I saw they were working. I told people, 'We are on strike! I'm the strike chairman, and I'm here to see what you are doing'. They disappeared and others started coming; and then they left and others came and left and went to others and called them to strike. Practically in front of my eyes, I could see how the whole shipyard slowly came to a standstill. Groups of workers stood together, putting their tools down and talking. I went back to my shipyard to put the final touches on organising the strike. We knew that it didn't matter which factory started it: the rest would follow. The lessons of 1970 had been learned. How can you imagine: there I am, a small man in filthy work clothes, coming out of a motor boat, saying 'we are on strike!', and in an hour 12,000 more people were on strike? It had been drilled into them that it had to be a general strike – and the fact that Gdańsk already stood helped.

Soon, other workplaces sent delegates to Warski to form an inter-factory strike committee.

> The next day, two factories joined us. On Wednesday, ten factories were on strike. That day, I was nominated by my workers to be their representative in Warski. They also sent me three couriers so I could send back information and messages. On Thursday, they also sent me two bodyguards – really huge men. Their duty was to be with me all the time and protect me from any harm.

As new enterprises joined the strike, a pattern became evident in the careful way that the workers chose their leaders and representatives:

> In 1980, there was not even one factory where the leader of the 1970 strike committee was elected. The feeling was that they were burned out, fearful. (They *were* paralysed with fear because they had been persecuted). But that attitude of mistrust was not directed toward the rank-and-file members of the 1970 strike committees. They were felt to have gained valuable experience.

> I myself was elected, in part, because I had been a member of the strike committee in 1970.

The workers recognised that solidarity with one another was necessary for their victory.

> Having formed the committee, we all went back to our factories to bring the demands that we created together in Warski. My crew and the other two accepted them with no changes as theirs. We decided we would not allow any profiteering or petty demands and details to break our solidarity, so the government would not be able to break us into little pieces and negotiate separate agreements.

The Szczecin MKS, centred in the Warski Shipyard, soon represented 380 enterprises – this figure increased to 740 by the last day of the negotiations.

The workers had learned the lessons of the previous confrontations with the Party and the government. They stayed in their workplaces, as occupiers. They did not go into the streets where provocateurs could have joined them to discredit them. They did not attack other buildings and sites, so they could not be portrayed as 'hooligans'. The government was forced to deal with their dignified selves, in their workplaces.

Negotiations

The workers' demands quickly centred on something hitherto non-existent in the Communist world: an independent union with the right to strike. 'For us', said Wałęsa to the government negotiators, 'the most important [demand] is that concerning...free, independent and really self-governing unions'.[36] They were stronger by virtue of the fact that the Szczecin strikers were co-ordinating with them and also demanding first an independent union. As Władysław Pawelec, a striker in the Paris Commune Shipyard, noted: 'We were not interested in a merely apparent victory, and that was why we were not particularly euphoric over the changes in the leadership of the Polish United Workers' Party. We thought it was a trick – like in December 1970'.[37]

> Tadeusz Pławiński: We explained continuously: 'Without independent unions, they will screw us again'. Nobody trusted them. You can only get something from the Commies with an organisation independent of theirs. If you dropped the free union, you dropped everything.

---

36. Kemp-Welch 1983, p. 69.
37. Pawelec 1981, p. 276.

Everyone recognised the significance of this central demand of the strikers. If granted, it meant that there would be a real power independent of the Polish United Workers' Party that would be able to force through policies contrary to those of the Party. It would change everything. Other workers cheered upon hearing about it. The government was openly hostile to this demand. A letter to Party members, from which the following excerpt was reprinted in the daily *Strike Bulletin*, was unambiguous in its attitude:

> the anti-socialist elements among the Gdańsk Shipyard workers made politi-
> cal demands and hostile stipulations in order to seize control of the strike.
> *Their demands threaten the essential security of the country. They put in dan-*
> *ger our national survival*... [They] demand the establishment of free trade
> unions... in order to obtain a platform for activities aimed against our Party
> and the People's Democracy.[38]

Jan Szydlak, head of the official unions, expressed succinctly the government's attitude: 'The authorities do not intend to give up their power or to share it with anyone else'.[39] But the government's options were limited. Karol Miller revealed that among workers in the Ministry of the Interior – whose job was to keep order – there was a 'frantic' and 'depressive' atmosphere: 'The scale of events brought the whole country to complete chaos, and in a situation like that, when people are under a lot of stress, and feel threatened, there was the possibility of bloodshed'. But in truth, this time the repressive agencies were not very useful, as secret-police Colonel Adam Sucharski recalled:

> It was a period when we did nothing. We met with agents, we collected infor-
> mation, we drank coffee, booze, we slept in our headquarters, we ate there and
> then we did nothing again. We prepared the police headquarters for a possible
> siege: the guards at the gates were doubled.

The government tried to distract them from the demand for free unions by offer-ing wage-increases. But these offers were brushed aside.

A sense of how the workers felt is evident by how they greeted the negotia-tors when they arrived by bus in Gdansk. They stood waiting for their arrival 'silent[ly] with folded arms and grim faces'. Even before the bus came to a stop, they moved forward in what had to be perceived as a menacing gesture – Wałęsa recalled that 'Jagielski stepped from the bus, pale and drawn'. The workers then shouted: 'Get out! Get down on your knees before the workers!'[40] Jadwiga Stan-iszkis, one of the strikers' advisors, said: 'Before Jagielski went into the meeting

---

38. 1983, 'Informational Strike Bulletin Solidarity', reprinted in *Labor Focus on Eastern Europe*, 4(1–3), p. 10, emphasis added; see also Sanford 1983, p. 53.
39. Persky 1981, p. 93.
40. Wałęsa 1987, p. 134.

he was forced by the workers to walk from the bus in which he arrived with the rest of the delegation along a few-hundred-metres-long line of workers loudly shouting the name of their leader, Wałęsa'.[41] The imagery evokes the so-called 'health path' imposed upon workers in 1976. No-one was physically threatening the negotiators, but it must have had an impact.

The government spokesmen attempted to divide the strikers and to structure the negotiations to their benefit. According to Anna Walentynowicz:

> Vice-Premier Jagielski...suggested having the negotiations *in camera*...in the offices at County Hall, or even in the county chiefs' private *dacha*. We refused because we understood that this was a good way to lose the struggle. We decided to hold the talks here, in the shipyard, so that at any moment we could call on the enormous mass of people who were crowded into the hall where the discussion was taking place. That helped us. It became apparent that our government was simply scared of meeting our community and they knew that it would act in our favour, so they tried very hard to hold out on that one.[42]

Meanwhile, in Szczecin, Aleksander Krystosiak recalled:[43]

> On Friday, the director of the Warski shipyard, Ozimek, announced that the government officials were ready for negotiations. They would talk with Marian Jurczyk, the head of the Warski strike committee, but not with people from other factories. Ozimek told the others to go back to their factories, and after the authorities had finished with the shipyard workers, they would speak to each factory separately.

All eyes now turned to Marian Jurczyk, the undisputed leader in Warski. How would he respond? Everyone knew that what he said would determine, in one way or another, how events might unfold.

> **Krystosiak:** Jurczyk stood up. A cold sweat came all over us as we waited to hear what he would say. For us, it was a few seconds of terror! Jurczyk's face was carved out of marble. It was emotionless. Our hearts were pounding: what would he do? Jurczyk took the microphone, looked at Ozimek and he said, in a voice as cold as the ice on the river, 'You go back and tell the government commission that they either talk with all of us at once, or they don't talk with anyone!' All our tension fell to the floor. We knew that a completely new direction in history had begun.

---

41. Staniszkis 1984, p. 52, n. 3.
42. Unpublished interview with Anna Walentynowicz by Ewa Barker, obtained through personal communication.
43. See Goodwyn 1991; Kemp-Welch 1980.

End of act one

Jurczyk's response forced Ozimek to consult with officials in Warsaw:

> Ozimek returned in the afternoon. By that time, there were representatives
> of 26 factories sitting there waiting. He came and spoke only to Jurczyk and
> to the Warski Shipyard Committee, treating us as though we didn't exist: he
> looked through us like we were thin air. He announced that the government
> officials would either negotiate with each strike committee in its own factory,
> or with no-one. It was 'take it or leave it'.

But then:

> As he was speaking, the representatives of five new factories entered the
> |room. Now there were 31 factories represented there. Within seconds, the
> phone rang: representatives from ten other factories were on their way.
> Now, we were 41. It was a huge boost of energy for us. Jurczyk responded to the
> government threat with his own: 'You see what is happening. You either talk
> with all of us or none of us. If you like, you can wait until we are ready to come
> to Warsaw and speak with you!' We just laughed Ozimek out. He left. That's
> how it stood overnight. Saturday morning, very early, they came to tell us that
> they were ready to talk. By then, we had representatives from 60 factories.

Thus, the coastal strikes were significant enough, and the strikers were adamant
enough about their demands that the government was forced to meet with them
and to send its top officials to the negotiations.[44] That was the strikers' first victory. They had made themselves into a new power to be reckoned with. They
now had to prepare for the next battle. As Krystosiak noted:

> We chose a group of negotiators. I was one of that group. The serious work of
> the inter-factory strike committee had begun. By Monday morning, 352 facto-
> ries in our region were on strike. We demanded communication with Gdańsk.
> When the government rejected that demand, we demanded two official gov-
> ernment cars to go to Gdańsk, with one of the ministers as a hostage, so that at
> least once we could speak with their strike committee and see what was hap-
> pening there. The minister and our couriers were sent to Gdańsk. There were
> two police-cars in front, with their sirens and their lights on, and everything
> got out of the way.[45] They returned the same day.

---

44. Ascherson 1982, p. 152.
45. Because of the blockade that had been thrown around Gdańsk, the delegation
from Szczecin was one of the few that were able to get in. A delegation from the Wrocław
inter-factory strike committee was arrested. Others were blocked. Later, a telephone connection was restored between the two centres, but Gdańsk was kept isolated from the
other areas; Kemp-Welch 1983, p. 181, n. 4.

The government did not want this communication to take place, and so they stalled. Only on 25 August, after the Gdansk inter-factory strike committee voted to refuse to resume negotiations with the government without re-establishment of phone links, was communication between Gdańsk, Szczecin and Warsaw permitted.[46] By then the strike had already lasted a week, and there were still no substantial concessions. The hard bargaining in Gdańsk did not begin until 23 August.[47]

When they began negotiating, the sticking-point remained the demand for free trade unions with the right to strike. The government tried mightily – but to no avail – to deflect them from that goal, urging them, just as they had done in 1970, to 'renew' the old trade unions by running for office within them. The workers refused. The government next attempted to retain its advantage by stressing that the union would have to accept and be subordinated to 'the leading role of the Party'. This formulation would not allow the workers to form an organisation independent of and possibly antagonistic to the Party. Tadeusz Pławiński: 'We stressed that without getting rid of that formulation, all the rest was unimportant. Nobody trusted them'. The daily *Strike Bulletin* recalled the experience of 1970:[48]

> Our own experience...after December, 1970 has shown that the agreement under which the Strike Committee was forced to join the existing trade union structure did not achieve a genuine representation of workers' interests. The proposal put forward by Mr Jagielski, for new elections to the workers' councils, does not therefore represent a solution: it is no more than yet another sly attempt to avoid discussion on the establishment of free trade unions.

In Gdańsk, according to Staniszkis, several of the advisors to the strikers did not believe that the government would or could grant unions total independence from Party control, and they tried to convince the workers to abandon this demand. She said that the advisors tried to convince members of the (strike) presidium that the phrase was meaningless.[49] But the workers refused to take this advice. Tadeusz Kowalik, one of these advisors, recalled: 'I did not meet a single striker or delegate who was willing to compromise on this issue'.[50] The strikers warned the government that they had learned from 1970: 'Gentlemen! You are no longer talking to those who...answered: "We will help you"...We

---

46. 1983, 'Informational Strike Bulletin Solidarity', reprinted in *Labor Focus on Eastern Europe*, 4(1–3), p. 15.
47. Ascherson 1985, p. 152.
48. Strike Bulletin 1983, p. 10.
49. Staniszkis 1984, p. 59.
50. Kowalik 1983, p. 145.

are different now, above all because we are united, and therefore stronger. We are different because ... we have learnt that promises are illusions'.[51]

They acted so boldly because the solidarity that the strike represented was far-reaching. Workers would defend one another. The unity they attained in this struggle had many manifestations. For example, the relatively well-paid shipyard workers fought for those in a weaker position – such as teachers, medical workers and others – who could not by themselves have won very much. They demanded increases in pensions, minimum wages, family allowances, and flat wage increases rather than percentages, which would have increased the differences between the higher- and lower-paid workers. As Ascherson has noted, 'the strikers' instinct ... told them that the regime's ability to control the working class depended upon its ability to hold that class divided'.[52] Krystosiak recalled that the 'workers started telling *me* how important a general strike was'.

Government counter-moves

In seeking to isolate the strikers from the rest of the country, the government permitted hardly any reports on the negotiations. With telephone connections between Gdańsk and the outside world severed, the MKS sent out couriers to spread the word, but many of them were detained by the police,[53] while the strike supporters were hit with a wave of arrests, beatings and vandalism.[54] In such situations, morale is fluid and malleable, being largely dependent upon how people perceive their chances from day to day. As the days passed, cracks began to develop among the strikers:

> **Aleksander Krystosiak:** The vice-chair of my strike committee resigned on the fourth or fifth day of the strike. His wife, a young woman with children, came and started crying about what could happen, that he could get killed, that he would be jailed, that they would send him to Siberia – and he quit. In other factories, sometimes as much as half the strike committee had to be replaced because people would quit out of fear. After two weeks of strike, some people who at first said, 'Either negotiate with all of us or none of us!' started giving in. People wanted some resolution, and the negotiations were dragging.

---

51. Strike Bulletin 1983, p. 17.
52. Ascherson 1982, p. 176.
53. Goodwyn 1991.
54. Strike Bulletin 1983, p. 16.

On the other hand, Krystosiak recalled:

> It went both ways. One woman came to visit her husband and he cried that he wanted to come home and be safe. She said, 'Just try to come back, and I'll trade you for a cat!' I would say that most women were very brave and supportive, and many times tougher than their men.

The government tried to encourage feelings of hopelessness, powerlessness and dissension.

> **Krystosiak:** They tried to negotiate separate agreements with other factories behind our backs. They created a competing strike committee to which they offered a 2,000 zloty raise. We sent two people there to educate them on what this strike was about: it wasn't just a stupid raise that would be given to them anyway because the government was scared. It was about Poland. It was the demand for change that would touch not only them but teachers, bureaucrats, clerks – everyone. The new strike committee that had begun talks was smashed against the fence and almost pushed through the holes to the other side because people were so angry. The government officials took off as fast as they could. The old strike committee was returned to power and stayed loyal for the rest of the time.

There were similar attempts in Gdańsk. Tadeusz Pławiński: 'The government tried to break up the strikes into single negotiations, to do anything to make an opening somewhere, to promise anything to one shipyard or a company, to sign any kind of agreement to break up the strike'. Early on, 17 factories held separate discussions with Pyka. These soon ended and such moves became impossible as the MKS attempted to become the sole negotiator.[55] Ten days after the strike began in Gdańsk, the government reshuffled. This did not impress the workers.[56] The negotiations dragged on and it was becoming evident that something more was necessary to prod the government into making concessions.

---

55. Garton Ash 1985, pp. 48–9; Ascherson 1982, pp. 151–2.
56. Potel 1982, pp. 134–5, pp. 140–1.

Chapter Eight
Social Solidarity and the Victory of *Solidarność*

Aleksander Krystosiak: There were weddings during the strike, and brides would come straight from the churches to hang their wedding-bouquets on the gates. It was a way of showing us: 'We are with you!' People cried when they saw these brides and grooms coming to place their flowers. What went on outside the gates was really important for the morale of the workers.

Grzegorz Stawski, a miners' leader: Real negotiations at the shipyards began only when the strikes in Silesia started.

These strikes built upon previously established social networks and helped to establish new ties and strengthen old ones. The vast social support for the strikers enhanced their resolve. As the negotiations proceeded inside the shipyards, a great mass of people avidly followed the proceedings and gathered outside to demonstrate their support. As Krystosiak recalled:

Announcements went over the inter-com outside, so everyone could hear. Half of Szczecin was standing in front of the gate, listening. There we were in that meeting-room, cut off from the rest of the world with our doubts. When Ozimek announced that they would speak only with Jurczyk, there was a grave silence. Not a word. Then Jurczyk responded, and after his few words, everyone outside cheered. The noise they made was so loud that we heard it. There were 12,000 people on strike in the shipyard, and at least ten-thousand outside, listening. So, when they shouted, that meant real support.

It is easy to imagine how that shout must have chilled the government-negotiators. Nevertheless, they dragged their heels, claiming they did not have the requisite authority for certain demands, while others were simply deemed impossible: 'Why don't we move to other issues that are more tractable and forget about these "political" demands?' Krystosiak once more:

> They would travel to Warsaw to get instructions. Sometimes they would act as though they had gone to Warsaw when we knew they hadn't. They would come back and say, 'regretfully, with great pain', that they had to refuse a demand, since 'Warsaw didn't agree, so the best would be to start negotiating again'.

But the strikers' outside support made it physically possible for them to continue. One farmer recalled: 'When the Szczecin strike began, the workers...turned to us for help. We [came]...into occupied factories and delivered bread, cucumbers, tomatoes'.[1] Krystosiak:

> The peasants brought livestock, food, bread that was baked in ovens in the villages.[2] Right by our shipyard, there was a huge, five-floor bakery that provided bread for most of Szczecin. The peasants brought flour to the bakers and told us, 'We brought so many tons of flour, and from one ton of flour, there are so many hundred kilograms of bread, so you should get that much from the bakers'. So, we said to the government officials, 'Go to Warsaw. Get their permission. Come back. We have time. We have food. We can wait'. And it worked!

Similar provisions were available to the strikers in Gdańsk and Gdynia.[3] Krystosiak:

> While in 1970, the government could fool workers into supporting them, in 1980 there was no way they could. As soon as the strikes started, it was clear that the government would never get any support, no matter how many teams were changed, and how many leaders were replaced. Students would come to me and say, 'I am at the university; I am in such-and-such department, and if you find any use for me, I am ready to help'. At that time, all the barriers

---

1. 1988, *UPNB*, 4: 13.
2. Farmers had bitterly and successfully fought against the government's efforts to take their land back in the 1940s and 1950s, and this same determination was now taking effect once again.
3. Staniszkis 1984, p. 48.

broke. There was no more 'we students', 'you workers'. It was all 'us'. It was an incredible psychological boost.

Out of this activity, a Farmers' Solidarity union was eventually formed and recognised by the government in 1981.[4]

The strikes became centres of activity. In Gdańsk, musicians performed a concert in the Lenin Shipyard in solidarity with the strikers. Actors and the Baltic Opera also performed there to express their support for the strikers. These were not merely performances: they were rituals that brought the workers together and graphically displayed the social support they enjoyed. These displays encouraged the workers not to back down during such a difficult period when little progress was being made in the negotiations. Anna Walentynowicz recalled that 'the solidarity which we felt in those moments, the experience of being in touch with people, the Mass performed on the shipyard premises . . . the Sunday communion and the daily prayers which broke out spontaneously among people even without a priest . . . gave us hope to hold out'.[5]

While the outside support buoyed the *strikers'* morale, for the *visitors* what happened inside the gates was also of great importance. The strikes became beacons of hope, and people flocked to them to both witness and participate in them. They knew that history was being made. Adam Dębski, an engineer from Kraków, recounted:

> I was on vacation on the Baltic Coast, and from the first days of the strike in Gdańsk I was there. We were sixty kilometres from Gdańsk and it wasn't easy to get there, but I went several times to the Lenin shipyards and, realising it was an historic moment, I took my wife and kids to show this to my family. My brother and I went on the last day of August and we heard the agreement announced by Wałęsa from the gate. I will remember this moment all my life!

The centripetal pull of these strikes led some people to change their lives. Mariusz Wilk had been active in the SKS in Wrocław and had graduated from the university. He was not sure what he wanted to do with his life: 'I wanted to start a childcare centre after vacation. In August, we went camping with some children to try it out'. While they were camping, the strikes began on the coast. Wilk was drawn to them:

> On the third day of the strike, we decided to go to Gdańsk. We borrowed a car, and in the evening we went to Gdańsk, leaving behind the girls and the children. We helped in the shipyard overnight. In the morning, we returned.

---

4. Nanowski 1984, p. 33.
5. Ewa Barker 1980.

The next evening, we went to the shipyard once more and we were active all night.

Wilk ended up staying in the Gdańsk Shipyard, where he edited the strike-bulletin. When the strike was over, he moved to Gdańsk to work with the union.

When the strikes broke out in Gdańsk, Grzegorz Surdy, a university student, was vacationing on the coast. Like others, he went to the shipyard gate where he spoke with the workers and the other spectators. He described it as a turning point in his life. When he returned to school in Kraków, he began to co-operate with the university-based Independent Student Union [*Niezależny Związek Studentów* = NZS] that was created in the autumn of 1980. A year later, when he went to the Polytechnic University in Warsaw, he joined NZS.

The strike spreads in Solidarity

Support for the strike spread way beyond the coast. In the Ursus tractor factory, according to Zbigniew Bujak:

> I went to the time-clock and posted an announcement on the bulletin-board that at 2:00 there would be a rally. Everyone who went to stamp his card read it and waited; the meeting was packed. I said, 'This is a rally to support the striking workers on the coast'. They applauded. 'If this isn't enough we will strike!' Applause again. I read the postulates from Gdańsk because no-one knew them. I asked for a show of hands of those who supported Gdańsk. When I asked who was against it, no-one showed his hand, even though party-members were in the crowd. I announced that we would collect money to help build the monument to the workers who had been murdered in Gdańsk. We pushed an electric car around and people piled money into it. People asked: 'Who is going to count that money?' 'You'. 'Who will carry it to Gdańsk?' 'We're going to mail it'. 'Who is going to mail it?' 'You!' We collected 27,000 zlotys, which at that time was a lot. When the Gdańsk strike ended, this committee became the Solidarity committee in Ursus. That was important because there was no question that we had the right, while in some other factories there were arguments over who was entitled to organise Solidarity.

But most of the rest of the plants in the country still worked, allowing the nation's leaders to hope for the strikers to falter. Rakowski acknowledged the following: 'No doubt the government was stalling because at the beginning many thought that the strikes would be limited to the Baltic Seacoast'. Workers were increasingly concerned that if the strikes remained isolated, the government might feel free to repeat the actions it took in 1970. Seweryn Jaworski, in the Warsaw Steel Mill, was one of those who worried:

> We decided to strike because we feared a blood bath. (After the strikes, I spoke with other people. In Silesia, they had the same feeling). The army and the police could pacify some factories, but not the whole country.

Jaworski and his colleagues planned carefully:

> We announced the strike during dinner. It was common for factory directors to have well-equipped liquor cabinets. When directors – and especially Party secretaries – came to talk to us, and we could smell alcohol, we would be furious. Then, even those who did not support us were turned around.

They proceeded with caution:

> There were loudspeakers and microphones in every area. You just press a button and everyone can hear you, but you could not tell where the voice came from. We did that. There were 2,000 working in the division and they stopped. When we saw that, we came out into the open. I was the leader of this group.

The Warsaw Steel Mill was on strike only a few days before agreement was reached in the negotiations on the sea-coast. By the time it ended, the strike was beginning to spread to other factories in the region.

Strikes broke out in Wrocław on 26 August, where the first MKS outside the coastal region was formed.[6] That was also the date that a strike of the bus and tram workers began in Łódź. Within a few days, the city was described as 'completely paralysed'.[7] By late August, there were strikes in every province, involving some 640,000 workers in hundreds of factories. The great majority of them were occupation-strikes in which the official union leadership had essentially no control.[8]

In the heated atmosphere of that time, people sometimes had to make very quick decisions that would change their lives. Mieczysław Gil, at the *Nowa Huta* Steel Mill just outside Kraków:

> As a journalist for the *Nowa Huta* paper, I felt it was a really good story, so I visited every section that was on strike to learn their demands. Then I came to the section where I had worked before I joined the paper. I was approached by a few of my colleagues, who told me that the workers were having problems

---

6. Goodwyn 1991, p. 235.
7. Cave and Latyński 1982–3, p. 53.
8. Sanford 1983, pp. 48–9.

voicing their demands, and asked for help. So I was faced with a choice. Until then I had been an onlooker, but by helping them with their demands, I would be acting as a striker. I couldn't refuse to help people I knew and had worked with. I also knew what a formidable opponent they were facing: the whole party-apparatus.

In the huge factory – thought to be the largest in Europe – the strike spread haphazardly. Gil said that it was 'organised on a friendship basis'. He noted that although these workers did not have the experience of workers on the coast, they had learned some of their political lessons: 'People felt that nothing could be fixed simply by changing the very top'. Edward Nowak, also at *Nowa Huta*, faced a situation similar to Gil's:

> I was a member of the Party and a foreman. One event decided for me. At a Party meeting, none of the items which were actually bothering the workers was on the agenda. I entered a Party meeting wearing a foreman's armband and asked why they were not talking about what concerned the workers in my section. They responded negatively, so I returned to my people. It was a decisive move. I wasn't conscious of this choice at that time, but it was obvious for me that my place was with the workers. When the strike ended in September, I realised that this was the choice that I had made, and I knew then that going on as a member of the party had no future.

The weight of Upper Silesia

During this period, eyes turned especially toward Upper Silesia. Would this area of such great importance to the economy, which produced most of Poland's energy and a large percentage of her foreign currency earnings – Gierek's base – weigh in? Or would the government, as usual, be free to act without having to fear what might happen there?

The government made every effort to keep the region in the dark about the strikes, which received no mention in the official press in Katowice (the commercial and industrial capital of Upper Silesia) until around 25 August,[9] and opposition publications were scarce there.[10] Andrzej Rozpłochowski, for example, who led the strike in the Katowice Steel Mill, knew nothing of the July strikes in Lublin and elsewhere.[11] But the news seeped in from various sources. People who vacationed in the North brought back information about the shipyard strikes. Eventually the official media spoke of the strike.

9. Kasprzyk interview.
10. Zbigniew Bogacz interview.
11. Rozpłochowski interview.

The decision to join the strike was not taken lightly. When the possibility of action arose in 1980, miners and their families recalled the killings in 1970. They felt that no moral or legal principles would restrain the masters of the country from using deadly force against them. Józef Pleszak recalled: 'There had been a lot of talk about it, and people thought that the same thing could happen here'. Official sources did all they could to contribute to fears and hesitations. The night the strike broke out in the July Manifesto Mine, one of the largest in the region, the local radio station broadcasted a discussion concerning the strikes. A woman, who said she was the mother of a young miner, urged miners not to strike and tearfully reminded them of the killings in 1970. The families of prospective strikers listened, terrorised about the possible fate of husbands, sons, brothers, fathers, lovers.

> **Zbigniew Bogacz:** On 25 August, the mines in Lower Silesia near Wałbrzych went on strike. Messengers from Lower Silesia came to Upper Silesia, bringing news about what was going on. Then, on 28 August, the Jastrzębie region went on strike, including its largest mine, the *July Manifesto*. Altogether, over fifty mines went on strike. Once the coal mines went out, the factories which produced machinery for the mines joined them. So did the salt-mines and the copper-mines.

Even before the miners struck, their representatives went to Gdańsk to state publicly their support, and to warn the government that if it did not negotiate in good faith with the shipyard workers, it would have to deal with them.[12] Some of these strikes were provoked by the blunders of officials. As Tadeusz Jedynak noted:

> Two weeks after the strike in Gdańsk had begun, our director spoke to us in his normal vulgar and rude way. The strike was started by the third shift on the night of 28 August in reaction to the way he behaved. People wanted him fired.

Ryszard Sawicki was in the Rudna copper mine in Lower Silesia:

> The government made its usual mistake. In the propaganda about the [Baltic coast] strikes, they spoke of ships waiting with oranges that were rotting while 'poor children with vitamin deficiencies' couldn't get them. They called the people who organised the strikes 'hooligans', just as they had in Radom. Just before I went to work on the night shift, they said that the miners in the Rudna Mine disapproved of the strike. That was the match that lit the fire. When I arrived, the miners were emotionally discussing what they had heard on

---

12. Potel 1982, p. 141.

the news. They said, 'I didn't say I was against the strikers or their demands'. Someone said, 'Let's strike'. And that's how it started.

Sawicki played a central role in organising the strike. It is apparent from his remarks that regardless of the ostensible cause of the strike, the workers were ready – perhaps even eager – to join the shipyard workers and others. Everyone understood the importance of the demand for an independent union with the right to strike:

> I made several hand-written copies of the shipyard workers' demands and gave them to friends in the mines, so they could see the differences between what the propaganda was squeezing into our heads through radio and TV and the reality of the demands. I sat down and wrote a letter to the shipyard workers, explaining that the government had lied about us, and therefore we were striking to support them. We collected money to send two representatives to Gdańsk. I told them that they should stay there until the strike ended. The director wanted us to go back to work. I said, 'You have to guarantee that our representatives will get safely to Gdańsk, and return. When they come back, we will go to work'. At the time, they were catching couriers. But because of this demand, ours made it.

Some strikes began without provocation, thereby further indicating the workers' readiness to join the shipyard workers and others. Grzegorz Stawski was a foreman in the July Manifesto Mine:

> The atmosphere was so tense that everyone was waiting for something to happen. On the night of 27 August, the second shift, which was finishing work, joined the third shift, which didn't start. The director of the mine angrily told the miners to go back to work immediately. I was the only supervisor who joined them. We sent messengers to the other mines to inform them about our strike. The next day, the first shift struck at the Borynia mine.

> **Zbigniew Bogacz:** When the workers learned that there were strikes in other mines, they struck at Piast. I was on sick-leave and had just left the hospital when I heard about the strike by telephone from one of the organisers. It wasn't long before the mine engineer, who had sent me to work in all kinds of difficult situations where he wasn't supposed to, called me. He had the nerve to ask me to call the strike committee and tell them to stop striking. I smiled. How could I stop the strike? I called them and told them, 'I'm with you'. After that, I was on the phone with them everyday.

The strike in the July Manifesto Mine began the night before Tadeusz Jedynak, who became the vice-chair of the negotiating committee, arrived to work on the morning shift. As he noted, others quickly joined:

Three delegates from the Borynia mine arrived to let us know that they were striking. I reached for a microphone and announced that we were no longer a *factory* strike committee, that we were now an *inter-factory* strike committee, and from that position we were ready to talk with the government delegates. That day, several other delegates joined us, and thus we established this inter-factory committee. After a couple of days, it was clear that the situation could not be dealt with at the level of the province.

In the Katowice Steel Mill, management appeared to encourage a limited expression of worker discontent. They organised meetings for the workers, asking them to express their criticisms of the company. Why? Andrzej Rozpłochowski speculated that the mine director, Szałajda, who was also a high official in the Party,

> was in the faction that hoped to succeed Gierek and get to power themselves. They needed some social unrest. Normally, you couldn't just meet somewhere in large numbers. But he called this big meeting for us, gave us time off from work and encouraged us to express our criticisms.

But once brought together, the workers set out in their own direction: 'Management's plan was to encourage people to complain about the factory and the country; then they would be sent back to work, and that would be the end'. In other words, Rozpłochowski was suggesting that management in his plant was attempting to use the strikes to strengthen their political standing in the bureaucratic manoeuvring. However, engaging in the exercise had some unintended consequences, as Rozpłochowski noted:

> All of a sudden 'Wacek' discovered that he thinks exactly the same as 'Franek' and 'Zosia', and there is a foreman who also agrees with them. We said, 'First, we'll talk among ourselves; then we'll meet with management'. The workers supported us, so they had no choice. Among the first few items on our demand list was free trade unions and the right to strike.

Still, as Rozpłochowski learned, strange activities were taking place:

> We went to the rolling mill, where they had stopped work; we saw several hundred people standing around. No-one knew who was in charge. Finally, we discovered that the leaders were in another room. We went to them and declared that our department was on strike and we were delegates to the strike-committee. We were told that a meeting with Szałajda was already arranged. At the meeting, the strike leader declared, 'We are striking against strikes'. We said that we *supported* the striking seashore workers. We had a sharp exchange of views, and the majority agreed to remove this strike committee and elect a new one, with me as the leader. The old strike committee went to a large department and told the workers that they were

the ones who had been rightfully elected and that they should not listen to us. We went after them, presenting our position. This contest lasted all night. In the largest department, the rolling mills, the former strike committee leader had earlier announced that there would be a mass meeting, so people waited to hear what he had to say. After I spoke, people themselves demanded that he come up and talk, but what they really wanted to do was to square accounts with him. He ran away.

At that point, events took a new direction:

> We announced that it was an occupation strike. We asked each department to guard its equipment so nothing was damaged or destroyed. We told them to make sure that there was no alcohol and no provocations, that food was well-distributed in the cafeteria. We placed guards at every gate. The whole atmosphere changed. Motorised police patrols organised blockades of every gate and every road to the mill. But people from other factories squeezed through the police cordon and found their way in, so we created an inter-factory strike committee. We had two overarching demands: free trade unions and the right to strike. Then we contacted management and told them we were ready to begin negotiations. We made two conditions: everything to be broadcasted through the internal radio system so that all the workers who were on strike could listen, and a guarantee of our personal safety.

So, in this case management appears to have started the action, in the evident belief that they could control events. But once the workers came together, they quickly joined the strikers and pushed their management and its agents aside.

Mieczysław Rakowski confirmed to me that the strikes in Upper Silesia both at the Katowice Steel Mill and at the mines in Jastrzębie forced the government to negotiate with them. Also, whole cities were paralysed by general strikes, including Wrocław, Łódź, Warsaw and Ursus.[13] By late August, over seven-hundred thousand workers had joined the strikes.[14] It represented a major challenge to the government.

Agreements

The entry of these new allies certainly buoyed the morale of the shipyard-workers. In Gdańsk, Zdzisław Kobyliński announced the strikes in the Warsaw Steel Mill, in the Lenin Steel Mill in *Nowa Huta*, and in the Jastrzębie mines. At the time, they were debating a government proposal to limit the right to form

---

13. Sanford 1983, p. 48.
14. Paczkowski and Byrne 2007, p. 10.

unions to the coastal workers. Kobyliński argued: 'It would be really crazy if those who have been helping us didn't get the same as us. It's impossible to imagine that we should have the right to form strong unions on the seaboard, and that they should not!' (Ovation).[15] These new strikes, and the threat that they might spread still further, evidently pressured the government towards bargaining more seriously. The workers certainly felt so. Tadeusz Jedynak: 'Allowing information about our strike on TV caused the strikes to spread faster, and eventually caused the agreements in Gdańsk and Szczecin to be signed'.

> **Ryszard Sawicki:** I was told that once they announced that the copper mine was on strike, it became a turning point in the negotiations. The government which, up to then, was playing around and not really being serious about the negotiations, sat down to the table ready to talk.

Other evidence also indicates that the miners and the steel-workers tipped the balance within the Party leadership in favour of making concessions.[16] Jadwiga Staniszkis, a sociologist at Warsaw University and one of the advisors to the negotiators in Gdańsk, said:[17] 'The government side was in a panic because of the miners' strike'.[18] It is certainly true that toward the end of the negotiations in Gdańsk, Jagielski appeared quite anxious to finish quickly. He said:[19]

> I have still to go to Warsaw, to the Central Committee Plenum and report Point One [dealing with the right to independent unions], by far the most fundamental, which we have initialled. Wouldn't it be a good idea ... to produce a communiqué indicating that we have reached agreement in principle?

Wałęsa responded coolly: 'It really won't be too much to go through these most important points. They won't take long'. But the Deputy Prime Minister pressed: 'The discussion should be completed today, when I return'. Wałęsa, however, refused to budge: 'Tomorrow is Sunday. I don't think there is such a hurry ... Sunday is not a working day'.[20] Rakowski, at that time on the Party Central Committee, recalled that:[21] 'The Party leadership was in a panic. At a Central Committee meeting, there was a call from Jagielski: what kind of agreement could he sign?' Gierek's answer was: 'Sign anything they want. If they ask

15. Potel 1982, p. 169.
16. Ascherson 1982, pp. 161–3.
17. Kowalik 1983, p. 166.
18. See the following for detailed accounts of the negotiations: Garton Ash 1985; Goodwyn 1991; Kemp-Welch 1983.
19. Kemp-Welch 1983, pp. 120, 122–3.
20. Kemp-Welch 1983, pp. 122–3.
21. From a speech given in Bloomington, Indiana, on 10 March 1998.

for a change in the constitution, do it'.[22] Evidently, the solidarity engendered by the strikers reached far and wide, indeed, even into the state apparatus of repression.[23]

The troops had not been – and often could not be – isolated from these events. Kazimierz Graca, a miner, was serving in the military in Gdynia at this time: 'We knew everything that was going on because the barracks in which I lived were just opposite the Paris Commune Shipyard. Until 3:00 we listened to official indoctrination, and after 3:00 we got leaflets from the strikers'. Of course, there was always the possibility of bringing in troops who had been less infected by the events on the Baltic Coast from elsewhere in the country. But as intended, as more sites joined the strike, such a strategy became more problematic.

The government negotiators continued to raise objections. Krystosiak again:

> The government officials claimed that Polish law did not allow free trade-unions. So, we had people in the provincial library digging through books and laws to provide us with information on the legal basis for free trade unions. Our lawyers dug out the documents signed for the Geneva-based International Labour Organisation. Amendment 78 says that the workers have the right to organise their own structure without asking for permission.

With this document the workers certainly appeared to have the upper-hand. What could the government negotiators do? What they actually did in response astonished everyone:

> Barcikowski stood up, and in front of the foreign press said openly that they had signed the ILO Accord to protect Poland's face in the eyes of the Western world – but they hadn't really meant it! The British TV cameraman dropped his camera! It was so incredible! It was a total, complete exposure. So we were dead locked.

Meanwhile, events outside were eroding the wall that the government tried to maintain against change. According to Krystosiak's recollection of events:

> We received a wonderful gift from our factories: two lists of names. One said that they had resigned from the old trade unions – practically the whole crew

---

22. According to Oliver MacDonald, despite Gierek's promise a decade earlier not to use deadly force, an attempt to crush the strikers was seriously considered: 'On the night of Friday the 29th, the Political Bureau apparently divided 8–5 in favour of military action against the Lenin Shipyard. Gierek was in the majority. But the security and military chiefs [Kania and Jaruzelski] refused to sanction such action, on the grounds that they could not vouch for the loyalty of security forces. The minority won, the Central Committee agreed to independent trade unions, the Gdańsk settlement was signed along with the settlement already agreed in Szczecin'; MacDonald 1981, p. 11.

23. Ibid.

of my shipyard with the exception of a few hard-line Party members. The other list was candidates for membership in a free trade union. The government officials were swept off their feet. The workers in these factories had already joined free trade unions that did not yet exist! With that support, the walls trembled.

The same thing happened in the Gdańsk negotiations. Tadeusz Kowalik recalled that there were those among the strikers who 'favoured a speedy founding of the new union, to present the authorities with a *fait accompli*. A preliminary list of the founder members of the new union began to be circulated among the strikers'.[24] So, the strike leaders tried a new tack:

> **Aleksander Krystosiak:** To prod them to give up, we said: 'This room is stuffy. We have sat here for so many hours. Let's go out and stretch our legs'. We walked through the meeting room where the inter-factory strike committee sat. What did they see? The workers in their work clothes, sitting around waiting, determined to fight for their cause. You could see them turning pale. When they returned to the negotiating table, they were ready to give up. They agreed that the new trade unions would be sovereign and independent of any governmental or party influence.

However, the government negotiators in Szczecin apparently thought better of their decision and sought to erase it. Krystosiak:

> The next day, they dropped off a letter saying that there was no legal basis for free and independent trade unions. You can imagine the reaction. There we were with the first document, signed by lawyers from both sides. And the next day, these idiots – what else would you call them? – dropped off this paper. If it were presented to the people, there would have been bloodshed.

How best to respond to such a move? In this case, it was ignored: it did not happen.

> We decided that the second document would never see daylight. We had a legal agreement, signed by both sides, which said that there was the basis for creating free trade unions in existing law. The first document was presented to Szczecin, and to the whole world, since there were all these journalists waiting for the news.

What could the government do now? The agreement had been signed already.

> You can imagine the government side: they were foaming with rage. They asked for permission to go to Warsaw to negotiate with the government. They

---

24. Kowalik 1983, pp. 156–7.

were gone for three days. We were hanging in limbo, waiting. They returned really tired – you could see that they had gone through a lot – and they were ready to talk again. They dragged the talks out. They knew that they had lost, that there was no way they could get out of it. Finally, they signed the agreement saying that free unions, independent of government and the Party, could be organised.

In Gdańsk, the negotiators' desire for haste aroused the strikers' suspicions. Wałęsa was unreceptive to Jagielski's call to come to an agreement quickly:

> It really won't be too much to go through these most important points. They won't take long. We have waited all this time. Let's work on Saturday and Sunday to finish it and have it all in writing... Why should we rush into agreement? [applause]

But the Deputy Prime Minister continued to press: 'The discussion should be completed today, when I return'. However, Wałęsa refused to budge. Now, Tadeusz Fiszbach, the Gdańsk Party Secretary, attempted a new line of argument: 'Mr Wałęsa I have a four-year-old grandson. I would like to see him'. But Wałęsa would not be moved: 'These eight hours won't save us. We want to do everything properly... to the satisfaction of both sides'.[25]

The workers approached the final agreement carefully. In Gdańsk, as in Szczecin, there were sticking points and near-reversals. The government at last agreed to everything save the release of political prisoners. The strikers refused to concede this point, fearing that the government could then arrest all of them, but Jagielski would not agree. The talks broke off. Jagielski informally promised Andrzej Gwiazda that the prisoners would be released, but he would not provide a date. Anna Walentynowicz: 'We refused to deal. Finally, he said that by the next day at noon all the people on our list would be freed. That was a compromise we had to make... but we stressed that if [they were not released] we would resume the strike'.[26]

Only later did it become evident that the government's haste was motivated by the strike's spread into the mines and steel mills. Anna Walentynowicz recalled: 'It turned out that *Huta Katowice* [the Katowice steel mill] had threatened to extinguish their furnaces'. That was not a threat to be taken lightly. What is more, in an act of solidarity the miners had sent a letter to the government stating that if all 21 demands were not met, they would flood the mines.[27] Both of these threatened to do serious and long-term damage to the economy.

---

25. Kemp-Welch 1983, pp. 122–3.
26. Barker 1980.
27. Ibid.

But even in victory the workers were wary, and they impressed their distrust upon the authorities. At the Rudna copper mine, the strike was to end when the couriers to the Gdańsk shipyard returned with the news that the agreement (as had been reported on television) was valid. Ryszard Sawicki:

> Because our strike was a rotation strike, one shift was always at home. The morning shift was told by management that the strike had ended and that they should go to work. People said, 'If the strike is finished, *Ryszard* should tell us about it. Until we see Ryszard here and he tells us that the strike is done, we continue striking'. They sent two people for me with a car. I lived thirty to forty kilometres from the mine. They came and got me up from bed. I was half-asleep, and thought they had come to arrest me. The people at work also thought I was arrested; that's why they insisted on seeing me before they went to work. The management saw that if anything happened to me, the whole crew of the mine would stand behind me.

> **Tadeusz Pławiński:** We were not going to leave the shipyard until our delegates came back. People saw the signing of the agreement and they wanted to go home, but we didn't let them. You don't know what they can put on TV. So we waited for the two guys to come home from Gdańsk.

Just days after the agreements were signed, Gierek's reign came to an end in what was becoming the normal mechanism of succession. He was deposed at a plenum of the Party executive that met without him. Stanislaw Kania, Gierek's successor, came to power as had *his* predecessors, through the direct-action of workers. That fact was a constant pressure on the government. Kania went out of his way to promise a new relationship. In his first speech to the Central Committee, which was shown on television, he promised to honour the Accords.[28] Among those delighted by the outcome were at least some of the regime 's police, one of whom later confided to an underground Solidarity publication during martial law: 'I remember when we were on duty in August 1980, greedily listening to and reading about the news on the strikes; I remember also how greatly afraid we were that we would have to go into the factories. We reacted with such joy, like children, when everything ended without force being used'.[29]

---

28. Mason 1985, p. 99.
29. 1983, 'The Policeman's Lot is Not a Happy One: Policeman Interviewed by Underground Publication', *UPNB*, 7: 22.

Extending the union's reach

The agreements in Gdańsk and Szczecin heralded the evolution of Soviet-style society into entirely uncharted realms. No-one could have known what would be the outcome of the agreements. The government sought to limit the applicability of the accords: it held that not everyone was allowed to form independent unions; they were specifically addressed only to those who had gone on strike and had won this right from the authorities. It sought to split the movement, forcing differing agreements in different places. Often it refused the right to form independent unions unless the workers struck, a policy that forced confrontations. (There is some evidence that the government preferred to be forced into making concessions so it could not be accused by the Soviet Union of being like Dubcek in Czechoslovakia in 1968 by encouraging these changes from above).[30] This stance did not, however, prevent workers from organising. Almost immediately after agreement was reached, appeals were made to other workers to form unions.[31]

Many people who had either visited or known of the strikes were determined to gain for themselves what the strikers had already won. However, since the administration was not disposed to grant this, they had to win it for themselves. Faced with intransigence on the part of local and national leaders, workers in many places struck. On the bus returning to Kraków, Adam Dębski stated: 'We read the papers about the agreement'. Dębski acted when he returned to work:

> In our factory, they attempted to renew the old trade unions. At their meeting, I said that someone should ask *us*, the crew of the factory, if we wanted to remain in these old trade unions. Maybe we wanted a new union. By the next meeting, we had collected signatures (illegally) with the demand for new trade unions. I had 300 people on the list, so I knew I stood for the majority. They tried to scare me, but I didn't give a damn.

The proto-union quickly began to provide aid and counsel for people who wished to become part of the burgeoning Solidarity trade union. Both Warsaw and Gdańsk became centres of information and guidance to others. Dębski recalled:

> The day before the meeting, I went to Warsaw to see Zbigniew Bujak. (I was scared to death). There were lawyers and others who gave me materials and helped teach me to organise a union. The result was a provisional group of the new trade-union established and I was elected president. So it began.

---

30. See Garton Ash 1985, p. 57; Persky 1981, p. 123; Ascherson 1982, p. 152; Staniszkis 1984, p. 55.
31. Persky and Flam 1982, p. 109; Cave and Latyński 1982–83, p. 54.

The Solidarity revolution was underway. On 11 September, Kania officially acknowledged that independent unions could be formed anywhere in Poland. Within weeks, vast numbers of workers – millions – left the official Party-controlled unions and enrolled in the new independent union. Two weeks after the agreements, 85 percent of the workers in the tri-city region of Gdańsk-Gdynia-Sopot belonged to the new union; the same was the case in the Warsaw region.[32]

On 23 September, delegates representing five million workers came together from over three-hundred cities and towns, and decided to organise a national Solidarity Union.[33] There was soon an average of sixteen strikes taking place at any one time.[34] Polish workers were clearly changing the balance of power in the country. And they knew it.

---

32. Sanford 1983, p. 75.
33. Sanford 1983, p. 76.
34. Ascherson 1982, p. 188.

Chapter Nine
The Solidarity Revolution

Solidarity programme, adopted in September 1981:[1] What we had in mind was not only bread, butter and sausage, but also justice, democracy, truth, legality, human dignity, freedom of convictions and the repair of the republic...Thus the economic protest had to be simultaneously a social protest, and the social protest had to be simultaneously a moral protest.

Alicja Matuszewska: For the first time since the Communists took power, people were united: there was no more 'Mr Engineer', or 'Mr Doctor'. A worker with a shovel used the familiar form when speaking with both. That was the greatest threat to the Communists. They could not divide the society any more.

Solidarity Strike Information Bulletin: People laugh, laugh, more and more, more and more freely!

Władysław Frasyniuk, leader of Wrocław regional Solidarity: We would be respected for our qualifications and not because we belonged to Party organisations.

Stanisław Handzlik, a Solidarity leader in the *Nowa Huta* steel mill outside Kraków: This democracy, this openness was bursting out day by day. Talents were released: organising, giving

---

1. Garton Ash 1985, p. 223.

speeches, artistic talent even. And because of all that, a lot of people grew more valuable in their own eyes.

Mirosława Strzelec, a nurse who worked in the *Huta Katowice* steel mill: Each worker realised that he was a valuable human being and not merely a source of labour.

The strikes of August 1980 were the beginning of a social-revolution. The nation emerged from those strikes transformed. Workers had beaten a Communist government – something never before accomplished. They were aware of what they had achieved, and this knowledge altered their self-image. They had seen a huge segment of the society stand by their side: not only fellow workers, but also farmers, intellectuals, students, their families, and many others. After the August strikes, more workers, emboldened by the outcome, made their own demands and struck to achieve them. It was clear that people intended to use the union to gain a say over a broad range of issues, and the reach of the union, as well as the social movement it had engendered and protected, quickly began to grow. Other segments of society – students, farmers, professionals, and so on – also began to organise themselves. With such self-activity came far-reaching transformations in social relations.

During the sixteen months of the union's legal existence, power moved from the Party and the *nomenklatura* to Solidarity. This shift resulted from the titanic *political* struggles that took place not just *between* the Party and Solidarity, but also *within* their respective circles. These struggles will be examined in what follows. But there is another element to this movement that is important to properly grasp: one that both affected and yet went well beyond the political realm. In a revolutionary situation, power is diminished not only via institutional reforms, but also through the lives of ordinary people who feel that they need no longer simply accept conditions that hitherto seemed inescapable. People become willing and able to take control of their lives, often to the dismay of their former rulers who find that those who had previously quaked in their presence now confront and challenge them. From below it feels like an end to the burden of fear and a vast expansion of liberty and possibility, as people grasp the levers of power which had previously been out of their reach.

This experience often transforms individuals, so that even when a new hierarchy develops (or an old hierarchy is able to reassert itself) they remain transformed. For example, when George Orwell joined the fight against the fascists in Spain, led by General Francisco Franco, during the Spanish Civil War, he noted such changes:

Waiters and shop-walkers looked you in the face and treated you as an equal. Servile and even ceremonial forms of speech had temporarily disappeared ... Tipping had been forbidden by law ... In outward appearance it was a town in which the wealthy classes had practically ceased to exist...There was no unemployment, and the price of living was still extremely low; you saw very few conspicuously destitute people, and no beggars except the Gypsies. Above all, there was a belief in the revolution and the future, a feeling of having suddenly emerged into an era of equality and freedom. Human beings were trying to behave as human beings and not as cogs in the capitalist machine. In the barbers' shops were Anarchist notices...solemnly explaining that barbers were no longer slaves. In the streets were coloured posters appealing to prostitutes to stop being prostitutes...In the early battles [women] had fought side by side with the men as a matter of course. It is a thing that seems natural in time of revolution.[2]

In Poland, both the strike victory and the solidarity that made it possible (and which continued afterwards) helped to create a sense of hope and personal self-confidence that armed people for future conflicts. Władysław Frasyniuk recalled: 'There was this great sense that workers would become the governors of their factories with the right to have organisations that would defend us'. Grzegorz Stawski: 'The very fact of the strikes caused people to feel their own value. They felt that they had the potential to change things, that they were not only objects of manipulation'.

One of the critical changes was that people became more self-assertive. To use a term frequently employed when discussing this matter, the people crossed the 'barrier of fear'.[3]

Bogdan Borusewicz: You have political hopelessness when you think that you must agree to everything they demand. Now, with this movement, hope and self-confidence grew. People lost a lot of their fear.

Zbigniew Bogacz: It was the first time that people could feel that the government was afraid.

Alicja Matuszewska: The most important thing was that people finally stopped being afraid. In the old days, if there was a worker who spoke out, they would find out who it was and fire him, and there would not even be a question about it. Not anymore.

Ryszard Brzuzy, a miner: People were not afraid to talk about political subjects. Until then, there had been a saying that if there were three Poles together, one of them was a secret-service man. But then, people who didn't know each other openly talked politics.

---

2. Orwell 1952, pp. 5–7; see also Bloom 1987, esp. chapter 5.
3. Lawrence Goodwyn used this term as the title for his 1991 book on Solidarity, *Breaking the Barriers*.

The workers now felt emboldened against officials who had once inspired fear. For example, anger was generated by a provincial governor's declaration of a state of emergency – a clumsy effort to block Solidarity from registering. Local Solidarity leaders threatened a regional strike if the officials responsible were not dismissed.[4] According to George Sanford:

> At a meeting at the local bus station, which was relayed to a crowd of 5,000 outside, the city officials faced public accusations that they had never really accepted the Gdańsk Agreement. The City President was blamed for a million zloty deficit on a pig farm and for having refused to renovate a centre for the handicapped run by nuns, while he had built a luxurious new Party headquarters... The deputy governors were accused of building villas for local notables and of assuring preferential supplies to shops catering to officials.

The upshot was that after suffering this humiliating experience, these officials were forced to resign.[5] Again and again, it was made evident in ways that could not fail to impress themselves upon the *nomenklatura* that power had shifted significantly. Hard-line Party Secretaries in Warsaw and in Łódź, who resisted giving up any of their power and prerogatives, were replaced. Solidarity members occupied the local government headquarters in the town of Bielsko-Biała in southern Poland, demanding that all the top local officials be fired.[6] Ginter Kupka, a miner activist in Upper Silesia, gave an indication of the workers' feeling: 'Nobody controlled us: the managers, the bosses, the foremen in the coal mines could do nothing to us now; *they* were afraid of *us*'. Ryszard Brzuzy and others described what these changes meant to them and their fellow workers:

> Management couldn't force people to break health and safety rules. Workers were not treated like slaves anymore. They had a greater opportunity to make decisions about their own lives. The power of the working class then was much greater than management's.

> **Staszek Handzlik:** Solidarity gave people courage. They demanded an explanation for this great 20 billion debt and fundamental reforms. We said, 'Of course we can work efficiently, but we don't want our work to be wasted by incompetent management'.

> **Alojzy Szablewski:** In the Gdańsk shipyard, I went to a room where there was no ventilation and the workers were breathing smoke. I told the director that if the situation didn't change by the next day, I would stop work on that ship. The next day the ship had many plastic sleeves, and great ventilators were

---

4. Garton Ash 1985, p. 85.
5. Sanford 1983, pp. 109–10.
6. Garton Ash 1985, p. 92.

taking the smoke out. In one of the huge work rooms, the heating was out of order, and the temperature was very low. We went to the director and told him it had to be repaired, and it was. Because he knew that Solidarity had power.

Grzegorz Stawski: With a real trade union defending workers' rights, we forced many changes in the mines, including the directors. From that time, workers couldn't just be fired. People were not badly treated any more. Working conditions, safety, health – all improved once a real trade union existed. We won free Saturdays and Sundays. We could better administer the work. We learned to speak with our own voice.

Years later, a miner called Alojzy Pietrzyk testified that during his working life there had been only one year, 1981, when no miner at his colliery died. This was thanks to Solidarity.[7] Statistics corroborate Pietrzyk's recollection: in 1979, there had been 47 fatal mining accidents, and in 1982 – the first year of martial law – in one mine alone, 41 miners lost their lives. But in 1981, no fatal mining accidents were recorded.[8]

As a result of their new power, workers found themselves able and, indeed, forced to confront matters that had previously been the sole preserve of the authorities. As Ryszard Sawicki noted:

Solidarity became a cure for all social ills. Everyone came to us with their problems. If they felt that the manager of a store did something wrong, they would come to us and expect us to take care of it.

People expanded the scope of their demands. They wanted public buildings turned back to public uses rather than being reserved for the privileged. They wanted a redirection of public funds into hospitals, schools, libraries and recreational centres. When these things were not forthcoming, a wave of strikes erupted.[9] Students occupied the University of Łódź, and after a month, they signed an agreement that included student participation in the representative bodies of those schools, independent curricula, increased humanities courses, as well as the right to study a foreign language other than Russian.

Solidarity was a huge social movement. Millions of people became involved and organised themselves: workers, housewives, students, intellectuals, professionals, farmers, even children. Within a few months, some ten million had joined the union, while many others belonged to associated organisations such

---

7. 1989, *UPNB*, 3: 14.
8. 1983, *UPNB*, 1: 28.
9. Wałęsa 1987, p. 163.

as the Independent Student Union. Aleksander Krystosiak vividly illustrated how power relations altered:

> About a month after the strike, the terrified deputy district attorney comes to my office. There *I* am sitting on the side of the desk that normally was *his*; he is sitting in a pleading position on the side of the desk where *I* would normally sit. He is telling me that they caught a worker who stole something. He is asking me if I would object to this worker being arrested. For some reason, I stand up. *He immediately jumps to his feet and stands at attention.* This is a psychological study of an official. A few days earlier, he was so self-important. And there he was standing in front of me, just a worker – and he looked like a sick rat – one of those you could step on and crush its spine, and it wasn't even capable of showing teeth or running away.

By this point, the Party had lost much of its control. Alicja Matuszewska:

> Almost immediately, I began receiving newspapers from the shipyards and elsewhere; I always took piles. Something like this would happen: someone would knock on my office door, and a young officer would come in. (I have no idea how they knew about me). They would ask me, 'Mrs Matuszewska, can we get some leaflets or newspapers?' So, I would say, 'Of course'.

In some cases, Solidarity leaders used their power to press hard against officialdom. Andrzej Rozpłochowski:

> I was a dangerous enemy in the eyes of the regional and central officials from the very beginning of Solidarity because I did not agree to any compromises. I felt that the only thing you talk about with bandits is how they will surrender. People in high positions did not want to deal with me because they wanted to make deals, and I was against it.

It must have been a terrifying and threatening experience that the apparatchiks dearly wished to end. Mieczysław Rakowski:

> For the whole Party, what happened in 1980 was unexpected, and therefore they were not prepared to accept the new situation. This was the tragedy: that neither side was prepared to understand – much less accept – this new situation.

> **Aleksander Krystosiak:** Among those people, the feeling of guilt and fear was born. The people accused them of signing false accusations and of doing wrong to innocent people. They felt not only that we had the power, but also that we had reason to put the noose on their necks. There was fear, and that's understandable. *They* were the ones who decided upon sentences. *They* signed papers and *they* looked at the 'evidence' – supposedly a gun – and *they* knew

as soon as they looked at it that it wasn't the gun of the man accused. It had been put there by the secret police. But they still went after that poor fellow. They were rats. People had scorn and contempt for them and were disgusted with their activities. *Even their children felt ashamed of their parents.*

There are many reports of family discord, as the children of officials had to endure questions and comments about their parents' activities and then brought these issues home. So, the new *status quo* brought a deep and continuing conflict with the *nomenklatura* system and its beneficiaries that would not be resolved until either the system or the union was eliminated. By late October 1980, the Soviet leaders were already demanding that the Polish authorities prepare for martial law.[10] As Zbigniew Regucki put it: 'The pressure put on us by our neighbours – Romania, Czechoslovakia, everyone else – was so strong that there was really no question in my mind that they were ready to come in'.

At the *Nowa Huta* steel mill they stated that the new union was upholding the values abandoned by the country's leaders: 'We ... believe ... that it is possible to restore the highest values: truth, justice, recognition for honest work and respect for man'.[11] The victory opened new horizons to the workers:

> **Aleksander Krystosiak:** People who built houses – architects, engineers, workers, foremen – came to me as vice-chair of the regional committee. They peppered me with all kinds of wonderful projects for making people's lives better that had never seen daylight under the Communists. They said, 'You want to build houses? We have a brick factory. It's yours!'

The union gave people a sense of great possibilities. Krystosiak:

> For forty-five years there had been unions. Everyone belonged. You got hired; you came to work; the first thing they did was put you in the union and take dues from your salary. Fifty percent of that money disappeared. No-one knew where it went. When you needed help from them, there was no money for you. Then, in a short time, just in my regional committee, we had 85 million zlotys in our account. We were getting ready to start building houses for people. I'm talking about this because I want you to see the depth and the breadth of the problems that were dumped on us. We took them on our shoulders and we were capable of managing quite well.

To some degree, this attack on the privileges and prerogatives of the *nomenklatura* became unfocused. Many people told me of the need to act as mediators at this transitional time, corroborating what Wałęsa had stated previously, namely that they had to:

---

10. Bernstein and Politi 1996, p. 250.
11. McDonald 1981, p. 139.

act as a buffer when the demands directly threatened the existence of certain power structures. In the course of dozens of meetings, I had to combat the general inclination to settle accounts with bosses, compromised factory managers, and government representatives as workers were carried away by a passion to clean up everything all at once.[12]

The movement that the creation of Solidarity unleashed not only changed relations between workers and their bosses or the Party; it also changed the character of social relations among the people themselves. This change was manifested in a number of ways.

Before the August strikes, people were often unpleasant to one another on the streets – on public transportation, in stores, at work, and so forth. But now people felt friendlier and treated one another better as a result of coming to know each other and working together in shared concern. In Upper Silesia and western Poland especially, people told me that as a result of Solidarity, their regions – composed of people from all over Poland who had remained strangers to one another – had become communities. My wife, Joanna, the daughter of a miner who became a Solidarity activist, told me how she experienced the difference:

> We moved to Silesia right after I finished second-grade, and I loved the spacious four-room apartment, having my own room, bathroom in the apartment and all to ourselves, unlike the apartment we had in Świebodzice, where the bathroom was a flight of stairs down and we shared it with our neighbours above.
>
> Then the beginning of the school-year came, and all the great things faded into oblivion as we found out that for the first few months we had to go to a school that was near the centre of town – a twenty to thirty minute walk. We were crammed into classrooms of 36 kids with not enough desks to go around. The kids in the school greeted us with hostility: we were the newcomers who were taking stuff away from them. They kept aside, spoke in the Silesian dialect to keep us out of any conversations, and many of the teachers did not hesitate to show us their disdain. We were '*osiedloki*' [people from the projects that had been built only for the newcomers – of the 44 families that lived in Joanna's building, only one was a native Silesian, and they had waited three years to get in].
>
> Because of us there was a shortage of everything, from classroom space to textbooks, to goods in the stores. The whole town was clearly divided into *osiedloki* (us), and the original denizens of Żory. We were the bane of their

---

12. Wałęsa 1987, p. 147.

existence, the ones with special privileges, since most of our parents did not have to wait for apartments for any considerable amount of time. (My parents got the apartment in three months because my father was a welder who had the qualifications for welding underground, a skill they really needed). But many of the people in town had been on waiting-lists for several years. Even in church, there were two distinct groups of kids: '*osiedloki*' and the kids from the old town, each of which stayed together. Basically, we were the pariahs because the natives did not have any choice in the matter.

Then Solidarity came, and all of a sudden things changed: the old antagonisms were forgotten, as we huddled together to listen to a transistor radio in school to hear about strikes and about decisions concerning our parents. Our mothers suddenly stood in lines together, and bitched about the thieving, the poor store deliveries, 'them' (the government) stealing and mismanaging. Our dads suddenly got together on Sundays after church to play chess, drink beer and talk politics.

I distinctly remember one of the kids in my class whose family had lived in our town for many generations inviting me over to her house. It was such a shock that both my mother and I fretted over what I should wear for half a day. Asia introduced me to her '*starzyk*' [grandpa] and then translated for me when I did not understand some of the things he said, since he spoke in the Silesian dialect. I was amazed and fascinated by his rich and beautiful language; this was not what we were taught to believe. It was not, as I had been told, a caricature of the Polish language with bastardised German and Czech thrown in for good measure. Asia lent me books by Gustaw Morcinek who wrote exclusively about Silesia, and used the dialect in his writings, and of whose writings I was mostly ignorant, except for some short story we had to read in school.

We became one community, united by Solidarity, educated by Solidarity about how the government tried to divide us, and how we needed to be united. And when martial law came, we were once again united. The native Silesians refused to be strike breakers, refused to take mid-management positions, and joined with our fathers in strikes, and then in being arrested. Once again, our mothers cried together, rode together to various prisons to find out if our fathers were there, made care packages. Us kids? We were joined by the shared hatred towards the soldiers and police who disrupted our lives, our school year, and took some of our fathers away.

This improvement in social relations began during the August strikes and continued thereafter. Marek Muszyński: 'Cars would stop at bus and tram stops and drivers would say, "I'm going to such and such a place if anybody wants to come with me". It was very common'.

Władysław Frasyniuk: People became friendly with each other, and less aggressive. For instance, if the bus didn't come on time, the bus driver was not rudely addressed. A great feeling of community developed.

Alicja Matuszewska: I worked for Solidarity in the evenings because I had a day job. Meetings would take place in my apartment until late. One time I hadn't time to stand in line to buy my ration and my refrigerator was empty. Eighteen people were at my home and we were all hungry. I had one loaf of bread and a little bit of oil, which was really terrible – black and filthy. One of the workers went to the kitchen, sliced the bread and fried it with that filthy oil. We all put salt on it and ate. If anyone has any doubts about what Solidarity was about, it was eating this loaf of bread together!

I said to them, 'Tomorrow, my daughter is coming home from Warsaw'. (She was a student there). 'I have nothing at home – no food. Not even bread'. One of them suggested that they work while I went to my job. I returned from work around 3:30pm and they showed me what they had written. It still needed work, so we started writing. Suddenly it was 8:30pm. I said, 'I'm sorry. I have to run to buy bread'. They said, 'No. At this hour there will be no bread. You'll go in the morning'. They left. I went to my neighbour and borrowed a half-loaf of bread and two eggs. I went home and opened the fridge and . . . everything was there! Even things that were not available in Poland: ham, salami, sardines, butter. It turned out that the wives of two of my workers – who didn't even know me – brought it all for me.

Aleksander Krystosiak: Before, people just growled and barked at each other. You stepped on someone's foot in a tram and you almost got eaten by that person. And now, people began seeing each other as human beings. In my opinion, this was the most important change that took place in society.

Sławomir Majewski: You could see the difference Solidarity made everywhere: we were all one family. I went to a meeting of the National Commission. On the train to Szczecin, we met a woman who said, 'You will arrive very early in the morning. Come to my place'. Then she left for work and we stayed in her flat and made tea for ourselves and felt at home. Of course when we left, the flat was absolutely clean. You felt immediate sympathy when you knew that someone belonged to Solidarity.

Ginter Kupka: During Miners' Day on 4 December, in the Julian mine, all the people at the celebration – wives, mothers and relatives of the miners – could go underground and see the mine. It had never happened before. It was important because people could really see the conditions of work. Before, many people didn't like miners because of the privileges they had, and now they could see how hard this work was.

Alojzy Szablewski: People who sold books, cigarettes, food in the shipyard asked Solidarity to see that these things were distributed fairly, so it wasn't the case that one person had several packs of cigarettes, and someone else nothing. Solidarity gave everyone a card, and he would take the card to the shop and get the same amount, so that everyone had food, and people knew it was just.

Alcohol-consumption, which had often been a major problem on and off the job, was now controlled by the workers themselves, and virtually disappeared at the worksite:

Władysław Frasyniuk: Drinking alcohol in the workplace entirely vanished. It was not from increased control from *above*. There was pressure from one's *workmates*.

Alojzy Szablewski: A man caught with vodka in the shipyard was brought to me. I told him, 'If you are ever again caught drinking vodka, then you will not be a member of Solidarity, and you will be fired'. Then I telephoned the director and told him to give the man one more chance. After that, no-one took any more vodka into the shipyard because they feared Solidarity more than the director. There were fewer accidents.

Aleksander Krystosiak: With lightning speed, the society rebuilt itself morally. In my factory, which wasn't any exception, there were four places where alcohol was sold. The director, the management, the foremen did whatever they could to get rid of them. But it wasn't possible. Why? Because the people helped hide them. But with the new trade unions, when the worker went to get vodka, he wasn't looking for the foreman or manager; he was making sure that no other worker saw him because he was ashamed of doing it. So these selling points just died out, like dinosaurs. What was really important was the change in the quality of the worker's mind.

This movement of moral regeneration was important in raising people's self-esteem. It was part of a much broader process in which people came to think better of themselves and of their fellows. In part, this sense was what underpinned the new attitude of co-operation and concern for one another. People's feelings of increased power and responsibility also helped generate a sense that they had grown, so that in their own eyes they were more valuable. In this context, many people began to undertake new tasks and new responsibilities. Increasingly, people who once had no voice or opportunity to affect their society now began to delve into areas they had previously not touched. As they did so, they discovered abilities they may never have imagined existed. As Mirosława Strzelec noted: 'The workers organised theatres, cabarets. They wrote articles, poems, and read them in public'.

Krystosiak: People who before didn't know how to build two sentences correctly now spoke sensibly and creatively before thousands of people. I was one of them. Many times, when people from my shipyard and from the Warski shipyard spoke at universities in Szczecin, they couldn't believe we didn't have a higher education.

Grzegorz Stawski: My first speech to the public broke a barrier of fear. I knew what I wanted; I knew what people wanted. The problem was whether I would be able to touch them. And when I did, I became more self-assured. I felt that having their support, I became stronger. I listened to them. We had to know what we wanted from each other.

Sławomir Majewski: Before Solidarity, people didn't know their factory income, its organisational structure, its economic problems. Only government-officials had been interested in the problem of how to run these factories and now ordinary people became concerned. As a member of a special group that prepared a new education programme for the university, I studied the economic problems of our university: its sources of income, how to organise a budget. It was a period of great efforts to improve our country, when *political* programmes were not so important, but there was a vast new *social* programme.

Helena Łuczywo: There was a great movement to improve our economy, our industries, cinematography, literature. People who had been completely apathetic before Solidarity were suddenly very active about how to improve education and health services. Someone organised a new programme of education for primary and secondary schools. A lot of activists went to improve the situation of prisoners. From the example of the independent trade-union, we had other independent organisations – like students.

Poles now became very protective of democracy in all realms of life, especially within Solidarity, for if they could not retain democratic forms there, how could they possibly hope to do so within the broader society?

Marek Muszyński: There was a sort of childish illness of democracy: every meeting, every gathering, every rally went on for hours because people wanted them to be strictly according to democratic rules. The common element was the belief that together by our own force, we could achieve something.

Sociologist and Solidarity adviser Jadwiga Staniszkis noted that the workers were very concerned about internal democracy:

People aren't looking for the sloganeering of a mass meeting: they want a flat technical description of what is happening. The workers have matured to such a degree that it is really impossible to manipulate them . . . For many weeks now, activists from regional chapters as well as rank-and-file union members have been complaining to union officials that many important matters are kept secret from the public.[13]

Democracy was manifested not just in meetings, but in everyday life. Feeling they now had a say in their country's life and trajectory, people discussed their conditions and options. Now that their opinions mattered, they were concerned about what they and others felt. Frasyniuk recalled:

> There were some controversial issues: should Solidarity demand free access to the mass-media like television, or should we reform the economy first? People talked about these problems everywhere: in lines, in the shops, at parties, in the buses. The regional Solidarity committee started work at seven in the morning, and we would finish at about ten or eleven at night, mostly because people would come to us to present their problem or their point of view, and we thought that they had the right to do it, so we listened.

When people become empowered, they often shed the feelings of apathy, the product of powerlessness. Great social movements frequently provoke a popular demand to learn – history, politics, economics – matters that had previously seemed remote and academic. In Wrocław, Solidarity organised a library for its members and established a 'workers' university' where lectures were given and particular skills taught. Władysław Frasyniuk:

> The demand for knowledge was spontaneous. For instance, the workers in Dolmel insisted on forming their own branch of the trade-union university on the territory of their factory because the building where we held meetings of the union's citywide-workers' university was too crowded. Academics, especially historians, were always asked to give lectures. They had no free time for themselves; they were to go anywhere in the region, and even to neighbouring regions. They spoke mainly of history; then economics and law; the traditions and history of trade unions in the world: how they work in different countries. The demand for knowledge about different trade-unions was so great that a permanent part of our magazine was devoted to the history and functioning of different trade unions in the world.

Jan Waszkiewicz headed the Solidarity information-bureau in Wrocław:

> People were interested in political, historical, constitutional issues – everything. There were lectures two or three times a week. Attendance varied: when it was somebody well-known, there would be a few hundred people.

---

13. Staniszkis 1983, p. 87.

A huge proliferation of publications came out from the underground, which, as Bogdan Borusewicz put it, 'wasn't really underground anymore. There was no workers' university in Gdańsk, but there were lectures in the factories, at the National Commission, and meetings in churches with interesting people'. In Kraków, according to Stanisław Handzlik, the 'hunger for education was enormous. We organised meetings with intellectuals to get to know the outlooks of the people in the opposition'.

> **Ginter Kupka:** We wanted every miner to be open to the world and not to think only about his work. We organised trips to different parts of the country, and we tried to attract people to visit places, to take part in cultural events, to go to different factories – to the Gdańsk shipyards to observe how ships were built; to Warsaw to see how cars were manufactured.

> **Andrzej Rozpłochowski:** Upper Silesia had very few enlightened intellectuals, so it was very important to create an independent publishing network to educate the workers. We also created a library in the region with a very rich collection of books, and we managed to organise smaller libraries in over one-hundred factories all over the region. These were large companies, and the books in those libraries also travelled around and were lent in other factories as well. We created a special network of communication through the phones and telexes in our region. Around mid-1981, we had regular lectures organised in factories and in cultural houses. Also, an independent network of lecturers and classes developed on the basis of the church. The number of people who came was large.

> **Ryszard Sawicki:** We emphasised educating people. We looked for independent presses and book publishers, and brought as much as we could into the mine for the workers. I figured that it didn't matter what they read or how much they understood. If they understood just a little bit, then even if at some point the government managed to scare them, later on what they read and learned would somehow be like an investment that brings you interest.

Many of these changes had permanent effects which carried into the period of martial law. Even with the arrest of thousands of activists and the suppression of almost all organisational remnants of the union, the government was never again able to reassert the same degree of control over individual behaviour and the expression of ideas that it had done prior to the Solidarity upheaval. Małgorzata Górczewska was 15 in 1980 and was very much affected by these efforts to educate broadly: 'I attended lectures at the university about the "white spots" in Polish history for about a year, and I learned about things I hadn't known about before. I met a group of young people at these meetings; I got newspapers and books from them'. Later, after martial law was declared, Górczewska became an activist: 'We published our own newspaper. Perhaps, if August 1980 hadn't occurred, and then the period where things were openly discussed, I wouldn't be here now'.

Chapter Ten
The Solidarity Offensive

Zbigniew Bogacz: Though we told people we were fighting for free trade unions, I knew it was a fight against communism. Solidarity wasn't only a trade union movement; it was a movement for independence.

Lech Wałęsa: My role lay in appropriately feeding the flame, tossing in the right ingredients, merging ideas, and maintaining unity, while at the same time not allowing a conflagration to break out... The communists had to believe that our actions and aspirations did not threaten the foundations of the system. They could not know that after taking one finger we would reach out in a moment for the entire hand under the right circumstances.[1]

The establishment of Solidarity was the beginning of a broad-based assault on the *status quo*. In the period after Solidarity was established, many battles broadened the power of the social movement at the expense of the Party/state. During the strike negotiations, the workers made it plain that they intended to challenge the *nomenklatura* system and its privileges. In the final negotiating session in Gdańsk, Jagielski insisted that the demand for a large wage increase was impossible as there were no funds to pay for it. Wałęsa responded:

---

1. Wałęsa 2007, p. xv.

'Prime Minister, we realise that money can't be produced without something to back it. But we would like to suggest where the money is: in the swollen state apparatus. It can be taken from them'. Here was a clear threat. If the union had the power to control the money, what power would it lack?

Many beneficiaries of the *status quo* saw the union as a threat. During the negotiations, Bogdan Lis brought up point 12 of the demands, which went straight to the heart of the *nomenklatura* system: namely, 'that people in leading positions be chosen on the basis of qualifications rather than party membership. To abolish the privileges of the militia, security service and party apparatus'. When the holders of the privileges denied they existed, Wałęsa responded: 'We'll investigate...We'll get to the bottom of it. Our journals will publish whatever is found'.[2]

Aleksander Krystosiak said that after the strikes the Party leaders were told: 'You can sit and do nothing, but draw the money for your salaries from the *Party dues*. We won't support you anymore'.

Workers challenged the power and the specific decisions of the *nomenklatura*, and they questioned their abilities. This trend escalated early in 1981. In mid-January, in the town of Kolbuszowa, the mayor was in jail and the Party Secretarywanted to resign,[3] while the region of Bielsko-Biała successfully struck to unseat corrupt officials. In February, workers in the Jelenia Góra region began a general strike, demanding the resignation of the Minister for Trade Union Affairs and insisting that a luxurious sanatorium (used for employees of the Interior Ministry) be handed over to the Public Health Service. They were successful.[4] Meanwhile, farmers began to agitate for their right to form a union, and they began to conduct sit-ins. Students and prisoners made their own demands.[5]

The many independent papers, journals and other publications to which Solidarity had given birth began avidly exposing corruption, starting with Gierek. It was revealed that he had a huge villa amid 4,000 acres of park, with a dining room for 40, a billiard room and a cinema,[6] while the former prime minister's son, according to Ryszard Brzuzy, 'lost a lot of money gambling in Monte Carlo'.

> **Zbigniew Bogacz:** We learned that the mine engineer was building a dacha for himself, using men who were supposedly working in the mine. The mine director had an orchard with 140 cubic metres of an endangered tree which

2. Kemp-Welch 1983, p. 131; pp. 132–3, 207–8.
3. Garton Ash 1985, p. 117.
4. Garton Ash 1985, pp. 141–2; Barker and Weber 1982, p. 38.
5. Barker and Weber 1982, p. 39.
6. Garton Ash 1985, p. 185.

grows only in Poland and is under strict protection – *but they were cutting them down to build his house.* So the noose was getting tighter.

New strikes began as workers demanded what others had already won but their local authorities refused to grant, even in the face of the Accords signed in Gdańsk, Szczecin, Katowice and Jastrzębie.[7] The most powerful sections of the unions protected smaller, weaker workplaces where the police were concomitantly more likely to be abusive. Management in those places was often far more autocratic than in the larger factories.[8] A Solidarity National Delegate Meeting spoke of 'fear of victimisation and reprisals'. The authorities used methods 'such as detention and interrogation by police surveillance' against Solidarity activists.[9] Zbigniew Bujak: 'The situation of *those* Solidarity activists was much more difficult than ours. People from small towns felt safe under our umbrella'.

> **Aleksander Krystosiak:** Our committee was created 'during the war', and we got elected and organised into an inter-factory workers' commission. In some provinces, the workers didn't trust the Inter-factory Founding Commissions that were created *after* the upheaval had taken place, so, factories from all over came to register with *us.* That meant that we had to travel frequently to the factories that asked us for help. There, the managers wouldn't allow new trade-unions to be organised. But when any of us came to the factory and said that we were from Szczecin, it was as though we had a gun in our hands. They realised that we would be able to stop the factory. They understood that unless they fulfilled these people's demands, they would really get kicked; that the big regions would support the small town factories up to and including a strike. People in small towns knew that there was a strong, well-organised, disciplined union standing behind them from the big regions.

The union grew as the movement spread throughout the country in what has to be described as an explosion of initiative from below. By mid-September, some three million workers from 3,500 factories had joined, even before the union was legally recognised.[10] They agreed to create *Solidarność* – 'Solidarity'.[11] The name expressed how the strike had been won, what the union stood for, and the basis of its strength.

---

7. MacShane 1981, p. 54.
8. Wałęsa 1987, p. 142.
9. McDonald 1981, p. 129.
10. Drzycimski 1982, p. 111; Garton Ash 1985, p. 75.
11. Sanford 1983, p. 76.

Counter-attack

Leaders of the Soviet Union were alarmed by this movement and the gains it was making in threatening the state's power. Leonid Brezhnev complained: 'There is truly a fully raging counter-revolution in Poland, but statements in the Polish press and by the Polish comrades say nothing about this'.[12] Their view of the matter was that 'Under the pressure of anti-socialist forces, who have managed to confuse significant strata of the working class, the PUWP (Polish United Workers' Party) has been forced to go on the defensive'. The response, they felt, should be: '*preparing a counter-attack and recovering the positions that have been squandered among the working class and the people*'.[13]

In Poland, Party officials, career soldiers, secret police and their families were isolated and often reviled by this movement. We now know that from the time of the August strikes that indicated just how serious the situation had become, the Polish government contemplated introducing martial law, an option that was rejected at the time by the Politburo because it was felt that the massive strike wave would make it impossible to implement.[14] Such considerations continued throughout the 16 months when Solidarity was legal. It is easy to understand why they hated Solidarity. Zbigniew Regucki:

> Solidarity's questioning of Party domains like the press, like censorship, like the fact that the Party was supposed to be representative of the working class, provoked two attitudes. One was fear: what will come next? The other was to wait for the reaction of the Soviet Union: would they intervene or not? Solidarity was viewed as a serious threat by the majority of the Party apparatus.
>
> **Grzegorz Stawski:** When Solidarity was created, it became very obvious that the Communist Party did not represent the workers. Solidarity did. The Communist Party was deprived of its right to speak in the name of the workers. Ordinary people put pressure on Party members to give back their Party cards. In some places in Upper Silesia they put dustbins in the streets where they collected Party cards.

The *nomenklatura* continually sought to undermine the Accords, to weaken the union and to take back – either by stealth or by force – what they had lost. These efforts continued in various forms until martial law was instituted. Janusz Onyszkiewicz recalled:

---

12. Transcript of CPSU CC Politburo Meeting, 29 October 1980, cited in Paczkowski and Byrne 2007, p. 123.

13. 'CPSU CC Politburo Report on Topics for Discussion with the Polish Leadership', cited in Paczkowski and Byrne 2007, pp. 83–4, original emphasis.

14. See Paczkowski and Byrne 2007, p. 13.

There was a fight with the authorities from the very beginning. They tried to limit the scope of the agreements to the coastline and to the coal-mining area of Jastrzębie – but that was obviously unthinkable. Then, they tried to split Solidarity. They signed about six hundred different agreements with different groups, granting each slightly different things; privileges, promises of pay. And then they tried to domesticate Solidarity by throwing favours at certain Solidarity leaders. They tried to implant seeds of discontent. They were very much afraid of the territorial [rather than craft] structure of Solidarity.

One tactic was to attempt to undermine the union from within. Tadeusz Pławiński:

> Our biggest problem at the beginning was that the *security police* organised Solidarity in small places.[15] In Słupsk, they made ridiculous demands, and then it came out that they were members of the security forces. After martial law, we learned that someone in the military shipyard, who acted as one of the strongest supporters of Solidarity, was a security policeman. In a lot of places, mostly small cities, that was what the police did. They also tried to bribe people – some got phones right away, which for most was impossible. A member of the MKZ [Inter-factory Founding Committee] applied for a car. Those cars were given only to Party members. A few weeks after the strike ended, he got it. He was kicked out of the MKZ.

> **Janusz Pałubicki:** They kept a close eye on what was going on in the factories. When they saw that there was enough upheaval to start something, then they would pick out people and extend their protection; therefore, these people felt freer to speak up and to denounce. So, they would become better known in the factory and people would elect them. They were not being paid directly by the secret police, but they were its pawns.

The official unions, which were rapidly losing their members, now called themselves 'reformed' and, like Solidarity, claimed they were 'independent and self-governing', but to no avail. Almost no-one was fooled or interested. The mischief-making was so pervasive that there were widespread suspicions about some of the people who had attained prominent positions in the union. As Zbigniew Bogacz put it:

> It seemed that the secret police worked from the bottom up: people who were their agents were elected in the factories and then pushed up. It took several months to clear up who was who. The Jastrzębie group was the most infil-

---

15. Both Rakowski and the secret-police with whom I spoke denied this happened.

204 • Chapter Ten

trated. Many were discarded during the elections in February. Only after that did normal activity began.

So, as Ryszard Sawicki reported, they took precautions to protect themselves:

> We were infiltrated by the secret police. So, we decided that before electing a leadership, whoever wished to become part of it had to tell his life story in great detail. Everyone heard it and could say if they knew something that person didn't tell. Once the person was verified, he could become part of the leadership. We also excluded anyone who had any disciplinary problem in the factory because we were afraid that later on they could be blackmailed by management. We decided that if there was suspicion that someone had cooperated with management, the police, or the government, he would be eliminated from the union. We felt that it would be better to wrong a few people than to keep in those who were hurting the union.

One way that they responded to Sawicki's efforts was by attempting to undermine his marriage. 'My wife got anonymous phone calls saying that I was sneaking around on her, screwing girls, spending wonderful nights in different hotels and having fun'. But they overplayed their hand:

> One time, I was supposed to go to Wrocław, but I got a phone call saying the meeting was off. So I just went to sleep. Meanwhile, she received a call saying that I was at some hotel in Wrocław having a good time with prostitutes and alcohol and all that. She came home and saw me sleeping, and that helped to clear the air.

The security forces seemed at a loss. Adam Sucharski: 'It was the beginning of disorderliness in our ranks, and it lasted a long time, about six months'. He blamed the Party leadership: 'I think our commanders did not know what to do. They were given no direction'.

But pressure was building from outside Poland. On 28 October, Czechoslovakia closed its border with Poland and, together with East Germany, pressed the Soviets for a crackdown. December saw reports that the Soviet Union had a massive force of three hundred thousand troops, including mechanised divisions, poised to invade, in addition to those already occupying the country.[16] East Germany sealed its border with Poland.[17] Kania was called to the Soviet Union where he was shown plans for military intervention in and the occupation of Polish cities and towns.[18] But they abandoned the project after mobilising their

---

16. Kwitny 1997, pp. 376–7; see also Sanford 1983, p. 117.
17. Szulc 1995, p. 349.
18. Bernstein and Politi 1996, p. 250.

troops. Apparently, warnings from the United States, together with the threat of an international union blockade of the USSR and an implicit warning by the Pope that he would denounce an invasion in uncompromising terms, led them to back off.[19]

The armed forces and Solidarity

It is not surprising that the military should attempt to prevent its civilian employees from organising themselves into Solidarity. Alicja Matuszewska worked in the military repair shipyard in Gdańsk, one of a number of civilian workers who worked for the military. As Solidarity was getting organised there after the strikes, she was called into a meeting by her supervisor, who was accompanied by two colonels. She was told that there could be no Solidarity union among the workers in the Ministry of National Defence. When she asked for a reason, she was told:

'Because Jaruzelski does not wish to have Solidarity there'. So I said, 'General Jaruzelski should have put into the agreement that there would be no Solidarity in the Ministry of National Defence. Let him write a letter saying there can be no Solidarity in the military and we will not organise it'. (After the Gdańsk agreements, Jaruzelski couldn't.) We argued for an hour, two hours. Finally, I had to go to work. Then, they started calling in workers who signed up for Solidarity and threatening them. When I heard of this, I went to the Paris Commune Shipyard and asked them for some kind of guarantee because if we went on strike, they would argue that Solidarity strikes were weakening national defence. They publicly threatened to strike unless the persecution stopped. They never called anyone again because they were afraid of the strike.

Throughout the sixteen months of legal Solidarity, the military continued to fiercely resist the efforts of workers under military jurisdiction who sought to organise themselves into the union. Matuszewska described some of the obstacles she and her co-workers faced:

In December 1980, the factory committee of the military shipyard was called to Warsaw. They said that the unions that had registered could have Solidarity. 'But you didn't register', they said to me. I said, 'Yes, I did', and I pulled out the documents. They didn't know what to do then. Jaruzelski's lawyer said that only civilian workers of military units with decoded names could register. I did not agree: 'because once we walk out of here, in one hour you can take

---

19. Weigel 1999, pp. 404–8.

away all the names of the units and put code numbers instead, and that will be the end of Solidarity in the military'. They stated that every unit that had already registered could stay. But we still refused to sign because we felt that other factories would be prohibited from joining if we signed.

A series of 'crises'

A sparring process continued over months, as the party sought Solidarity's weak points. But in almost every case during its first six months, the union emerged stronger than ever as it progressively encroached on state power.

Registering the union

The first conflict was over legal recognition of the union, a promise embodied in the Accords. Without registration, people who joined could be targeted by the police. Jan Ciesielski, a Solidarity leader in the *Nowa Huta* steel mill, recalled that: 'People were very cautious about joining this movement. The question was one of courage and trust'. Zbigniew Bujak discouraged the timid from joining: 'I said, "This union will fight for you, but you will also have to fight the police, the Party and the administration because this is a union of changes"'. The government insisted that registration was a matter for the courts to decide, and the courts demanded that Solidarity write into its bylaws that the Party had the 'leading role'. Janusz Onyszkiewicz:

> The Gdańsk Agreement accepted the leading role of the Party, *limited to state affairs*. But according to the Party, it should play the leading role *everywhere*. To limit this 'leading role' to state affairs was to say that we accept that the Party had the final say in big political issues: national defence, foreign policy, internal security, strategic economic decisions. But the Party is not supposed to play the leading role in every aspect of our lives. And, in particular, certainly no leading role in Solidarity.

So, Solidarity limited the Party's influence in the union:

> We introduced into our charter a clause saying that nobody in an elected office in the Party could hold an office in Solidarity. You had to choose. They tried desperately to force us to admit this leading role of the Party in our charter, which would give them some leverage. We argued that loyalty must be with Solidarity, while an official with the Party would be bound by Party discipline.

People grew increasingly angry as the dispute dragged into October. When Solidarity called a one-hour general strike on 3 October, the country came to a halt virtually everywhere. It was an impressive show of power as the workers were able to see just how powerful they were. Many workers who had not yet joined were drawn in. Mieczysław Gil: 'There were certain circles that sympathised with Solidarity but did not display it openly, like teachers, municipal services, officials responsible for culture in the city. It was a turning point when they joined the strike'. In Adam Dębski's factory:

> It was the first time that the factory management had to give power to our committee. We had everything at our disposal: all entrances, internal communication, all telexes, all phones. I had the right to make all decisions in the factory for one hour.

In the *Nowa Huta* steel mill, noted Jan Ciesielski:

> Almost everyone joined this strike. At the gates, they put up a banner that read 'Solidarity Strike', but obviously certain sections, like the furnaces, were exempted. There was considerable opposition by management, and party-members were told not to strike. In my section, all the machines were inactive except for two, which were operated by Party members. The rest of the group gathered around and ridiculed them, so they had to stop.

This demonstration of Solidarity's strength yielded results: immediately afterwards, Kania reiterated to a meeting of the Central Committee that the August strikes had been legitimate.[20] Now, the problem of the courts was suddenly resolved and Solidarity was registered a few weeks later without having made any concessions. Janusz Onyszkiewicz recalled of that action:

> It was rather funny. We knew exactly what was going to happen before we went to court. Everything was fixed in advance by the Central Committee, showing the 'independence' of our courts.

But the controversy did not end there. The presiding judge simply read 'the leading role of the Party in the state' into the Solidarity statutes. This move outraged people and provoked a new threat of a general strike, scheduled for 12 November. Journalist Denis MacShane wrote: 'Leaflets were prepared by regional Solidarity committees, instructing workers to occupy plants, to bring food and bedding with them, banning alcohol, and other preparations for the strike'.[21] But the Supreme Court overruled the lower court, removed the offending clause, and inserted instead an appendix of the relevant points of the August Accords, which

---

20. Garton Ash 1985, p. 80.
21. MacShane 1981, p. 57.

conceded that place to the Party.[22] This was an acceptable compromise.[23] Within a short time, the union grew to the strength of some ten million, encompassing almost the entire working class – blue-collar and white-collar.

But registration did not end the constant conflict between the Party/state and the union. Workers and others continued their activism. Medical workers in Gdańsk went on a sit-down strike that drew support and the threat of sympathy strikes throughout the country; students and faculty at the universities raised their own demands. Within a short while, the government was faced with a railway strike, negotiations in the textile industry, and other areas of discontent.[24] At the same time, the government was not really ready to come to an accommodation with the union.

> **Ryszard Sawicki:** Once the union became registered, it seemed that everything came to a standstill. You could not get anything out of the government. They stalled: they would say, 'Yes, but...' and they would go round and round, and you couldn't get them to commit to anything. It seemed like they were testing to see what they could get away with. And we saw that in all cases we got nowhere: it was a stalemate.

Police powers

In the autumn of 1980, the Warsaw Prosecutor General issued a secret document with the charge that Solidarity was connected to the pre-Solidarity opposition, which was guilty of 'anti-Socialist' activity.

> **Zbigniew Bujak:** It showed that the government was preparing for a confrontation. Mr Narożniak got it, Xeroxed it and spread it around. In November, the police invaded the union's Warsaw headquarters and searched until they found a copy of the document.[25] The prosecutor put him in prison.

Narożniak was threatened with a five-year prison sentence for disseminating state secrets. Moreover, Bujak noted:

> There was the more general question of whether the prosecutor and the police had the right to enter Solidarity headquarters and search without asking permission and whether we had the right to publish it. They claimed the documents were secret and Solidarity was not allowed to publish them.

---

22. MacDonald 1982, p. 15.
23. Garton Ash 1985, pp. 81–4.
24. Sanford 1983, pp. 107, 110–11.
25. Garton Ash 1985, p. 90.

Here was a direct challenge to the union. Solidarity insisted that Narożniak and the clerk who had supplied him with the document be freed and the prosecutors and police restrained from invading their offices.[26] Twenty Warsaw factories struck and Bujak threatened a regional general strike to secure Narożniak's release and support new demands to punish those responsible and to curtail the activities of the police.[27] Workers striking in Łódź for wage-increases also demanded that Narożniak be released, showing that the strike was spreading beyond the Warsaw region.[28] The government did release him, although the legality of disseminating such documents was left unsettled in theory by these events. But the arena of practical activity open to the union had broadened. Solidarity's authority was now edging beyond that granted by the Accords and certainly extended far beyond a simple trade union.

One result was that now smaller and more vulnerable places felt freer to organise Solidarity and to take a more aggressive stance. Bujak: 'The police stopped entering Solidarity headquarters in small towns. The prosecutor's office stopped calling in activists for interrogation. People felt like we beat the police'. On the other hand, the government's very attempt to prosecute made some people more cautious. Poznań Solidarity leader Janusz Pałubicki cautioned that the 'Narożniak Affair' was also 'harmful':

> because in truth, it was a warning to people who worked for the government: you do something like that and you'll go to prison. So, anyone who wanted to follow suit had to think twice: is it worth it? Will the region stand behind me? People who thought so would act. But most people were doubtful, and they wouldn't do it because they were afraid. I think that from then on, the leaks diminished.

Similar battles were fought in other regions. In Szczecin, the government censored the Solidarity paper by cutting out a cartoon that showed Poland with scaffolds for repair works. The caption read: 'No trespassing for strangers' – an obvious allusion to the Soviet Union. Printers rebelled and refused to print any official paper that day, while they did print the cartoon. In a similar fashion, printers threatened not to print the Warsaw daily *People's Tribune* unless the ban was lifted on showing Andrzej Wajda's film, *Workers '80*.[29]

In response to these assertions of popular will, the members of parliament exhibited some unaccustomed signs of independence, calling for the resignation

---

26. Ibid.
27. Garton Ash 1985, pp. 91–2; MacShane 1981, pp. 57–8.
28. Cave and Latyński 1982–3, p. 56.
29. Sanford 1983, p. 122.

of the Ministers of Agriculture and the Food Industry.[30] Just a few weeks later, a poll published by the Polish Academy of Sciences corroborated the social pressure the deputies were feeling: 58 percent of the population favoured Solidarity and distrusted the authorities; 62 percent held the authorities responsible for not fulfilling the Social Agreements, while only 1.1 percent blamed Solidarity.[31] But the party-leadership, under pressure from the Soviets and the *nomenklatura*[32] escalated its rhetoric. Kania called Solidarity's continual resort to strikes 'blackmail', and suggested that the union was exercising a form of dual power.[33] The term evoked images of revolution, which could be used to justify a crackdown against the union.

Free Saturdays

By the New Year, another open conflict emerged. In the negotiations in Jastrzębie, the government had agreed that the workers need not work on Saturdays. Many workers there had been required to work every Saturday for months or longer because the coal-mines produced much of Poland's energy, heat and a large amount of its foreign reserves. Suddenly, in an attempt to rewrite the social-contract unilaterally, the government decreed that those who did not work on the Saturdays that fell on 10 and 24 of January, and two Saturdays a month thereafter, would effectively forfeit much of their pay and benefits for the month. The Solidarity leadership insisted that all Saturdays be work-free until further notice. In Upper Silesia, Solidarity banned Saturday work. Grzegorz Stawski recalled that when some miners attempted to work, despite the union's call not to:

> Pickets were organised, and some workers were even thrown out of the mines in wheelbarrows; sometimes, the workers would cut off the pants of those who worked on Saturdays. [Both were ritualistic acts of humiliation]. They were a very small group, hostile to Solidarity.

The union once again threatened a national one-hour strike if the government insisted on its demand. The strike threat brought about new negotiations that resulted in a compromise on free Saturdays: workers would work only one Saturday a month.[34]

------

30. Sanford 1983, pp. 112–13.
31. Sanford 1983, pp. 123–4.
32. Sanford 1983, p. 124.
33. Sanford 1983, p. 120.
34. Jonathan Kwitny has stated that, at that meeting, the government shared secret data with Solidarity, showing the extent of the shortages of production that resulted at least partially from taking Saturdays off, and that having seen the numbers the union

Provocations

While these political wrangles proceeded, there were a series of apparent provocations. They were carried out locally, but there were so many, of such a similar character, that it was natural that suspicions would be directed toward the central government. Within a few months of the Accords, shortages of goods became apparent in the stores. There were reports that the authorities were withholding goods from the market, which engendered suspicions that the shortages were artificially created. Grzegorz Stawski: 'People began telling us that they were destroying food; large amounts were found in illegal dumps'. In early 1981, in hundreds of factories, workers either struck or threatened to strike, despite efforts of the Solidarity leadership to calm things. Increasingly, the sense of control that Solidarity had inculcated was dissipating. Zbigniew Bogacz:

> The region of Bielsko-Biała went on strike for a week, demanding that the governor and the deputy-governor of the province, and the director of the Fiat factory be removed. They had embezzled large amounts of money, but the government was protecting them. In Jelenia Góra, the Party Secretary had defrauded, and they couldn't get him to resign or be fired. So again, the whole region went on strike for a week.

The strikes worsened the shortages and made life even more difficult. Suspicions grew that they were being purposely provoked.

> **Bogacz:** The losses in production were incredible: car factories, textiles. We could see that the government's strategy was to negotiate, negotiate, with no results. People were growing more and more emotional, and we felt helpless.

Faced with the situation in Jelenia Góra, Ryszard Sawicki, who served on the Solidarity National Commission, felt that:

> The government provoked the strike so as to blame Solidarity for shortages. In Jelenia Góra, there is no industry of real importance to the government, but there are a lot of little factories that produce consumer goods. The whole strike was a provocation, but the workers there handled the matter foolishly. Some of the demands were ridiculous, like insisting that virtually everyone who had the title 'Director' be dismissed. I understood that if they struck, it would be the government's victory because then they would be able to say 'It is not our fault that you cannot get carpets, clothes, crystal and other consumer goods; it is because Jelenia Góra is on strike'.

---

agreed to more work on Saturdays. Kwitny provides no source for this statement; Kwitny 1997, p. 380.

Sawicki felt that these provocations were part of a broader pattern. But regardless of intent, the effect of these repeated demonstrations of a lack of faith was to shatter any residual popular trust in the government.

> **Zbigniew Bogacz:** The resistance from the government side showed people that the Communist system had to be changed. People saw that they couldn't win what they wanted within the system. So a different kind of feeling grew: a demand for radical change, once and for all.

> **Grzegorz Stawski:** The majority of ordinary people had felt that perhaps the authorities had been deceived about our working and living conditions. But that view very quickly changed when we tried to carry out the agreements. They cheated, which radicalised people.

Still, the charge that Solidarity was responsible for all the country's troubles resonated, especially among the nation's elderly. As Stawski noted: 'There were some people who turned their backs on us, like pensioners. The government convinced them that we were responsible'. But this was still a small counter-current amid the growing flood that moved in Solidarity's direction.

The growing strength of Solidarity

In this first period of Solidarity's existence, most of the government's moves were unsuccessful, largely because of the overwhelming public support for the Accords: a survey in late 1980 found 91.7 percent in favour and only 2 percent against.[35] By the end of November, 7.5 million people had joined the union; within another six weeks, a million more joined. These included a third of all party-members, especially younger workers.[36] Near the end of 1981, the vast majority of workers belonged to Solidarity.[37] The government's continual conflicts with the union mainly served to further discredit the country's leadership and to infuriate most of the population.

> **Grzegorz Stawski:** At first, it was all about a trade union. Then the government's obstructionism broadened the range of issues that Solidarity had to deal with, and the conception of a social movement was born. People knew

---

35. Adamski et al., cited in Mason 1985, p. 93. Mason also pointed out that 58 percent of Party members supported the agreements, almost the same as in the general population (60.1 percent).
36. Mason 1985, p. 94.
37. Ibid.

who was responsible. That's why there were all those radical demands to get rid of directors.

Over time, the movement's influence increased. Aleksander Krystosiak:

By the spring of 1981, the process of divorcing the basic Party organisations from the factories had begun. It wasn't our directive to do it. It was the workers by themselves who decided that these organisations had to be got rid of.

Adam Sucharski agreed:

I could see that the Party had no control over its activists. The basic Party organisations just existed on paper; they did nothing. The provincial Party committee was just spinning its wheels.

This breakdown produced a psychological demobilisation that was felt particularly acutely within the enforcement apparatus. In the secret police, according to Sucharski:

This situation led to an oscillation of moods, almost as if the service was suffering from manic-depressive disorder. People seemed to have two faces: there was an 'official' opinion, which they presented at Party meetings; but when you met these people privately, they presented a totally different view. I believed for some time that if the Party made some concessions and followed through on the agreements, it would have a chance to control the situation. A few weeks later, I changed my opinion and started believing that it was the end. And that was true with most people.

In Gdańsk, Andrzej Jarmakowski told me that Solidarity had a contact within the secret-police who provided 'lists of secret-police workers with their names and telephone numbers':

We used that information when someone was arrested and we learned that he had been beaten by the police. We published the information that Captain such-and-such beat him, and that he lived at this address, and there was his phone number. So everybody who was listed had to change their apartment and move out.

Colonel Sucharski corroborated Jarmakowski's claim: 'We learned that they had agents among us. A lot of our workers and the militia sympathised with their ideas; so, there were leaks'. Moreover, the police had their own grievances and could not be sealed off from the rest of society. One policeman confided to the Solidarity underground press in 1983: 'We read ... the independent press with interest and hope, passing it around among ourselves. After August 1980, we also began forming an independent self-governing trade union'.[38] Karol Miller, a colonel in the Ministry of the Interior:

> I'm torn inside. My mother goes one way, my father another. They fight every time they sit down. I can see that my mother is right *and* my father is right. I know that others were being torn, just like me.

Solidarity estimated that as many as 40,000 police out of a national total of 150,000 were engaged in unionisation,[39] while whole units of the military were declaring themselves in favour of Solidarity.[40]

This trend threatened the government's ability to carry out repression. Rakowski acknowledged the government's difficulty: 'In the early months of '81, we were very weak because the Party was divided in many different ways. Therefore, at this time, we couldn't adopt a strong policy towards Solidarity'. Some Solidarity activists, like Ryszard Sawicki, encouraged this development: 'I was distributing Solidarity leaflets and periodicals not just to factory committees but also to police and the military'.

> **Andrzej Rozpłochowski:** We printed and delivered leaflets directed especially to the police. We called upon them to stop serving the system. We had great results: the first attempts to organise a free trade union of police were in Silesia.

However, when police did attempt to unionise, Solidarity activists responded warily. They worried that attempts would be made to place agents inside Solidarity. Rozpłochowski:

> A guy came to talk to me. He told me that he was a police officer and they were interested in organising a free trade union for themselves. I didn't believe him. I sent him away.

> **Aleksander Krystosiak:** The police and lower-ranking officers wanted support from Solidarity. Why? I'm not sure that all of a sudden they stopped loving the Communists and fell madly in love with Solidarity. It was a kind of calculation. They saw a new emerging power and they wanted to make an alliance with it. Three policemen told me they wanted to organise a trade union. At first, I was very withdrawn and distant.

Later, they learned that they had been wrong in their judgment. Rozpłochowski:

---

38. 1983, *UPNB*, 7: 22.
39. Garton Ash 1985, p. 237.
40. Szumowski interview.

The police did organise a union: one station organised an occupation strike of their building. I learned of it when someone told me that the station was covered with Polish flags and the police were all inside. They registered with us and had representation at the national congress, where they were very warmly greeted by the delegates. When martial law came, a lot of police who were engaged in free trade unions were arrested.

Aleksander Krystosiak: Only much, much later we learned that there was a constant struggle between the criminal police and the secret police. The secret police were like a master and the criminal police like a servant.

There probably were agents in some of these groups, but Solidarity's strength was in its openness and democratic form. No-one could stealthily lead this movement. There were no great secrets to be uncovered.[41] The movement thus had some in-built protections, as Krystosiak recalled:

It was incorruptible and impregnable against infiltration. Even stuffing our governing bodies with secret-police agents wouldn't work. We were teaching people how to demand their rights publically. We discussed making some of our moves more secret, but we decided not to do that especially because the government here works in constant secrecy.

One policeman recalled that:

Immediately after the Warsaw court rejected the motion on the registration of the union, 500 policemen were thrown out of work – the union's founders who refused to sign a declaration stating that they would discontinue their activities … On December 13 (1981), several dozen of them went on protest hunger strike at Szczecin's Warski Shipyard. And after the strike at the shipyard had been suppressed, they were interned.[42]

Premier Jaruzelski: The crisis appears to ease

The new union's influence was continuing to grow as the government's diminished. Tensions were rising in Poland due to this growing polarisation. It appeared that as each week went by, the ability of the government to use repression against the union diminished. The Soviet leaders knew what was happening: they heard a report in January 1981 that Solidarity represented a 'great force', and that the

---

41. See Cave and Latyński 1982–3, p. 64.
42. 1983, *UPNB*, 7: 22; see also Cave 1982b, p. 18.

Polish Party had 'lost a true creative link with the people'. The report warned that the Party was losing control over the mass media because the 'people who directly prepare information materials sympathise with Solidarity', and that if this situation did not change, 'the fight for public opinion will be lost'.[43]

Defence Minister Wojciech Jaruzelski became Premier. A poll in early March found 85 percent in approval,[44] as the General (and the army under his command) retained a respect that eluded all other institutions within the Communist state. Jan Ciesielski recalled: 'The people trusted Jaruzelski. They thought the situation could evolve in the direction it had in Czechoslovakia in 1968'. Jaruzelski appointed Mieczysław Rakowski as Deputy Premier, and gave him the sensitive job of dealing with Solidarity. For many years, Rakowski had been the editor of the liberal and respected weekly *Polityka*, and was a man thought to have a 'European' worldview, so this appointment could be seen as a move to achieve a *rapprochement* with the union.[45]

Premier Jaruzelski immediately called for a three-month strike moratorium. Although many recognised that the disputes were often provoked by the *nomenklatura*, people were growing tired of the continual disruptions, and many were sympathetically disposed to the General's plea. Perhaps some social calm would ease things. Moreover, all these tests of will were exhausting the workers and the society. Denis MacShane heard from a worker in the Ursus tractor factory in December 1980:[46]

> We have been on strike five times in five months...Now we are tired of strikes. I think if we were asked to strike again, we wouldn't, unless it were of exceptional importance.

Solidarity responded favourably to Jaruzelski's request.[47] Rakowski immediately began negotiations with the union and quickly made an agreement with farmers to move toward a farmers' union.[48] The gridlock of confrontation began to pull apart. Miners in Jastrzębie offered to work on all Saturdays for the three-month period. An agreement ended several student strikes. On 8 March, a plaque was erected to commemorate the repression of 1968. A dispute with hospital workers in the city of Łódź ended with an accord, as did the threat of a regional strike.[49] The truce was falling into place.[50]

---

43. Bernstein and Politi 1996, p. 256.
44. Garton Ash 1985, p. 145.
45. Szczypiorski 1982, p. 129; Sanford 1983, pp. 145–6; Wałęsa 1987, p. 180.
46. MacShane 1981, p. 59.
47. Garton Ash 1985, p. 146.
48. Wałęsa 1987, p. 181.
49. Sanford 1983, p. 153.
50. Garton Ash 1985, pp. 145–7; Sanford 1983, p. 147.

Still, the possibility of military intervention remained if Jaruzelski's efforts to pacify the country did not succeed. At about this time, as Adam Sucharski recalled, the secret police started to become re-energised. It was, he said, 'a new breeze'. Anti-Semitic propaganda began to appear, with instructions of how to tar Solidarity union leaders as Jews, while arrests and beatings of activists became more widespread.[51]

51. Barker and Weber 1982, p. 43.

Chapter Eleven
Bydgoszcz: the Turning Point

> **Andrzej Rozpłochowski:** After the Bydgoszcz provocation, I felt that I had to stand up and fight. Being humble in front of a tyrant does not protect *you*; it emboldens *him*.

There are times in the course of social movements when participants are confronted with choices, the outcome of which can have more far-reaching consequences than anyone could have anticipated. Leon Trotsky described such a moment during the 1917 February Revolution in Russia when, as he put it, the soldier was 'clearly shaking off his soldiery'.[1] He noted that while 'the psychological moment when the soldiers go over to the revolution is prepared by a long molecular process', nonetheless, 'the critical hour of contact between the pushing crowd and the soldiers who bar their way has its critical minute...when the grey barrier has not yet given way, still holds together...but already wavers, and the officer gives the command: Fire!', whereupon the soldiers then have to decide what to do. Trotsky held that these critical moments may decide 'not only the fate of the street skirmish, but perhaps the whole day, or the whole insurrection'.[2]

What happens when the dynamic of a movement shifts in direction, as one or another side gains a clear advantage? The future is then structured by this turning point. Here, Trotsky's example becomes most relevant.

---

1. Trotsky 1960, p. 386.
2. Trotsky 1960, pp. 121–2.

There may be a lengthy period of preparation, involving: changing structures; perceptions of and reactions to those changes; thinking, consciousness and changing attitudes; tactical and strategic efforts and inter-relationships – all of which could be understood as Trotsky's 'long molecular process'. But at some point, a decisive step may turn the whole balance of forces, depending on how the actors respond. Such situations create turning points in social movements, after which nothing is the same.

If turning-points are so significant, what are they, and how are we to understand them? The concept is not new in sociology, where it has long been used primarily as a way to understand life histories. The argument applies as well to macro-historical phenomena, and has been used in political science, economics and the history of science.[3] I argue here that it is also relevant in understanding social movements. Andrew Abbott claims that a turning point involves the move from one generally steady trajectory to another different trajectory.[4] 'Trajectories', he notes, 'are interlocked and interdependent sequences of events in different areas of life'. He calls them 'master narratives', comparing them to E.C. Hughes's idea of 'master statuses', which override subordinate statuses (for example, race over occupation).[5] Similarly, Abbott contends that 'a master narrative is an over-arching social process that has the character of coercing processes within it, and indeed of preventing those processes from creating combinations that disrupt it. It is this coercive characteristic that makes trajectories master narratives'.[6] While these trajectories are important, Abbott argues that:

> the 'regular' periods of the trajectories are far less consequential and causally important than are the 'random' periods of the turning points . . . precisely because they give rise to changes in overall direction; . . . they are the crucial sites of determination in the overall structure of a life course or an organisational career because they change its parameters.[7]

Abbott holds that while such a turning point often may not be discerned at the time of its occurrence, in retrospect 'it becomes clear that direction has indeed been changed'.[8] An initial lack of clarity results from the fact that a turning point itself is not instantaneous: it is itself a process that takes place through time and results from the choices that actors are forced to make when confronted with situations that demand decisions.[9] 'What defines a turning point as such is the

---

3. Abbot 1997, pp. 88–9.
4. Abbot 1997, p. 92.
5. Hughes 1945.
6. Abbott 1997, p. 93.
7. Ibid.
8. Abbott 1997, p. 88, p. 95.
9. Abbott 1997, p. 96.

fact that the turn that takes place within it contrasts with a relative straightness (both before and after)'.[10] So, Abbott argues, as a result of the turning point, afterwards things are different.

This chapter uses the concept of turning points to examine one of the key developments in the course of Solidarity's struggle with the government. Later, in the third part of the book, I will examine one other crucial turning point in that conflict.

On 4 March 1981, Jaruzelski and Kania were summoned to the Kremlin to meet with Brezhnev and much of the Soviet leadership. They were pressured to 'deal much more strictly with the Church and the "hooligans" in Solidarity'.[11] Not long after this meeting, the truce that Jaruzelski had requested began to break down. KOR was deemed the cause of Solidarity's belligerence – despite its efforts to moderate Solidarity's demands – and it was smeared as a 'Jewish' organisation.[12] Deputy Prime Minister Rakowski complained about conflicts in several cities, as well as Solidarity's criticisms of the military and the security police. A frequently-cited example was the appearance of a leaflet depicting a gallows 'with an explanation of who is going to hang from it', as well as a factory paper that wrote '90 days of Jaruzelski's government, 90 gallows for 90 leaders of the Party'. 'It is difficult', Rakowski complained, 'to call this partnership'.[13]

At this time, farmers were becoming more insistent on forming Rural Solidarity, and in this they were supported by Solidarity activists. Peasants owned 80 percent of the land and produced an even greater share of the country's food. They could, if organised, extract new concessions from the government. So the government, of course, did not wish to allow the farmers to form such an organisation. This dispute was to become the flashpoint: the events that began in the city of Bydgoszcz in north-central Poland in mid-March became discernibly *the* turning point in this struggle.

The provocation

Without regard to the authorities, farmers created their Rural Solidarity organisation, and a week later, in mid-March, they occupied the building of the Peasant Party in Bydgoszcz, demanding legal recognition of their organisation. The authorities planned a strong response. They certainly seemed to bring in the equipment for one. Bydgoszcz Solidarity wrote that soon:[14]

---

10. Abbot 1997, p. 89.
11. Bernstein and Politi 1996, p. 271.
12. Kwitny 1997, p. 386.
13. Barker and Weber 1982, pp. 40–1.
14. Persky and Flam 1982, p. 156.

The atmosphere in the city becomes tense. Trucks full of armed functionaries of the Ministry of Defence cruise the city. Inhabitants of the city hear that special military units are now stationed near Bydgoszcz. The atmosphere of fear is heightened by the closing of Poniatowski Street in the vicinity of the militia headquarters. Now... it becomes a holding area for vehicles equipped with special gear, such as water cannon.

Peasant activists, accompanied by Solidarity leaders, appeared at the meeting of the Bydgoszcz provincial council to present their case. Although Jan Rulewski, the leader of Bydgoszcz Solidarity, had received assurances from the provincial council chair that Solidarity representatives would be allowed to speak at the end of the meeting, the council suddenly adjourned. Rulewski jumped up to explain why they had come to the meeting, but the microphone was cut off. Then, the delegation refused to leave despite the mayor's demand that it do so. They asked for the right to read their *communiqué*, but the police attacked. The activists, as Solidarity reported:

are now pressed against the walls, against window frames, against railings... The shout of Antoni Tokarczuk is heard, as he is pinned against the stair railing. One of the militiamen is stuffing his mouth shut... One can hear the noise of bone joints as limbs are twisted... Two plain-clothes men lead out 68-year-old Michael Bartoszcze... Suddenly a third man comes up to him. He hits him hard across the face. One, two, three times. Then pummels him with his fists... A group of plain-clothes men is milling around [Rulewski]. They hit him blindly, wherever they can. They kick him. Whenever he falls, they pick him up and begin to beat him again... They work like machines, systematically and mercilessly... On the streets of Bydgoszcz, the patrols of the militia are cruising. Armed vehicles are seen everywhere. The atmosphere of terror will last a few days.[15]

The sight of these men with their injuries, transmitted on television, was shocking. All three of them required hospitalisation; Bartoszcze was even said to be 'near death'.[16] Solidarity activists, the general public and many Party members were enraged by this action: it was the first time since the start of the August strikes that the police had used violence.

Speculation was rife as to who had authorised this attack and for what purpose. Most felt that it was a provocation. Journalist Andrzej Krzysztof Wróblewski, who arrived in Bydgoszcz the day after the beatings to cover the events for the weekly *Polityka*, recalled:

---

15. Persky and Flam 1982, pp. 156–60.
16. MacDonald 1982, p. 19.

I asked police, who were all over the city, where was this or that street, to learn that they were not from Bydgoszcz. I asked them when they were brought to the city: it was before the incident. So, that would indicate that it was a provocation.

Wróblewski saw it as a dangerous situation:

There were no fewer than ten to fifteen thousand people on the streets, and it was clear that they were ready to do anything that was called for by one of the people beaten by the secret police. That night I called Rakowski and said, 'Mietek, the protest may spill over any moment. Send someone out here'. Rakowski said, 'Don't be naive. Do you think I don't realise the danger? I am alone here', meaning that he was surrounded by comrades who wanted a tougher line – not to negotiate with the crowd but to disperse it.

People's opinions diverged over who was the *provocateur*. While some saw it as a move on the part of the Party hard-liners to force Jaruzelski to move in their direction, a significant segment of Solidarity saw it as an attempt by Jaruzelski and the Party leadership to test Solidarity. Rakowski denied that the government bore any responsibility for the attack: 'We prayed every day for social peace, and we were not interested in such a provocation, for what reason? We had just started'. But he acknowledged that the provocation could have come from others in the apparatus: 'Maybe the secret-police', or, he suggested, 'Maybe Rulewski himself organised his own beating!' Meanwhile, as the crisis escalated, the Ministry of Internal Affairs – the site of police power – went on full alert.

Facing crisis

The pressing issue for Solidarity was working out how to respond to this situation. Solidarity activists, the general public and many Party members were angered by recent events: indeed, there was a wave of resignations from the Party. Now, with the union stressed as never before, the first serious cracks in Solidarity began to appear:[17]

Andrzej Rozpłochowski: The powerful pictures of the men being beaten were visible proof that it could happen to any of us. Government propaganda was getting more and more aggressive toward us. Many of us believed that there was only one way out of this situation: to show them we were ready to fight for our rights. Not doing anything would have given the government a clear

---

17. 'Shall We Call a General Strike?', Transcript of the Meeting of Solidarity's National Commission in Bydgoszcz, 23–24 March 1981, cited in Persky and Flam 1982, pp. 161–6.

signal that the union was unable to defend itself, and therefore, whenever they felt like it they could just go in and kick anyone they wanted.

Rozpłochowski, described as 'one of Solidarity's most radical activists',[18] and others insisted that the Solidarity National Commission meet:

> As I spoke with other regions through telexes and phones, there was the feeling that we had to call a special meeting. I knew that Wałęsa and some of the 'experts', did not want a collision with the government. But the leaders of the three most important regions – me in Katowice, Bujak in Warsaw and Lis in Gdańsk – demanded this meeting and were prepared to call it even over his veto.

Wałęsa was cautious. As Rozpłochowski recounted: 'I phoned him and said it was necessary to call a meeting of the KKP [*Krajowa Komisja Porozumiewawcza* = National Co-ordinating Committee: the Solidarity national leadership], but he absolutely refused, and the conversation turned into a quarrel. Wałęsa accused me of wanting bloodshed'. These differences became increasingly significant in the life of the union. One side feared that failure to respond forcefully would mean that Solidarity could not protect them against government repression. As one Solidarity activist put it: 'People understood that one day it was Rulewski who was beaten and tomorrow it could be you and me'. They proposed that the union threaten a general strike. KOR member and Solidarity leader Zbigniew Romaszewski recalled visiting the mines in Wałbrzych at that time: 'The miners kept saying: "stop this knocking about half an hour here, half an hour there; we are ready to go down for two weeks, but let's have peace afterwards"'.

The other side felt that the Soviet threat required the union to tread very carefully. The government had certainly suggested that a general strike could bring about Soviet intervention of a military kind.[19] They noted the potentially open-ended character of the conflict: once a general strike began, exceptions would have to be made for food production and distribution, transportation of necessary goods, steel manufacturing until the furnaces could be banked, emergency medical care and other matters. The union would have to take measures to ensure that necessities continued to be produced and were fairly distributed. In this way, such a strike would ineluctably force Solidarity to begin assuming powers ordinarily reserved for governments, and therefore to become a rival to the already-constituted government. Thus, the general strike had inherent within it an insurrectionary potential. Janusz Onyszkiewicz:

---

18. Paczkowski 2003, p. 414.
19. Paczkowski and Byrne 2007, p. 20.

If you have a general strike and the country is brought to a standstill, either you take power or another group does. Solidarity was determined not to take power, so if we called for a general strike, what if the government simply sat it out? Yet nothing short of it would work.

Rozpłochowski's account of the National Commission meeting sharply illustrates the tensions:

It was a scandalous meeting. Wałęsa and his moderate advisors and supporters tried to scare us with some bishop who talked to us about the 'dangers of what we were doing'. But most of us felt that we should make our demands upon the government, and that if we could not get what we wanted, we should be ready to carry out a general strike.

With the stakes so high, when it became clear that the majority at the meeting of the National Commission favoured a general strike, Wałęsa stormed out of the meeting, slamming the door in the process.[20]

The union demanded recognition of Rural Solidarity and punishment of those responsible for the provocation, guarantees of security for all union members, annulment of a government directive giving only half-pay to strikers, and the closure of all cases pending against people arrested for opposition activity between 1976 and 1980.[21] The negotiators were given very little latitude. In this situation, as Janusz Onyszkiewicz noted:

The negotiating team only had the authority to *negotiate* – not to make a deal. If the government refused to make concessions, they were supposed to come back to us and only *we* [the Solidarity leadership] would be able to decide what would happen next.

On 20 March, half-a-million Solidarity members in the Bydgoszcz region held a two-hour warning strike, and a week later the union carried out a similar action across the nation.[22] The National Commission (KKP) gave notice that unless there was some effective response to its demands, the union would call an open-ended general strike on 31 March. Janusz Onyszkiewicz: 'A general strike in this situation was more or less like a national uprising. It is always a very risky business'. Risky, indeed! For how would a national uprising be met? Winicjusz Gurecki: 'I was for the general strike, but at the same time, I was afraid of it. It was possible that it would end in bloodshed'. Still, the government remained resolute. When the National Commission demanded to know who was

---

20. Wałęsa 1987, p. 187.
21. Garton Ash 1985, p. 155.
22. Sanford 1983, pp. 156–7.

responsible for the outrage, and to have them punished, Rakowski refused, claiming it was a closed question. Alicja Matuszewska:

> We could not make any deal with the government. They delayed, they detoured, they did everything possible not to answer us. We talked about some issues for half a day. Then we would go out to dinner, and when we returned, there were different people to talk to. We would say, 'Let's start with what we agreed upon before dinner'. They would say, 'We don't know what you agreed upon before dinner'. There were many such cases.

As a result of this standoff, preparations for the general strike were underway. As Onyszkiewicz recalled, workers 'prepared like they were going to war'. They brought food and sleeping bags to their factories and, in some instances, they prepared weapons.[23] Instructions concerning what to do in various circumstances were duplicated and widely disseminated. Zygmunt Cieślicki said: 'We decided that sick people and women should not take part, but everyone wanted to stay, and they were angry with us for wanting them to go home'. Aleksander Krystosiak recalled: 'We had all the petrol stations under our control, all the phone-exchanges, all the cars of all the factories, and at that point society was psychologically ready for the final battle with the Communists'. Tadeusz Pławiński: 'We probably had 95 percent support to strike – even Party members. We were so sure that the strike was coming, that two ships left the shipyard the last day, even though the work was not finished because they feared that otherwise they might not get out'.

> **Władysław Frasyniuk:** We organised a strike-committee in the combined factories of *Pafawag* and *Dolmel*. It was safer there, easier to protect from possible attacks. Then we insisted on the autonomous activities of the factory commissions, so that in case the leaders were arrested, they would be able to continue on their own. We prepared bottles with acetylene gas to defend ourselves in case tanks came.

What would be the result? Rozpłochowski: 'At that time, the outcome of such a contest was by no means clear. Nor was the allegiance even of the bodies of state repression certain'. As Bujak noted, 'Party committees were declaring themselves in favour of Solidarity; many police stations were on Solidarity's side; soldiers were publically announcing that they supported Solidarity'. Ryszard Sawicki: 'I don't know what would have happened if the government had decided to resolve the strike by force because at the time, Solidarity had the support of at least half the police and the military'. Jaruzelski did not attempt to use troops, despite the urging of a majority of the Politburo.[24]

---

23. Garton Ash 1985, pp. 157–9; Persky 1981, p. 207.
24. Barker and Weber 1982, p. 43.

But Wałęsa worried that the government drew 'only one conclusion from the mobilisation: that it was itself threatened and that, within the space of twenty-four hours, the whole population would rise against it'.[25] Adding significantly to the tensions was the menace of invasion. Some one-hundred and fifty thousand troops were poised on Poland's borders.[26] Intense war-games were underway in the western area of the Soviet Union. Leszek Maleszka, a Solidarity journalist, recalled: 'Thousands of Soviet troops were relocated on Polish territory. We were getting information from US intelligence about the concentration of Soviet forces on the Polish border'. Many feared the worst if the strike actually took place.

At the height of its fear of disintegration, the government offered to meet some of Solidarity's demands. It agreed to punish those responsible for the beatings (although no punishment actually happened) and stated that Rural Solidarity could act as if it were legal. Two months later, Rural Solidarity was registered.[27] There was no mention of dropping charges from offences going back to 1976. Not all of the union's demands had been met. Would it accept the offer? Or would the conflict escalate? Now, Wałęsa announced a 'postponement' of the strike without consulting the National Commission,[28] because much had been won and the dangers of continuing the confrontation were too great to proceed: 'We weren't armed and we didn't want to fight. We would simply continue along the path we had chosen'.[29] It was, to say the least, a controversial act.

---

25. Wałęsa 1987, p. 160.
26. Bernstein and Politi 1996, p. 274.
27. Ascherson 1982, pp. 265–6.
28. The matter is a complex one. Carl Bernstein and Marco Politi state that Robert Gates, then deputy head of the CIA, claimed that Poland's Primate, Cardinal Stefan Wyszyński, 'who was dying of cancer, fell to his knees in front of Wałęsa, grabbed the coat of the Solidarity leader, and threatened to remain kneeling in prayer until death'. Wałęsa, he said, called this gesture 'emotional blackmail'. If this story is true, it sheds new light both on Wałęsa's actions and on the role of the Church; Bernstein and Politi 1996, p. 288. But Jonathan Kwitny, also citing intelligence sources including Admiral Bobby Inman (then Gates's superior at the CIA), asserts that Wyszyński went to Jaruzelski and 'dropped to his knees, took hold of [Jaruzelski's] uniform [and] begged him never to invite Soviet troops [or] use Polish troops against Polish citizens'. Did Wyszyński use this gesture twice? Have the sources been confused? Did the gravity of the situation lead him to general use of this dramatic display? Besides these encounters, apparently the Pope was engaged in some diplomacy with the Soviets via the Soviet ambassador to Italy. According to Kwitny, Wyszyński informed the Pope of the union's decision not to strike *before the decision was announced*. The Pope then suggested a no-strike pledge 'if the Soviets pledged not to invade'. They agreed. The agreement between the union and the government followed; Kwitny 1997, pp. 386–7.
29. Wałęsa 1987, p. 187.

Rifts in Solidarity

The differences within Solidarity, which hitherto had been seen as peripheral, now became central. Thirteen years later, activist Winicjusz Gurecki was still deeply affected by the experience. He had spent the evening sitting by the telex, receiving messages from factories reporting on their state of readiness all over Poland:

> A decisive majority felt that it was time. We waited all night; then when we heard on television that there would be no strike, I saw how people reacted: disbelief, crying, throwing hats on the floor, and really, really cursing Wałęsa. *My feeling was that it was the beginning of the end of Solidarity, that we had to confront the government or Solidarity would be eaten. It was either be prey or predator.* People felt betrayed.

After hearing this announcement, people rose and left. Gurecki:

> I felt that we had lost. You don't win battles by running away before you start. There is no doubt that a lot of people felt relieved, but I was just broken apart, tired, discouraged.

Many people were angered that Wałęsa had bypassed the rest of the leadership. At the subsequent meeting of the National Commission, he was bitterly excoriated for having acted without consulting either the rest of the negotiating committee or the National Commission.

> **Janusz Onyszkiewicz:** They should have called a meeting of the National Commission to present their proposal and then we could have decided what to do. But they did not. They signed an agreement, although it was not as they had been instructed, and they called off the general strike. Once they declared that the strike was over, it would be extremely difficult to say then that we thought we should go on with the strike.

In reaction, Karol Modzelewski resigned his position as Solidarity's press-spokesman, calling the agreement 'a very bad compromise'. He complained angrily about the undemocratic manner in which the matter had been handled:[30]

> The most important decision for both the union and Poland was made behind the union's back... The mechanism of decision making is... monarchic... There is a king and a court around him... and... he governs by himself and with his court.

---

30. Persky and Flam 1982, p. 170.

Andrzej Gwiazda, another long-time activist and one of the founders of the Free Trade Unions, protested that a 'dictatorship in the union is an essential (and sufficient) condition for the absorption of Solidarity by the system, returning us back to square one'.[31] He resigned his position as deputy chairman of Solidarity. Anna Walentynowicz lost her position as a union-delegate because of her vehement opposition to the agreement.[32] Małgorzata Celejewska:

> Many workers believed that the decision to call off the general strike was made by the National Commission and not just by one person. And even though they disliked it, they complied with the rules. Wałęsa's decision was the worst mistake made by Solidarity, and people were really upset with him. So was I.

Part of the reason for the differing reactions had to do with conflicting senses of what the fight was about. Wałęsa's side stressed especially the progress made in getting official recognition of Rural Solidarity. One poll showed that 92 percent of Solidarity members believed this to be the most important issue in the conflict. The Solidarity leaders who supported Wałęsa agreed with this view.

> **Onyszkiewicz:** The most important issue was not who was actually responsible for the beatings; it was the registration of Rural Solidarity. After all, the whole Bydgoszcz crisis resulted from the struggle to get these farmers registered. In this agreement, their existence was accepted as a fact. They did not get legal registration then, but the authorities agreed not to harass them and to allow them to function – which was basically an admission that they existed, and which resulted fairly soon in legal recognition.

The other side felt that the key issue was the attack itself. Alicja Matuszewska: 'Wałęsa said "I could not make the country stand still because Rulewski lost some teeth". The issue wasn't Rulewski's teeth but the union's safety in the future'. Małgorzata Celejewska: 'The clear goal of the general strike was to punish the people who were guilty of what happened in Bydgoszcz'.

> **Ryszard Sawicki:** I do not feel that the demand to register Rural Solidarity was the most important one. More important, in my view, was the demand of free access for Solidarity to the mass media, and also that those guilty of beating Rulewski be punished, or at least that there be a decent investigation into it.

Wałęsa's defenders felt that since a Soviet invasion could not be precluded, he had done the right thing. Ryszard Sawicki acknowledged that it was 'a big decision, of tremendous importance. I myself was scared'. Edward Nowak:

---

31. Barker and Weber 1982, p. 59.
32. Barker and Weber 1982, p. 44.

The general strike had to be called off. There was a real threat of Soviet military intervention. I had no illusions that the army would eventually be used.

Grzegorz Stawski: 'The most radical regions were for the general strike, but the majority were against; they were afraid of the possible consequence: civil war'. It was an issue that deeply divided Solidarity.

> Leszek Maleszka: After the agreements were signed and Wałęsa returned to Gdańsk, he was attacked by Solidarity activists, who held that his action had weakened and demobilised the union. In response, Wałęsa produced a number of telexes with messages of support for his solution to the crisis from meetings all over Poland. People were grateful to him for easing the tremendous tension.

This discussion took place throughout the country, on telex machines and phones. Alojzy Szablewski: 'Some wanted a confrontation: people were so angry that they were ready to fight with knives. But it would have meant a massacre'. He was among those who brought this discussion into the stormy meeting that the militants had demanded: 'I received many letters, especially from older people, asking that there not be a confrontation. People came and cried and asked us to call off the strike'. Polls by government- and Solidarity-sponsored institutes reported overwhelming support for Wałęsa's decision.[33]

Rozpłochowski conceded that it was a difficult decision: 'Everyone was afraid of a general strike. We all knew what the consequences could be, and none of us was eager to jump in front of a cannon to block it with our own bodies'. Nonetheless, in his view, a strike was the right thing to do:

> In each nation's history, you get to the point where these decisions have to be made, where there is a risk in taking up the fight. You get defeated, with or without honour. To call it off was a question of honour.

Rozpłochowski admitted that Wałęsa's move had mass support, but highlighted dissenting voices from elsewhere: 'Our side also had letters and telexes and documents from factories all over Poland saying that they rebuffed Wałęsa's decision'. Note Rozpłochowski's suspicion and distrust:

> None of us knows if they were *real* telexes or *fakes*. It could be that they were written in the factory *Party* committees and signed as factory *Solidarity* committees. There was no way to check.

This distrust was something new, and over the ensuing months it would only increase.

---

33. Mason 1985, p. 123.

Bydgoszcz as a turning point

It is possible that the views of both sides were correct. It is true that the demand for Rural Solidarity, which was what precipitated the crisis, was ultimately won. But backing off from the brink of the strike, regardless of whether it was necessary or not, damaged the union, leaving its members psychologically demobilised. Onyszkiewicz:

> The results were fairly good, but they were not *felt* that way, and that was very important. It was felt as a failure: that the union was stopped in its advance. The Bydgoszcz crisis was the moment we lost momentum. I think the main problem was a certain crisis of confidence in the leadership. And that was because the way the whole thing was handled by the negotiating team, and by Wałęsa in particular, resulted in a crisis.

People on both sides of this dispute believed that the union had been damaged. Whereas up until that point support for the union had been growing, afterwards the direction was reversed. Maciek Szumowski: 'Bydgoszcz was a Party success. They created an image of Rulewski as politically irresponsible, and he became the personification of this irresponsible element that they claimed existed in Solidarity and was pushing for tragedy'. Zbigniew Bujak spoke for many:

> I didn't realise the impact calling off the strike would have. Afterward, it would be impossible to threaten another general strike. It's as though someone had picked up a gun, pointed it and then didn't shoot. After that, no-one would take him seriously. If the strike had failed, you could prepare another one because we would know what had gone wrong. But having called it off, you couldn't prepare another.

The divisions that emerged in the union as a result of this crisis never healed. Rather, the internal union dynamic was now set on a new trajectory. Rozpłochowski: 'By the end of that meeting, there was one thing clear in my mind: that the biggest achievement of the Communists in the Bydgoszcz provocation was that they split our union'. Zbigniew Bogacz: 'Since Bydgoszcz, there has been a split which practically exists until now [1993]'. Andrzej Jarmakowski:

> We held ten million people in tension, and after a week to tell them to go home without giving them any reason why... There were a thousand, maybe two thousand people shouting that the Solidarity people were traitors. They shouted 'Traitors!' – at *us*!

> **Aleksander Krystosiak:** From then on, Solidarity was split. Those of us who wanted a confrontation with the communists felt that if we went into action alone, *we* would be breaking solidarity, even though solidarity was already broken. We felt that we could not win a confrontation alone.

Disagreements that had been submerged now became central to the union's dynamic.

> **Józef Pinior:** After Bydgoszcz, there was pressure from the bottom toward radical changes. At the same time, the Solidarity leaders did not want revolution, for fear of the Soviet reaction.

> **Aleksander Krystosiak:** We lost some of the army and the police because they saw that we were weak. The aggressiveness of the secret police re-emerged. They were no longer afraid to arrest you, to detain you, to interrogate you.

> **Tadeusz Jedynak:** It was the start of serious conflicts between Solidarity leaders. Some factions became more and more radical. The decisions of the centre were not respected in the regions. It was increasingly difficult for us to force Solidarity leaders on the local levels to call off strikes. We lost the unity that we had.

The feeling of defeat after these events was palpable. Alicja Matuszewska recalled her return to work the next morning:

> Can you imagine how we felt with the cheerful smiles on the officers' faces? *They* won and *we* lost. There were moments when we could not look into each other's eyes.

Moreover, she affirmed:

> After Bydgoszcz, the government spoke to Solidarity in a completely different voice. Repression against the military's civilian workers who tried to organise themselves intensified. They knew they had taken the weapon out of our hands. They felt they had won and they started fighting us openly. They spied on us; they followed us.

> **Tadeusz Pławiński:** Bydgoszcz was the beginning of the end. After that, we weren't able to negotiate anything to our advantage. Anything we tried to gain with any government office, industry, the Party – everything went down the drain.

> **Małgorzata Celejewska:** When the strike was called off, the atmosphere changed completely. They felt defeated. You could see that not just among the people, but also in the organisation of the union itself. For example, when I went to the headquarters of the regional commission, I saw complete chaos there. No-one knew what they were supposed to do.

A sense of how things were changing can be gleaned in the fact that shortly after these events, on 1 April, meat-rationing commenced; the rationing later spread to butter and grain products, and later still to a variety of other commodities, including alcohol and cigarettes.[34] The limited access to these products created more distress and tension.

A measure of the outcome of this clash between the government and the union could be seen in the popular mood. Before Bydgoszcz, people were solicitous of one another. But in its aftermath, they were increasingly inclined to bark at one another. Aleksander Krystosiak: 'If you went to an office before Bydgoszcz, the clerks felt obliged to be nice. After Bydgoszcz, they returned to their routines: you would get into the bus and someone would yell at you'. However, one should not make too much of this trend, because such levels of incivility did not approach anything like what had existed before the strikes that had established Solidarity. Of course, the authorities sought to take advantage of this turn. As Jan Cieślicki noted:

> After the strike had been called off, there was strong propaganda on television by the Party. They concentrated on the main leaders of Solidarity, revealing how many times they had been married, how many houses they owned, how much money they got from the West. People thought that there could be truth in the propaganda, and they were not as trusting of Solidarity as they had been before.

The view from above

While the Solidarity activists felt that they had lost ground and that the government was increasing its control, government leaders saw the union as being more aggressive. Rakowski argued that after Bydgoszcz, Solidarity had ceased to be merely a social movement and was now seeking power. According to a report by Soviet Marshall Viktor Kulikov, Warsaw Pact Commander-in-Chief, immediately following the Bydgoszcz crisis Kania claimed that the Party was too weak to lead an offensive against Solidarity (although Jaruzelski was reported to believe that 'the Polish party and state leadership had won a strategic battle in Bydgoszcz').[35] As the Soviets saw it, Solidarity had gotten what it wanted, namely, acceptance of a union for farmers and a promise on the part of the government to investigate and punish police who had attacked the Solidarity activists. Two days after the resolution of the Bydgoszcz crisis, Brezhnev informed the Soviet Politburo that 'a counter-revolution is taking the offensive on all fronts'. After dressing down Kania, Brezhnev reported on the phone:

---

34. Paczkowski and Byrne 2007, p. 22.
35. 'East German Report of Discussion with Marshal Viktor Kulikov', in Paczkowski and Byrne 2007, pp. 249–50.

Comrade Kania acknowledged that they had acted weakly, that they needed to be tougher...I told him: 'But how many times have we told you [that] you needed to take decisive measures, that you mustn't forever be giving in to "Solidarity". You all insist on the peaceful way, not understanding or not wanting to understand that the sort of "peaceful way" you support can lead to bloodshed'.

Yuri Andropov, head of the KGB and a member of the Soviet Polish Commission, was equally grim in his assessment: 'Solidarity is now starting to grab one position after the other. If an extraordinary session of the Polish parliament is called, then there's no excluding the possibility that it will be completely in the hands of the representatives of Solidarity, and at that point, in a bloodless coup, they will take power into their hands'.[36] The next day, 3 April, Kania and Jaruzelski were summoned to a meeting in the Soviet Union that lasted most of the night, during which Yuri Andropov and Dmitri Ustinov, the Soviet Minister of Defence, demanded stronger action on their part and threatened intervention if matters did not improve.[37]

It is easy to understand why the Soviets put pressure on their Polish 'comrades'. And it is also easy to comprehend the fears of the Polish leaders as to what might happen if they didn't handle the situation to the Kremlin's satisfaction. I asked Rakowski about the threat of a Soviet invasion:

There was a real threat. Don't forget that Jaruzelski and I belong to the generation that saw the events of '68 in Czechoslovakia. For our generation, the vision that we would have a new cemetery was the most important factor. I have no documents in my hand, nor have I seen any, saying that the Soviets planned an invasion. But I think a responsible politician had to take into account that this invasion was possible.

It may be that Soviet pressure prevented the government from following through on its promise to find and punish those responsible for the beatings. If so, we have a picture of a leadership that was simply responding to the pressures on all sides. Moreover, if Bydgoszcz was a provocation, then the investigation would have run counter to the interests of the responsible parties.

Everyone looked at the matter through his or her own lens. From the point of view of the government, the Party and the secret police, the Bydgoszcz affair was not a turning point; rather, it was just another in a series of conflicts that were tearing apart the fabric of society. They apparently did not perceive the impact that these events had on the Solidarity activists. As Rakowski noted:

36. Bernstein and Politi 1996, pp. 276–8.
37. Bernstein and Politi 1996, pp. 279–84.

Before we signed the Warsaw Agreement on 31 March, there was a discussion about what could happen, that this could be the beginning of some clash between Solidarity and the Party. But the Bydgoszcz affair was over. It was not an important subject in the next months because starting from April the Party was involved in its own problems: the Party Congress. The Party units discussed less about Solidarity and much more about the situation in the Party: leadership, democracy.

But the Bydgoszcz events had a bigger impact on the Party than they first realised.

Chapter Twelve
The Party at War with Itself

> **Maciek Szumowski:** The Party was the army through which Moscow controlled Poland. So, it was extremely important for Moscow to know that the Party did not fall apart.

> **Leszek Maleszka:** The Party apparatus interpreted Solidarity activities as counter-revolution. People at the highest level had dirty hands. They were suspected of embezzlement of public funds. So the Party apparatus felt itself threatened by the situation of dual power. A competitive source of power was emerging.

Solidarity had come to represent the nation in a far more meaningful way than the Party ever had. Given Solidarity's extensive following and influence, even in a would-be totalitarian country like Poland, the state had limitations to its power. Modern analyses of social movements have appropriately employed the concept of *political opportunity structure*. Such structures are seen to either constrain or enable a movement's development and mobilisation.[1] One of the key variables usually considered here is the role of the state, which is seen as constraining or facilitating social movements. The analyst asks: has its control weakened for some reason? Does it repress, attempt to co-opt, or is it willing to accommodate the social movement's demands?

---

1. Kriesi et al. 1995; McAdam, McCarthy and Zald 1996; Tarrow 1998.

Less often considered, in this calculus, is whether the state itself is subject to the constraints of political opportunity structure by the social movement it confronts. In the unusual situation of mass upheaval that confronted the Polish state from August 1980 until the military coup in December 1981, the Party/state was limited in its options for a lengthy period. Therefore, it was not free simply to choose whether to repress or not, and instead was forced to struggle with the new social support that was enjoyed by Solidarity. This struggle took place not just between Solidarity and the Party, but also within the Party itself: the Party came to have a significant constituency that supported the social movement outside of the Party, and that drew support from that movement. Until the conflict between this tendency and the rest of the Party was resolved, the Party and state leadership were limited in their options.

On 24 August 1980 – one day after serious talks began in Gdańsk – the battle over the future direction of the Party began. There was a major reshuffle of the government, and many of Gierek's allies fell, thus handing the strikers their first victory. Soon after the accords were signed, Gierek, too, was ousted from office. Who was to replace him? It soon became evident that there were different factions within the Party; they deeply disagreed over how to respond to the challenge presented by Solidarity. The centrists, led by Stanisław Kania, Gierek's successor, sought to carry out some of the Accords and thereby regain social standing for the Party. The Party simply could not afford to consider the hard-line strategy at that time.[2] Kania reportedly said that the Party could not use force. Maciek Szumowski said of Kania: 'He remembered the shootings in Gdańsk. He was very clearly against any kind of use of force'. Perhaps because she had been an eyewitness to the killings in Gdynia in 1970, Alicja Matuszewska saw the matter more starkly:

> The nation had stood them up against the wall so they had no choice. They could either shoot us (and there were too many of us) or compromise. This concession was essentially playing for time.

For the moment, the compromisers were dominant. The fact that the Party negotiated with the strikers was acknowledgment of an entirely new situation. Members of the Polish *nomenklatura* felt menaced by this movement, and they strongly opposed it.[3] However, there was also a reformist wing that sought an accommodation with Solidarity, as Dorota Terakowska, a well-known political journalist, recounted:

---

2. Ascherson 1982, p. 162.
3. Sanford 1983, p. 83.

Our opposition was aimed at the Party apparatus – the people who hold steady jobs, who work at the Central Committees at various levels, working out and applying the Party line – professional officials. *We fought for the preservation of Solidarity because it was the only organisation with broad enough popular support to control the Party.*

These opposing factions disagreed over whether and how quickly the agreements should be fulfilled, how much of the Party officialdom should be purged and how to relate to Solidarity.[4]

The Solidarity leadership perceived these divisions, as Janusz Onyszkiewicz noted:

The [Party] reformers saw a chance to change the functioning of the whole political system. Another group, the majority, wanted to 'domesticate' the Solidarity movement. They tried to use the British method of absorbing the leading figures into the establishment and giving favours such as cars, secretaries, offices. The third group felt they had their backs to the wall, so: 'We must sign anything, but later we will try to crush them'.[5]

The factions other than the reformers hoped to ride this social movement until its force was spent. Apparently, at one point Kania suggested to the Politburo that Solidarity might be absorbed into the system, as he referred to a 'compromise of a structural kind'.[6] Zbigniew Regucki, as Kania's Chief of Staff, was the most highly-placed official with ties to the reform-movement. He told me:

When Solidarity started questioning the Party domains like the press, censorship, the Party as the representative of the working class, it provoked two responses. One was fear; the other was to hope for the reaction of the Soviet Union: would they intervene or not? Opinions expressed by Party apparatus members: Solidarity was a competitive power source to the Party and would gradually assume all the powers that had hitherto belonged to the Party.

---

4. Sanford 1983, pp. 87–8. For a compelling example of shifting factions forming in a leadership group when confronted with a powerful social movement, and for a discussion about how the administration at the University of California at Berkeley responded to the social movements of the 1960s, see Smelser 2010.

5. George Sanford saw a breakdown of the Party during the Sixth Party Plenum in October 1980 that was similar to Onyszkiewicz's; Sanford 1983, pp. 92–3. He reported that in a briefing to top security men in Silesia in early 1981, Party leaders acknowledged that they had acquiesced to the workers' demands because they had no choice: 'The aim was to quench the strikes, calm the nation and consider the situation later'; Sanford 1983, p. 67. Years after, in 1983, Jerzy Kołodziejski, the former Governor of the Gdańsk province and one of the signatories of the Gdańsk Agreement of 1980, stated: 'The authorities suffered from the conviction, based on past experience, that such agreements could be broken with impunity'; 1983, *UPNB*, 17: 4.

6. Paczkowski 2003, p. 415.

Solidarity was viewed as a serious threat by the majority of the Party apparatus. They charged that the union aimed at breaking the Soviet system from within. Kania could not disregard the powerful neighbour that we have.

The Party/state had little organic attachment to society, whose distrust was such that Admiral Janczyszyn, head of the Navy, was forced to swear that the armed forces would not be used against the workers[7] – a promise that was ultimately belied. Given that it ruled not by consent but rather by *raison d'état* (read: Soviet tanks), what strategy could the Party leadership have? By now, both its ideology and promise of prosperity were discredited. These issues were wrenching the Party apart. From the August strikes that first won the right of workers to organise themselves independently, through to the shock of martial law, around a million people quit – one-third of the Party's membership. That lurch outward was heavily concentrated among workers and young people, a sign that the Party was losing touch not just with its base, but also with the future.

Worse still from the point of view of the *nomenklatura*, in seeking to improve the Party's social standing, Kania announced that Party officials who had misused their offices to enrich themselves would be investigated. Within just ten weeks of the Gdańsk and Szczecin Accords being signed, one-third of the District First Secretaries and prefects had been replaced, and people were demanding more.[8] Charges of corruption played a role in the resignations of the First Secretaries in Wrocław, Tarnów, Koszalin and Radom.[9] Some of their replacements were Solidarity members.[10]

Thus, a threat that had originated *outside* had now extended *into* the Party itself. Regucki: 'There were plenty of Party activists, usually at the level of the provincial Party committees, who really hoped that the system would become more democratic'. These differences brought about contradictory policies as the different factions vied with each other. For instance, the new chief of propaganda, the liberal former First Secretary of the Party in Krakow, Józef Klasa, permitted pro-Solidarity journalists a good deal of leeway in their reporting, while Olszowski, the national head of censorship, demanded that the media carry the Party line.[11]

Many Party members were so disillusioned that they just quit. By March 1981, over two hundred thousand had already abandoned their Party membership.[12] Many Party members joined Solidarity without concern for Party policy. Witold

---

7. Garton Ash 1985, p. 48.
8. Ascherson 1982, p. 200.
9. Hahn 1987, p. 291, n. 36.
10. Hahn 1987, pp. 58–61.
11. Kasprzyk interview.
12. Garton Ash 1985, p. 170.

Sułkowski, a Solidarity leader in Łódź, recalled that Party members were 'loyal to Solidarity and took the union's side during any conflicts with the authorities'.[13]

But for a long time most remained in place – some out of inertia, some because they were not yet ready to give up on the Party, while for others, like journalists, leaving the Party also meant leaving their profession. A significant number stayed in the Party because they were asked to do so by Solidarity activists who wished to have both inside information concerning the Party's activities and influence on the Party's direction. Stanisław Płatek, one of these Party members, recalled:

> I wanted to leave the Party the moment I joined Solidarity. But Solidarity persuaded Party members not to leave. They wanted to know what was going on in the Party.

Party reformers demanded free and open elections and massive purges of the so-called '*betons*' – 'cement-heads' – meaning dogmatic hard-liners. They fought to give Solidarity space. Maciek Szumowski edited the Kraków Party newspaper at that time:

> We, the party-opposition, wanted to give life to the Gdańsk agreement. We wanted the Party to negotiate with Solidarity. The movement *outside* the Party gave strength and protection to the dissidents *within* the Party. The only safeguard for the reforms was the fact that Solidarity existed. We knew that without it, the Party would not change much. So we fought to strengthen Solidarity, not to assume power within the Party. We saw ourselves connected with Solidarity. That I could survive as chief-editor of the Kraków Party paper I owed to the support of Solidarity and the Party grassroots, who heavily supported our paper. I had several visits from tough *apparatchiks* from the Warsaw Central Committee, who came to Kraków to fire me. But each time they learned what the reaction of the Party masses in the larger factories in Kraków would be if I were fired: they would strike. So, they couldn't fire me. It was a cold political calculation.

> **Krzysztof Kasprzyk:** The Party Congress had just been held in February of 1980, but rank-and-file members were already demanding a new congress. There were hundreds of resolutions from Party organisations of the lowest level: in the academic world, in the factories, and so on. Also, some grassroots party-cells began to communicate between themselves.

---

13. Cave and Latynski 1982–83, p. 62.

This stance forced Szumowski and his collaborators into open conflict with Party conservatives: 'We were charged with acting as agents of Solidarity in the Party when we were expelled'.

For a while, the Party reformers appeared to be a real contender for power. They assaulted the *nomenklatura* principle. Stefan Bratkowski, one of the best-known Party reformers, asserted that Gierek had encouraged 'thieves and embez-zlers', and that the Party was run as an oligarchy.[14] Krzysztof Kasprzyk insisted: 'We wanted to push reforms from within the Party, which was perceived by the people as the major source of all problems. We said that the *nomenklatura* must be abolished in most aspects of social life'. This was a battle that the Party leadership affirmed from the very beginning that it could not afford to lose: 'We cannot give up the *nomenklatura* mechanism',[15] they insisted. Some Solidarity leaders, including Zbigniew Bujak, who were aware of these strains, saw the Party reformers as allies:

> We were looking for people from the other side to make an agreement. With the Party first secretaries from Gdańsk and Poznań, an agreement was pos-sible. The horizontal structures in the Party [see below] were certainly ele-ments with which we could have discussions.

The Party reform-movement

By autumn, Party reformers in Kraków were already organised into caucuses. Kasprzyk recalled:

> Hard-liners talked all the time about democratic centralism. We felt that the Party must evolve toward a more alive political structure. We discussed end-lessly what should be done to prevent the full-time bureaucrats from dominat-ing the Party, like limiting *apparatchiks* to one or two terms.

Almost immediately the reformers began to demand a new Party Congress in order to force through changes.[16] The conservatives sought to postpone it for as long as possible, so that, as Szumowski put it, 'the wave of support for Solidarity would abate and the balance would shift again in favour of the conservatives. We insisted on calling the elections earlier – while the wave of support was still prevailing'.[17]

---

14. Sanford 1983, p. 76.
15. Staniszkis 1984, pp. 217–18.
16. Kasprzyk interview.
17. Sanford 1983, p. 144.

There were significant indications of the impact of Solidarity within the Party. In Toruń, the 'horizontal movement' began to formalise and provide a theoretical framework for local Party organisations to meet and collaborate. This normally-tabooed form of organisation in a Party which was organised vertically – so that the centre communicated directly with the Party bodies, without the latter communicating with one another – had the potential to form a substantial counterweight to the leadership. This movement, whose form was influenced by Solidarity's inter-factory committees, spread by example and emerged independently by other names elsewhere.[18] By December 1980, there were such linkages in 17 of the 49 provinces, centred especially in the big cities.[19] Zbigniew Iwanow, the leader of this movement in Toruń, had led the strike that established Solidarity in the Towimor ship-machinery plant in that city. After the strike, he won control of the local Party organisation, and he and his colleagues created an inter-factory Party commission. Within a few months, 7,000 of the city's 17,000 Party members were affiliated to the commission. This movement was perceived in very stark terms. Yuri Andropov, who before long became one of a group of rapidly expiring Soviet leaders, said that the horizontal movement would 'lead...to the collapse of the Party'.[20] Zbigniew Regucki explained why he felt this way:

> The horizontal structures were a threat to the centralist idea of the Party. They were treated as an attempt to break the Party from within, since they initiated a discussion regarding the Party's prerogatives, and how the Party apparatus should be elected.

Iwanow was soon expelled from the Party, but the Towimor members re-elected him as First Secretary anyway, thereby defying the Party leadership. They then presented a list of demands, which included: free, secret and competitive elections, with at least two candidates at all levels; acceptance of the horizontal structures, with organised factions permitted; term-limits and a ban on multiple office-holding; and separation of the Party from the government. One item – namely, punishment of the 'guilty in recent years', – threatened the position of some powerful members of the *nomenklatura*. How could they respond to this rebellious attitude? For the moment, they had to accept it.

The comrades in Toruń were not alone. In Łódź, the horizontal movement commission said the Party was 'so compromised that transformation is not

---

18. Garton Ash 1985, p. 171.
19. Jerschina interview.
20. 'Transcript of CPSU CC Politburo Meeting', cited in Paczkowski and Byrne 2007, p. 276.

possible; it can neither regain the confidence of society nor renew itself'.[21] In the town of Kolbuszowa, the mayor was jailed, the First Secretary wanted to resign, and no-one wished to replace them.[22] In the Gdańsk Shipyard, rank and file members took control of the Party organisation, which then became openly hostile to the central leadership. Around the country, worker-members complained about the Party's lack of internal democracy.[23] It became increasingly difficult to keep internal debates secret. In several places, reformers had control of important city and provincial positions.

As the reform-movement was growing, liberal party secretaries felt the need to co-operate. They may also have approved of its activity, but they had never tried and could never have succeeded in reforming the Party without Solidarity. Tadeusz Fiszbach, the First Secretary in Gdańsk, had sought a *rapprochement* with the strikers from the beginning. 'We need a new Party', he avowed, apparently genuinely moved by the determination to reconstruct the nation politically, economically and morally.[24] In Kraków, the First Secretary appointed a special commission to collect proposals for Party reforms. It received hundreds of resolutions from all over Poland. All of this activity profoundly worried the Party leadership, according to Rakowski, who said that the 'centre was a prisoner of the old dogmas: that any group in the Party was a danger'. Szumowski noted: 'When the mass of words were put aside, the most important difference that emerged in the Party was negotiations versus the use of force'. I commented to Szumowski that it was a difference drawn in blood. He responded:

> Yes, it was very dramatic. It was our opinion that it would be better to break up the existing structures from within than to attempt to set up structures outside the system. That meant we tried to get control over Party newspapers rather than to create a new political party.

They had few other realistic choices. Jan Jerschina was one of those active in these discussions:

> We discussed whether we should organise a new political party. But we would have lost half of our followers, who were not prepared to take such a drastic step, which would weaken the reformers who stayed in the Party; and we ourselves would be very weak because it was too late to organise another party.

---

21. Garton Ash 1985, pp. 98–9, 171–2; Ascherson 1982, pp. 201–2; Persky 1981, pp. 155–6.
22. Szumowski interview.
23. Garton Ash 1985, p. 117, pp. 170–1.
24. Persky 1981, p. 145; Goodwyn 1991, p. 223.

Journalists

Many journalists supported reform, and the party-leaders had difficulty in rein-forcing the Party line to the population through their regular communication links. There was intense conflict over what they called 'propaganda'. For example, when Krzysztof Kasprzyk returned to Kraków from vacation on 30 August, the eve of the signing of the Accords, he immediately saw 'lots of typical propaganda rhetoric, more and more pressure to publish things against the strikes, like commentaries of "deep concern" about what might happen if the strikes went on. But we resisted'.

Reformers took over the Journalists' Union both in the nation and in many local areas, so that the press opened up considerably. Kraków journalists, as Kasprzyk noted, 'called an extraordinary meeting to try to push a new character into the media, censorship, relations with the party, everything'. They did not join Solidarity, but, instead, opted to 'renew' the official trade union. But this 'renewal' brought little comfort: many journalists felt that Party policy destroyed their standing and damaged their ability to do their jobs, and they were determined to alter this situation. Kasprzyk:

> The credibility of the media was extremely low. We wanted to end the propaganda of success, control by the Party *apparatchiks* and officials, censorship. Some one hundred and fifty journalists from Kraków unanimously adopted a resolution which included: sympathy for the working class and a welcome to the new trade unions; freedom of the press and an end to censorship; democratisation; an extraordinary congress of the Polish Journalists' Union. We demanded that the whole resolution be published the next day in the Kraków newspapers. It was revolutionary.

The Party later expelled Stefan Bratkowski, who had been its own candidate to lead the union.[25] Soon, a petition circulated nationally that called for an extraordinary congress of the Polish Journalists Association. The 'renewed union' was obviously affected by the horizontal movement: it adopted elements of the horizontal approach, as Krzysztof Kasprzyk recalled: 'Horizontal communication between media communities all over Poland began, mostly among younger journalists, [aged] 28 to 40, who had previously had some trouble with censorship or the apparatus'. In the midst of this conflict, Solidarity's influence obviously extended more deeply into the Party, as its supporters engaged the leadership in open debate.

The *apparatchiks* felt besieged by the internal and external opposition. From the Soviet perspective, this trend was very dangerous. In a letter to the Polish

---

25. Report on the meeting from Kasprzyk interview.

United Workers' Party Central Committee, they stated that 'the adversary has gained control over the mass media, most of which have become the instrument of anti-socialist activities . . . The Party has not won the battle as long as the press, radio and television work not for the PUWP but for its enemies'.[26]

An example of how this battle was played out is evident in the conflict over Maciek Szumowski's appointment as editor of the Kraków Party newspaper *Gazeta Krakowska*, after his predecessor, Zbigniew Regucki, had left to become Kania's chief of staff:

> When Solidarity appeared, the Party suddenly had to find people who had popular trust to move to the front line. Suggesting me was a calculated risk on Regucki's part. I took the job because of the pressure of colleagues and friends – I was not looking for a position in the hierarchy.

Szumowski saw a unique opportunity in this offer:

> Solidarity created a chance to make a better press. I knew it was a big risk to accept this position: I would either have to turn my back on all my journalistic achievements or I would have a collision with the system – and I was aware that I would lose. I decided to publish a good paper and to defend my moral credibility up front. So, I had to assume my own defeat from the start.[27]

He turned *Gazeta Krakowska* into an independent journal that quickly became an organ of the reformers. He brought the Party's disagreements into the open, thereby informing the public about them and enabling that same public to influence Party policy:

> *Gazeta Krakowska* presented the opinions of both the hard-liners and the moderates. We ran them on the front page. Such factional fighting in the socialist countries is usually played behind the scenes. The *official* press *extracted* all the elements which indicated the existence of factions within the Party, while *we* took the full texts and printed them out. This Party usually has a monopoly over the whole spectrum of political life; then it had to make allowances for public opinion.

For example, Szumowski's exposés of the environmental damage caused by the *Huta Skawina* aluminium factory forced the factory to close within a few months.[28] *Gazeta Krakowska* came to be widely respected and sought after throughout Poland:

---

26. Paczkowski and Byrne 2007, p. 296.
27. Sanford 1983, p. 65.
28. Garton Ash 1985, p. 138.

We created something new in this system: a local party-paper whose duty was not only to inform about the Party but also about Solidarity and the current situation in the country. Isn't it strange? *It was the official organ of the local Communist Party, but its new, open policy made it the unofficial, un-named Solidarity organ.* The reds had claimed that the socialist press represented the nation. Then it became true. The people who stood in long lines every morning to buy this paper claimed it as their very own.

By all accounts, the claim that people queued to get the paper is true. Under Szumowski as editor, it may have been the most widely-circulated daily paper in Poland at that time.

It soon became evident that Szumowski and his colleagues were regarded as enemies by Party loyalists:

Gazeta Krakowska followed a formula of dialogue and a search for compromise. And because the authorities more and more damaged this dialogue, our sympathy shifted more and more toward Solidarity. The hard-liners in the Politburo called us the official organ of Solidarity and of the Bishop of Kraków. We printed their opinion in the paper and answered it. So we openly debated the decision-makers of Poland.

Szumowski's strategy of bringing Party business into the open, limited the hard-liners' room to manoeuvre: 'The workers supported the more moderate line and the message was telexed from factories to the centre. So for a while, hardly anyone spoke openly in favour of confrontation with Solidarity'. Szumowski openly defied the Party leadership. When Stefan Bratkowski was expelled for his activity as head of the Journalists' Union, Szumowski publicy challenged the decision:

I published an open letter defending Bratkowski, demanding that he and people like him be kept within the Party. So I broke Party discipline. Then, we published the local Party committee's and others' responses. *The Party had to respond to the opinion of the editor of its own official organ, thus giving proof that they had lost control of the paper.*

The *nomenklatura* was plainly frustrated with its inability to undermine Solidarity, whose authority and stature rose as it responded to each challenge placed before it, while the morale of the Party loyalists fell. The population was growing angrier with the evident refusal of the government to fulfil the promises embodied in the Accords. Meanwhile, the hard-liners increasingly demanded that rank-and-file Party members carry the line. Kasprzyk, as the leader of the Journalists' Union in Kraków, felt these pressures with particular intensity:

We were in a very tough position, walking on a tightrope, because we tried to embody the values of Solidarity, but we had to deal with the Party. Sometime in February or early March, ten of us were summoned to Stefan Olszowski's office at the Central Committee in Warsaw. It was an extraordinary meeting that lasted some four or five hours. We said that we didn't want to undermine the position of the Party or to remove the Party as our political sponsor; we simply understood the role of the media in a different way than these bastards. We weren't trying to make people more radical; *we simply didn't want to lie any more*. But Olszowski saw that as meaning that the media were escaping Party control, as happened in Czechoslovakia in '68, so we realised that our position was very delicate.[29]

Olszowski was under serious pressure from the Soviet Union. In January 1981, Leonid Zamyatin, head of the Soviet Central Committee's Department of International Information and a member of the Soviet committee on the Polish crisis, visited Katowice. According to a Polish report on the visit, while there 'Comrade Zamyatin emphasised several times, outside of official meetings as well, that he did not understand why the party did not act firmly to isolate the enemy. According to him this is particularly needed in the mass media'.[30]

Counter-attack

The Party leadership was being challenged from two sides: on the one side by Solidarity supporters within their ranks, and on the other by Party *apparatchiks* who felt their positions were under threat. As early as September 1980, lower-level Party functionaries revealed their anger about the concessions made to Solidarity.[31] They sometimes took action against the union on their own. For example, the Party First Secretary in Częstochowa proclaimed a local state of emergency to prevent the registration of Solidarity,[32] while the former Warsaw First Secretary sought to organise the *apparatchiks* against Kania's policies.[33] By November, the hard-liners were beginning to reassert themselves within the

---

29. George Sanford reported that the Party had a very hard line on this matter: 'Polish Communists had always stressed, in private conversation with me during the 1970s, that the main mistake in the Prague Spring had been their noisy mass media and that they would not allow this to happen in Poland'; Sanford 1983, p. 58.

30. 'PUWP CC Report on Leonid Zamyatin's Visit to Katowice', cited in Paczkowski and Byrne 2007, p. 180.

31. Sanford 1983, p. 69; Hahn 1987, p. 64.

32. Sanford 1983, p. 108.

33. Sanford 1983, p. 110.

Central Committee. Żabiński, a Politburo member, laid out a strategy to corrupt Solidarity leaders by according them privileges and status.[34]

But upheavals in January once again demonstrated the strength and determination of the Solidarity movement, and strengthened the hand of the Party reformers.[35] By early February, when Jaruzelski ascended to the premiership, forces in favour of an early Party Congress were reaching a crescendo. Solidarity activists were charged with using the union to destabilise the Polish society and economy. Politburo member Kazimierz Barcikowski told a meeting of Party activists: 'Don't be afraid to use polarising methods!'[36]

Szumowski became a target. Since they dared not fire him, they instead tried to buy him off:

> At a party, with much liquor flowing, they offered me a position in Rome. They said my wife could go, too, and also be a writer there, and that we would be paid in dollars.[37] I told them to fuck off.

Then, they attempted to destroy him by going after his adolescent daughter:

> I wasn't rich, but my daughter was in the worst period of immaturity. One evening, a security officer came and told me that she had been captured during an attempt to hijack a plane, armed with a hand grenade and a pistol. The plane had been surrounded by the anti-terrorist military units. The girl and two boys were led out and a press conference was called on the spot. My daughter was interviewed on tape. They made it appear that the whole thing was because her parents were busy with the newspaper and paid her no attention. The tapes were then copied and hundreds of cassettes were sent to factories for people to hear.

But this scheme was undercut because of Solidarity's widespread support. Szumowski:

> Many prosecutors who belonged to Solidarity had the courage to oppose the secret police. The criminal police and the secret police hated each other. The

---

34. Sanford 1983, p. 65, p. 67.
35. Sanford 1983, p. 128.
36. Staniszkis 1984, pp. 73–4.
37. To appreciate the significance of this offer, it is necessary to understand the significance of dollars in Poland at that time. They were a most coveted commodity. On the black market (which was quite open) a dollar was worth a great deal. Many wages translated into less than $100.00 a month or even considerably less. In 1988, for example, it cost about one dollar (at the black market rate) for a full meal at the best restaurants in the finest hotels. Everyone wanted them. One of the most coveted benefits was to be sent abroad so as to be able to earn dollars. Some Poles who spent their working lives in America would return to Poland after they retired. Their social-security benefits permitted them to live quite well there.

criminal police found out that the grenade was made of wood. It had been prepared for students to use during lessons. The young man who started the whole thing was an acquaintance of hers. He co-operated with the police because earlier he had, while drunk, stolen his father's car and had an accident. So the police had something on him. They forced him to improvise this game and to draw in Kasia. It turned out to be a primitive provocation on the part of the security office in Kraków. She was still expelled from school.

Bydgoszcz

The Bydgoszcz events were just as pivotal to the conflict within the Party, whose divisions became deeper and more visible,[38] as they were to the struggles between Solidarity and the Party, and those within Solidarity itself. Mieczysław Gil: 'Before Bydgoszcz, the Party hadn't demanded that we declare ourselves either for the union or the Party'. Now, the Party leadership demanded that its members leave Solidarity, and that they refuse to participate in the Solidarity warning strike on 27 March.[39] But there were very few who heeded this appeal.

> **Leszek Maleszka**: Lower-ranking Party members supported Solidarity. The Tarnów committee, one of the factories to which I was connected, said: 'Until the matter is settled, we suspend our allegiance to the Central Committee'. It was unheard of before for such a low-level body openly to declare its independence from the Party leadership.

Tarnów's action was joined by many factory Party organisations. Local First Secretaries and worker-members on the Party Central Committee were among those who opposed the Politburo's orders.[40] At the March Party plenum, Kania announced that he had 350 local Party resolutions and angry calls for changes in the Politburo, with some insisting that the whole body resign and demanding a fuller explanation of the Bydgoszcz events.[41] Party members in the Gdańsk shipyard occupied the same building the strikers had taken over in August, and sent telexes of protest to the Central Committee. They were still there nine days later, at which point Kania showed up to endure a seven-hour barrage of complaints. Activists especially charged that the leadership represented only the apparatus, from which half of it came, with another 25 percent drawn from managers, although these groups made up only 5 percent of the Party membership.

---

38. Hahn 1987, pp. 90–1.
39. Garton Ash 1985, p. 157; Staniszkis 1984, p. 190.
40. Garton Ash 1985, pp. 157–9; Persky 1981, p. 212; Goodwyn 1991, p. 296.
41. Sanford 1983, p. 158; Hahn 1987, pp. 96–104.

The reformers were finally able to set a mid-July date for the Extraordinary Party Congress.[42] Democratic election rules would prevail: secret elections with all candidates able to compete. The *Horizontal Movement* continued to grow. In a plenary session of the Party, the hard-liners tried to change direction. But, as Szumowski noted: 'The workers in a mass supported the more moderate line and support for the moderates was telexed from factories to the centre. The telexes were constantly running'. This intervention was decisive: 'The matter was decided within hours in a more peaceful way'.

Preparing for the Party Congress

So it appeared that the Party reformers were becoming stronger. This sense was strengthened when the horizontal movement held a national conference which called for, among other things, an end to censorship and guarantees that democracy would be respected in choosing delegates to the Party Congress.[43] With the date for the Congress set, the apparatus and its opposition struggled over a broad range of issues, including how delegates would be elected to the Congress, what programme the Congress would adopt, what should be the relationship between the Party and the government, and who would be elected to key positions. In many places, the Party was becoming democratised from below.

> **Szumowski:** Normally, the Party committee would go, say, to the *Nowa Huta* steel mill and suggest ten people as delegates and would then read out the names. Then the audience could add a few more names. But the Gdańsk and Kraków Party committees proposed that every factory with over one thousand Party members should convene its workers and simply allow them to propose candidates. Knowing that if direct elections were held, people who supported Solidarity would be chosen, the Central Committee delayed accepting such a democratic procedure. But the Gdańsk and Kraków committees conducted their own elections and elected representatives for the Party Congress, presenting the Central Committee with a *fait accompli* – also an exception in the system.

During this period, the reformers had considerable influence:

> For a few months, the totalitarian Party had to reckon with pressure put on them by non-Party members. *Gazeta Krakowska* had considerable influence on the delegates coming from other factories; we could expose the hard-liners and thus contribute to their defeat, and promote those who were more liberal.

---

42. Hahn 1987, pp. 33–9.
43. Paczkowski 2003, pp. 430–1.

One critical article could remove a person from his active career in the Party. We had decisive personal influence until the Party Congress.[44] So, the mechanisms of democratic regulation within the Party were first, the pressure on the part of Solidarity; second, democracy within the Party; third, this free press.

The Party reformers maintained close ties with Solidarity and regularly consulted with Solidarity leaders. Tadeusz Pławiński was among those who was invited to and regularly attended Party meetings before the Party Congress.[45]

The election campaign was intense. The atmosphere within the now openly factionalised Party grew increasingly nasty. For example, in Toruń, where Iwanow sought election as a delegate to the Party Congress despite having been formally expelled by the leadership, he won in the city Party conference by a vote of 363 to 354. More than half of the losers then threw down their Party cards and walked out. First Secretary Zygmunt Najdowski, who was one of those who walked out, returned, but vowed that with such a vote he would not run for election. Later, Najdowski asked that those who had walked out be readmitted. The delegates refused and voted to strip Najdowski of his position as a deputy to the parliament (*Sejm*).

The Party apparatus again insisted that divided loyalty was unacceptable. Dorota Terakowska: 'There was a call at the election meetings for an open declaration from those who belonged both to the Party and Solidarity to declare themselves: either, or'. But Solidarity still carried great influence[46] and officials often found that members of their own families (especially their children) were infected with the general condemnation of their activities. Even the secret police were affected. Colonel Sucharski recalled that many of their workers were 'sympathisers of Solidarity':

> At the same time, we were having a hard time recruiting new people. In fact, we had situations where our own workers were trying to leave the service. We found out that this Party Secretary sympathised with Solidarity; that one did something wrong; the other one built a dacha. And we were obliged to make reports on these things to the provincial Party Secretary. As he got this information, it showed him that half of his people were against him and the other half was unfit, and it made us the bad guys because we knew it. So, it got to the point where we stopped informing about these matters.

As the Party Congress approached, the reformers were quite strong in some places; indeed, the reformers were so strong that at the Kraków Party Regional Conference in June, they took control:

---

44. Rakowski denied that Szumowski held such influence.
45. Pławiński interview.
46. Mason 1985, pp. 148–9, 152–3.

Szumowski: We demanded that Catholics and non-partisans in general have equal access to higher posts with Party members. Rotation of posts in the Party apparatus was also coded in the new statutes. The purpose was to end the control of the Party apparatus.

They carried this programme into the election for the new Party Congress where, as Szumowski recalled: 'A fight went on, influenced both by *Gazeta Krakowska* and its audience, for every sentence, almost every word'. The reformers' programme included the 'acceptance of Solidarity as a social movement; the policy of seeking a consensus with Solidarity; and creating a new social covenant that would enshrine these policies'.

By the time of the elections, the Party leadership had accepted the reformers' demand for unlimited nominations from the floor, which several called 'a real victory for democracy within the party'.[47] Newly-adopted statutes stressed the power of elected Party committees over the apparatus. Party leaders often had to consult with locals before making appointments, and now their proposals were regularly rejected. A significant new rule prohibited a candidate defeated in one Party conference from standing in another. As a result, only 71 of 236 Central Committee members won election as delegates to the Congress,[48] although most members of the Politburo and the Secretariat did manage to get elected.[49] Kania, who himself had difficulty in being elected, had to plead with the conferences to elect people known and trusted by Moscow.[50] Some conservatives were outraged by this demeaning spectacle.[51] Zbigniew Głowacki stated indignantly that the leaders 'cannot be petitioners running from conference to conference seeking someone kind enough to nominate them'.[52] In the end, 90 percent of the delegates were new – a fact that provided hope to the reformers and fear to the Party leaders.

In April, 322 basic Party organisations in Bydgoszcz replaced their first secretaries; only 71 incumbents managed to retain their positions.[53] Only about seventeen percent of the incumbent provincial Party secretaries managed to get re-elected. In twelve provinces, all the secretaries were replaced, and in thirteen all but one were replaced.[54] New people now comprised 80 percent of

---

47. Mason 1985, p. 155.
48. Sanford 1983, p. 188; Hahn 1987, pp. 43–4, 47–51.
49. Garton Ash 1985, p. 172; Mason 1985, p. 151; Sanford 1983, pp. 186–7, p. 189.
50. Garton Ash 1987, pp. 177–8.
51. 'Nowe Drogi' 1981, cited in Hahn 1987, p. 77.
52. Ibid.
53. Garton Ash 1985, p. 172.
54. Hahn 1987, p. 69.

the regional Party organisations, 65 percent of the village, town and factory organisations, and 50 percent of the first secretaries of all the basic Party organisations.[55] As Szumowski stated:

> *The Soviet Union and the security forces in Poland were afraid of one thing: that the political ambitions of Solidarity would join forces with the political ambitions of the reformist elements within the Party.* If such a thing happened, there would be no pretext to intervene militarily because the Party would still be officially in control and supported by a mass movement.

Thus, it was not yet evident how things had changed since Bydgoszcz. Kasprzyk remembered sensing that Bydgoszcz '*even strengthened our democratic movement* because we realised what kind of threat for us and the Party as a whole these Bydgoszczes could be'. But by the end of May, with most of the Party delegates already chosen, it was becoming evident that despite the large number of new people elected to the Party Congress – many of whom wanted significant changes – the reformers would not dominate proceedings. Both reformers and the most conservative candidates were often defeated, since neither could achieve a majority of votes, so the new delegates often had no connection to the reformers. Many of their perspectives were akin to those of their predecessors.[56] At the Congress, it became clear how strong the *centrist* party forces were.

In early June, the Soviets sent an angry letter to the Polish Party, warning of a possible 'attempt to deal a decisive defeat to the Marxist-Leninist forces of the party and produce its liquidation'.[57] Evidently, they were unaware of the constellation of forces that the elections had produced. Only days later, at the eleventh Party plenum, Kania's conservative opponents attempted to depose him. He survived thanks largely to the support he received from military-officers, who constituted 10 percent of the Central Committee.[58] Zbigniew Regucki said: 'Moscow wanted all the liberals removed from power. The Soviet letter was widely circulated, and this was the atmosphere in which the preparation for the Party Congress took place'.

> **Szumowski:** The conservatives aimed at taking power in this session. Whereas before, hardly anyone spoke openly in favour of confrontation, now, as psychological warfare, rumours were spread that they should assemble ten or twenty trains and ship away all the Solidarity leadership – all ten thousand. In *Trybuna Ludu*, the possibility of confrontation with Solidarity was openly discussed. Rakowski was implicitly suggesting either the use of force or a military

---

55. Mason 1985, p. 130.
56. Sanford 1983, p. 203.
57. Hahn 1987, p. 116.
58. Garton Ash 1985, pp. 175–7.

intervention by the Soviets. Someone said that it would be enough to arrest 5,000 people in the country and calm would return to the streets. The threat of imminent Soviet military intervention was a tool of this psychological warfare waged against Solidarity.

While the reformers' strength was in the industrial centres – where Solidarity was the strongest – almost half of the Polish population still lived in small towns and villages of ten thousand or fewer.[59] Here, invisible to outsiders, is where the hidden strength of the apparatus was most strongly felt. Jan Jerschina:

> The Party apparatus won the elections because it was able to direct the provincial areas against the great cities. We didn't control who was sent from the provincial areas to the regional congresses. And during the Party Congress, the so-called 'green' provinces opted unanimously against the industrial provinces. Among the two-thousand at the Party Congress, there were about seven hundred who represented reformist attitudes similar to ours.

Warsaw and Upper Silesia were also strong supporters of the Party leadership.[60] What further undermined the reformers is the fact that since the strikes of 1980 the Party had gradually been losing members – up to some three hundred thousand, or around ten percent of the entire Party.[61] The vast majority of those who left were workers.[62] It is reasonable to assume that most of those who left were Solidarity supporters, so their departure weakened the reformers within the Party who sought an accommodation with Solidarity.

The atmosphere was one of increasing polarisation. On 12 June, at the summer Sejm session, Premier Jaruzelski spoke of the need for more discipline and respect for law and order. He vowed that anti-socialist and anti-Soviet activities would be punished. The deputies passed a resolution calling for firm action against Solidarity 'extremism', which they said was pushing the country towards a 'national tragedy'.[63]

These constant attacks alienated Solidarity. Disgust with the Party led many of Solidarity's activists to lose interest in the intra-Party struggle, especially after Bydgoszcz, and they voted with their feet and left.[64] Many workers who were Party members refused to seek election as delegates to the Party Congress because they would be isolated among their fellow workers if they did so.[65]

---

59. *Rocznik Statystyczny* 1990, pp. 46–7; Zaklad Wydawnictw Statystycznych.
60. Szczypiorski 1982, p. 136, and interview with Szumowski.
61. Sulek 1990, p. 500.
62. Sulek 1990, p. 501.
63. Sanford 1987, p. 201.
64. Interview with Jan Jerschina.
65. Garton Ash 1985, p. 173.

As a consequence, few of them realised that the reform-movement was losing strength.

The Party reformers felt the support of Solidarity ebbing away. This made victory more elusive given that Solidarity's support had sustained the reformers and made possible their efforts to change the Party. As Szumowski noted: 'Solidarity lost interest in what was going on within the Party. The tragedy of the Party reformers was that Solidarity was occupied with itself: they became more and more convinced that they alone could do something'.[66] Kasprzyk:

> Solidarity treated the Party as one big structure that obstructed the whole reform-movement. But I thought from the beginning that the only chance for the whole thing to succeed lay within the system, that this system could not be reformed from the outside.

This polarisation weakened the reform-movement, as those who left the Party were its supporters. Jan Jerschina recalled that after Bydgoszcz: 'There were fewer and fewer in the middle, and fewer chances to get more followers from this middle'. By ignoring the Party reformers, Solidarity was unknowingly strengthening the hand of the hard-liners who would, soon enough, turn their full attention to the union. Virtually none of the Solidarity activists with whom I spoke was aware of the adverse effects of their turning away from the Party struggle. At the same time, party-members were leaving and being expelled.[67]

Party Congress

At the start of the congress, the reformers still appeared strong. Professor Hieronim Kubiak, a liberal from Kraków, was elected chair of the programme committee, which could be a powerful position, as he set the timing of discussions. As Kubiak explained: 'All documents went through my hands and without my acceptance, they couldn't reach the congress'. During the congress, Szumowski wrote a column for *Gazeta Krakowska* entitled 'Behind Closed Doors'. Each day, he summarised the events, including reports on closed meetings from which, as a delegate, he could not be excluded.[68] From his point of view, the Extraordinary Congress was a bust, despite whatever strengths the reformers had:

> The reformers made no progress at all. *Gazeta Krakowska* and I were attacked. There was even a proposal to throw me out of the congress because I was no longer 'really in the Party'. In the back of everyone's mind was Moscow. The

---

66. Goodwyn 1991, pp. 292–3.
67. Paczkowski 2003, p. 433.
68. Hahn 1987, pp. 132–3.

reformers were afraid of the shadow of the shadow of rabid radicalism falling on them. They were conscious that Moscow was watching the congress and every verb, every adjective was very, very closely monitored. So, the reformers stepped back in their rhetoric. They all spoke not so much in real terms, but in 'newspeak'. So, only those who really understood the nuances knew what people were for.

In this atmosphere, many elected as reformers backed away from the reform camp. Szumowski:

> It was very fluid because there were 'opportunistic reformers' who had thought that what they read in *Gazeta Krakowska* was the course that the Party was going to take. They did not realise that, to a great extent, what was happening in *Gazeta Krakowska* was my personal doing and it was actually rejected by the Party. But when they looked around and listened to Jaruzelski and others, they realised that they were swimming upstream, so they changed course and suddenly stopped being reformers.

In the elections, the reformers were outmanoeuvred by the Party leaders who allowed them to take over the job of preparing the resolutions to be voted on, while the leadership concentrated on retaining control of the Party apparatus. The outcome, as Jan Jerschina recalled, was a 'very beautiful document with everything there':

> self-management, restructuring of industry, changes in Party statutes, free Party elections, democratisation of the state. But Mr Olszowski was very happy that we were doing this. He was wise enough to know that in a short congress, if the reformers prepared the resolutions, they would not have time to partici-pate in the plenary sessions. Two thousand people voted on the document, with no time to read it and not much time to discuss it. The main thing in the Party is to elect a leadership. Paper, conclusions, documents – who cares about all this? If you have power, you do with documents what you wish.

Although Kania was easily re-elected to his position as First Secretary,[69] he was weakened by attacks on his policies and character. Most incumbents were turned out of office: only 8 percent of the old Central Committee was re-elected.[70] A significant number of reformers and liberals were elected to the leadership bodies. But as Regucki recounted, 'both the radical wing and the conservative wing in the Party were cut down in the election process. What was left was the middle, which could be easily manipulated'.

---

69. Garton Ash 1985, pp. 178–9.
70. Mason 1985, p. 157.

Janusz Onyszkiewicz: At the Party Congress, the Party apparatus was more or less wiped out of the Central Committee. The people who replaced them were newcomers who didn't know the rules of the game. They were completely atomised and they didn't know their way around. So the remaining representatives of the old guard could keep control. The Central Committee had 100 people of whom twenty to thirty were from the former Committee. And you had 70 who didn't know each other, and who knew nothing about how the whole thing functioned. So, they were easily handled. As a result, while it looked very much like a defeat of the Party apparatus, in fact, it was not because the *apparatchiks* retained the ability to manipulate. The Party became even more centralised because of that.

The Politburo – a smaller body that comprised the actual leadership – was much less changed than the Central Committee.[71] Moreover, in some cases the new people did not last long. Andrzej Krzysztof Wróblewski claimed that the 'Party leader in the Gdańsk shipyard was promoted to the Politburo as a desperate attempt to present the Party as younger, more democratic. In a few months, he was dropped because he was too close to the workers and too far from the Party hierarchy'.

When all was said and done, the Party leaders had succeeded.[72] They still controlled the Party. In addition, after the Extraordinary Party Congress, the horizontal movement began to dissipate.[73]

After the Party Congress

The opposition movement within the Party had been contained, leaving party-conservatives freer to continue its offensive against Solidarity. With the challenge to its authority over, the leadership now turned on its adversaries, both inside and outside of the Party. At the Central Committee meeting following the Party Congress, Jaruzelski warned that the time for concessions had passed and that the Party would defend its power against Solidarity.[74] Party reformers, as Andrzej Wróblewski recalled, were characterised as 'naive and threatening possible normalisation. People were reminded that the Warsaw Pact would not tolerate the largest country besides Russia falling into anarchy'. A number of the most prominent reformers were now expelled. Hieronim Kubiak, who had been put on the Politburo as a gesture to the reformers, was attacked:

71. Garton Ash 1985, p. 179.
72. Garton Ash 1985, p. 236.
73. Kolankiewicz 1981, p. 372.
74. Sanford 1983, p. 217; Garton Ash 1985, p. 197.

In a booklet entitled, 'Who Really is Hieronim Kubiak?', a so-called biography, there is information about Americans whom I really met, openly and professionally. So, adding fiction to reality, and mixing it together, they produced a kind of cocktail which was quite explosive. And remember what it meant to be accused of working with the CIA.

Kubiak received threatening letters:

They would send a postcard that spoke of the punishment we would get for what we 'did to Poland'. There was supposedly a capital sentence issued for me at least twice, with a statement when it would be fulfilled, under what circumstances, and that no-one would be able to prevent it. On another occasion, I was told that my four-year-old son was not necessarily safe. I had to be in Warsaw away from my family for a week, two, without any direct contact with them, so how critical it was psychologically! And step-by-step, the pressure grew, with the intention to force us to resign. I had a conversation in my university office, late in the afternoon. No-one else was present. It ended and I left immediately. The next morning, I got a phone call at my hotel in Warsaw that Jaruzelski wanted to see me as soon as possible. I learned from him, to my astonishment, that I shouldn't speak any longer with that man. He repeated fragments of our conversation.

Kubiak found himself increasingly isolated on the Central Committee, as more and more of the reformers were eliminated from the body. Ultimately, once martial law was declared, he was removed from his position as a Central Committee Secretary, although he remained in the Politburo. But by that time, such a position was irrelevant, as power had passed into the hands of General Jaruzelski.

Szumowski had a similar experience as his supporters backed away from him:

The Party First Secretary in the military-equipment factory, who had supported me, slowly withdrew his support. I asked him why. He was really terrified; he never spoke in detail. But he looked around and would point to the ceiling, and he gestured ears were listening in his office. He stopped helping me out. So, I saw how the pressure was put on people one-by-one.

Szumowski's opponents were unable to remove him from his position before the military coup that ended the era of legal Solidarity. But the opposition movement within the Party had been contained, leaving Party conservatives with greater freedom to pursue the attack against Solidarity. The efforts to get at Szumowski did not cease:

There was constant pressure on me to withdraw, from threats to my daughter's life and freedom, to petty interferences, where they would cut my outside phone line, so I could not call to stop a piece that was censored. I had to stay in my office until five in the morning, to make sure the censors would not just slice up my paper. I was told that they actually prepared a file for every member of the Central Committee with the most radical snippets from the paper Xeroxed and put together. They said that Moscow was really concerned. The Russian Consul invited Dorota [Terakowska] and me over. He served us chicken soup, and he fed us stories about Siberia: that in Siberia you have to use an axe to cut the bread because it is so cold. It was a thinly-veiled threat that it could happen to us. He pulled my paper out of his desk, really greasy and disgusting by then. He turned it over to me, and it was all coloured with permanent markers, in six different colours. He said, 'Look. We are keeping an eye on you: these are all the mistakes you made'. I asked him what the colours were for: 'That's none of your business'. Later, the Polish Consul-General to East Germany came to me, tearing out the hair on his head, saying, 'You are endangering Poland!' Olszowski stands up in the autumn of 1981, 'The counter-revolution is spreading and we need to act!'

In mid-August, Kania and Jaruzelski met with the Soviets in the Crimea and accepted the Soviet view that Solidarity was an enemy. They promised a 'full-blooded struggle' against 'anarchy, counter-revolution and anti-Sovietism'. News of the meeting and its conclusions was published in *Trybuna Ludu*.[75] The assault on Solidarity and its activists now became more open and virulent, as the 'extremists' were blamed for all social problems in an effort to sap the union's social support. Ryszard Sawicki:

> I remember Rakowski from the summer and his harsh speeches against Soli-darity. He broke off negotiations. Before, they had kept the veneer of diplo-macy, and now, after the Party Congress, they were abrupt and nasty.

It was then announced that the Party would continue to appoint factory-managers, a stance that enraged the workers.[76] At the Fourth Plenum, in mid-October, Kania's resignation was accepted, leaving General, Minister of Defence and Prime Minister Jaruzelski to add 'First Secretary of the Party' to his litany of titles. Once again, Party members were warned to leave Solidarity.[77]

---

75. Sanford 1983, p. 225.
76. Ibid.
77. Sanford 1983, p. 226.

Chapter Thirteen
Approaching Open Conflict

Aleksander Krystosiak: The *nomenklatura* understood what was going on; they felt that from the bottom up there was a huge tidal wave coming to sweep them into the abyss. They realised that there was no way we could coexist peacefully.

Józef Pinior: People accused the authorities of causing the shortages; they were sure that food was stored in army warehouses. I remember street gatherings from 1981 when people were so hot that if we had told them to go and take food from the warehouses, they would have done it. We told them to be calm. This is the drama of Solidarity: the situation pushed us toward revolution, but the Solidarity leadership did not want it.

Virtually everyone in the opposition with whom I spoke separated the period of legal Solidarity into two parts: before and after Bydgoszcz. Before Bydgoszcz, the threat of a general strike, together with the élan they had discovered, had enabled the union to set the agenda. Now, its members no longer had that weapon. Before Bydgoszcz, Solidarity had been on the offence; after, it was on the defence. Just as Solidarity had a significant influence on the Polish United Workers' Party's internal life, so too had Solidarity become increasingly beset with factional struggles as the government now carried out a propaganda barrage:

> **Zbigniew Bogacz:** They blamed whatever was wrong on Solidarity. Hungry people who have nothing to put into their pots for dinner look for someone to blame.

> **Andrzej Wróblewski:** This is how it was presented: People do not respect their managers; there are strikes everywhere; in village X or Y, people who were desperate for bread took over the bakery. Fear was cultivated among pensioners that, due to this 'anarchy', there would be no money to pay pensions, no milk for babies. The atmosphere built by the Party-controlled media was that our entire country might disintegrate.

> **Zygmunt Cieślicki:** The propaganda made up unbelievable stories about Solidarity leaders: that they had been married many times, that they supposedly owned many houses and got much money from the West. Unfortunately, some people thought that there could be truth to these stories.

This approach was by no means ad hoc; it was purposeful.

The Party's impact on Solidarity was not that it had infiltrated the organisation. Rather, the Party was able to widen the rifts that had emerged within the union during the Bydgoszcz events by the pressure it was able to bring to bear on the Polish people. The union's position was made all the more difficult by the inflation that was now surging through the economy, threatening pensioners' standard of living. The country's foreign debt necessitated selling domestically produced food abroad. Shortages, especially of food, were becoming too much a feature of normal life.[1] People spent more and more of their time in long lines, simply trying to get the basics. Rationing was introduced in April and its promise of more equitable distribution won the support of most Poles.[2] But as Onyszkiewicz noted: 'They wanted to cut the rations quite drastically, without consultation, and you often couldn't even buy your ration'.

These grinding pressures constricted everyone's choices and possibilities day after day – becoming weeks and months. Zbigniew Bogacz recalled:

> People felt that 'because of your strikes, we get nothing'. In June, there were food shortages in Silesia – the region that never had shortages – while they wanted the mines to produce more. A miner had a sandwich with only margarine or lettuce in it. We felt it was a provocation.

In late July, the situation was made even worse when large price-increases for consumer goods, on the order of two hundred to three hundred percent, were announced.[3] Solidarity leaders feared that strikes would turn people against the

---

1. Ash 1985, p. 187.
2. Mason 1985, pp. 165–6.
3. Norr 1985, p. 112.

union. As early as October 1980, a decline in support for strikes began to show up in the polls. In the *Poles '81* survey, over 46 percent expressed support for the government banning strikes. Moreover, there was significant opposition to various other forms of protest, including street demonstrations, occupying public buildings, blocking traffic and resisting the police.[4] So the Solidarity National Commission urged union members to avoid confrontations.

These trends provided the context of union elections for local and regional positions and for delegates to the upcoming Solidarity Congress. The elections were necessary to legitimate the union. Janusz Onyszkiewicz recalled: 'The situation of the Solidarity leaders was rather precarious because we were still not elected, so at some stage; they could argue that we were imposters. That is why we thought it very important to formalise the situation and to have our elections'. But with the growing shortages, basic human survival became more and more a concern, and people had correspondingly less energy for or interest in the union debates. Surveys in late 1981 found a desire for an improved standard of living having displaced all political demands as the most important goal.

Provocations?

People grew increasingly angry at the government's behaviour and suspicious that the shortages were created by government in order to undermine Solidarity. Władysław Frasyniuk: 'The government was on strike, and it was creating anarchy in social life. They stopped delivering food to the shops as the shortages grew'. Stories circulated of food being held in storehouses (*even to the point of rotting*), of cigarettes dumped, of mail from abroad thrown into a lake.

> **Grzegorz Stawski:** We fought to get the right to check the food warehouses to see if more food could be sent to the stores. When we did, we found that *they were filled to the brim*. The government's idea was quite simple: create shortages. Their line was: 'Solidarity is creating anarchy'.

> **Władysław Frasyniuk:** In the chicken factory here, the workers told us that the cooler was full. We insisted on sending the chickens to Wałbrzych, where the food shortages were much worse than here in Wrocław, but the manager wouldn't allow it because of 'orders from the centre'.

> **Alojzy Szablewski:** We found plenty of chocolate in the warehouses, even though there was none in the stores. The director said it was for export. That night, they moved it to the army warehouses.

---

4. Powiorski 1983, pp. 110–12.

Since the government blamed Solidarity for the shortages, some turned to demonstrations because they were thought to be less disruptive than strikes. Within a few days after the Extraordinary Party Congress, Solidarity locals began to organise 'hunger marches'. Thousands demonstrated in Kutno and Łódź (where only butter and flour could still be bought).[5] Yet the government cut the monthly meat ration to three kilograms per person,[6] and hunger marches spread to other cities.[7] In August, buses blockaded the centre of Warsaw for two days, shutting down most commerce. Rakowski called the marches a dangerous escalation of the conflict that showed that the union sought the 'liquidation' of the government.[8] However, according to Sucharski, the secret police were carrying out systematic provocations during his period. He said: 'That was our role! That is what we were created and paid for!' The widely held belief that the shortages were planned from above arose naturally in a society where the opaqueness of policy *was* policy, and where distrust of everything the government did or said was taken for granted.

Yet most of the Solidarity leadership did not share this view. They proposed that Solidarity be allowed to check the supplies:

> Janusz Onyszkiewicz: Then we could say that the government was right in cutting rations and raising prices, or that they were merely trying to increase the tension in the country by hiding food and trying to exploit this tension. We proposed this idea to the government. We thought it would be a lifeline for them, because it would actually be *us*, the leadership, who would say 'Sorry, but there is no food'.

This was the beginning of the development of a new line of thinking: Solidarity would offer concessions on the *economy* in exchange for *political* concessions by the regime.[9] Onyszkiewicz continued:

> We wanted two things to compensate us for our commitment to an unpopular price rise: a more or less independent judicial system and free elections to the local councils. Price rises would be acceptable only in a situation in which we would be able to say: 'All right, we must accept it, but we are firmly established on the road to democratisation'.

5. Cave and Latyński 1982–3, p. 59.
6. Ash 1985, pp. 185–6.
7. Ash 1985, p. 196.
8. Ost 1990, p. 127.
9. Ash 1985, p. 194, p. 256.

But Onyszkiewicz noted:

> The Party took our proposal as an attempt to seize power. They wanted Solidarity to accept responsibility for the situation in the country – without any influence. It was signing a blank check. We could not take responsibility for reducing the food rations just on their say-so; we had no reason to have such confidence.

In response to this demand, Deputy Premier Rakowski demanded that Solidarity back off strikes, street demonstrations, and 'false messages about hunger in Poland'.[10] In Solidarity's view, Rakowski's response was disingenuous. Onyszkiewicz:

> In Polish, there is no difference between the English words 'check' and 'control'. There is only one word – *kontrolować* – which can be understood either way. Rakowski said 'Who *controls* the food holds the power'. We wanted to *check* it. It was a bizarre situation. We thought we were putting our heads on the chopping block by making this offer. But they considered it a bid for power and flatly rejected it.

Thus we can perceive how differently each side saw the world. For Solidarity leaders, their proposal was the *minimum* required to co-operate with the Party leadership, while the latter felt the union vastly overstepped its bounds. From the point of view of the government, a proposal to check the availability of supplies would give Solidarity access to more information about the economy, which would then enable it to make more demands. Journalist Andrzej Krzysztof Wróblewski said: 'The dynamic of such a process makes it that when you *check*, in a minute you *control*. It was not a *linguistic* but a *political* problem. Solidarity was on the move, and with every step backward made by the power, Solidarity made a step forward'. Onyszkiewicz called the situation a 'stalemate: we were negotiating with the government on economic reforms and other things, but we were getting nowhere'.

Corrupting the union

As noted in Chapter Twelve, the government also sought to undermine the union with bribes. Ryszard Sawicki recalled:

---

10. Ash 1985, pp. 195–6.

I read Andrzej Żabiński's directives to factory directors about how Solidarity leaders were to be dealt with:[11] give them offices, secretaries, cars, drivers. Some Solidarity leaders *did* take bribes. In the copper mine in Lubin, they received a beautiful office and they had a Fiat at their disposal.

Because of the strategic economic and political importance of miners, the government made a real effort to lure them into breaking ranks with the rest of the workers. Zbigniew Bogacz:

> The government gave miners special perks: 'Decree 199' gave them three and a half times as much as for their work on Saturdays and Sundays as on any other day in the week. If a miner worked for four Saturdays in a month, he got double his monthly salary. Some of the money could be deposited in a hard currency account. They created special miners' stores. Miners also got extra rations of cigarettes, vodka and sausage for working on Saturdays, while the supply of goods in regular stores dropped.

Individual coal mines made their own barter deals with farmers, exchanging coal for food. Zbigniew Bogacz: 'We did not agree to these transactions. We knew that the food sold to the mines came out of the pool of food for the whole society'. They feared that such arrangements would undermine the basic trust that had come to exist among the workers.

> **Bogacz:** In November 1981, one month before martial law, the minister of mining gave us 10,000 cars to distribute. I convinced the commission that we shouldn't distribute those cars. I found out later that some of the factory commissions did it despite our orders.

> **Sawicki:** We won many things for the miners. But I would hear from women working in the sewing factory who asked: 'Do my children have different stomachs than miners' children? Why do miners get a kilogram of sweets and I get only 100 grams?' These are little things, but they were important to the people.

The mechanisms of negative selection

Solidarity's new power ignited new ambitions:

> **Bodgan Borusewicz:** I began to see how ambition and position were going to the heads of people: colleagues who used to be co-operative were turning into bosses who destroyed their opponents. Unfortunately... the movement began to acquire all the negative characteristics of the system: intolerance toward

---

11. This speech was secretly taped and distributed; see Hahn 1987, p. 91.

people with different opinions, stifling criticism, primitive chauvinism... The cult of leadership flourished: first, the *supreme leader*, Wałęsa, whom one couldn't criticise; then the leaders in every region and virtually every factory.

Jan Waśkiewicz: It was a very speedy revolutionary career from the bottom to high office. I can understand the feeling of people coming from the bottom of society to the height of conversations with government ministers. It is really a shocking feeling to feel your social position rise so much.

Mariusz Wilk, a Solidarity journalist: Imagine a man who was a simple worker before August, and now he has contact with Western journalists, he lives in hotels, and has the feeling of doing high politics with the government. The mechanisms of *negative* selection began to act. Everybody thought they were doing high politics, beginning with Wałęsa, and ending with the typist.

Małgorzata Celejewska was treasurer for the Gdańsk region of Solidarity. She recalled how 'it seemed that the staff's only job was to make sure that the cafe upstairs did not go out of business: they spent all their time there discussing political issues'. Celejewska proposed that these workers be on leave from and paid by their companies rather than the union. And she served notice that their perks would be ended. In response, the staff quit *en masse*. Then, she said, 'They left the regional commission and went straight to the National Commission to work – in the same building, so they didn't even have to move. They sat, drank coffee and smoked and argued – paid for by us!'

When Alicja Matuszewska became the union's national treasurer, she very quickly began to clamp down on expenses:

> I remember a young woman came in, really elegant, about 22. She wanted to be paid for being separated from her family. She said she worked with Maciek. After she left, I asked the book-keeper where she lived: 'In a hotel where the National Commission pays 5,000 zlotys a month'. – which was almost the average monthly salary. So I said, 'Not a penny more'. I asked Maciek why he hired this girl. 'Because we needed her'. (We hired experts: a lawyer, an economist, a professor. We brought them to Gdańsk and we paid for their stay at the hotel. I suppose the girl was a specialist in bed). So I said that we would no longer pay for the hotel. I regularly reminded people that this money came from the workers.

This problem appears to have been pervasive within Solidarity. Witold Sułkowski, a member of KOR who also served as a Solidarity leader in Łódź, felt that the paid leaders 'wanted to surround themselves with as much staff as possible'.

> Altogether, I guess there were about 80 paid officials attached to the Presidium by the end... Many of their functions were... unnecessary to

the functioning of the union...Various research units...basically didn't research anything...Many posts were filled with the wrong people. Something which...existed...only in Łódź, and which made us look...ridiculous...was the security section of the Founding Committee. All these people got fairly high salaries, above the average wage[12]

Verification by radicalism

The constant daily difficulties made people angrier and more open to radical appeals. Dissidents viewed the union leadership as too timid and vacillating, too willing to compromise. As Solidarity's elections approached, challengers to the then leaders responded to the growing mood of frustration and anger by calling for greater militancy. They criticised the leaders and their advisors for being soft on Communism when they counselled caution, and workers reacted with increasing anger and distrust of their leaders. 'The government has its back to the wall, but so do we. Our walls are the rank-and-file', said one Solidarity leader.[13]

> **Władysław Frasyniuk:** This situation radicalised people. It made some people feel that the Solidarity leaders were ineffective. We did not want to overuse the strike weapon, but to keep it ready.

> **Lech Kaczyński:** The more radical you were, the better. This was connected to the fact that Solidarity was a place of enormous promotion for many people; in such a situation, there are always more aspirants than places, so some verification was needed. That was done through radicalism.

> **Mieczysław Gil:** Anyone who tried to limit the influence of the radicals was immediately called a collaborator who feared confrontation. Expectations outgrew the union, which had to pursue a centrist course to stay in the country's political spectrum.

> **Jan Ciesielski:** Lower-ranking activists wanted to have an action associated with their names. A series of small wildcat strikes followed. We tried to stop them, but we obviously could not reach every single factory.

Aleksander Krystosiak acknowledged that these tactics by people whom he called 'screamers' were effective. In Szczecin:

> We lost about twenty real good activists who got out-auctioned by loud mouths. The 'screamers' wanted positions. Jurczyk as chairman, and I as vice-chairman of the regional committee, were paid about double what an average

---

12. Cave and Latynski 1982–3, p. 55.
13. Garton Ash 1985, p. 141.

worker got. For such money, we worked 24 hours a day. If I left at 7:00am one day, sometimes I came back at 7am the next day to change and go back. If they wanted to pay us extra hours, they would probably have had to pay us more. We travelled at our own expense. But ever since the new people came in, the plucking of the union began. These people never forgot to take money.

Alicja Matuszewska: People were quite visibly pushing themselves forward, trying to get some position in Solidarity.

Bogdan Borusewicz: Old friends who had sacrificed when free unions were just flimsy ideas were being shunted aside ... I was disgusted to see people change when ambition went to their heads how modest and decent friends became bosses who savagely destroyed their opponents.[14]

But while people rose on radical rhetoric, once in positions of authority, they often avoided conflict. Krystosiak: 'once the careerists had a position, their main goal was to lower the scale of demands of the union and they scared people by speaking about bloodshed'.

Zbigniew Bujak: Those who joined Solidarity at the beginning had courage and knew they were risking being fired and police harassment. Before they joined, they had to overcome the barrier of fear. But, those who joined later, when it was legal were still afraid of the police. They saw that organising a strike was safe, so they wanted to do it on every occasion. But, when martial law was declared, these people did not join the strike in Ursus, but neither were most of the original people there because they had *stepped back* to give the newcomers the opportunity to back up their words. If the original activists had struck, there would have been many more than there actually were. The same happened in virtually every factory in many regions.

The growing anger made life difficult for the union leaders. Ryszard Sawicki: 'We felt we needed peace to prepare for the Solidarity Congress. The government did everything possible to prevent it. They even provoked strikes which we had to stop'.

For most of 1981, the leadership felt itself pressed by the rank and file, which demanded militant action, even as the leadership was attempting to move beyond individual grievances and more carefully to plan demands and strikes. The whole situation was ripe for mischief-making by the secret police. Many people spoke of it. Mieczysław Gil: 'The tactic of the authorities was to try to make people demand more than Solidarity could really win to show that Solidarity did not

---

14. Kaufman 1989, pp. 13–14.

have control over its members, that the state was plunged into anarchy and that the only viable solution was to introduce martial law'.

Self-government

Although the union leadership was attempting to avoid constant warfare with the government, people were growing increasingly insistent that Solidarity become more aggressive in the face of the government's tactics.

> **Onyszkiewicz:** We found ourselves under increasing pressure from below to do something because there was a general feeling that there was food, and we could not say there was not. So we were sandwiched between this increasing pressure and a certain sense of helplessness because we knew we could not threaten another general strike.

Solidarity had originally stated that it did not 'intend to...encroach upon the prerogatives of management'.[15] But inevitably a movement emerged seeking to replace unqualified managers, to allow workers to develop economic plans, and to decide what to do with the profits their enterprises gained. This programme did not come from the union leadership; rather, it emerged from below, especially from the ranks of skilled and technical workers.[16] Edward Nowak was one of the leaders of the 'self-government' movement and chief of the self-governing body in the *Nowa Huta* Steel Mill near Kraków. He described how it grew until 95 percent of factories of over a thousand workers belonged to 'The Net', as it was called. By August 1981, this movement was represented in some 3,000 workplaces:[17]

> We set up a club in Kraków region to create a new economic structure. Other cities soon followed suit. In March 1981, a group of delegates came from the Gdańsk shipyard with the suggestion to form a network of representatives of the biggest factories in Poland to exert pressure on the authorities. It included Ursus, Cegielski from Poznań, the Gdańsk shipyards, Pafawag and Dolmel from Wrocław, Warski from Szczecin, the Silesian coal mines.

This movement threatened radically to reduce the control of the state apparatus. As Henry Norr put it: 'state ownership of the means of production in practice meant ownership by the apparatus...The only way out...was through the genuine socialisation of the means of production'.[18] Nowak:

---

15. Norr 1985, p. 97.
16. Ibid.
17. Stefancic 1992, p. 79; Barker and Weber 1982, p. 64.
18. Norr 1985, p. 109.

The first step of the programme was that enterprises should be self-financing, self-governing and independent. For example, at the city level, an enterprise that dealt with funerals should be controlled by the municipal authorities, with its income allocated for municipal needs. Instead, every enterprise pays taxes to the central treasury and from there the funds are allocated according to the whims of those in charge. *But they are not responsible to anyone.* We are opposed to the state setting prices. There should be a normal free market.

The programme was a lunge for the throat of the *nomenklatura* system, and was often so presented by its advocates. Nowak: 'We fought against the *nomenklatura* system, where the most important thing is that a factory manager be a faithful Party member. Sometimes people who were put in charge had no organisational abilities'.

Many Solidarity activists and leaders felt that this self-management movement was necessary to get the economy working properly again. Workers were often not willing to make sacrifices when they felt that their exertions were wasted. Seweryn Jaworski, the vice-chair of Warsaw Solidarity:[19] 'Workers today no longer believe that their effort will really produce results unless they have organised it themselves'. Party-leaders called upon the rank and file to oppose this growing demand from below for power, but it continued to develop.[20]

The Solidarity Congress

By early September 1981, when the Solidarity Congress opened in Gdańsk, shortages of food and other commodities were substantial. A medical study reported that the Polish diet was 'approaching critical protein deficiency'.[21] The day before the Solidarity Congress opened, the government announced substantial rises in the prices of beer, alcohol, tea, coffee and tobacco. Worse yet, noted Bogdan Lis:

> The government wanted us to agree to price increases for alcohol, cigarettes and coffee. We refused unless this action was one item of a reform package. But, finally, we signed. The government then introduced the price-rises during the Solidarity Congress, without any warning or any reforms. They said that Solidarity had agreed to it, showing the documents we had signed on television. The whole next day of the Congress was dominated by discussion on this subject. I think that many of the delegates did not believe that Solidarity had demanded conditions to approve this.

19. Barker and Weber 1982, p. 66.
20. Norr 1985, pp. 105–6.
21. Wałęsa 1987, p. 191.

At the time of the Congress, the Soviet military carried out what were called the largest military exercises since the end of World War II. Delegates to the Congress could see Soviet warships near the port of Gdańsk. Moreover, the Party launched a series of attacks in an apparent attempt to divert attention from the union's proceedings, and to disorient the congress. Zbigniew Bogacz:

> The congress starts. The journalist Bronikowski goes from Warsaw to the striking Szczygłowice Mine in Upper Silesia. He ignores Solidarity, but speaks with the leader of the old trade unions. Arent, the local Solidarity leader, and others get angry; they take the old trade-union leader out of the mine in a wheelbarrow. Arent gets arrested. In reaction, all the mines from the Zabrze region go on strike. At that time, I was in Katowice at my post. We got calls from mines all over, saying that they were ready to go on strike to demand Arent's freedom. I phoned Wałęsa and presented the situation to him: at any minute, all of the mines in Silesia could go on strike. So here was the Congress, which had so many problems to take care of, and all of a sudden everything stops and the whole Congress does nothing but deal with Arent's arrest. I knew that they were trying to get all the mines to strike, so I called the Solidarity leaders from the mines to explain to them that it was a provocation. The situation in Silesia radicalised the mood in the Congress.

There were also reports of secret-police officers infiltrating the Congress. Ryszard Sawicki: 'A delegate from the police told me that he counted 30 secret police just from this one region of Poland'. More ominous was the news of Soviet naval and military exercises in the Baltic Sea and on Poland's borders.

It was evident at the Congress that the social movement was reaching deep into the security forces that were supposed to safeguard Party control. Sawicki said:

> Early in the Congress, there was a letter from Solidarity supporters in the military. Solidarity never tried to organise the police or the military. The government went hysterical, emphatically denying in the press that the letter existed. Because of these denials, two representatives of the Solidarity union for the military came to the second part of the Solidarity Congress, stood at the lectern in their uniforms and said, 'There are 40,000 of us'.

Sawicki felt that these defenders of the social order supported Solidarity because:

> The police were fed up with the whole system. They were tired of being ordered to prove someone's guilt falsely. Throughout the history of Communist Poland, the police were isolated from the society. Ordinary people did not want to socialise with them. To have a friend or an acquaintance who was a policeman

was deemed shameful, something you did not want to admit. If you had a policeman in the family, at gatherings, you did not talk about certain things because you had a black sheep living among you. And they wanted to end it.

In truth, Solidarity's influence was so pervasive that it reached even into the homes of the police, through family members. Sawicki:

The wives of the police were nurses, store clerks: they were Solidarity members. Through them, we knew what each policeman felt. They would relay to us what they had to say, and they educated their husbands about Solidarity. We said to them, 'You play an important role in the society, and you will be needed'.

In fact, Solidarity's divisions were evident. Wałęsa was criticised for having negotiated a compromise with the government over the wording of a bill establishing the workers' self-government, and a formal motion was passed criticising his conduct and that of his advisors.[22] Critics resented the advisors' counsels of caution to Wałęsa. Discontent crystallised as opposition to electing Wałęsa president of Solidarity, and he received only 55 percent of the votes. In Ryszard Sawicki's view:

Wałęsa was elected because of the West. We felt that it would look really strange if we kicked out the guy who had received 17 honorary doctorates, was already a candidate for the Nobel Peace Prize and was *Time Magazine's* 'Man of the Year'. We figured that the West would feel that Poles must be crazy to kick him out, so many people voted for him who otherwise would never have done so.

Nonetheless, there was a significant turnover of leaders at the Solidarity Congress; a less experienced leadership came to the fore. There appeared to be an odd symmetry with what had happened at the Extraordinary Party Congress. Sawicki:

The hundred people who were elected at the Congress to the presidium of the Solidarity National Committee were essentially all new; they did not grow out of the strikes in 1980. Not very many people from the National Commission were elected to the governing body. It was easy for Wałęsa to control them since they did not have the experience of being 'active under fire', Wałęsa was, for them, a half god. He was left alone in making decisions and he could essentially do whatever he wanted.

It is certainly true that Wałęsa, and the moderates he represented, won at the convention, but much of the base was moving away from moderation.

---

22. Garton Ash 1985, pp. 214–15.

After the Solidarity Congress

By the end of the Congress, the Party attacks were escalating. The Party leadership called upon the *Sejm* to grant emergency powers to ban strikes and to suspend work-free Saturdays. But in the prevailing atmosphere, non-Communist deputies could be more independent: they refused to vote for the bill and it failed.[23] The Party was thus even losing control of the state institutions, which provoked Rakowski's contention that: 'The structures of government were coming to zero. This was for us, the government, a huge danger'. Even before the Solidarity Congress, plans for martial law were printed in Moscow and were in Warsaw by early August, perhaps sooner, according to information passed to the CIA by Colonel Ryszard Kukliński, who was serving as an American informant.[24] The existence of these plans did not mean that martial law was inevitable, but it was clearly an option. Meanwhile, the secret-police were beginning to shake off the torpor that had affected them since August 1980. Adam Sucharski:

> Three to four months before martial law was declared, there was a visible and significant change in the atmosphere, where our activities became more vigorous and we started very aggressively and actively creating files on the Solidarity leadership. We once again entered the factories and demanded that they follow our directives.

Leszek Waliszewski, the regional head of Solidarity in Upper Silesia, recalled activists being arrested for putting up posters and for selling union publications.[25] Zbigniew Bogacz: 'The secret police dumped vials of poisonous gas by the Sosnowiec mine. About sixty people were hospitalised. It was a clear provocation. The mine went on strike, and others were ready to join it'.

Meanwhile, the shortages were growing more extensive.[26] Solidarity leaders worried that the general population would blame the union. Jan Ciesielski: 'In September, the Party started provoking a series of strikes, which they then used as propaganda against the union: "Solidarity has no real programme but strikes". Food shipments were delayed, which created empty shelves. People really began to think about Solidarity as the authorities wished them to think'.

The Solidarity leadership tried to prioritise issues and to pick their battles, but they had less and less control as conditions deteriorated. In some places, workers threw the Party apparatus out of the factories. At the Kazimierz Juliusz Mine, located in the Zagłębie region, Solidarity activists gleefully told me how they had ejected Party activists from the premises while Rakowski was present, thereby

---

23. Garton Ash 1985, p. 242.
24. Bernstein and Politi 1996, p. 312.
25. Waliszewski 1983, pp. 54–5.
26. Mason 1985, pp. 164–5.

humiliating him. Official sources claimed that there were similar efforts in 21 provinces.[27] Many of Solidarity's leaders felt that these actions were unwise.

> **Ryszard Sawicki:** I told activists that we couldn't replace every director in every factory. All these fights to dump the Party from the factories were ridiculous. We should have spent our time building the grass roots and left the fights for later. After we changed the system, we could look into changing directors or dumping the Party from the factories.

The union leadership's efforts to avoid confrontations made it increasingly suspect in many people's eyes. According to Zbigniew Bujak, in Warsaw there was increasing distrust of the Solidarity leaders: 'We had to hide money. But . . . there were constant accusations of misappropriation and wastefulness, demands that people account for every penny. Given this level of supervision . . . how was I to conceal anything without having the presidium or the entire Regional Board vote on it?'[28]

Strikes persisted, often provoked by the authorities and demanded by the rank and file, even as social support for them diminished.[29] Władysław Frasyniuk: 'A mine in Wałbrzych refused to work because of food shortages. I went down there to try to convince them not to strike. I argued that these local strikes tired people. We should first plan economic reforms and then, if needed, go on strike'.

Solidarity leaders felt that the difficulty in settling grievances was intentional: to exhaust the society and to argue that Solidarity was being unreasonable. Andrzej Żabiński seemed to confirm this view when he told police chiefs in early 1981: 'Let them go on striking, that will compromise the strikes. We shouldn't be in such a hurry to end them'.[30]

> **Zbigniew Bujak:** In Zielona Góra, workers called for a regional strike to fire one director! The authorities refused. After a few hours, government negotiators left, not to return until noon – four days later. The government didn't want an agreement because this strike was hurting Solidarity.

> **Alicja Matuszewska:** Nothing from the Gdańsk Accords was being realised, and there was nothing we could do about it. Representatives of the National Commission would go to a strike and negotiate while the people went to work. But their demands were not met and weeks and weeks would go by.

---

27. Mason 1985, p. 161.
28. Łopiński et al. 1990, p. 10.
29. Mason 1985, p. 173.
30. Solidarity News Agency, cited in Garton Ash 1985, p. 241.

The crime rate rose by a third over the previous year, increasing people's desire for a return to order.[31] Meanwhile, the verbal attacks against Solidarity and its activists were escalating. Leszek Maleszka: 'In October 1981, the evening news stepped up its campaign against Solidarity. To avoid strikes, Solidarity developed the idea of writing graffiti on the walls, like "TV lies". The police beat these people up, which provoked another series of strikes'.

> Ryszard Sawicki: Right after our Congress, very harsh voices spoke about bringing order to Poland. These plenums were never public, but they allowed the information to leak out because they wanted to show the society that there was at least someone who wanted to bring about order and peace to social life.

These attacks on Solidarity had some effect. By September 1981, one survey found as much as sixty percent of its sample felt that Solidarity bore some of the responsibility for the conflict with the authorities.[32] Clearly, a corner had been turned.

Preparing a military solution

In retrospect, it is not difficult to find evidence that a military solution was becoming more and more likely. By the autumn of 1981, Zbigniew Bujak later told the *New York Times*: 'It was becoming clear that the authorities were planning a sizeable operation against the union'.[33] Jaruzelski warned that 'The party cannot be removed by force. There may be force to meet force'.[34] The Solidarity press reported the formation of a 'Committee of National Salvation', and that special army and militia units had been assigned the task of suppressing popular resistance. Adam Sucharski confirmed that behind the scenes the government was preparing to strike:

> We already had plans to take over radio stations, but now those plans were made more precise and concrete. We had a state of heightened alertness, which meant that we were not allowed to leave the city we lived in; no vacations; and we had to be at their disposition at any time. In routine exercises, everyone had to show up at headquarters as fast as possible. Our equipment was upgraded.

---

31. Mason 1985, p. 176.
32. Mason 1985, p. 183.
33. Garton Ash 1985, p. 248.
34. Mason 1985, p. 161.

The government sent troops into two thousand villages,[35] accompanied by a pro-paganda barrage.

> **Andrzej Krzysztof Wróblewski:** They would enter state farms and see corrup-tion or waste or disorganisation, and they would remove it by military means. That built up the authority of the army as the only un-corrupted organisation to lead the country. It was shown as the healthy purification of our social and economic life.

One poll found 91 percent supporting these military moves, most because they thought the soldiers would end corruption and incompetence.[36]

> **Alicja Matuszewska:** Jaruzelski said that he had sent 'operation troops' to every village, every little town, every city to 'check the economic situation of the country'. We did not believe even one word of it. The National Commis-sion began receiving reports that Solidarity banners and posters were torn down, notices of meetings and other things were destroyed.

Soldiers who had been conscripted for the regular two-year period of national service in the autumn of 1979 now found their term extended for two months. This was an important sign for those who cared to read it. So far, there had been no reports of Solidarity affecting the army's ability to use its troops as it saw fit. As far as the government was able to, it prevented information about what was going on in the society from reaching the soldiers. But could the generals be certain of the next batch of conscripts? The new draftees who would be com-ing into the army would have been in the general population throughout the Solidarity period and would surely have been affected by it. They might be less trustworthy than the troops they would replace – troops whose two-year hitch began before the August strikes, and who therefore would have been more iso-lated from the surging currents of opinion that flowed through Polish society. Even many of these soldiers had clearly been affected: Ryszard Sawicki recalled that 'After martial law, I found out that the prisons were half-filled with soldiers and officers because they supported us'. How much worse might it have been with a new round of conscripts? Adam Sucharski: 'This draft extension was a clear signal that something was coming'.

On 4 November, a meeting between General Jaruzelski, Primate Glemp and Wałęsa – representing the three institutions with a claim to authority in Poland – produced little because Jaruzelski offered little: a continuing dialogue with the government, Solidarity, the Church, and the old unions. 'Consultation' was the

---

35. Garton Ash 1985, p. 238.
36. Mason 1985, p. 189.

word, not 'power-sharing'.[37] Zbigniew Bogacz recalled: 'The meeting brings nothing; in fact, it has a negative result. From then on, essentially all negotiations with the government end'. But from the Party leadership's point of view, Jaruzelski's offer was quite reasonable and the union's refusal to accept it was a dangerous sign, an indication that the most intransigent elements in the union were now driving its policy. Rakowski: 'Wałęsa's answer was negative. When we asked him why he said no, his answer was, "I was under such who pressure from the radical wing that I couldn't do it"'. Colonel Ryszard Kukliński, who served in the central apparatus, began to work with the CIA in hopes of avoiding a repeat of the 1968 Soviet-led invasion of Czechoslovakia. He stated that he had been working on martial law for 380 days – that is, almost from the time when the right to Solidarity was won. He said that on 7 November 1981, 'the preparations for imposing martial law had been so highly advanced that pressing the proverbial button would have sufficed to mobilize the entire police-and-army machine. The only remaining problem was preparing a pretext acceptable, at least to part of the society'.[38] Then, at the Party plenum on 27–28 November, General Jaruzelski announced that he would ask the *Sejm* to grant him emergency powers.[39]

One might ask: why, with all these signs, did Solidarity's leaders fail to see what was being prepared? Some of it was done fairly openly, as Adam Sucharski confirmed: 'How do you keep a secret about being more closely tied to the military when you have military officers in your headquarters working with you all the time? You could not hide that from an observer'. But as Sucharski noted, the procedures they followed certainly tended to lull the observers' senses:

> We had drills very often – essentially, every week – where we were all called in at 3:00 in the morning. We came in, our presence was checked, we went back home, and a few hours later, we had to be there in the morning. The first drill, we got all excited; the second drill, we got excited; the third: surely, something will happen; after the fifth: 'The same again?' By 12 December, the real alarm, it was: 'Oh, it's more of the same'.

It seems reasonable to suppose that observers would also experience this loss of excitement.

---

37. Bernstein and Politi 1996, p. 315; Ash 1985, p. 243.
38. Kukliński 1998, p. 8.
39. Ost 1990, pp. 143–4.

A death list?

As the year's end approached, word spread in the military, among the police, members of the Party and the *nomenklatura*, and among their families, that the union was creating a 'death list'. According to sociologist Jadwiga Staniszkis, the list was alleged to have 50,000 names of 'future victims' on it,[40] a number large enough to threaten not only national and regional, but even local leaders and members of these bodies. This claim was verified, in some instances, by the appearance of crosses on some people's doorposts, supposedly indicating that they were marked for death. I spoke to several people in Solidarity about this threat; they all dismissed it as a government ploy to help the regime prepare its supporters for the military steps that by then were in an advanced state of planning, and to secure backing from the apparatus of repression.

> **Zbigniew Bujak:** The authorities started a propaganda campaign in the administration, party, police and army. They said that Solidarity was preparing to take power by force and that Solidarity was preparing lists of soldiers, police and Party members to *liquidate*, that Solidarity *would even hang children*! They were told that Solidarity members were marking crosses on their flats to indicate which families were to be hit. Those crosses actually did appear – because the secret-police were doing it! We had proof of this: we caught one of them in Kraków making these crosses. We published this fact, but the credibility of the Party apparatus was higher than Solidarity's among the professional soldiers and the police.

> **Władysław Frasyniuk:** After martial law was imposed, we learned that during autumn, Party secretaries on the local level were given guns and told that the authorities could not ensure their safety if they did not accept them.

> **Aleksander Krystosiak:** They had special meetings with the families of army officers. Those who lived on the second floor and up were given ropes so that if Solidarity attacked, they could escape.

How widely was this threat believed? There were, certainly, people who felt endangered. When I asked Mieczysław Rakowski if he believed the threats, he answered: 'You can't exclude such a situation because when there are such historic changes, very often people lose their common sense'. Colonel Adam Sucharski was emphatic in his certainty that the menace was real:

> I absolutely exclude the possibility that it was ordered to create a sense of endangerment in the families of our workers. There was a poem spread around

---

40. Staniszkis 1984, p. 192.

which ended, 'On the trees, instead of leaves, we'll hang the Commies'. There were slogans being painted on doors and phone calls made to families, with threats. I myself was in a commission that worked on protecting these families from anticipated dangers. We created a support network between families, and we prepared certain buildings where families could be gathered so the military and police could protect them.

These threats were *perceived* as real by many of their designated targets:

Aleksander Krystosiak: After I was already detained under martial law, I was sitting in my cell, reading in the newspaper how my own shipyard was supposedly armed to the teeth with swords and knives in every worker's locker, in every drawer, everywhere. There were even pictures of these 'weapons'. How did it happen? The director had us make swords out of very thin tin to be used for official ceremonies. The knives were needed to cut rubber to seal leaks, and to open cans.

But as Zbigniew Bujak pointed out: 'Wives of the soldiers came to Solidarity about this propaganda programme, and so did some officers, because not everyone swallowed this story'. While it is true that some threatening statements were made, as far as I can determine, there was neither any effort nor intention to follow through on them. In very few cases did the leaders ever make such statements, and they were *never* policy. As Adam Michnik noted, 'No people were molested or killed, not one drop of blood was shed by people working for the Polish revolution'.[41] As David Mason notes: 'When a public statement is made by a member of the Party's Politburo or Central Committee, it reflects the official line. This was not the case with Solidarity, where factional disputes were out in the open, and where the centre had considerable difficulty coordinating and restraining actions in the regions'.[42]

Approaching counter-revolution

In this atmosphere, the *nomenklatura* pressured the party-leadership to do away with Solidarity. By this time, there was general consensus among the party-leaders for declaring martial law.[43] The *Poles '81* survey found that in counter-distinction to all other groups, those who were both members of the Party and in managerial positions were ready to restrict freedom of speech, ban strikes

41. Michnik 1982, p. 94.
42. Mason 1985, p. 121. This minority consisted of those most hostile to the regime and least willing to compromise with it.
43. Paczkowski and Byrne 2007, p. 28.

or use the army to break them, require farmers to sell their produce (presumably at government fixed prices), suspend free Saturdays, strengthen both the criminal and the secret-police, and ban demonstrations (with harsh sentences for demonstrators).[44] On 28 November, the Party Central Committee called for giving the government emergency powers.[45] The US soon had satellite photos of military vehicles, personnel carriers and tanks gathered not far from the Gdańsk Shipyard, and of Warsaw Pact troops approaching the Polish border.[46]

The population was deeply split over what to do. The *Poles '81* survey found that 70 percent supported Solidarity, while over 40 percent felt that Solidarity shared some of the blame for the worsening economy.[47] A Solidarity poll found only two-thirds of the union's members still believing that the union needed the strike as a weapon in its arsenal.[48] Stanisław Handzlik felt that 'people started doubting their successes and lost hope as each approach, each effort, every round of talks failed', and as the economic situation of the country deteriorated.

But strikes continued. During November, one report had 105 strikes in progress, with millions of workers involved, none approved by the national leadership.[49] On 2 December, while a strike was taking place at the Firefighters Academy in Warsaw, and a regional strike was threatened to support it, police stormed their academy and arrested everyone there. Wałęsa was visited by Minister for Trade Union Affairs, Stanisław Ciosek, as the attack was taking place. Wałęsa wrote of that meeting:[50]

> When he was called to the telephone for a moment, Ciosek left a piece of paper on his chair with a simple hand-written note: *Keep Wałęsa in his hotel at all costs* [italics in original]! ... After a time we learned that, while this conversation was taking place, a spectacular attack by special police units, supported by tanks and helicopters, had been launched on the Fire Service Officers' School. Several hundred students were striking there ... I had intended to forestall this action by trying to end the strike quietly. I was convinced then that we were seeing the final preparations before martial law was declared and that we had just witnessed a spectacular dress rehearsal; the strike had been quelled by force and I had been kept out of circulation, so that the authorities could now proceed unhindered, to a programme of large-scale repression. Ciosek had only come to my hotel to keep me holed up there.

---

44. Powiorski 1983, p. 114.
45. Łopiński et al. 1990, p. 15, n. 1.
46. Bernstein and Politi 1996, p. 323.
47. Powiorski 1983, pp. 116–17.
48. Mason 1985, p. 127.
49. Bernstein and Politi 1996, p. 317.
50. Wałęsa 1987, p. 202.

The next day, the Solidarity National Commission met in Radom amid a perva-sive sense of what Wałęsa called 'extreme emergency'. There was talk of build-ing a workers' militia, and of overthrowing the government. Wałęsa, usually a moderate, adopted the radical rhetoric: 'Confrontation is inevitable and it will take place ... Today things have reached such a point that I see no other way out: People must be ... told what game we're playing'. Wałęsa later insisted: 'At Radom, I became the most radical of the radicals, letting myself be carried away by the atmosphere in the hall. If I hadn't spoken as I did, I would have ... rendered myself powerless in Solidarity's future'.[51]

> **Alicja Matuszewska:** Karol Modzelewski stood up to make a proposal. I listen to it and I don't believe my own ears. He said something like this: 'We have to put the government up against the wall. We have to show them that it is *their* "final conflict".[52] I went nuts. I said to Rulewski, 'It *will* be their last fight. They will shoot just one series and they won't have to shoot anymore'.

By the end of the meeting, according to observers, Wałęsa grew silent: 'he sat there, as though resigned, seemingly far away'.[53] The Solidarity leaders threat-ened a 24 hour warning strike on 17 December, the anniversary of the 1970 kill-ings, if the parliament granted to Jaruzelski the Extraordinary Powers Bill he was seeking. So now the government had another deadline to worry about. This meeting took place on the same day that the Soviet Minister of Defence warned the Polish comrades: 'We shall never agree to the removal of the Polish People's Republic from the defensive system of the Warsaw Pact ... This is no longer your problem alone ... We shall never allow interference with the vital interests of our alliance'.[54]

They also decided to call for an all-out general strike, not contemplated since the Bydgoszcz crisis.[55] Jaruzelski later wrote: 'The same kind of demonstration in Budapest in 1956 set off a chain of tragic and bloody events'.[56] Rakowski painted the picture the government felt it faced: 'We were surrounded by the Czechs and East Germany, backed by this huge bear. In the Kremlin, there were old people who didn't understand what was going on. Even Gorbachev, when he first came to power didn't understand'.

---

51. Wałęsa 1987, pp. 202–3.

52. This is a reference to the *Internationale*, which has a stanza with the following refrain: 'Tis the final conflict / let each stand in his place / the international working class / shall free the human race'.

53. Łopiński et al. 1990, p. 2.

54. Szulc 1995, p. 373.

55. Łopiński et al. 1990, p. 15, n. 1.

56. Bernstein and Politi 1996, p. 333.

It turned out that the government had bugged the room where they Solidarity National Commission had met, and they had a tape recording of the proceedings, which was appropriately edited to remove comments that mitigated the more inflammatory remarks. The tape was played relentlessly on the radio, on television, and in the factories and workplaces, and provided the rationale for martial law. Rakowski said: 'The Radom session was the last straw. Jaruzelski and I felt they had broken the small, weak bridge between Solidarity and us'. And as if that were not enough, Rakowski continued, there was also a sense that the government itself was falling apart:

> They planned that the whole of Constitution Square should be full for the demonstration on 17 December. For us, this was very dangerous because in such a situation, it would be possible to lose control. Solidarity had become a very huge power; people were looking to see who would be the winner. And that situation can paralyse the government.

Zbigniew Bogacz described the atmosphere in those days:

> It was like being hunted: the hunters make noise so the animals are driven forward. Now, Solidarity is the animal being chased. People are terrorised by stories of the coming winter: that there will be no coal, no warm water, no electricity – because of Solidarity. And what do *we* have? One national publication and a few regional presses. If all you see on TV is that Solidarity is guilty, it is understandable that some people began to believe it. In the last week, we got information about the movement of Polish and Russian troops, of military convoys moving at night. I travelled from Katowice to Pszczyna to get to Brzeszcze, and I could see convoys of military troops moving.

As this polarisation was taking place, many Poles were beginning to pull back from the brink. A variety of surveys of the time showed willingness to compromise:[57] a majority of workers were willing to abandon free Saturdays temporarily, and many Solidarity members were willing to relinquish strikes.[58] In this atmosphere, Matuszewska recalled that, as Wałęsa returned to Gdańsk by car, 'people knew ahead of time through which cities he would be going. Women would come out, saying "What have you done? You want all of us to be killed?" People demanded that we explain. They felt that Wałęsa wanted to push them into bloodshed'.

Yet Solidarity activists' sense of safety was still so widely held that when the declaration of martial law came in December 1981 many people at first refused to believe it. The Wrocław leadership, almost alone, recognised the signs and acted upon them in advance. Józef Pinior, the Solidarity treasurer in the Wrocław region,

57. Mason 1985, pp. 194–7.
58. Staniszkis 1984, p. 327, n. 12.

said: 'In December, we had information that martial law would be introduced. Therefore, we took all the money – 80 million zlotys – from the bank before it happened'. Pinior withdrew the money on 3 December, nine days before martial law was declared. This money was later put to good use by the union.[59] Wrocław Solidarity prepared an underground even before martial law was established. I asked Pinior why they had not alerted other Solidarity chapters of the forthcoming coup, since he had so clearly foreseen it. He answered: 'We did, they didn't believe it. Our friends in Warsaw saw us as radicals'. Aleksander Krystosiak was one of those who Pinior told, but 'when I tried to tell my presidium about it, they just screamed me out'. Indeed, most people seemed to feel that reports of such dangers were merely another example of the regime's 'psychological terror[ism]'.[60] Frasyniuk cautioned that even in Wrocław their preparations were not really adequate: 'People weren't mentally prepared. Nobody imagined that this seemingly weak government would prove strong enough to turn the police (who had set up their own independent trade union) or the army (our workmates and neighbours) on us'.[61] Zbigniew Bujak had deposited in the bank several thousand dollars that had been sent from abroad just a week before martial law was declared.[62]

In the gloomy atmosphere that permeated the days before martial law, Alicja Matuszewska met her daughter for dinner at a restaurant in Warsaw:

> I said to her, 'Ania, I think that it is just a question of days before we get arrested'. The dinner went by in a very solemn atmosphere. By Monday, the tapes from the Radom meeting were being played on the radio all day long, including Wałęsa's speech. People made the appropriate deduction – that it was Solidarity who did not want to talk to the government and *we*, not the *government*, were just playing for time. At the end, they said that Solidarity was pushing for confrontation. It was a masterpiece of provocation.

In truth, there was some openness on the part of the public to the governmental crackdown. People hoped that life would get better, that the government could deal with corruption, that as the strikes stopped more would be produced, that life could return to some semblance of normality.

---

59. The government line was that Pinior had stolen the money and used it for himself. But their tiny one-room apartment, mostly filled with boxes and crates, so there was little room even to sit, suggested that he had not benefited from that money. And Wrocław's Solidarity had a lot of financial resources during the martial law period.
60. Kaufman 1989, p. 13.
61. Łopiński et al. 1990, p. 12.
62. Kaufman 1989, p. 27.

Part Three

A Resurgent Opposition and the End of Communism in Poland

Chapter Fourteen
Counter-Revolution!

> **Jan Jerschina:** The whole Party apparatus wanted to get rid of Solidarity. Members of the *nomenklatura* were afraid to go to the factory, the office, so they lived through this period terrorised. You can imagine how angry they were, waiting for the good times to return. They pushed for martial law.
>
> **Adam Michnik:** This [Party] leadership watched as the national movement grew, as it sought the removal of the Party from factories and institutions, they felt threatened by the impending elections to local government councils, they had nightmares about the coming referendum on the shape of self-government in the factories and they were one step from bringing in drastic price rises. The December coup was their answer.[1]

The coup – carried out under declaration of martial law on the grounds that Poland was in a 'state of war' because the Polish constitution had no provision for a state of emergency – officially began at midnight on Saturday 13 December, the night winter began in Poland.[2] That winter was one of the coldest in memory, with an unusually heavy snowfall of more than a metre. The government's riot police were sent to

---

1. Michnik 1982a, pp. 22–3.
2. General Jaruzelski claimed that 'remarks by then-Vice-President George Bush were interpreted ... as a green light for martial law'. Jaruzelski said that the deputy chief of the Polish general staff had been told by Mr. Bush 'that martial law was a better option than Soviet intervention'. Jaruzelski said: 'We took that as a sort of signal. Do it yourselves or there will be the most feared option'; see Perlez 1997.

Solidarity regional centres to destroy communications and printing equipment.[3] Most of the military and the police learned of the crackdown only at the last minute. Colonel Sucharski recalled:

> A state of highest alert was declared, where everyone had to show up in full uniform and fully armed at 9pm. We thought it was a drill, so when we walked into the conference room, we were shocked because all our superiors were there, fully-equipped in field uniforms. We were told that at 2400 hours martial law would be declared. Every group commander received a file containing signed arrest warrants; and the rationale we were given was that at the meeting in Radom, the Solidarity leadership had decided to move aggressively against the government.

> **Captain Krzysztof Klas:** We got the alarm at four in the morning of 13 December. There were some five thousand of us and five thousand police. It was organised so that before 6am we would be in front of the mines. They expected the miners to strike, and they wanted to demonstrate the power of the army in front of the entrances.

Sucharski's orders were:

> If we met with any kind of resistance, we had the right to use all available means of enforcement, *except weapons*. We left at 2300 hours to get to the addresses by midnight. It was a really cold night. One guy was brought in long johns because he jumped out the window. There were a few cases where doors were broken down. We were surprised that we were able to carry out the action so successfully, that there were no leaks in advance. One guy was having a party. We knocked on the door. He came, and we heard him say, 'Don't open the door; let them get lost'. So I say very sternly, 'You are under arrest; open the door immediately'. Finally, he says, 'Oh, a joker. Go ahead. Open the door'. She opens the door; we walk in, in uniforms. We present the warrant, and you can see the guy's face go long. I told him he was under arrest; he did not believe it.

The government deployed a huge force to detain Solidarity activists and supporters all over the country. It included 70,000 soldiers, over 30,000 people from the Ministry of Internal Affairs, over 40,000 people from the reserve armed forces, 1,750 tanks, some 1,900 armoured vehicles, more than 9,000 cars, also cargo planes and helicopters and scores of warships to block the ports.[4] Despite all this force, Ryszard Sawicki was taken by accident:

---

3. Paczkowski 2003, p. 446.
4. Paczkowski and Byrne 2007, p. 33.

I decided to take back roads. It was bitter cold, and there was a snowstorm. I drove into a valley where an unploughed road wound around. When I went over a railroad crossing, I saw a roadblock: I had no chance to escape. The officer came; I showed him my documents. He looked them over, and when he figured out who I was, it was as though he had been kicked in the ass. He pulled out his gun. I said to him, 'Just take it easy. I'm not going to run away. There is nowhere for me to go'.

The operation was largely a success: most people were unsuspecting, despite the fact that the American government had been warned in advance of the coming roundup by Colonel Ryszard Kukliński, who had defected but weeks earlier with the information.[5] Some ten thousand were arrested, and Solidarity records, funds and equipment were seized. Sucharski: 'When cars started pulling up in front of the prison, the line seemed to have no end'. Ryszard Sawicki: 'The jail was filled, so they had no room to lock me up'.[6]

As the military manoeuvres proceeded, people got signals that something untoward was happening. Sawicki was visiting with miners in Wałbrzych:

> We got a phone call from the Solidarity headquarters, saying that a telex from Wroclaw had come. It was cut off in the middle, and they couldn't get it back. The telex read: 'We are being attacked by the *ZOMO*'.[7] So before anything was announced officially we knew that something was happening.

The National Commission was meeting that evening in the Gdańsk Shipyard. Aleksander Hall, leader of the Young Poland Movement, said: 'we kept discussing the need for preparing for some kind of confrontation with the authorities, while downtown the first detentions were being made and telephones were being disconnected'.[8] Zbigniew Bujak had a similar feeling: 'The atmosphere ... was ... a bit strange from the start ... On the one hand, the blustering statements made by many people, and on the other, Lech looking pityingly at the whole situation'. Around 10pm, Bujak received a call from his deputy, Wiktor

---

5. Bernstein and Politi 1996, p. 322. But the American ambassador to Poland, John R. Davis, stated that he had known nothing of Kukliński's revelations. Years later, Jerzy Urban, the government's spokesman, claimed that had the American government revealed the plans for martial law, they would not have been carried out.

6. Then-Deputy Prime Minister Rakowski told me that he thought it foolish to have made so many arrests. He felt that 'it would have been enough to have interned a hundred people to provide conditions that were sufficient'. Jaruzelski, who was the one in control, later acknowledged that these mass arrests were 'an indefensible idiocy'; Szulc 1990, p. 374. But it is certainly not the case that arresting only a hundred would have sufficed to put the union on ice; Barker 1990, p. 1.

7. *Zmotoryzowane Odwody Milicji Obywatelskiej* = Motorised Reserves of the Citizens' Militia. They were the riot troops called in to suppress the strikers.

8. UM Conference, CNC.

Kulerski. Kulerski decided that a dangerous moment had arrived and he quickly ran home to inform his wife that he would disappear: he did not return for five years.[9] Just before midnight, Wałęsa received a telegram: '*all communications by telephone and telex have been cut*. At that point I announced that the meeting was over'.[10] Outside, Aleksander Hall learned that the police had been to his apartment and realised that some kind of round-up was taking place.[11] Most of the Solidarity national leadership, which was in Gdańsk for a meeting of the National Commission, was detained.

It is clear that no-one had any idea of the scale of the internments until they were officially announced at 6am on Sunday, when Jaruzelski appeared on television and radio to explain his move:

> Our Fatherland found itself on the edge of the abyss ... Our waning economy receives new blows every day ... Strikes, strike readiness, actions of protest have become the norm ... Cases of terror, threats, and moral lynchings multiply. There are cases of direct physical violence ... Words spoken in Radom, conferences in Gdansk revealed without a doubt, the true aspirations of Solidarity's leadership circles ... Such ambitions are proven true on a mass scale in daily practice, the extremists are growing more aggressive, there is an open effort for the complete demolition of Polish Socialist statehood. Continuation of the present situation would have led to unavoidable catastrophe, complete chaos, abject poverty and starvation ... In this situation, doing nothing would have been a crime against the nation.[12]

He proceeded to explain the measures he was taking: 'Today, the Military Council of National Salvation has been constituted. The council of state ... declared a state of war at midnight on the territory of Poland'. He contended that they were 'not substituting the constitutional government'. Rather, he promised, the Council 'will be disbanded when law governs the country and when the conditions for the functioning of a civilian administration and representative bodies are created.'

Jaruzelski maintained that by his act he had saved Poland from a far worse fate: 'Perhaps someday our history will ascertain that the third World War did not start thanks to Poland'. But many in the opposition felt that a military invasion was improbable given that the Soviet Union was already burdened with a war in Afghanistan. The Polish population was more than three times the size of Hungary's or Czechoslovakia's, and there was a real possibility that many units of

9. Kaufman 1989, p. 25.
10. Wałęsa 1987, p. 206
11. Lopinski et al. 1990, pp. 3–4.
12. www.konflikty.pl/a,395,Czasy_najnowsze,Przemowienie_gen._Jaruzelskiego.html. Translation by Joanna Bloom.

the Polish army would fight the Soviets. After their presumed defeat, the Polish economy would be crippled, the Polish people unquestionably sullen and resentful, and the Soviets would have to bear the economic consequences alone.

Moreover, we now know that, just days before, the Soviet Politburo had decided against invasion because, as Anatoly Gribkov, then Chief of Staff of the Warsaw Pact, claimed, 'one Afghanistan is enough for us'.[13] After the disintegration of the Soviet Union, a high-level commission, led by the Party's chief ideologist Mikhail Suslov, concluded that the Soviet authorities had ruled out armed intervention in Poland.[14] Mark Kramer, Director of the Harvard Project on Cold War Studies, said: 'All the Politburo transcripts and everything else I've seen suggest that they were desperate not to go into Poland. I think if Jaruzelski had ... stood up to the Russians, he could have gotten away with it'.[15] Kramer's statement is based on considerable evidence: retired Army General Anatoly Gribkov, who had been for many years Chief of Staff and First Deputy Commander-in-Chief of the Warsaw Pact, insisted that the Soviet Union had no intention of invading Poland.

But Gribkov averred that Jaruzelski had requested backup if the imposition of martial law ran into trouble. Mikhail Gorbachev affirmed this assessment, saying that Jaruzelski had requested backup but was told that Soviet troops 'would continue to protect Poland against external threats, but would not be used against internal dangers'. Kramer noted that, according to Gorbachev, this response 'came as a shock to the Polish leader who tried in vain to persuade Suslov to change his mind'.[16]

In any case, the crackdown specifically included: curfews; permission from the police before travel, and those who got such permission had to report to the police within 12 hours of arriving at a new area; shutdown of all telephone and telex communications for a month; a ban on publication of all newspapers and magazines; strikes and public meetings other than religious services were prohibited (special permission was required even for weddings); reduced radio and television programming; most newspapers and periodicals were suspended; schools and universities closed; all organisations 'whose activity threatens the interests of the security of the state' suspended; bank accounts frozen; mail censored. Theatres and cinemas were shut down, while the purchase of typewriter ribbons and typing paper required permission. Any actions that were 'socially dangerous' or that threatened 'the security of the state' – including union activ-

---

13. Kwitny 1998, p. 62.
14. Hayden 1994, p. 136.
15. Kwitny 1997, p. 411.
16. Kramer 1998, pp. 5–6.

ity, assemblies and demonstrations, wearing buttons or emblems – were prohibited. Violators could incur prison sentences of up to ten years.[17]

People listened in astonishment. Sawicki recalled: 'They seated me in the hallway near the front desk. The radio was turned on. As I sat there, I listened to the speech of our "national Messiah"'. Piotr Polmański, not detained, turned on his television: 'Suddenly, there appeared General Jaruzelski, and he declared the imposition of martial law. I went into the other room and I started to cry'.

Cardinal Glemp, Poland's Primate, called upon Poles not to resist for fear of the consequences. But there was resistance, which will be discussed in the next chapter.

Capture

Most of the targets were apprehended because they had no idea what was awaiting them. In Gdańsk, the police went through the hotels housing the delegates to the National Commission room by room, systematically arresting them. Wałęsa was visited at his home by Gdańsk Party secretary Tadeusz Fiszbach and the provincial governor Jerzy Kołodziejski, who delivered an 'invitation' to Warsaw to negotiate with the authorities. He refused until all arrestees were released. They left to report to their superiors and returned about 3am. Wałęsa recalled: 'When Kołodziejski told me that I'd be better off going to Warsaw of my own accord than being taken there by force, I realised that I had no choice'.[18]

> **Andrzej Jarmakowski:** We let them take us like sitting ducks. Right across the street from the Solidarity building, there is a post office; at 9:30pm, it was taken by the army. So there was proof that something was happening, but no-one was interested. At 10:30, our connection to the outside world was cut off. I went home about then and went to sleep around midnight; at 12:05 I was awakened and taken to prison.

Jacek Kuroń had attended the meeting of the Solidarity National Commission in Gdańsk. He was taken in his hotel there. Later, he described what happened:

> I heard the turning of the key. They came. Later, we rode in the 'bitch' through the city at night. There were tanks and armoured vehicles on the streets. They didn't even handcuff me. My loyal guardian Major Leśniak asked: 'And so, Mr. Kuroń, was it worth it?' 'Do you remember, Mr. Major, when three years ago

---

17. Wałęsa 1987, p. 211; Lopinski et al. 1990, p. 16, n. 8; Bernstein and Politi 1996, pp. 334–5; Cave 1982, p. 7; 'Movement Restrictions Eased', in *UPNB*, No. 1, 10 January 1982; 'Workers on Trial: Defense Speech of Jerzy Kaniewski', *Committee in Support of Solidarity Reports*, no. 2, 19 May 1982, p. 2; Paczkowski and Byrne 2007, p. 33.
18. Wałęsa 1987, p. 208.

you came to get me from here, from Gdansk?' – (I answered his question with a question). – 'You came then in four Fiats. And today, as you can see for yourself, how many tanks and military did you have to lead into the streets to get me?'[19]

Małgorzata Celejewska returned home around 10:00pm: 'We saw lots of police vans. The driver said, "Something is wrong". But we thought they were just trying to scare us'. Her son was watching television. A short while later, the picture on the screen disappeared. They went to bed not long after:

As soon as I fell asleep, there was knocking at the door. I looked out the window and saw a police car. So I put on my robe and opened the door. One guy was a military lieutenant. He told me to get dressed. He said that martial law had been declared. I realised I had no choice.

Alicja Matuszewska: When I came home from the National Commission meeting, I entered the building from the rear. For the first time in this whole Solidarity period, I was scared. I went in, carefully closed all the doors and only then I turned on the light in the kitchen, which had no window. In the morning, I was awakened by the doorbell. I went to the door and looked out the peephole. A navy lieutenant and a private stood there. They threatened to break the door down, so I opened. I got dressed but because I was so upset, I forgot to put on my panties; I only put on my pantyhose, and then I suffered from the cold. As we were walking out, he said to me, 'You did not turn off the gas in the bathroom. Please do it'. So, I knew that I would not return soon. I turned off the gas, locked the door and I banged on my neighbours' doors and said, 'Take care of my daughter when she comes back for Christmas'. Downstairs, a black Volga awaited us. They put me in the back. I look around and see nothing on the street. I had no idea that Jaruzelski had already declared martial law. I was taken to a really tiny room, a little larger than my bathroom. At that point, my legs felt soft, and I asked if I could sit down. He said I could. We sat there maybe 5 minutes, not longer. They took away my documents and then led me to a courtyard, where a police-guard and two policemen stood.

Aleksander Krystosiak: I had just returned home from a meeting; there was a house full of guests because it was my name day. We talked for a while and the guests left. I had a glass of vodka, some fruit; I went to bed. I hadn't even managed to fall asleep when they started banging on the door.

---

19. www.wiadomosci.dziennik.pl/wydarzenia/artykuly/370780,stan-wojenny-w-polsce-30-rocznica-wprowadzenia-stanu-wojennego.html,3. Translation by Joanna Bloom.

Leszek Maleszka, who lived in Kraków, was visiting friends in Warsaw at the time of the round-up, so he initially escaped:

> Someone came to tell us that martial law had been declared and they were rounding up Solidarity activists. We went to someone we hardly knew for cover and waited until morning. Then we began to plan how to return to Kraków.

But he was not free for long:

> I was in hiding for ten days when I decided to report to the police, since my wife was to be operated on for her pancreas – it was a serious operation. I had to sign a document in which I declared that I would obey the martial law regulations. Then, I was released. I later started writing articles for the underground press and going to meetings. In mid-January, I was again detained by the police and sent to an internment camp.

But the police operation was far from perfect. Janusz Całka: 'We analysed the list of people who were taken to internment camps. People who were no longer active were interned, while others who had become active were not'. There were many such mistakes, including people who were dead or were out of the country, despite all the checking and rechecking that the secret police did in the months preceding the crackdown. Because of these errors, many people were convinced that the lists had been drawn months earlier, and that therefore Jaruzelski had long been planning to declare the state of war. In fact, it is now known that before December, 1980, under the direction of Party secretary Kania, preparations had begun to introduce martial law in Poland, and to arrest key people in Solidarity and their supporters, and progress in preparations was continually monitored.[20] Moreover, one of General Jaruzelski's former military associates told the German magazine *Der Spiegel* that the state of war had been meticulously planned beginning in December 1980.[21] Already by mid-September 1980, the main details had all been worked out: to be done on a Saturday night before Sunday, when most workers would be off; to begin at midnight, six hours before the proclamation of martial law over the media; major round-ups for detention.[22] These preparations did not mean that martial law was inevitable then – simply that it was prepared as an option.

---

20. Kania's speech to the meeting of the Warsaw Pact Leadership in Moscow, 5 December 1980, in Paczkowski and Byrne 2007, p. 144; also Meeting of the Homeland Defense Committee, 13 September 1981, in Paczkowski and Byrne 2007, pp. 350–6.
21. General Leon Dubicki in *Der Spiegel*, cited in Sanford 1986, p. 119.
22. Message from Ryszard Kukliński to CIA, in Paczkowski and Byrne 2007, p. 364.

Escape

For the most part, people who escaped did so by luck. Sławomir Majewski had attended the National Commission meeting:

> My flat was far away. That night, I was very tired, so I went to a hotel. I later learned that the secret police had been to my flat three times. They didn't think about looking in the hotel, where I was registered under my own name!

> **Zbigniew Bujak:** My friend, Zbigniew Janaś, decided to leave the National Commission meeting in Gdańsk and go back home. I had to go back with him, because if my wife found out that he returned and I didn't, there would be a storm. We went to the train station, and from there we could see the hotel where the National Commission was meeting. The *Monopol* Hotel had been surrounded for two hours when we went to ask what happened. We learned that the presidium and the whole leadership of Solidarity had been arrested, handcuffed. Then we headed for a quiet place to survive.

Bujak stayed underground in Gdańsk for a week before he ventured to return, in disguise, to Warsaw to build the underground there.[23]

> **Mirosława Strzelec:** I had been in Hungary and was returning by bus when I learned about martial law. I got off near my house, where my neighbours told me the police were waiting for me in my apartment. So I got back on the bus and went straight to *Huta Katowice*.

Bogdan Lis was warned by friends 'to get out . . . because . . . the hotels were surrounded, Solidarity's regional headquarters too'. So he escaped, as did Eugeniusz Szumiejko and Jan Waszkiewicz, although they had both stayed in the Monopol Hotel after the meeting had adjourned. Somehow, the police missed them. Władysław Frasyniuk and several other activists were in a train on the way home when they were informed by the conductor that the police awaited them in Wroclaw. They jumped off the train as it neared the city. Helena Łuczywo and her husband were just a step ahead of the police who came to shut down *The Warsaw Regional Weekly*:

> We saw the police surrounding the Solidarity building, and my husband and I decided to escape. We left through the back exit. When we went out, we saw the soldiers in back, and we realised that we wouldn't be able to get past them. We saw the janitor of a nearby building and we asked him to hide us. They broke into our apartment that night, then stayed away for a few days, and they returned. We began to move from one apartment to another.

---

23. Kaufman 1989, pp. 22–3.

Leszek Budrewicz had been involved in a student strike at Wrocław University that had ended the day before:

> The next day I came home, but I needed to talk to someone. I was very tired, but I got dressed and left. Forty minutes later, they came for me. I went back to the university, where people were finishing up after the strike, and I helped them. Someone called and said that the police had grabbed the leader of Solidarity in a tram. When we turned on the radio, they played the national anthem. I knew that was it! We turned on the radio at 3, at 4, at 5 and at 6. At 6am was the first information that there was martial law, and Jaruzelski's speech. I went to a friend the police didn't know.

Bogdan Borusewicz had noticed that petrol was not being sold that night, the police were engaged in 'strange manoeuvres' and the phones were not working. When he saw a police van in front of his apartment building, he realised what was happening and disappeared:

> I went to a friend's, and then to the shipyard. It had been pacified once; I organised the second strike. On 16 December, the shipyard was pacified by tanks and by the *ZOMO*, but I and some friends managed to escape.

The Nowa Huta Steel Mill struck in response to the proclamation of martial law (see next chapter). Jan Ciesielski:

> We had divided ourselves into groups a little earlier in case the strike was broken by force. Some would try to escape and go into the underground to organise Solidarity structures, and some would stay to be captured by the authorities. Staszek [Handzlik] and me were supposed to enter the network of electrical lines, which was large enough to accommodate people, and through these, we were supposed to leave the plant. But we entered the sewer system by mistake and spent about ten hours there because we lost our way. Finally, someone alerted us that they knew that people were trying to escape that way. He helped us get out. The resistance was finally crushed, but we managed to slip through the *ZOMO* patrols and go to a small room they had prepared for us. We cleaned ourselves, spent the night, shaved, changed our clothes and on 16 December, in the evening, we left the factory.
>
> **Bogdan Lis:** At first, we had to decide if those who managed to escape being arrested should go to the shipyards, knowing that the *ZOMO* would probably enter and subdue them. We decided that some would go, and some would stay in the underground to reconstruct the organisation. Some of

my friends and I felt that it would be a long period, and we decided to stay underground.

Solidarity sources estimated that some two hundred activists escaped capture, including a handful of nationally known leaders of the union.[24]

Repression

There was no wholesale slaughter; the corpses did not pile up. According to underground Solidarity sources, in the next two years, only 56 people are said to have died or committed suicide in response to state pressures.[25] (Another source suggested that perhaps a hundred were killed).[26] Nonetheless, the repression was substantial and sustained, including not only detentions without trial, but also wholesale firings from jobs – some 800,000 people – while thousands were arrested or beaten, and thousands more were drafted into the military or sent to work camps and dubbed parasites. Huge numbers of journalists and professors were purged.[27] Some 900 of Poland's 3,000 judges had joined Solidarity. Some of them were interned or sentenced to prison; others suffered house searches and threats.[28] One risked a prison term of three months for possession of one piece of contraband literature. Lawyers who tried to defend those charged with violating the martial law rules sometimes risked retribution.[29] Many Party reformers were incarcerated and some were charged with counter-revolutionary activities – a very serious charge. Regardless of whether legal charges were brought, the invocation of martial law enabled the authorities to expel trouble-some members from the Party. Wholesale expulsions occurred.

Mirosława Strzelec fled the Katowice Steel Mill, as the military moved in to crush the strike:

> I stayed with private families and in churches all over Poland. I spent almost two months hidden in the apartment of a man who was on the Central Com-mittee [sic!]. I was sure that there were people who helped my children, but they had been left alone. There were charitable organisations, but they only helped people in prisons or detention centres, not those of us who were in

---

24. Cave 1982c, p. 18.
25. Barker 1990, p. 1.
26. www.20years.tol.org/2009/10/05/wojciech-jaruzelski/
27. Barker 1990, p. 1; 'Education', in *UPNB*, no. 6, 22 March 1984, p. 25.
28. 'Let Us Be Just to the Judges: Article in Underground Tygodnik Mazowsze', *UPNB*, no 10, 20 May 1983, p. 27; Sanford 1986, p. 134.
29. 'Workers on Trial: Defense Speech on Behalf of Jerzy Kaniewski', *Committee in Support of Solidarity Reports*, no. 2, 19 May 1982, p. 3.

hiding. I learned that one of my daughters was in the hospital, and I had such depression that I wanted to go to the nearest police station and say, 'Please let me see my children'. When the first amnesty was declared, and the Church authorities started talks with General Kiszczak [Jaruzelski's right-hand man], they told him that my daughter needed help. I simply wanted to go home; on 10 January, my father took me to the police station. They questioned me for six hours without a break. They threatened me, blackmailed me, tried to buy me: they told me they would send my daughter to hospitals abroad, and they would publish all my poems, that I would get paid for the 13 months I had been underground and that I would be able to go back to work – if I would only co-operate. If I didn't, they would destroy me and my children.

I refused. They told me to report to the police-station every day. They questioned my qualifications as a nurse, so I couldn't work. I had nothing to live on. The first time I missed going to the station, they came to my home, forced the door open and thoroughly searched my flat, destroying a lot of things. They told me that whenever I didn't report by myself to the station they would come back and do it again. Nobody helped me – neither neighbours nor friends – because everyone was afraid. The police watched my flat and followed me all the time. In March, I had to go to the local government to get a ticket to work. I was sent to a home for sick and retired teachers, because there it didn't matter who I spoke with. For half a year, they made me work at night. I was threatened all the time and my life was made very difficult. When my daughter was in the clinic, I couldn't take her home for a few days. My husband left me and started to live with another woman. They tried to persuade the headmistress of my daughter's school that I was a bad mother who didn't take care of her children. They would search my locker at work; they wanted everyone to stay away from me.

Strzelec contracted incurable cancer. When I interviewed her in 1989, her illness was in an advanced stage, requiring shots of morphine twice a day. She purposely did not have her shot the evening I spoke with her to allow herself to be lucid with me.

Nine strike leaders in the Katowice Steel Mill (*Huta Katowice*) were each sentenced for three to seven years, with large fines,[30] while hundreds were fired and some 1,600 demoted. Over 1,500 lost their jobs at the Warski Shipyard in Szczecin, and about 2,000 at the Gdańsk Shipyard.[31] Rumours alleged that suspected oppositionists were being drafted into the army. KOR leaders were charged with treason, potentially a capital offence.

---

30. 'Calendarium', *Uncensored Poland*, No. 1, 1982, p. 7.
31. Cave 1983, p. 24.

Over 2,000 journalists, including some of the best known in Poland, lost their jobs.[32] The government also attempted to bribe, blackmail or coerce respected journalists, but with little success.[33] The Polish Journalists' Union was dissolved. Nowhere was this policy more devastatingly applied than in Gdańsk. Grzegorz, who when I interviewed him in 1986 did not wish me to use his last name, had served in the leadership of the local journalists' union in Gdańsk:

> When the state of war was declared, all papers stopped publication. We received our salaries each month, without being allowed to do any work. One day in April 1982, I was summoned to come the next day to the 'verification'.[34] The commissioner from Warsaw was an *apparatchik* journalist who had been fired for incompetence years earlier. He said that he was here to beat down the 'counter-revolution' in Gdańsk. That meant me and my co-workers. I had been vice-president of the Association of Polish Journalists and chair of the workers' council for the newspapers. It meant that I had no chance at all. That was the end of my professional career.

This verification procedure was applied to the mass media, government, judiciary and education. People were questioned about their ideas and their allegiance. They were asked to sign a declaration of loyalty and to resign from Solidarity; refusal to do so resulted in dismissal.[35] For those who refused, persecution did not end with loss of jobs.

> **Grzegorz:** I know a very good writer who worked as a bricklayer. Another became a professional driver. Some of us got off with a disability pension, thanks to help from our doctors – not much money. Those who were old enough got old age pensions. We tried to organise a co-operative to make posters. They didn't even allow one meeting. I have heard that Jaruzelski said that he would never allow these 'counter-revolutionaries' to meet. Some who were not fired formed a new weekly: they are faithful to the government and therefore they get lots of money.

Teachers were required to prove that they 'are in a position to guarantee the socialist content of education at their schools', which the basic Party organisations

---

32. Kalabiński 1984, p. 76.
33. Lechowicz 1982, pp. 41–4.
34. Wałęsa wrote that the verification 'left only those on editorial staffs who had declared themselves fierce critics of the "period of anarchy created in Solidarity"'; Wałęsa 1987, p. 263.
35. 'Loyalty Declarations', *Poland Watch*, no. 1, 1982, p. 88; 'Circular from the Head of the Council of Ministers' Office, Warsaw, 17 December 1981', *Poland Watch*, no. 2, 1982, pp. 3–4; 'Archbishop Glemp's Letter to General Jaruzelski, 28 December 1981', *Poland Watch*, no. 3, 1982, pp. 15–16.

were then required to 'thoroughly check'.[36] According to one account that appeared in an underground journal *Wola*,[37] they had to answer the following questions:

1. In what way do you contribute to the promotion of secularism?
2. How do you practice secularism in your home?
3. Why do you not belong to the Party?
4. Why do you not belong to the new trade unions?
5. In what way do you encourage others to join the new unions?
6. How do you contribute to the ideological development of your pupils?
7. Are you for the removal of crosses from schools and boarding schools?
8. Are you for the socialist system?
9. Have you organised youth groups in your school?

The article goes on to point out that the 'verification does not evaluate the teacher's work or his morals; it does not aim to improve the quality of a teacher's job performance'. A year later, another article in another underground journal *KOS* noted that another document, different from the above, was being used to 'verify' teachers, raising the possibility that there were different documents circulating about this matter. This one, called 'Topics for Discussion with Teachers', included the following point:[38]

The teacher's ideological-political position [is to be evaluated by his or her]: wholehearted support and acceptance of the principles of the system of the socialist state and active adherence to those principles; defence of the principles of socialist morality (humility, honesty, responsibility); acting on the decisions of the Party, government, and educational authorities; identifying with those directives; strengthening and developing the secular character of the school and secular morality.

Large numbers of teachers lost their jobs in this process. Still, the authorities did not feel that their goals had been accomplished. Over a year later, the Minister of Science and Higher Education called for a renewed verification campaign 'to complete what the first wave in 1982 failed to achieve'. The renewed purge was to go after deans and assistant deans, the directors of scientific institutes and leading professors.[39]

---

36. 'The Party's View on Education in Poznań', *UPNB*, no. 9, 14 May 1982, pp. 15–16.
37. 'How Teachers Are Verified', *Committee in Support of Solidarity Reports*, New York, no. 34, 28 June 1985, p. 23.
38. 'On Verification: "They Want Teachers to Fight Children"', *Committee in Support of Solidarity Reports*, no. 43, 30 July 1986, p. 28.
39. 'The Bane of Verification', *UPNB*, no. 17, 2 September 1983, p. 32.

Members of the judiciary and their employees who had joined Solidarity were among those subject to repression. Supreme Court Justice Stanislaw Rudnicki, who had joined Solidarity, was dismissed from his post, followed by some forty others. 'Several judges were interned, one high ranking judge was sentenced to three and a half years in prison; others suffered house searches and threats on their lives'.[40] The new regime was felt in the Party also, which expelled a number of the reformers, put many of them in jail, and charged them with counter-revolutionary activities – a very serious charge. It also centralised administration, putting much greater power into the hands of a small group.[41]

In some areas, factories closed after the strikes. When they were later reopened with new workforces, those suspected of having taken part in the strikes were not readmitted.[42] Andrzej Sokołowski, a coal miner recalled that:

> Only ten people were arrested, but the 'red spies' made lists of who went on strike, so the director could fire them. In mining, you have to use explosives. There were hundreds who had that skill, but only a few such jobs. It is a well-paying job, so if you take it away from them they lose money: strikers lost this job.

Many suffered imprisonment. Conditions were considerably worse for workers than intellectuals or leaders whose names were well-known in the West. While Wałęsa was well fed and taken care of, workers whose names were not known received considerably harsher treatment, as indicated in a letter smuggled out of one of the internment camps:

> Except for a short break [they] remain locked in cells; eight people to a cell. Each person has about two square metres of space in the cell with hardly any room left for walking. Sanitary conditions are extremely bad: a bucket for excreta is kept in the middle of the cell. Food is very poor. No specialist medical care is available; there is only one prison GP and a dentist... Walks: once daily.[43]

Some suffered considerable hardships, including cold, overcrowding, lack of water, pest infestations, filthy cells and deplorable lavatory conditions, insufficiently nutritious meals, lack of exercise and inadequate medical care, especially

---

40. '"Let Us Be Just to the Judges": Article in Underground Tygodnik Mazowsze', UPNB, no. 10, 20 May 1983, p. 27; appeared originally in *Tygodnik Mazowsze* no. 44, 10 March 1983.

41. Lamentowicz 1982, p. 23.

42. 'Dismissals From Work, Expulsions From University', UPNB, no. 20, 5 November 1982, p. 5.

43. 'Internment Centre in Potulice/leaflet/19th January 1982', UPNB, no. 4, 5 March 1982, p. 23.

for the aged and those with serious medical problems. There were reports of beatings, solitary confinement, denial of visits, threats of dogs being unleashed to attack them, but radio broadcasts spoke of country-club-like conditions.[44]

When martial law was declared, Krzysztof Młodzik participated in an underground strike in the Piast Mine that lasted for two weeks (see next chapter). What he best remembered of the whole experience was what happened to him after the strike ended:

> After we left the mine, we were allowed to get in the bus. We had gone only about four kilometres when they stopped it to examine our identity cards. We were taken to Katowice. In the police van, we weren't allowed to move our heads from right to left. There were about thirty people and we couldn't see who they were. One person made some noise, like sneezing or something, and I recognised his voice. Someone else yawned, and step-by-step, we knew who was in the car. The policemen knew what was going on, so they didn't want us to sneeze, yawn or anything.

> When they stood us against the wall, if you didn't spread your legs you were kicked. The policeman would come to someone and hit him on the wrists or in the back of his head, and we stood near this wall and couldn't even turn our heads. They searched very thoroughly, to such an extent that they would even be able to find a pin. We were told to undress totally. Then our clothes were carefully examined. A Solidarity pin was found under the collar of my suit. I had simply forgotten about it and it was missed in the mine, although they searched us there, too. They called me a tough guy. Then, for the first time, I was hit with a truncheon. I was told to bend over and count my toes. The guard started to hit my ass, shouting 'Solidarność'. One hit was 'S', the next 'O', and so on.

> I was taken to a detention centre and left in a small cell. I heard people shouting and hitting doors from various cells. After some time, the shouting stopped; it turned out later that they had been beaten, and then they didn't shout anymore. We had only five minutes to walk all day. There were seven people in a cell for two. If someone was sick and he didn't want to go for a walk, everybody had to stay in the cell or the sick person had to go for a walk too. The windows were never opened. When it was very cold, we asked them for some heat. So they made it so hot we couldn't stand it.

44. Cave 1982c, pp. 20–3; 'Notes from a Polish Internment Camp', pp. 25–8; 'Conditions at Internment Camp in Wierzchowo Pomorskie', *UPNB*, no. 6, pp. 20–2.

But Młodzik and his fellow prisoners found ways to survive their prison ordeal:

> A philosophy professor was put into our cell; he told us not to be depressed, and he said that we would win against all odds. I owe this man a lot. He made me a believer, although he was a Muslim. He asked us to make him a star and crescent. He put it on the eastern wall; he prepared his blanket, and this was the first time I saw a Muslim doing his prayers. He would say them aloud. He did it so vividly that we all admired him. At the same time, he was a good talker. It was as if it was a holiday all the time in our cell.

> I think the Communists made a mistake by putting workers together with intellectuals in prison. The intellectuals had a lot of information. A 'university' came into being. There were mathematicians, historians, physicists, people who knew languages, and they gave us lectures. When my wife came to visit me and asked me if she should bring me a book, I told her I didn't have time for books. This was the first time I met people in the opposition.

Ryszard Sawicki described a different prison experience:

> When we were arrested, no-one from our families knew where we were. After a while, we were told that we had the right to write a letter home once a month. So I wrote a letter saying where I was, and that I had been arrested. That was it. Because I did not write to my wife, they called her to the police headquarters. The officer on this case said, 'Your husband doesn't love you because everyone writes from prison but him'. My understanding of the situation was quite clear: the more you wrote, the better they got to know you: your weaknesses, your character. I told my cellmates not to write, but they did.

> In my cell were 13 men; the cell was very small. Sleeping in those conditions was very hard: there was not enough oxygen; it was cramped. So we had a headache all the time. The building in which we were kept had no basement and not even a slab underneath. There was nothing to insulate it from the ground. The walls were wet up to about three feet, so the conditions were very unhealthy. I slept in the lower bunk, and because of the conditions there, I got rheumatic problems. I still have rheumatism in my shoulder. I was not the only one who suffered from those problems.

A variety of measures were used to sap prisoners' morale, including: withholding letters, limiting visits, harsh interrogation, isolation, lack of information about the outside world, limitations on movement and exercise, and poor quality of food, to name only some. These methods varied in their success, but generally unless people were facing desperate circumstances – such as children or very sick relatives with no-one to care for them – they were not moved by the efforts to get them to inform or sign loyalty declarations.

Because several of the people in the jail were strangers to one another, they sought to find out who were possible agents who may have been placed among them. Sawicki:

> Until the middle of January, the Głogów prison became an internment prison only for the activists from the Legnica region. There were only 24 of us. We managed to get rid of people who we didn't know as activists. It happened on 24 December. They allowed us to get together in one cell and we organised it so that it would be a traditional Christmas Eve. We had some bread to give ourselves best wishes. Andrzej Kosmalski, who was an atheist, actually made a cross out of some wood, and we prepared a table which looked as much like a Christmas table as we could get it under the circumstances. Since we all sat at the improvised Christmas table, and some people were strangers among us, and we didn't want to hurt anyone's feelings with suspicion, I proposed that since we didn't know each other well, each of us should tell the story of where they were active and what they did during Solidarity.

> These people told us stories that were out of this world. We continued this happy creativity, even though it became clear very quickly who they were and what they really did. They also knew that they had discredited themselves in our eyes, so they quickly left prison, some of them as soon as the next day – because there was no point in them staying there.

The efforts to punish these activists were wide-ranging and long-lived. Sawicki continued:

> I got out of prison in July 1982. Right after my release, our financial situation wasn't so bad because my wife still held her position as lead accountant in the company, and at the time she earned enough money to support the two of us. But that did not last long. After the quarter ended, and she balanced the books, the next day the office was sealed and she was told that there was no work for her. She applied to many companies for a new job; in most places they were happy to hire her, but the next day there was no job for her. I looked for work; I even applied for a job as a rubbish collector; I felt that it might even be good because I would become a walking stain on the conscience of the people in the region. But I ended up having to leave Poland because I had no other way to survive.

On 1 April, bills were introduced into the legislature against what were called 'social parasites', defined as those who did not work in sanctioned employment for a period of three months or more. They would be required to register at the local government office. The government would compile a blacklist of people who 'consistently' avoided work for 'socially unjustified' reasons and held independent sources of income. One of the clear aims of this bill was to get at those who were doing work for, and earning a living in, the underground. These people were then to be ordered to perform 'public works' for up to sixty days a year, more in 'exceptional circumstances'. Failure to report could result in fines or prison terms of up to three months; failure to perform the labour could result in up to two years in jail.[45]

---

45. 'The Proposed Law on "Social Parasites"', *Poland Watch News Bulletin*, no. 15, 1982, pp. 25–7.

Chapter Fifteen
The Resistance

Resistance to the '*State of War*' began almost immediately, as those not detained gathered at their workplaces and universities. By 14 December, strikes had broken out in a number of places.

In the Lenin Shipyard in Gdańsk, as Bogdan Lis recalled, there was organisational chaos with local, regional and national committees all attempting to function, while at best they were leading only a couple hundred workers, supported by some 1,500 people outside:[1]

> Passages were blockaded with railroad cars; the gates were welded together. The port was protected by a barricade of railroad cars. Tugboats armed with water cannon were moored in the canal and ready to fire at the police.

Ultimately, the strikers surrendered. By Wednesday morning, the strikers had negotiated surrender with the security forces. The printing presses had earlier been slipped to the underground that was already being organised.[2] The loss of the Gdańsk Shipyard had an importance that went beyond the place itself. Bogdan Borusewicz recalled:[3] 'I was certain that if the strike in the shipyard collapsed, the fact that a coal mine or steel works was on strike wouldn't make any difference because people think in terms of symbols and would hang on as long as the shipyard did'.

---

1. Lopinski et al. 1990, p. 30.
2. Lis 1982a, p. 17.
3. Lopinski et al. 1990, p. 31.

At the Paris Commune Shipyard in Gdynia, Tadeusz Pławiński, who escaped the first sweep, found others who were still determined to resist:

> During the day, the police did nothing. They worked at night and got whoever they could. Then they left. We went to see who they got.

Many were fearful to go on strike. Pławiński argued with them and eventually a strike began:

> We had something like 4,000 people. I was surprised at how many stayed to the end: women who didn't have to; some who were not in good health and definitely couldn't afford to be beaten by the police; some who had good positions whose loss would cost them a lot.

However, staying in the shipyard eventually became impossible:

> They ordered us to leave. We had about fifty tanks coming at us from two directions, plus a lot of big trucks from the special police forces. They started scare tactics: they hit the shields with their clubs in a certain rhythm so it sounded like shots. A lot of people ran away. They ran a tank at full speed toward the gate until it touched it, then backed it up and did it all over again. They pushed us back to the piers. We had tanks on one side, the ZOMO on another and water on another. You could fight and get killed, or you could leave. We said we would leave if they allowed us to go as a group. There were about 2,500 people. I was really proud that no one from the shipyard was arrested that day.

In Wrocław, most of the larger factories struck. At the *Pafawag* factory, the atmosphere evoked the strikes of August 1980, with pictures of the Pope and the Virgin Mary hanging on the gate, along with flowers and a red and white banner.[4] In those early hours, there was hope that a mass strike would materialise, but the police and the military were brought in.[5] Frasyniuk and others formed a Regional Strike Committee: 'They would surround a factory; then tanks came through the wall and the police surrounded the workers and pulled them out. Some were arrested, others questioned and let free'.[6] Some workers wished to fight the police, but Frasyniuk urged them not to.[7] Once the police entered the factories, Frasyniuk said:

> People were questioned and their names written down. All this took four hours; they were made to stand in the open air all that time, although it was

---

4. Lopinski et al. 1990, p. 21.
5. Lopinski et al. 1990, p. 22.
6. Interview with Frasyniuk.
7. Lopinski et al. 1990, p. 22.

bitter cold. Then the *ZOMO* left the factory. In the Lenin Steelworks, they still refused to work. The police came three times to the large factories before they decided just to shut them down.

This was clearly an extraordinary contest: the police 'pacify' the factories, take away those whom they consider the ringleaders and then leave, expecting the others now to go back to work. But the workers reconstitute the strike, so the police must return again and again. At last, they close several factories entirely and keep them closed for a month.

In the midst of this turmoil, Frasyniuk, who participated in several of the strikes, managed to avoid getting arrested because the workers hid him. At Solidarity headquarters: 'They broke down the doors, smashed up the print shop with crowbars, and then they destroyed everything – cupboards, desks, telephones, radios, tape recorders ... They even smashed all the equipment belonging to the government unions'.[8]

Marek Muszyński, who worked at Wrocław's Polytechnic University, was awakened at about 4:30am by friends who had learned of the crackdown:

> They heard from the BBC that the army was in the streets. Our buildings weren't yet taken. Only nine of the forty members of our commission were in prison. I managed to contact some, and we began to evacuate secret documents. You had to be cautious because there was fresh snow on the streets, which were empty, so a trail could be seen.

They prepared to resist:

> The next morning we met at 9:00 and we decided on an occupation strike. By the evening, there were about 1,000 people: two to three hundred workers, and the rest students. The *ZOMO* attacked by force on Tuesday night, so I went into hiding.[9]

In Kraków, Jan Ciesielski helped to organise the strike in the *Nowa Huta* Steel Mill:

> We proclaimed an occupation strike. By morning, practically the whole factory was paralysed. About a hundred people came, armed with truncheons to escort us in case of a police attack. After noon on 15 December, I received a report that huge columns of tanks and armoured personnel carriers were coming.

8. Lopinski et al. 1990, p. 20.
9. Author's interview with Muszyński.

They began to prepare defences:

> We welded together the main gates and blocked them with old cars, and anti-tank contraptions welded together. The plant has its own transportation system, a network of rail cars. We had every railway crossing blocked by a long line of cars.

But they were only stalling the inevitable. Ciesielski:

> It ended by force. Around midnight, one tank broke through the main gate, cut in half the bus that was blocking the way and behind it followed armoured personnel carriers and other tanks. People then scattered through the plant. The gate was about 500 metres from the rolling mill, which was where the strike committee was centred. There were about eight railway crossings between this gate and the strike committee. It took quite a long time to separate the trains from each other to make room for the personnel carriers. The *ZOMO* searched the rooms, but didn't find us.

In Colonel Sucharski's province, the three largest factories struck:

> We had at least two to three police for every striker. We threatened them with the use of force over loudspeakers; we gave them a time limit, and then, at 2 am, the gate was opened and a tank turned its canon on the mass of strikers, creating great panic. Most of the strikers, save for about a hundred of the most determined people, left. The *ZOMO* came in, fully equipped with tear gas and batons, and chased them out. By dawn, when people in the other two factories learned that this factory had been pacified, they called off their strikes themselves.

By the end of December, work had been suspended in more than twenty of the nation's largest factories until 4 January.[10]

> But what they were doing upset some of the people who were charged to do it. There were sporadic reports of soldiers refusing to carry out orders. In a town near Kraków, according to Solidarity sources, 'a whole unit... rebelled and all officers were put under arrest'. In Bydgoszcz, Solidarity reported 'armed clashes between army and ZOMO units'. There were also reports of officers turning in their Party cards, and of army units having to be withdrawn because the soldiers were fraternising with the workers.

---

10. 'Solidarity Information Bulletin No. 9', Warsaw, translated and reprinted in *UPNB*, no. 1, 10 January 1982, p. 28.

Upper Silesia

In Upper Silesia, resistance was more determined. The miners and other industrial workers in the region, having once been mobilised, were not easy to quell. Their strikes set an example for how the rest of the nation might have responded, and did much to restore the region's reputation. Józef Pleszak recalled that on Sunday morning, after hearing about martial law, he and others soon headed to the July Manifesto Mine, where many others had gathered. They set about building barricades, but the police broke in the next day: 'We were attacked by the ZOMO, who had no mercy for anyone', he said. The attackers used 'clubs, shields, hammers, then water cannon, tanks', while the miners had 'clubs, chains, fire-extinguishers'. The police responded with bullets; at least 14 workers were killed, while many more were injured:[11]

> On 16 December between 1:00 and 1:30am, the whole plant was surrounded by army units. The strikers were given 10 minutes to leave. Then . . . tanks smashed the fences and several hundred ZOMO personnel entered the grounds. A great number of tear gas grenades were thrown. The gassed workers were attacked by the police. Several were badly beaten. The workforce was gradually shoved out through the main gate.

Wujek Mine

Deadly force was not limited to the July Manifesto Mine. The worst casualties were in the *Wujek* Mine. Adam Skwira 'quickly went to the mine to see what was happening, but no-one knew until 6am, when we heard the first news on the radio'. About 9 that morning, someone came to Stanisław Płatek's flat to inform him that much of the Solidarity leadership had been arrested. Płatek, Skwira and others spent Sunday digesting the news, trying to decide what to do. On Monday, Płatek said:

> The workers decided to strike. We wanted the decision to be democratic, so when the afternoon and night shifts reported, it was up to them to join us or not. If somebody didn't want to, he could go home. Around midnight, when the night shift came to work, the strike committee was formed with representatives of all the departments and of each shift.

> Skwira: The strike committee was responsible for food supplies, communication with neighbouring factories, coal mines and cities; each department was

---

11. 'Information Bulletin of NSZZ Solidarity, Warsaw Region', translated and reprinted in *UPNB*, no. 1, 1982, p. 11; see also *UPNB*, no. 2, 1982, p. 16.

responsible for maintaining order and keeping the machinery in good shape. It developed demands like the abolition of martial law and freeing political prisoners.

The *Wujek* miners built barricades for protection. Skwira: 'We realised that while the barricades were good against the police, who were on foot, they wouldn't hold against tanks'. Płatek:

> The next day, many people left. We voted to continue the strike and to forbid workers from leaving without a pass from the strike committee. We heard about the pacification in the July Manifesto Mine, so people began looking for sticks, shovels, chains, rubber pipes for self-defence. During the night of the fifteenth, the army and police surrounded the mine. The next morning, army officers told us that our mine was the last place in the country on strike, and that they would soon start pacification. The crowds gathered around the mine were told to leave.

They attacked shortly before noon. Skwira said that gas came not only from the ground, but also from helicopters. Many people were beaten, including medical personnel.[12] Płatek:

> After the spectators were gone, they started shooting live ammunition. They broke through our first barricade and began to fight with the miners. We heard shots. I saw a miner on the ground; I tried to get closer to him, but I was shot in my right arm. Practically, it was the end of my participation in the strike.

The use of deadly force quickly brought an end to the strike. Skwira: 'After the shooting, there was silence. Officially, we know 38 were hit, but there were many people injured who didn't report it because they didn't want to get in trouble'.

> **Płatek:** The bullet had stopped in my left rib and my arm was seriously injured. They tried to take me to the hospital but at the next corner, the ambulance was stopped and the police took me out. One of the colonels went to hit me, but the military doctor, who realised that I was really injured and I was not pretending, stopped him. I was operated on and then went straight to the prison hospital. I was sentenced to four years in prison.

Solidarity sources said the police would not allow the doctors to get to some of those who were shot, and as a result some died who need not have. Skwira noted that after the attack, the 'atmosphere was very depressing; the terror was starting. A few days later, they began to arrest people'.

---

12. *UPNB*, no. 2, 1982, p. 20.

Katowice Steel Mill

In the Katowice Steel Mill, where Mirosława Strzelec worked as a nurse, she began to organise resistance there:

> We met in the slab yard and founded a strike committee. There was nothing to eat – not even a grain of rice. Doctors and nurses brought as much food as they could to us. On the second day, we got food brought by taxi drivers, farmers and the families would bring parcels of food through holes in the wall.

The government tried to use psychological pressure on the workers. Strzelec:

> They asked wives to cry into microphones; they tried to persuade us that some-one was ill, that someone's wife was giving birth at the moment – anything. On 17 December, someone informed us that people had been killed at the *Wujek* Mine. We began to collect money for their families. Some were afraid and left. I don't blame them: the story had been spread that we wanted to blow up the oxygen department and that half the city would be destroyed. There were accidents: some people got burned; some legs were broken or sprained, and some people got sick.

The government denied that anything unusual was happening. Strzelec said: 'We heard the official announcement on the radio which proclaimed that the steelworks was working normally. It was not until the fourth day that Polish television admitted that there was a strike'. During the second week of the strike, the government pressure intensified: 'Every department of *Huta Katowice* was surrounded by many *ZOMO* men and soldiers and approaches to the mill were blocked by tanks'.

But after a while it became clear that some of these workers were simply not going to surrender. They apparently had some co-operation from the soldiers: Strzelec: 'Departments surrounded by soldiers could communicate with one another because the soldiers let them; they helped us with supplies of food, and they ate with us'. So, the government needed to replace these troops:

> The *ZOMO* troops took away these soldiers and replaced them. By then, there were only three places on strike: the Katowice Steel Mill and the *Ziemowit* and *Piast* coal mines. The majority of troops went to the steel mill because it was not underground, like the coal mines.

Now came a military assault:

> They entered a hall where about 2,000 people worked. When the workers saw the soldiers, everyone stood near his workshop and began to sing patriotic songs. The soldiers joined them. Then they left and the *ZOMO* attacked. They

completely destroyed the rooms of the Solidarity committee: burning flags, destroying all the equipment they had. If they saw someone, they would throw tear gas at them. Helicopters were flying with people on ladders hanging from them, throwing tear gas bottles onto the ground. Some people were seriously beaten.

Faced with this situation, Strzelec decided to act:

> I phoned one of the ambulance drivers and we went together. He was afraid to go in, so I went. I had sheets with me and I put all the money and the documents into them, tied it all up and took it downstairs. I was lucky to get everything; everyone was surprised that I managed to do it. (Later, I was accused of taking money from the steelworks because I took the money and the documents from the Solidarity building).

Strzelec was among the few who decided not to surrender, but to go underground instead.

> A few of us left in the last functioning locomotive. We got off the train into the snow, where we lay for a long time, until it got dark. Then, we went to a village where priests took us to an apartment where the police would be unlikely to look for us. We spent the night there. As a result of lying in the snow for so long, I got a fever and was unconscious, so I was taken to a convent. I spent three days there. I pretended I was a nun.

Piast mine

Zbigniew Bogacz attended a party the night martial law was declared, so he avoided capture when they showed up at his home around 12:30am. Like others, he learned of martial law on television the next morning. On Monday morning, he said:

> the morning and afternoon shifts met and we organised a demonstration demanding freedom for the interned. The director, the First Secretary and some other officials were all very stiff and pompous, so they were whistled down, had mud thrown at them and they had to leave. We decided to go underground without even changing clothes: we just grabbed helmets: so I go underground in slacks and a nice shirt and tie. As we go, we meet people: in one place, about six hundred, in another, about four hundred – on strike. I went out and quickly changed into miners' clothes, and in 15 minutes I was back underground. That was a signal that they could trust me. There were more than 2,000 of us. We decided not to allow more people to join the strike. Instead, we asked them to send us food.

But while they were safe from assault, they were beset with a logistical night-mare: How to feed people? How to keep up their morale? How to see that no-one was injured? How to keep up the repair of the mine? And what would be the long-term consequences to physical and mental health of being underground for an indefinite period of time? Bogacz responded:

> The electricians created electric stoves from chain saws. We had big pots that could cook fifty litres at once, so we started cooking soups, so we could keep something in our stomachs. We had to service the pumps that keep out the underground water, and we had to organise safety. We didn't know how long the strike would go on.

I wondered why the authorities hadn't cut off the miners' electricity. Bogacz:

> If they cut off the electricity, they would drown us because of the water that comes into the mine. So the pumps had to work 24 hours a day. If they cut off the electricity, the mine would be flooded in hours. Plus huge ventilators pump air into the tunnels. We didn't think they would kill us all.

According to Krzysztof Młodzik, on the second day of the strike:

> a member of the local Party Central Committee who worked in our mine came down and urged us to come out. People wanted to throw him into the shaft, but we stopped that. We accompanied him to the elevator. I had never before seen a man so scared.

On the next day, Bogacz recalled that they gained some succour: 'A delegation from the Ziemowit Mine [which was also conducting an underground strike], joined us where our tunnels met. We had psychological backup from the fact that two mines were connecting underground'.

The authorities attempted to persuade Bogacz to end the strike, offering him special benefits if he cooperated: 'The director of the ministry called to tell me that I would get whatever kind of work I wanted if I ended the strike'. Bogacz refused: 'how would I look in the eyes of the people who trusted me?'

> We learned that there were mines and factories on strike not only in our region, but everywhere in Poland. We found out that *Wujek* and several other mines were on strike, and the Katowice Steel Mill, the Gdańsk Shipyard and the Lenin Steel Mill, in *Nowa Huta*.

They got this information through a radio they rigged up underground, with wires secretly run to the top. With it they listened to western and Polish broadcasts.[13] Bogacz:

---

13. Interview with Młodzik.

> I think the deciding influence on the length of the *Piast* strike was the events at the *Wujek* mine on 16 December. We heard of the killings. They said that people were only wounded, but there was no way to verify it. By 20 December, the other strikes had all been forcibly ended.

Knowing that they were alone, and aware of the prior use of deadly force and that now they would be targets, the miners grimly prepared. Bogacz: 'Near the shaft we had water under high pressure. I told them that if they came underground, they wouldn't get out because we would be prepared'. They learned that an anti-terrorist group was being considered for use against them. Bogacz continued:

> We had people above ground, and if the anti-terrorist group showed up, we would get a signal. If the elevator came down, the highly-pressurised water would tear them apart. Maybe they would kill a few of us, but we would get their weapons. I told them that was how they would be greeted if they came down. They couldn't cut off the water supply because it was in the shaft. Then we learned that they had another idea – paralysing gas. I told them that if they did, I would open the shaft ventilation traps, and they would get that gas immediately above ground.

The efforts to persuade or to force the miners to abandon their strike, continued:

> They waged psychological war: they had wives and children crying for the strike to end, while we were supposedly beating people to keep them underground. Now, suddenly, in every family, there were said to be some sick, some injured, some dying. We knew these were phony when one of us who wasn't married was told that his supposed child was very seriously ill! So, we decided that the best way to make people aware of what they were doing would be to read the letters out loud and give people examples of the bullshit.

When they learned of the assault on the Katowice Steel Mill, the tension grew. Since a group of priests had led some workers out of the *Ziemowit* Mine, the government wanted priests to go down into the *Piast* Mine as well, and suggested that the miners were refusing to permit them to do so. So they made it clear that clergy were welcome. Bogacz:

> They asked Bishop Bednorz, to go into the mine to get people to leave. On Christmas Eve, the bishop and priests were underground with us for about six hours. He tried to talk people into ending the strike. Only about 12 people left. The bishop gave the rest of us the last rites. We asked him to tell our families about the atmosphere underground, so they wouldn't panic. We just wanted him to tell the truth.

The strike continued through the Christmas holiday.

> Christmas Eve was typically Polish: a very warm atmosphere. We had soups, bacon, sausages, but a shortage of bread. We wanted to show that we were determined enough to sacrifice even our family holiday to fight for our rights. At least we knew we were all together and our families knew where we were. We knew of the wives and families of miners who would never again sit at the table for Christmas – the *Wujek* miners. We had a radio connection, so we could listen to the traditional midnight mass from Warsaw. We heard the priest mention us – the miners in Silesia who were still on strike. It went to all of Poland, and they all knew that there was one mine still on strike.

As the strike dragged on, they were concerned:

> How long could a person stay underground without damage to health – mental or physical? We spoke about it with doctors. We hadn't had any accidents up to then, and we wanted to finish the strike that way. People had to safeguard the coal, the machines, to take care of ventilation, to get rid of the water. The electricians worked with high-voltage electricity – and there were no accidents. We knew we couldn't keep it up forever, that it was stretching our luck.

So they began to talk about ending the strike, which occasioned serious divisions:

> About three hundred were strongly for continuing. I said I would stay with them, but it would be better if we ended the strike together, as one crew, rather than to become a smaller and smaller group. We decided that we would all go out together at 7:30 pm, after the TV news. There was snow on the ground outside: we had been in darkness for a long time; we were afraid that the collision of our eyesight with daylight plus white snow could blind us. But in the evening when it was dark, if they attacked, we would be able to get out through dark corners in the mine which they didn't know, so there wouldn't be a massacre.

The two-week strike finally ended:

> About 7:30 pm, we started going up. I stood near the shaft as people were leaving with tears in their eyes. It took several loads before I left in the last cage, to be sure that no one remained underground. The news spread around so quickly that families were tripping over each other, running to the mine to meet their men. A few thousand people – family members and friends – came to the mine to meet us. They were a kind of guarantee that nothing would happen there.

Once the strike ended, the police went after the leaders. Bogacz:

> They took me to the interrogation building, stripped me naked, called me names: bandit, murderer! They screamed at me about how I kept so many people and made them suffer underground. One of them hit me in the face with his fists, then with a club. I was defenceless: it was just me and them. I was lucky that I was the last one, and they were already tired. Because all my friends who were arrested before, were also beaten, worse than me.

At least two thousand workers are estimated to have lost their jobs at *Piast* as a result of this strike.[14] A total of almost a hundred and fifty striking factories found the military and the police used against them. As indicated, tanks were sometimes used, workers were fired upon. The whole process took about a week, not counting the coal mines that experienced underground strikes. Some of the strikers were arrested.[15]

Continuing resistance to martial law

Resistance continued long after martial law was imposed. For example, Tadeusz Jedynak, the vice-chairman of Solidarity in Upper Silesia, was interned during the round-up in December. He was kept in prison for a year. After his release, he went underground. He was arrested again in 1985 and charged with treason, but in September 1986 he was again released as part of the general amnesty proclaimed then. He later explained what he did when captured in 1985:[16]

> When I was thrown into Rakowicka [prison] in June 1985, I did not say a word. It was not I who had a hard time dealing with them but, on the contrary, it was my jailers who had the hard time. When I was captured, I immediately wanted it to be known: I had an appointment schedule a few days later with Zbyszek Bujak and I was afraid he might be caught in a trap. So when they proposed that I appear on TV, I said that I had to consult my wife. They bought this line and they brought her in. When she saw me I knew that I had succeeded. I shouted to her that there was no question of my appearing [on television], and they took me away. I was all the time aware that they could film me with a hidden camera, so when they gave me a shaving kit, I played a trick on them and shaved my head: let them show me bald-headed on television. The guards were furious because I changed my appearance so much that they couldn't even stage a confrontation.

---

14. Paczkowski 2003, p. 453.
15. Paczkowski and Byrne 2007, p. 34.
16. Jedynak, 1986: p. 7.

Similarly, my wife was a teacher in Upper Silesia at the time, having begun her career after the invocation of martial law. She was not subject to verification, nor were the other teachers around her. They talked openly about Solidarity and what had happened in Poland. Her mentor opined that this was the case because the opposition was so great in their region that if they did do a verification, they would have to let the janitors do the teaching. (Of course, the janitors themselves might not have passed). According to my wife's mentor, the other option for filling the vacancies would have had to be 'łapanki' (random street round-ups carried out by the Nazis during WWII).

The nation's political leaders were left with an angry and sullen population. Colonel Sucharski recalled: 'The Party leadership was declaring "We won!" But what kind of victory was that? It created great bitterness among the workers'.

The declaration of martial law and the round-ups associated with it moved another generation into opposition. That was why Bogdan Borusewicz called it a 'Pyrrhic victory'.[17]

> **Piotr Rozbicki**: Everything was turned upside down. I was too young in the Solidarity period to understand what it was all about. The declaration of martial law opened my eyes: that you should oppose everything.

> **Paweł Adamowicz**: I started taking food to the shipyards and preparing information. After the shipyard was pacified, we took part in demonstrations for three days, fighting with the police. Later, I printed and distributed leaflets and papers and during the breaks between classes, everyone would sit silently on the floor.

Such actions – which were carried out in many schools – produced an eerie atmosphere in a context that was normally filled with the normal sounds of youth. I wondered if Adamowicz, a high-school student at the time, was aware of the severe penalties he was risking? He responded: 'My brother was interned and my family was worried about me, but it was my duty'. So, on May Day, when his school director ordered the students to join the government demonstration, he and his collaborators:

> organised a boycott. Some thirty went, out of about seven hundred. There was no leader; we were simply a group of friends who trusted each other and did everything together.

Resistance took many forms. Shortly after 13 December, Deputy Prime Minister Rakowski met with about twenty leading intellectuals. All but one opposed martial law; as a result, that person's 'friends refuse to acknowledge him and even

---

17. Lopinski 1990, p. 36.

members of his family call him ... Kola (for *colla*borationist)'.[18] Actors refused to appear on television or radio, and the leaders of the dissolved journalists' union called upon journalists to refuse to join the new union the government was forming or to write for government publications, stating: 'The knowledge that our present actions will be assessed in the future should be a warning to those who think that the time of contempt for decent work and honour will last forever'.[19] Bogdan Lis:[20] 'Leaflets are constantly thrown onto the streets ... On the thirteenth day of each month at 9:00 pm, many lights go off in people's houses'.[21]

Some people rebelled by hooking up to the electric grid directly, thereby bypassing the meter to avoid paying the charges to the government.[22] In Upper Silesia, when people disembarked from the buses and trams, they handed their already-punched tickets to those entering, enabling them to ride without paying. This was done *en masse*, so the government was systematically denied these revenues. The anger and alienation filtered down even to children, including high-school and even grammar-school students around the country, many of whom created and distributed their own underground leaflets and papers, despite the penalties for doing so. Slogans were spray-painted on walls, overpasses and other public places at night, and after being painted over in the daytime, they were repainted at night, so a battle of wills continued. A widely-used slogan that appeared on walls and on signs, promising an ongoing struggle, read as follows: 'The winter is yours; the spring is ours!' A guerrilla war of signs and graffiti persisted for a long time. Ryszard Brzuzy:

> We managed to hang six-metre cloth signs. On the way from Warsaw to Katowice, there was a big sign: 'Solidarity is alive!' and it made them furious. We hung them under bridges or high on electric wires. They were afraid to take them down. First, they switched off the electricity to get them, which is a very complicated operation. We had no schedule so they couldn't catch us.

One day in late January, a Solidarity flag flew for three hours in the Cegielski factory in Poznań before a special unit arrived to cut it down. People tried, even in symbolic ways, to keep the union alive. Miniature Solidarity buttons appeared; high-school and university students wore black to school; at football matches,

18. 'Rakowski and Kubiak Meet Intellectuals, 25 February 1982', *UPNB*, no. 7, 1982, pp. 22–3.

19. Bratkowski 1982, pp. 23–4; 'Unofficial Publications: Information Extracted from Information Service of Warsaw Solidarity, no. 47, 14 May, 1982', *UPNB*, no. 10, 4 June 1982, p. 13.

20. Lis 1982a, p. 18.

21. In Communist Poland, because leafleting was illegal, leaflets were thrown into the air or down from buildings rather than being handed out.

22. *UPNB*, no. 1, 1 January 1983, pp. 3–4.

cries of 'Solidarity' were frequently heard.[23] People demonstrated against the government by turning their lights out, or by ostentatiously going outside 'for strolls' when the television news was broadcast. Union dues and other contributions were collected and used to aid the repressed and pay for printing and other such necessities.[24]

Stefan Bratkowski, the head of the Polish Journalists' Union before the coup, recorded opposition tapes and sent them all around Poland, where the tapes were copied and replayed over and over. Soon there was a whole apparatus of underground Solidarity organisations, newspapers, even guerrilla television and radio broadcasts, that would break off before they could be found and repressed, and an underground network of videotapes made illegally for VCRs. Books, journals and underground publishers appeared, and by the late 1980s they rivalled the official press in both quantity and quality of titles – of course, they published things that the official publishers would not publish, including material translated from the West. By the mid-1980s, much of this material was openly sold, at least on university campuses. And people frequently listened to foreign broadcasts into Poland.

Several Solidarity activists, who had been abroad when the crackdown was carried out, stayed there and continued to aid the opposition from without. Local cells in factories, universities, schools and elsewhere organised petitions and protests, boycotted official propaganda meetings, and publicised the names of government collaborators.[25] There were organisations in almost every large factory, and at universities and scientific institutes.[26] Bogdan Lis recalled:[27] 'Solidarity had left an awareness, that one can be free, that it was possible to live differently. It had allowed people to get off their knees'. Frasyniuk: 'Everywhere you would turn, people kept on discussing things in the food lines. That is why the police started to attack the lines and told people to disappear'.

Production figures in the wake of the coup were disastrous.[28] According to official figures, production in January 1982 had fallen 13.6 percent since January 1981, when Solidarity strikes were alleged to have caused considerable damage, thus already cutting production; and it had fallen 17.5 percent since December 1981.[29]

The coup also occasioned prominent defections. Rakowski's son, who was studying in West Germany, took asylum there. Dozens of sailors refused to

---

23. 'The Everyday Reality of Martial Law', *Poland Watch*, no. 2, p. 116.
24. Lopinski et al. 1990, p. 66.
25. 'Solidarity Organisation Under Martial Law', *UPNB*, no. 16, 3 September 1982, pp. 31–3.
26. 'Organisation of Solidarity Under Martial Law', *Committee in Support of Solidarity Reports*, no. 7, 1 October 1982, pp. 4–5.
27. Hayden 1994, p. 48.
28. 'The Everyday Reality of Martial Law', *Poland Watch*, no. 2, p. 115.
29. Kuroń 1982a, pp. 7–8.

return to their ships in various ports of call. Poland's ambassadors to America and Japan defected.[30] Less prominent was the sixteen-year-old daughter of a military officer who wrote to Radio Free Europe:

> Almost all of us hate our fathers...I am branded by my school friends on account of my father...I cannot go on listening to my father's views, and his attempts to persuade me that all is well. He forces me to watch the news on television. He forbids me to be friends with young people, who are – in his opinion – rabble or whores. He chooses friends for me who are the children of the military. I am sixteen and attend a secondary school... Teachers are liars and treacherous... A dreadful atmosphere prevails at home... If I speak in a slightly raised tone of voice, or criticise anything – my father hits me or beats me with his belt... If I could escape from this country – I would do so.

These sentiments were reflected within the Polish United Workers' Party, where Party members, especially workers, who had retained their membership through all the conflicts and tensions, now left in droves. They were heavily concentrated among the young and among workers. Jan Lityński: 'The general view was that the Party was falling apart'.

> Bujak: People threw their Party cards out of the window. The boldest threw them into the wastebasket near the Party room. There were not many young people left in the Party at that time, and cases of young people joining the Party then were really exceptional.

From the declaration of martial law, the Party grew increasingly moribund. Very few new people joined until 1985, when the Party slowly began to grow, but not enough to rejuvenate it. By that time, some 700,000 workers alone had left the Party since the strikes in August 1980. Year after year, the median age of its members rose: it was becoming a gerontocracy.[31]

---

30. Jain 1983, p. 185.
31. Sulek 1990, p. 504.

Chapter Sixteen
Rebuilding the Movement

> **Zbigniew Bujak:** We guessed that in the first few days, 300 to 500 editorial boards formed around the country. Within weeks, secret committees formed in the factories. They collected fees and organised underground publications. A second, spontaneous organisation emerged to help interned prisoners and their families.

How can a movement respond after it has been forcibly suppressed through what amounted to a *coup d'état?* How do the activists who avoided being captured regroup to begin to recreate the movement? They could not go home – the police had been there and would return. They did not know who else had survived or how to find them. What was possible? These were the dilemmas that faced those activists who managed to survive the military coup. Their initial problems concerned how to hide, where to go, how to find others who were also free. Subsequent matters included where to stay – first for days, then weeks, months, and finally years – how to arrange for publications to be produced and distributed, how to combat the Party and state that had driven them underground. The most fundamental of concerns was how to keep the movement alive, and how to keep the mass of union participants and supporters feeling a part of the movement and involved in those discussions. First, individuals and local groups had to arrange their own solutions. Later, Solidarity members had to find how to meet, discuss and pass on the decisions that emerged from discussion. Broader questions of strategy had to be discussed. There was also the problem of how to translate decisions made by 'leaders' into mass action.

In effect, a war was waged between the opposition and the government, which continued to search for people who had escaped, and to pressure those whom it had already caught. The government tried to get public declarations of loyalty in exchange for freedom. There were some who signed, often out of duress: 'a Solidarity activist who had left a sick child at home . . . One . . . was taken from his mother suffering from cancer and told that there would be no-one to give her a cup of tea'.[1] Still, as Bujak noted, that effort on the part of the authorities 'collapsed, and very rapidly too'.[2]

Surviving

Basic survival required a safe place to stay. At first, this was an individual problem for each who had escaped detention. By the time Marian Terlecki, a Gdańsk Solidarity leader, found that he had the wrong keys to an apartment he had been lent, it was too close to the curfew to risk going out, so he prepared to camp out in the stairwell. But a couple in the building sheltered him. Later, he stayed with a friend who no longer wished to be politically involved:

> I left their house just as soon as there was a chance of hiding somewhere else . . . I didn't know where I'd be living in the coming weeks, and more importantly, I didn't know with what kind of people – because people had changed. They became more elusive, more ambiguous, more uncertain of themselves.

He found a safe place and stayed there for two months: 'Now, the first serious dilemma was . . . posed: was it possible to do something safely? Without jeopardising myself, or my hosts? Because, after all, I wasn't there just for the sake of hiding. I had to renew severed connections; I had to meet with people'.[3]

Especially in the early days, it was common for people to move frequently, despite the dangers of doing so. Sławomir Majewski: 'First I stayed with friends, but I had to move from one flat to another: it was dangerous to stay in one place because people who lived in the building could find it strange that a man they did not know stayed for such a long time'. In Wrocław, at first the activists had a hard time finding a place to stay; they slept five or six to a room, often going hungry. They established networks of communication, only to have their

---

1. Zagozda 1982, p. 20; *Poland Watch*, no. 2, 5 February 1982, p. 11.
2. Bujak 1982, p. 39.
3. Terlecki 1983, pp. 83–6.

couriers arrested or drop out from fear.[4] Over time, finding places to stay grew more difficult. Occasionally, a host's indiscretion forced someone to evacuate quickly. Zbigniew Bujak recalled: 'Sometimes an apartment may be "clean" but it turns out that half the occupants of the building are in the underground, which makes it easy to be caught by accident'.[5] Bujak further noted the difficulties of having to deal with day-to-day living, among strangers:[6]

> The greatest problem I experienced was what I would call the emotional burden of living with people one didn't know... Even now when I go to a new apartment I always recognise straight away the place where the head of the family sits. It was so important not to be a burden on the family... never to occupy the position of the head of the family, or to sit where he (or she) sat.

The combination of all this – state repression, the isolation and insecurity to which those who were underground were subjected – made life very difficult, as Marian Terlecki stated:

> The situation of many friends and acquaintances, interned or arrested... was simply unknown... The streets were filled with depressed people, ZOMO patrols, tanks and military transporter trucks. The worst part, however, was the lack of hope... The Christmas holidays were approaching, but instead of good cheer, this time they brought only further depression. Contact with family, haunted by the Security Police... was out of the question. Friends who had escaped the tempest were hiding somewhere, and there was no way to reach them. And I had no certain place of refuge. There was always the fear that 'they might look for me here, too'. Trying to scrape together anything was a thankless task. People were lost, paralysed with fear.[7]

Helena Łuczywo organised housing for many of the leading activists in Warsaw:

> We needed I don't remember how many apartments every two weeks: for people to stay – you had to live with other people, and apartments in Poland are small. We needed several places to meet – because you didn't meet in the apartment where you slept or worked. One place was needed for the editors of *Tygodnik Mazowsze*, places to print, from which to distribute, and so on. We had to find dozens and dozens of apartments. At some point, I calculated that I went through 300 different apartments.

---

4. Lopinski et al. 1990, pp. 41–3. In Wrocław, the first translator I had quit after my first interview, as he feared that the assignment was too dangerous. This was in 1988 – over six years after martial law was first invoked.
5. Lopinski et al. 1990, p. 67.
6. Hayden 1994, p. 81.
7. Terlecki 1983, p. 83.

Part of the problem was getting people food. Frasyniuk recalled: 'Once we sat depressed for two weeks, eating rice and macaroni because there was nothing else in the house'.[8] It was dangerous for them to go outside, where they might be recognised. While inevitably they did go out for a variety of reasons, including changing apartments, it was preferable to keep such trips to a minimum. Łuczywo:

> We found a woman who did all the cooking for us. She got food from people through the church; then she would cook for a few days. She froze everything and she would write what each thing was on the plastic containers. Once a week, on Mondays, we would have lunch together – which was not very safe but we couldn't resist it – and she would deliver a week's worth of frozen food. She did it for years.

Remaining underground for weeks, months, even years, was difficult. As Łuczywo remembered:

> Only later did I realise how isolated we were. We didn't work in an office, a factory or somewhere, so we didn't see our former companions turn either into collaborators, or become concerned just with their private lives. Nor did we see how much of a legend we were becoming because we didn't go to parties and places where people talked about us. We just moved from one apartment to another and tried to find new places, which was awful work.

Did they have any enjoyment during the lengthy period they remained underground? Łuczywo: 'The first months were wonderful, in spite of being separated from my daughter. Later, it was awful because then it was just routine: one year, two years, a third year, the fourth year . . . It lasted until the round table talks in 1989'.

Zbigniew Janas, recalled that hiding in the underground was 'horrid':

> [I]n the beginning it meant nearly total isolation. In order to be active and survive, you need quite a number of people to help you find lodgings, to serve as liaison, to organise meetings. I did not want to make use of the people around the underground regional committee, who were stretched anyway. I had to form a quite new group for myself. This took me about a year. Only then, I could say, did I become really active.[9]

Some people changed their appearances. Men, for example, could grow a beard or a moustache, or shave them off; women could cut their hair or grow it long.

---

8. Lopinski et al. 1990, p. 151.

9. 'Interview with Zbigniew Janas', in *Tygodnik Powszechny*, 24 January 1988, reprinted in *UPNB*, no. 4, 1988; 'A Conversation with Zbigniew Janas', *UPNB*, no. 20, 9 October 1985, p. 26.

Others did not disguise themselves, but got away unnoticed. Regardless, all had to have fake documents, as they were frequently checked, and that meant establishing illegal operations and making contact with them.[10]

Reconstructing the opposition

Zbigniew Bujak: We knew that some activists had managed to hide; the problem was, how would they meet, given the conditions of martial law? How would they get in touch with each other? We had no telephones – they had been cut off by the government. People were not allowed to leave their town or district without permission. And there was a curfew.

Having avoided detention, Solidarity activists now began to construct an underground. It seemed imperative that their first step should be to present some kind of public presence after the devastating arrests[11] – to be able to show that Solidarity was still alive. Bogdan Borusewicz recalled that after he escaped from the Gdańsk shipyard:

We found people who printed several thousand leaflets which were distributed on Christmas Eve. People were frightened, so I signed the leaflets with my name just to show that there were people who were not afraid of Jaruzelski. My acquaintances, who were also hiding, saw the leaflet and knew that I wasn't in prison. We got in touch with one another, but it took a long time because of the risks.

Eugeniusz Szumiejko was in Gdańsk during the arrests, but had managed to escape: 'It was during midnight mass on Christmas Eve that I discovered that ... Borusewicz was active; someone had left a lot of leaflets in the church signed by him'.[12]

Everyone attempted to find and make contact with others who had escaped. Borusewicz:

We contacted people we trusted who had contact with somebody else in a whole chain that finally connected us with somebody who knew where someone else was hiding. They organised a meeting. You had to be very careful. When you knew the person who carried the information it was all right, you could trust him. But if not, it could be a trap.

---

10. Łuczywo interview.
11. 'An Authorised Interview with Zbigniew Bujak and Wiktor Kulerski', *UPNB*, no. 6, 1982, p. 7.
12. Lopinski et al. 1990, p. 38.

It was a process that had to be repeated by each person who had not been detained and wished to resist. Jan Ciesielski: 'First, we had to learn who had escaped, which was done through our network of friends and acquaintances'. Sławomir Majewski: 'One had to look for those who had not been arrested. And then you look for his acquaintances, because perhaps he was an agent'. Jan L., a member of underground Solidarity's Committee for Social Resistance, which organised aid to the repressed and published information about the repression, recalled:

> Within the first two days of martial law a group of us met almost accidentally to exchange information and to examine the possibilities for further action. We started meeting regularly, every few days and each time in a different flat in order not to arouse suspicion.[13]

Edward Nowak was arrested on 13 January, but during the month before they caught him, he helped to lay the basis for the underground in Kraków: 'We arranged that whoever escaped would meet at a given time and place. Everyone – at first, there was fewer than twenty – went about the city in disguises, looking for people'. Władysław Frasyniuk:

> It was extremely difficult because we didn't even have a place to sleep. Some people quit because of the extreme repression; others were arrested. To renew contact with a given factory sometimes took two or three months because you had to check people.

Ryszard Brzuzy worked in the brown coal fields away from the cities:

> Two or three of us would get together at a time; we didn't meet together at once. After a month, we organised broader meetings of about thirty in the churches. The older people were more afraid; they had less energy and less will to be active than us younger people. The first thing was just to give people information; when someone got an underground paper there was a feeling that we had not been not destroyed, and that we could not be destroyed by tanks. We were still alive. We had to search for paper, which we stole from work-places. We had old ink, but not enough, so once we made it from shoe polish and oil. Our printing press had been seized, so we made primitive equipment. Over time, we managed to improve the quality. We were arrested at the end of June, after three months of printing by very primitive methods.

In the first months, there was a chaotic character to this activity, in which some-times two or more underground groups were active in the same factory, without

---

13. Jan L. 1983, p. 15.

knowing about each other.[14] Gradually, in many factories they began collecting dues again and publishing. At first, all they could do was to indicate that Solidarity still existed. In Warsaw, the first call for resistance urged people to boycott the official press and to turn out their lights on the thirteenth of every month in a symbolic gesture of opposition.[15]

They were joined by young people who were moved into activity by the government's betrayal of its promise. Thus, a new generation became active. Małgorzata Górczewska was one of those:

> In 1980, I was 15; I met a group of young people from Toruń with whom I co-operated during martial law. I got newspapers and books from them, and during the martial law period, we published our own newspaper.
>
> **Paweł Śliwiński:** Getting involved [in the underground] was a gradual process. First I read the underground press, which was hard to get. Later, my friends and I made our own leaflets and distributed them around the town. My contacts with the underground became more frequent. First, I read these things; next, I would carry them somewhere. It was all based on personal acquaintances.

Thus, primary groups were crucial to maintaining an opposition just as they had been in giving birth to it. But some who had not been active before martial law, because they did not trust the government, were willing to undertake underground activity, so new people were activated by the crackdown.

The reconstituted national leadership called upon its supporters to 'organise a mass, society-wide underground resistance movement', and to resist in any way possible, other than violently.[16] Helena Łuczywo resumed underground publishing in Warsaw, and created what became the official organ of the Solidarity underground. *Tygodnik Mazowsze* ('Mazovian Weekly') began coming out in February 1982:

> A few of us who survived martial law started *Solidarity Information*, which was a daily bulletin, of whatever news we could get. We immediately began to distribute it outside of Warsaw, and also to smuggle it out of the country. There was a huge hunger for information. People typed and retyped it and it got out of our hands totally. After a while, some people began to print it independently of us. Later, we got in touch with the printers; we could pass them information directly.

---

14. 'Solidarity Underground: Secret Factory Commissions', *UPNB*, no. 18, 1982, p. 13.
15. Lopinski et al. 1990, p. 45.
16. Appeared originally in *Tygodnik Wojenny*, 11 February 1982, cited in Sanford 1986, p. 254.

Tygodnik Mazowsze grew into a 'huge organisation, printed in 20 locations all over Poland', Łuczywo recalled.

These publications had an immeasurably important role in that period, providing an alternative source of information from the official censored media.

> Łuczywo: The problem of the Solidarity Underground was that, if you wanted to keep an organisation going, you had to have something for people to do. There were not that many things to do after martial law was imposed. One of them was producing and distributing underground publications, which involved thousands of people. It was very labour-consuming.

Bujak felt this activity was important:

> The history of the beginnings of the Warsaw underground is the history of the underground press . . . We have been told by many people that when we finally began publishing a weekly, many other organisational details improved, including the payment of union dues and the creation of several factory papers.[17]

Through the underground press, as Andrzej Tymowski noted:[18]

> Rumours were confirmed or disproved, news spread of upcoming demonstrations, and opinions exchanged on the effectiveness of proposed tactics. Analysis and debate were conducted via the underground press, since severe curfew restrictions prevented even small groups of people from meeting privately and public meetings were obviously out of the question.

In April 1982, *Tygodnik Mazowsze* estimated that some 1,700 underground periodicals were circulating, some with a considerable readership (the paper of the Lenin Shipyard workers in Gdańsk had a circulation of 60,000, while the Wrocław regional organisation distributed 20,000 copies per issue):[19]

> The 18 months of Solidarity created such a need for freedom of expression that, despite the internment of the majority of the union's journalists and printers, despite the confiscation or destruction of printing equipment, four months after the introduction of martial law we can observe an unprecedented growth in the underground press.

Over time, these papers became increasingly adept at getting information about conditions in the internment centres, and about strikes and demonstrations. Local groups, ranging from professionals to workers to high-school students and even elementary-school pupils created their own publications, including

---

17. Lopinski et al. 1990, p. 47.
18. Tymowski 1983, p. 96.
19. 'Statement of the Regional Strike Committee of Solidarity in Wrocław, 1 February 1982', *Poland Watch News Bulletin*, no. 4, 1982, p. 19; Cave and Sosnowska 1982, p. 64.

pamphlets and eventually books.[20] (In 1988, I met with a group of elementary-school students in Wrocław who published an underground publication for the classmates in their school and in other schools.) One publication explained how to establish an underground factory commission.[21] Another gave advice on how to plot, withstand a police interrogation, survive in prison. A publication in Katowice told workers: 'Stick religiously to the most idiotic instructions ... a senseless rule is your ally ... If you are told to break any rules: demand that the order be put in writing; complain about it, prolong the whole process'. Slowdowns and sick leave appear to have been common methods of resistance in the first year of martial law.[22]

Beyond the underground press, in the early days the most important activity on the ground was providing aid to the families of detained workers. Andrzej Sokołowski: 'Until the men who were imprisoned got out, we helped their families because the wives were not working'. In some places, this was the beginning of underground activity. Aiding those who were imprisoned was seen as a moral necessity: they were sacrificing for all. Helena Łuczywo:

> The fact that people stayed in prison for Solidarity was an important reason for people to do something. You had always to look at why you did this in the name of Solidarity. Very few people believed that it would be reborn. But you had to go on, and one of the reasons was that those people were in prison, so you did it for them.

One of the measures the government took as part of its crackdown was to close the universities to preclude student protests. They remained closed until February. When Grzegorz Szwetyn returned to his studies at Wrocław University; he immediately set to work to build the underground:

> I began creating new structures because most of the activists had been arrested. These structures were built mainly through the distribution of the press. We were given papers, and we distributed them to the people around us. At the beginning, we had several hundred copies. People who are not residents of Wrocław took those papers out and distributed them in their places. The Independent Student Union [Niezależny Związek Studentów = NZS] dealt with two matters: first, it helped those who were detained; and second, it provided a political context with the newspapers. NZS was also engaged in a battle for greater autonomy of the universities.

---

20. 'Unofficial Publications: The Current State of Play', UPNB, no. 10, 4 June, pp. 7–9; 'Popularity of the Official Press', UPNB, no. 7, 27 March 1985, p. 42.

21. 'Solidarity Underground: How to Set Up Secret Factory Commissions', Poland Watch News Bulletin, no. 18, 1 October 1982, p. 14.

22. Cited in Cave and Sosnowska 1982, p. 66; Jarosz 1982–83, p. 115.

By the spring, the first stirrings of self-education groups emerged, initiated by people who felt the need to rethink Solidarity's experiences and to consider the future.[23] These blossomed into underground 'universities' often organised through the churches, as well as lectures and meetings where a wide variety of topics were discussed. A report on these circles appeared in *Tygodnik Mazowsze* in mid-1984:[24]

> Private courses are usually initiated by people who were most active in Solidarity at their place of work... based on friendship and trust... In a self-education group usually a strong sense of community develops. Before a lecture starts there is an exchange of information about recent developments, actions, planned events, and so on... Often they exchange underground publications... We do not keep addresses or any other data about participants. Everybody is an acquaintance or a friend of somebody, so he can always be contacted. When there is an urgent need for help, or someone needs a hideout, these are people one can turn to.

Frasyniuk noted that there were constant efforts to disrupt organising:

> Management is fairly strict in implementing the blockade between the different sections of plants (for example, people have to put their names down when they leave their workroom), and security men are trying to infiltrate the plants. We could say that, apart from regular production teams, there are whole 'security sections' whose job it is to interrogate and intimidate workers all the time.[25]

This effort to reconstruct the opposition was sometimes interrupted. The police were constantly searching for those who had avoided detention, as well as for new activists, and they frequently succeeded. For example, in March they arrested a number of key operatives in Wrocław, which made the work of recreating the network more difficult.[26] Nonetheless, by spring, regional leadership bodies were being recreated in several areas.

Nowhere was this effort more difficult than in Upper Silesia where the repression was great. Adam Skwira: 'Those who had trials all lost their jobs, including me'. Skwira found another job elsewhere, but he kept in touch with his friends at the *Wujek* Mine, where, he said, there was a lengthy period of terror. Ginter Kupka: 'In March 1982, when I left the detention camp, many people were afraid

---

23. 'Underground Education Courses', *UPNB*, no. 11, 3 June 1983, p. 32; appeared originally in *Tygodnik Mazowsze*, no. 46.

24. 'They Know What They Want', *UPNB*, no. 11, 1984, from *Tygodnik Mazowsze*, no. 83.

25. Frasyniuk 1982, p. 16.

26. Lopinski et al. 1990, pp. 60–1.

to do anything connected with Solidarity. There were no meetings, no lectures, nothing'.

Stanisław Płatek: It was not until mid-1983 that the Solidarity underground began to be active in Upper Silesia. There was no chance to start underground activity in the *Wujek* Mine. I was observed by the secret police, so I couldn't act. We published a periodical, *The Voice of Upper Silesia.* We concentrated on giving help to people in prisons and detention centres.

Józef Pleszak: In 1982, we organised a secret underground at the July Manifesto Mine with a group of 15 who weren't close friends but knew each other. Each of those 15 was to get others to join the group. After three months, there were 50 of us. But there was no underground publication until February 1983.

At first, local oppositions proceeded without much guidance from or connection to the national leadership. Borusewicz: 'Resistance was concentrated in demonstrations in December, January and February, and we had absolutely no influence over their emergence or the course they took'.[27] Thus, he noted: 'Those who, because of their union mandate, should have been actively leading, and not ... hiding while society actively stepped out, were in the position of fans'.[28] He said: 'Until March everyone was independently active. Many groups had no contact with each other. Social activity was so enormous that no structures were needed, no organisation in this sense'. But these groups 'didn't protect themselves well enough, so by the summer of 1983, they were arrested. Gradually, the spontaneous resistance declined and the structures had to take on themselves the responsibility for resistance. By the summer of 1983, the underground structures of Solidarity were fully responsible for organising'.

Reconstituting a national leadership was also a difficult undertaking, noted Wiktor Kulerski, Bujak's deputy in the Warsaw region: 'We were motivated by fear. Not the fear of getting caught but the fear of making some mistake. I did not want to make one false step that could have terrible consequences later'.[29]

Borusewicz, Lis and Aleksander Hall were unable to meet before 1982. By then, each had his own couriers, networks of safe apartments and other necessities.[30] Frasyniuk: 'In February, we managed to reconstruct the Solidarity Temporary Coordinating Committee [*Tymczasowy Komitet Koordynacyjny* = TKK] from four regions: Warsaw, Wrocław, Gdańsk and Kraków'. Borusewicz: 'We began forming wider contacts with various ... conspiratorial groups in March, and the first

27. Lopinski et al. 1990, p. 39.
28. Borusewicz 1983, p. 13.
29. Kaufman 1989, p. 94.
30. Lopinski et al. 1990, p. 40.

declaration of the TKK appeared on April 30. In late March/early April, we established permanent contacts with other regions'.[31] Zbigniew Bujak: 'The leadership
body was drawn mainly from former leaders or from the people who were the
most famous. I was the leader of the Warsaw region; Frasyniuk was the leader of
the Wrocław region'. This was the basis which allowed them to move forward.

The opposition finally began to cohere. Bujak: 'The largest of the regional committees each was represented in the national committee. Below them, there were
factory committees'. Connections between local areas developed, so that gradually a framework for national action was reconstructed and more co-ordinated
efforts became possible. Those from the national leadership who had escaped
met first on 13 January and issued a statement in which they called upon people
to continue to resist non-violently, and to 'adhere to humanitarian aims', to 'distance themselves from terrorism and illegality', and to 'always act in accordance
with the principles of Christian ethics'. They urged people to take care of the
families of the interned, the dead, the injured and those who had lost their jobs;
they encouraged them to ostracise collaborators.[32]

> **Bogdan Borusewicz:** The basis of the TKK was the old opposition because we
> knew and trusted each other. We decided that there should be a centre which
> would co-ordinate activity in the whole country. There were many strikes;
> many were fired. But one had to fight.

The first months of martial law were taken up with debate over what kind of
organisation should be built. Some argued that the growing underground movement should constitute itself as a centralised organisation that would prepare
for a confrontation with the authorities, if necessary.[33] Bogdan Lis expressed a
contrary view:

> Here in Poland, immediately after World War II, the organisation *Freedom and
> Independence* was infiltrated and all the commanders, excluding one person,
> were from the secret-police. We feared that creating any centralised structure
> would make it easy for the police to infiltrate. In the end, we founded the
> TKK to *co-ordinate* activity in the regions; we decided that the regions would
> be autonomous.

Elsewhere, Lis noted that the 'arrest of small circles doesn't carry great consequences precisely because the different regions are connected very loosely'.[34]
Borusewicz: 'By the spring we could have created a single, enormous organisation,

---

31. Borusewicz 1983, p. 12.
32. *Poland Watch*, no. 2, 5 February 1982, pp. 7–11, 14.
33. Tymowski 1982, pp. 81–2; Tymowski 1983, pp. 98–9.
34. Lopinski et al. 1990, p. 74.

only what would have been the point? From the security point of view also this would have been a bad idea'.[35]

The TKK called for a fifteen-minute work stoppage and a one minute halt to traffic at noon on 13 May, the fifth monthly anniversary of martial law, and promised that the thirteenth of every month would be a day of protest until the people interned and arrested were released.[36] They threatened a general strike should Solidarity be de-legalised and not merely suspended. The authorities went to considerable effort to prevent these demonstrations, including threats to fire workers, detentions, special guards. But the demonstrations proceeded in several places.[37]

These Solidarity leaders were dealing with a government that was determined to prevent them from having any influence. Interior Minister Czesław Kiszczak insisted that while the government was willing to leave alone those individuals who ceased opposition, there would be no negotiations, no agreement with the opposition as an organised entity.[38]

Spirit of resistance

What gave people the heart to build an underground despite the draconian penalties they faced if caught was that many believed that, before long, Solidarity would be triumphant. The slogan: 'Winter is yours, Spring is ours' resounded with this sentiment. Eugeniusz Szumiejko recalled: 'I functioned under the illusion that the struggle would last only a couple of months and that we'd be victorious. Even in my worst imaginings, I still told myself, the spring will be ours'.[39] People simply refused to concede defeat. They built the underground; they insisted on voicing their convictions – in the streets, in the shops, on public transport, in classes. In some workplaces, people engaged in slow-downs. In some areas, such as Warsaw and Wrocław, they managed to obtain radio and even television broadcasting equipment, and they carried out guerrilla broadcasts for brief periods, as well as continuing to organise demonstrations. Classes outside the official channels were still held in churches, in people's homes and elsewhere.

The unending pressure from Solidarity loyalists limited the government's ability to manoeuvre even under these conditions of martial law. Borusewicz:

> There was deep-rooted mass resistance on the part of most groups of the population. Thus the authorities were unable to make an about-turn that

---

35. Lopinski et al. 1990, pp. 39–40.
36. *UPNB*, no. 9, 14 May 1982, pp. 3–4.
37. Cave and Sosnowska 1982, p. 72.
38. Sanford 1986, p. 152.
39. Lopinski et al. 1990, p. 37.

would have lessened social pressure, meaning some civil rights relaxations and a simultaneous improvement in the economic situation. Instead, the 'war' entered a new stage.[40]

From Colonel Sucharski's point of view, the government was not hard enough on the social movement:

> Martial law didn't change anything. The society shook off the original shock and depression because the limitations were removed – phones were reinstated, goods became available once more, and Solidarity started to revive. Some activists would sign a loyalty oath and be released. Right before the holidays, large numbers got out, and eventually there was just a handful left. The Solidarity leadership was taken over by what we called 'the second suit'. They learned from the Polish underground during the occupation, and they were prepared for such a situation.

There were also problems when new conscripts were brought into the military. Jerzy, an engineer who later worked with the self-governing councils in the factories, was one of them:

> I think they were afraid that they wouldn't be able to cope with us. They preferred to avoid any discussion with us; but we had quite fierce arguments with many of them. They kept their distance from us. Seventy percent or more shared my views, so we could talk with them, and they were unable or didn't want to punish us for what we said.

They did not try to use these new conscripts to suppress Solidarity: 'We were not the right people for them to use in such actions. They were not sure of us. This assessment concerning the impossibility of using us originated from the political officers, who felt we would be politically unreliable'. Jerzy recalled continual discussion between people who had been touched by Solidarity and soldiers who had been apart from it, perhaps because they lived in rural areas where Solidarity was not to be found, or they had been too young to appreciate what was happening around them.

The statement of Colonel Wiślicki, the military commissar at Polish radio and television, at a meeting with party-activists indicate the grim situation that the authorities saw themselves facing. Colonel Wiślicki said:[41]

---

40. Ibid.
41. 'The Military Commissar at Polish Radio and TV Speaks Out', *UPNB*, no. 8, 30 April 1982, pp. 16–17. The meeting was surreptitiously recorded and excerpts were published in *Le Monde* in France, on Radio France International, and on Radio Free Europe in Polish. (The Polish government denied that the recording was valid.)

The state of war cannot be lifted until the Party can take over the political direction of enterprises, which means that ... it is not a question of months but of years ... I'm not talking about acceptance ... We are far away from being accepted. So when answering the question – how long will the state of war last we can answer: a long time.

The struggle for a presence

Inevitably, there were differences among Solidarity activists concerning how to proceed. Jan Lityński:

> Gdańsk wanted to organise very quickly and have a general strike. In Warsaw, we were thinking about long-term organisation, and we did not think right away about striking. We wanted to build a structure which would work for several years, not one ready for the last struggle in a few months. This difference was important.

> Edward Nowak: The most important thing was to recreate the factory structures, so actions could be taken in the factories themselves, and so workers could meet and exchange opinions freely.

> Józef Pinior: In Lower Silesia, we wanted a confrontation with the authorities. But in this approach, we were alone. Colleagues in other regions of Poland saw it differently. It produced a very different political landscape here from the other regions in Poland. In Lower Silesia, because Solidarity really fought here, it was strengthened. With the 80 million zlotys we had withdrawn from the bank a few days before martial law, we could compensate people who had been fired; we could subsidise the activity of the underground publishing houses; we could support people painting on the walls; we could start immediately to act without needing to wait for help.

There was debate about whether the opposition should concentrate on activity in the factories or in the streets. They had learned in the past how easy it was for provocateurs to infiltrate street demonstrations. But in the streets, you were anonymous; in the workplace, opposition activity was easily caught. Władysław Frasyniuk:

> In 1982, we found it essential to direct our attention toward the factories, which made it easier for the police to catch us. But they were indispensable if you were dreaming of rebuilding the factory structures. For some period, we opposed street demonstrations.

It soon became evident that shop-floor activity bore its own hazards, as strikers were fired. This happened frequently in Gdańsk, which carried out monthly 15 minute strikes: during the February 1982 strikes, hundreds were arrested and many fired.[42] Lis recalled that 'over a period of six months, several hundred people were fired, interned or arrested'. In Gdańsk, and probably elsewhere, slow-downs became normal; they tried a form of strike in which workers came to work and then refused to do anything, went home after their shift was over, and returned to do the same the next day.

In Wrocław, Kornel Morawiecki, who had not played a public role before martial law, now pushed strongly for street demonstrations.[43] But Frasyniuk, the region leader, opposed them because 'the Reds can choose the worst-organised region to provoke an outburst, crush it in a bloody fashion, and thus undermine the confidence of those regions that are better organised'.[44] Janusz Onyszkiewicz also saw it differently: 'This radical approach would not work. We must change the tactic from confrontation to a long march: slow changes, building pressure, creating parallel structures'. But many accepted that the goal should be to work toward a general strike to force the government to make concessions and to negotiate a new accord.

In Kraków, in mid-February 1982, a huge demonstration materialised as individuals one-by-one (to get around the ban on gatherings) came to lay wreaths and candles at a monument in the city. When access was blocked, they went to another monument, and then another. The symbol of Polish resistance during World War II had been an anchor; now, this symbol was appropriated by the opposition,[45] and drawings of anchors appeared on the walls of public buildings. Scattered demonstrations were held in Gdańsk, Poznań, Bydgoszcz. Bogdan Lis: 'The authorities reacted in a brutal fashion, often lashing out blindly in all directions'.[46]

There were mass demonstrations in several places on 1 May 1982, where the official demonstrations were boycotted. In Gdańsk, the unofficial May Day parade was massive – perhaps 30 people wide and stretching beyond where the eye could see. Two days later, on 3 May, the anniversary of Poland's 1791 democratic constitution,[47] they marched to commemorate Polish democracy and, by implication, to oppose the current undemocratic regime. In Gdańsk and Szczecin, these demonstrations lasted more than a week, and thousands were arrested or subject to other forms of punishment.[48] In several Warsaw enterprises, factory

---

42. Lopinski et al. 1990, p. 43.
43. Lopinski et al. 1990, p. 59, p. 62.
44. Lopinski et al. 1990, p. 96.
45. 'Solidarity Press Underground: Some Examples', *UPNB*, no. 6, 1982, p. 11.
46. Lopinski et al. 1990, p. 93.
47. Cave and Sosnowska 1982, p. 71.
48. 'Arrests, Internment, Sentences After Demonstrations', *UPNB*, no. 10, 1982, pp. 6–7; *Committee in Support of Solidarity Reports*, no. 2, 19 May 1982, p. 1.

managements attempted vainly to prevent the stoppages by threatening their workers.[49] June demonstrations were also apparently widespread.[50]

The government responded by attacking the demonstrations; curfews, just recently lifted, were reimposed; telephone services were again interrupted.[51] It was not clear that the demonstrations gained anything. Bujak recalled that 'hundreds of activists were fired'. Onyszkiewicz:

> In the past, when the working class showed its muscle, this Party felt obliged to make some concessions. But now, even powerful street demonstrations won nothing. This showed that the ruling group was immune to these pressures, and that even if we escalated these demonstrations, nothing would happen; they would simply try to crush it with force, as they did. So I think this was important as proof that certain methods were not applicable.

Solidarity's strength remained in tact especially in the largest factories in the biggest cities: they were the underground's strongest supporters, just as they had been the base of Solidarity when it was a legal, recognised union. This situation was a problem for the Communist state, which claimed to represent these workers and to be based upon them.

In late June 1982, the TKK called for a suspension of protest to see if the authorities would be ready to deal. But about a month later, when Jaruzelski made it clear that there would be no negotiations or concessions, the TKK called for protests in August. Despite official efforts to prevent them and Primate Józef Glemp's admonition not to go into the streets,[52] on 31 August, large numbers did just that.[53] Over 5,000 people were detained and, according to official sources, four were killed by bullets,[54] while some KOR members were indicted on charges of 'preparing a violent overthrow of Poland's socio-political system'.[55] But the Solidarity leadership felt that the turnout was insufficient. Looking back at the end of the year, Bujak said that the 31 August demonstrations, which saw only some 15,000 turn out in Warsaw, were 'the last chance for saving Solidarity's right to legal action. And when it appeared that there were not 150,000 manifesters,

---

49. 'Protests on 13 May in Warsaw', UPNB, no. 11, 18 June 1982, p. 5.
50. 'Demonstrations on 13 June', UPNB, no. 11, 18 June 1982, p. 3.
51. 'Statement by Solidarity Officials in Hiding', and 'Demonstrations of 1st, 4th, 9th and 13th May', UPNB, no. 8, 30 April 1982, p. 4, p. 6.
52. 'Calendarium': Poland, 13th August–3rd September, UPNB, no. 16, 3 September 1982, p. 16, p. 11.
53. Cave and Sosnowska 1982, p. 73.
54. 'Calendarium: Poland, 13th August–3rd September', UPNB, no. 16, 3 September 1982, pp. 17–18; 'Demonstrations on 31st August: Scope', UPNB, no. 17, 17 September 1982, pp. 3–4. Some say five were killed: Lopinski et al. 1990, p. 180, n. 1.
55. 'Calendarium: Poland, 13th August–3rd September', UPNB, no. 16, 3 September 1982, p. 19.

but only 15,000 or 50,000, then the authorities' decision to de-legalise proved ten times easier'.[56]

On 8 October, the *Sejm* passed a new trade-union law that outlawed Solidarity and its associated organisations, including Rural Solidarity, and that authorised the formation of new trade unions under very restrictive conditions. They were prohibited from having the kind of regional structure that had made Solidarity so powerful. Rather, a union could only represent an individual workplace; regional and national unions were prohibited until 1984. Permitted unions were required to accept 'socialism', recognise the 'leading role' of the Party – the issue that Solidarity had fought so hard against – and to take responsibility for meeting production quotas, as unions had done in the past. The right to strike was severely limited to bread-and-butter issues, and then only after going through a detailed arbitration procedure, and only if the *Sejm* did not prohibit their strike. That right was denied to a long list of occupations.[57]

Would they be able to impose this new stance? Could Solidarity defend itself? The response was confused, with strikes called for and implemented on Monday in Gdańsk, Wednesday in Warsaw and Kraków, Thursday in Wrocław.[58] The TKK then called for 10 November to be a four-hour general strike, but workers in the Lenin Shipyard in Gdańsk struck immediately and were soon joined by the other shipyards in Gdańsk and Gdynia, while thousands gathered in the streets by the shipyard gates. Their presence provoked street battles with the police.[59] After a few days, the TKK called for other workers to join the strike, and despite the fact that the telex and telephones lines to Gdańsk were shut down and the roads blocked, workers in several cities joined the strike.[60]

During the period leading up to 10 November, would-be strikers were confronted with threats to militarise more workplaces, while individuals were called in for 'discussions' with management during which they were threatened with serious consequences if they should join the strike. A large number were actually drafted into the army and the ZOMO (some six hundred workers from the *Nowa Huta* steel plant alone were drafted before 10 November); many others were detained. On 8 November, Jaruzelski met with the Primate, Archbishop Józef Glemp, and the two agreed that the Pope would be invited to visit Poland the next year (with the implication that if the strike were successful, the Pope's visit might not be permitted).[61] A week earlier in Italy, Glemp had stated that the

56. Bujak 1982, p. 40.
57. Sanford 1986, p. 159.
58. Lopinski et al. 1990, pp. 169–73.
59. Hauser 1982–3, p. 12.
60. Hauser 1982–3, pp. 12–17.
61. Tymowski 1983, p. 99.

Church opposed the strike because it 'might lead to disastrous consequences'.[62] On 9 November, there was a massive display of police at the workplace.[63]

Workers were informed upon arrival at the Gdańsk Shipyard on 10 November that it had been militarised. Effectively, what that meant was that they had been drafted and were then subject to military sanctions for breaking discipline. They faced up to twenty-five years in prison as the penalty for having anything to do with 'messages, leaflets, recordings or films containing information liable to provoke public unrest or weaken the Defense capability of the Polish People's Republic'. Anyone leaving the job would be charged with desertion, and, as the government stated plainly: 'There is no appeal against a given order'.[64] The shipyards were not the only workplaces subject to this tough approach. The now-militarised *Nowa Huta* Steel Mill was surrounded by soldiers and riot police armed with machine guns: 'Workers entering the plant had either to sign a statement saying they would not strike, or they had verbally to answer the shop foreman's question, "Are you going to strike today?"'[65]

It was now apparent that a general strike would not come soon.[66] As Bujak put it, looking back six months later, 'The debacle of November tenth became the turning point for the union. It became clear that the general strike was an illusion'.[67] Many others agreed with him. Sociologist Andrzej Tymowski saw a significant victory for the government:

> By the end of November 1982 . . . Solidarity had not only been driven from public life, but it had failed to mobilise its 'ultimate weapon' the general strike, the underground leadership was in disarray, and the opposition in general appeared to have been outmanoeuvred by an accommodation between the Church and the state.[68]

> **Jan Ciesielski:** The central leadership was indecisive about when to stage a protest and what it should look like when they banned Solidarity. We, in Kraków, suggested that a national general strike should be set for the first working day after Solidarity was declared illegal. Instead, they waited a month, by which time the emotions had dissipated. People were afraid to strike; they preferred to be on the streets. This failure to respond in November was a very

62. Hauser 1982–3, p. 18.
63. 'How the Authorities Prepared for the Demos on 10th November', *UPNB*, no. 1, 15 January 1983, p. 33.
64. Hauser 1982–3, pp. 14–17.
65. Ost 1982–3, p. 72.
66. 'Calendarium' and 'Summary of Events', *UPNB*, no. 21, 19 November 1982, pp. 5, 8–9.
67. Bujak 1983, p. 14.
68. Tymowski 1983, p. 99.

heavy blow for the activists, for the printers, for those who risked their freedom distributing leaflets. People finishing work were supposed to gather in
the main market square. But the market was sealed by the ZOMO. People
feared walking in a large group, so they tried to slip out through alleys; they
went by trams, by buses. It didn't work.

This defeat allowed Jaruzelski to say that Wałęsa was 'no longer a threat to
public order' and that he would be released. Then, on 12 December, Jaruzelski
announced the suspension (not lifting) of martial law. But many elements of
martial law were preserved, including people suspected of oppositionist sympathies being drafted into the army, despite otherwise prohibiting disabilities.
Moreover, there were reports (denied by official spokesmen but taken seriously
by the Church) that union activists were put into special penal battalions and
forced-labour camps.[69]

Despite all these setbacks, the underground structures persisted. Solidarity
did survive. Many people continued to pay union dues – even if the number
was diminishing. Publications continued to appear. They continued ostentatiously turning off lights between seven and eight in the evening and going out
for walks during the broadcast of the evening news. The government continued
to lack legitimacy. In that sense, the situation was at a stalemate. It was a far cry
from what Jaruzelski and his collaborators had expected when they launched the
'state of war'. At that time, they apparently hoped that the Solidarity movement
would disappear, or re-emerge tamed and toothless with a new, more accom-
modating leadership, as Janusz Onyszkiewicz speculated:

> They thought that once they introduced martial law, then (this is based on
> interviews and statements given by representatives of Western financial
> institutions) once they crushed Solidarity they would get more credits. Their
> second belief was that with the leadership eliminated, the sound core of this
> movement would find out that they had been hijacked by this experience,
> and Solidarity could be restored, but under different leadership. And then,
> after this first shock of martial law, they would regain the confidence of the
> people.

This whole period changed the feelings of the union activists. It had become
evident to them that they had little chance of reforming the system, that it must

---

69. 'Former Internees and Solidarity Activists Imprisoned by the Army?' and 'Some
Western Reports on Imprisonment by the Army', *UPNB*, no. 1, 15 January 1983, pp. 10–11,
p. 20, based on articles that appeared in *Le Monde* on 23 December, and in the *Herald
Tribune* on 24–25 December.

be transformed. Tadeusz Jedynak: 'Unless the system is changed, we'll achieve nothing worthwhile'.[70] Bogdan Lis:[71]

> Our goals are no longer the same as they were during the first strikes against the imposition of martial law. Solidarity will never be the same as before the 'war'. A trade union isn't enough, because the regime can always dissolve it whenever it likes. What we need are structural changes in the system.

Through it all the question persisted of how to keep the Solidarity leadership from becoming isolated from the mass of the population at a time when the Solidarity leaders could not act openly? This could be a serious problem. As Wałęsa noted, 'the harsh reality of martial law' made it difficult to 'maintain the mass nature of the movement underground':

> Organisationally, that was impossible. It was easier to work at the elite and individual level. I felt, however, that the power of Solidarity lay in the masses. I have always tried to emphasise this so that propaganda would not relegate us to the role of radicals and marginal players. The nation would not trust hecklers, as we were then called. I spoke publicly about the independence of the labour union, about its scale, about the need for dialogue between the authorities and society, so that our fight would continue to be the fight of the entire nation, if not directly, then symbolically. At the same time, our union was active in secret, our underground printers carried out their tasks, and organisations supporting and maintaining Solidarity's ideas and the everyday activities of the union were sprouting near parishes. The aim of the fight was to enable the many to identify with the struggle of the few.[72]

How to accomplish this difficult task was the central problem that remained.

70. Lopinski et al. 1990, p. 227.
71. Lopinski et al. 1990, p. 223.
72. Wałęsa 2007, p. xv.

Chapter Seventeen
'To Kill a Priest'[1]

Bogdan Borusewicz:[2] Perhaps the Jaruzelski group thought that six months would be long enough to exhaust society, capture all the activists, infiltrate various groups, then do a U-turn toward liberalisation, and then... new foreign credits, normalisation, renewal... Yet somehow the issue wouldn't go away. There was deep-rooted mass resistance on the part of most groups of the population. Thus the authorities were unable to make an about-turn.

As the months and then years went by, the hopes of Solidarity activists sagged. By 1984, amnesties had freed most prisoners, thereby removing one of the underground movement's reasons for existing. Weariness became evident. Bogdan Borusewicz recalled:

The underground structures had already begun to lose people in 1984. The society was tiring. There were no open demonstrations, so the resistance was not seen in the streets. But the boycott of the government, of television, of the new unions still held.

It was estimated that only five percent of the workers continued paying Solidarity union dues, although levels of participation varied, reaching as high as fifty or sixty percent in some factories, while in others the ranks of

---

1. This title came from the movie of the same name, written and directed by Agnieszka Holland.
2. Lopinski et al. 1990, pp. 36–7.

the activists were decimated.[3] In April 1984, Bogdan Lis estimated that 10 percent of Polish workers remained active in the movement. He did not see that number as a great achievement. As he put it: 'Solidarity ... wasn't destroyed by the tanks and soldiers after December 1981 ... It exists, and this is the ... only success'.[4] (But 10 percent was still a large number for an organisation that once had over nine million members. Bujak estimated that some 10,000 in the Warsaw region were devoting most of their time to underground activities, and perhaps as many as 100,000 spent some time on such work).[5] In mid-1985, General Kiszczak, in charge of the police, estimated that the opposition was made of small groupings, 'each containing between a few and a dozen or so persons: all in all, about 1,500 declared enemies of socialism'.[6] Generally, strikes were not successful.[7] Many people were discouraged. Zbigniew Bujak recalled:

> Doubts entered our ranks as to whether Solidarity was capable of bringing us victory. Had some general come to ... the ... leadership during martial law [and] said 'my division and I are at your disposal', we would have considered it more seriously. But there were no such serious proposals, and therefore ... no opportunities for an open fight with the government.[8]

People continued to find ways to demonstrate popular opposition to the government:[9]

> lighting candles in windows on the thirteenth of each month; ... boycott of TV news with demonstrative walks in the streets; demonstrations of disapproval for collaborating artists (clapping so they could not perform) or writers (depositing piles of their unwanted works before their doors); harassing known collaborators in factories.

But these were mainly symbolic actions. Janusz Onyszkiewicz recalled that people did not have 'a clear idea what they should do in concrete, practical terms'.

---

3. 'Solidarity in the Warsaw Region', [published originally in *Tygodnik Mazowsze*, no. 71, 8 December 1983]; 'Solidarity in Słupsk', [published originally as 'Two Days in Słupsk', *Tygodnik Mazowsze*, no. 70], *UPNB*, no. 2, 26 January 1984, pp. 29–30, pp. 34–5.
4. Lis 1984, p. 24.
5. Kaufman 1989, p. 88.
6. 'Interior Minister on Security Situation', *UPNB*, no. 11, 22 May 1985, p. 23.
7. 'Poland Needs Us: the Underground Factory Press', *Poland Watch*, no. 5, April 1984, p. 102.
8. 'Communism's Negotiated Collapse: The Polish Round Table, Ten Years Later', A Conference Held at the University of Michigan, April 7–10 1999.
9. 'Unusual Signs of Defiance', *UPNB*, no. 10, 24 May 1984, pp. 19–20.

The Church and the opposition

The Church now stood as the only openly independent institution, and many saw it as part of the opposition. David Ost noted that: 'In the first few weeks of martial law, churches were often transformed into emergency Solidarity head-quarters as people gathered there to exchange strike information, read leaflets, plan further actions and flee ZOMO'.[10] Recall that the first leaflets announcing resistance appeared in the churches, which in many cases responded favour-ably to pleas for help. Churches compiled lists of prisoners and of people whose whereabouts were unknown; they collected money to help the injured or pris-oners' families; they provided meeting places; priests ministered to prisoners; people acting for the Church sometimes paid fines for detainees.

Father Zalewski felt that during martial law 'the churches became a haven for the opposition, at least morally'. A new form of Church activity came to life: 'Masses for the Fatherland'. These were specifically political Masses, which con-stituted the one form of open opposition that the authorities found themselves powerless to stop. Attendance at Masses increased, and demonstrations were often organised from the crowds who were leaving. Frasyniuk worried that this trend could undermine support for Solidarity:

> A lot of people began to seek protection in the Church, believing that it could guarantee safety for them. When well-known Solidarity activists acted within the Church, it convinced people that the Church was the only institution that could fight for us. It made it easier for the Church hierarchy to manipulate Solidarity. The Church tends to speak in the name of society, and so in the name of Solidarity as well. So Solidarity activists are very often under pressure to be quiet.

In this period, the government allowed many churches to be built in the hope of gaining the Church's co-operation.[11] Within a year of the proclamation of martial law, hundreds of new churches were being erected, while the Church also won new concessions from the government exempting it from taxes.[12] While many priests supported Solidarity, Primate Józef Glemp, in particular, appeared to co-operate with the government. The day martial law began, he delivered a televised sermon in which he seemed to blame Solidarity for the conflict: 'Opposition to the decisions of the authorities under martial law could cause violent coercion, including bloodshed...That is why I myself...shall plead, even if I have to

---

10. Ost 1982–3, p. 78.
11. Warecki 1982–3, p. 122.
12. Warecki 1982–3, p. 119; 'The Building of New Churches: Successes and Failures' and 'Tax Concession for the Church', *UPNB*, no. 1, 15 January 1983, pp. 29–30.

plead on my knees: Do not start a fight of Poles against Poles'. Although Glemp called for liberties to be restored, release of the interned and amnesty for the imprisoned, he continued to resist opposition activity. He spoke against demonstrations: 'Street is not a place for dialogue, enough blood has been shed on our streets. A table is the place for dialogue'.[13] In December 1982, he called on actors to end their boycott of radio and television. The Primate disparaged Solidarity: 'To think of Solidarity as a bloc of pure ideals is a mistake', he said. 'Solidarity lost its bearings in defence of the workers'.[14]

Among many Solidarity activists and supporters, Glemp's stance earned him the informal titles of 'Comrade Glemp', 'the Red Cardinal', or 'Comrade Cardinal'.[15] At the same time, the government fumed and demanded that priests who openly supported, encouraged, and even aided the opposition, be silenced.[16] Glemp seemed once again to side with the government. He asked 'those who wish to use the churches for other purposes: respect holy places!.... We do not want political slogans...in our churches'.[17] He took action against individual priests who he felt had gone too far in their support of the opposition. One of these priests, Father Nowak, who had been repeatedly called in by the prosecutor for interrogation because of the political character of his sermons, was moved from the politically sensitive Warsaw suburb of Ursus to a small village some sixty miles away. Some of his parishioners responded with a hunger strike, demanding that Father Nowak be returned to the Ursus parish.[18] Ultimately, the Solidarity leadership asked the parishioners to give up the hunger strike on the grounds that the Church was not an appropriate area for the confrontationist tactics that were used against the Party.[19]

In a meeting between the Primate and some three hundred of his priests in December 1982, Glemp insisted that the Church must not become identified with either side, and certainly should not create a 'neo-Solidarity'. He rejected the idea that the Church should be encouraging the opposition.[20] Glemp then took a lambasting from the priests. One argued that Glemp appeared to be making deals with Jaruzelski, as when he had attacked stone-throwing by the crowd, but not the police's use of truncheons against the people. The speaker complained

---

13. Walendowski 1982, p. 61.

14. Glemp 1984, p. 10.

15. Ost 1982–3, p. 80.

16. 'Some Official Remarks on the Polish Church', *UPNB*, no. 22, 1982, p. 19; Latyński 1984, p. 16.

17. 'Other Important Statements by Polish Bishops', *UPNB*, no. 10, 20 May 1983, p. 33.

18. 'The Cardinal and the Priest', *UPNB*, no. 4, 23 February 1984, pp. 27–8; Glemp 1984, p. 14; 'Calendarium', *UPNB*, no. 6, 22 March 1984, p. 7.

19. Ibid.

20. 'Archbishop Glemp Criticised by Priests', *UPNB*, no. 1, 15 January 1983, based on a detailed report of the meeting carried in *Mazowsze Weekly*, no. 37, 18 December 1982.

that priests who had not suffered were not allowed to help those who had. Another argued that people felt the Church collaborated with the regime. The Primate's call to actors to return to work was cited as a reason for young people losing interest in the Church.[21] One priest suggested that 'the Episcopate spoke a language different from that of the Vatican', referring to the perception that the Pope had a decidedly different attitude toward Solidarity. Glemp denied that there was any difference between himself and the Pope on this matter.[22] One priest whom I interviewed (who asked to remain anonymous, for obvious reasons) told me that 'The head of the Church in Poland, Cardinal Glemp, doesn't have much respect among the clergy as a whole'.

At this time, Poland's most prominent dissident priest was Father Jerzy Popiełuszko, who made his huge church in Warsaw into what amounted to an open centre of opposition. He held monthly Masses for the Fatherland – termed 'séances of hatred'[23] by the government – at which attendees were exhorted by prominent actors, priests, people of international repute, often from abroad, to keep their faith in themselves, their ideals, their movement. These masses became very popular. Delivered outside, on the church grounds, thousands of people would turn out for them – many more than could be contained within the grounds, and they would spill out into the surrounding streets, made possible because of the impressive voice amplification system the church installed. Each of these masses became a demonstration, to which Solidarity supporters came flocking, with banners and signs – this was virtually the only place where such overt demonstrations could take place. This form of political-religious ceremony spread, and other priests around the country made use of them. The churches thus served not just as venues of worship, but also as community centres, where the opposition could organise. Fr. Popiełuszko was denounced by name in the Soviet paper *Izvestia*.

Despite the admonitions of Cardinal Glemp to stay out of politics,[24] Father Popiełuszko encouraged workers to continue their resistance. He supported Solidarity's election boycott. He frequently met with steel workers, miners, actors and others[25] from around the country, encouraging and aiding their activities. One of those with whom he worked was Andrzej Sokołowski, who recalled that 'Fr. Popiełuszko helped me a lot with material aid and moral support and advice on how to organise'. Piotr Polmański said: 'Father Popiełuszko's masses

---

21. 'Archbishop Glemp Criticised by Priests', *UPNB*, no. 22, 10 December 1982, p. 19; 'Archbishop Glemp Criticised by Priests', *UPNB*, no. 1, 15 January 1983.
22. Ibid.
23. Kaufman 1989, p. 148.
24. Latyński 1984, pp. 17–18.
25. Kaufman 1989, pp. 138–9.

supported us in creating the underground structures. The support of the "unconquered walls" of the church made us braver'.

None of this activity would have mattered if the opposition were disappearing from Polish life. But it persisted. On 31 August 1983, the third anniversary of the Accords that established Solidarity, there were demonstrations in at least sixteen cities, the most significant of which saw some 10,000 workers clash with the riot police.[26] The underground continued its activities. Those who worked for and supported the underground press were a much larger number, and there were many youth who did not belong to Solidarity but who were opposition activists or supporters.[27] So, the stalemate continued. Then, near the end of 1984, an unexpected tragedy dramatically changed the situation: Fr. Popiełuszko lay dead, murdered by operatives from the Ministry of the Interior, who were soon exposed.

Murder

> **Janusz Onyszkiewicz:** They killed Father Popiełuszko partly because they were not getting anywhere, and there was a sense of frustration in the ranks of the police. Imagine you are in the police. You must trace these 'counterrevolutionaries'. But we had an amnesty in '83, '84, '85 and '86. That created quite a lot of frustration, and the authorities were simply not strong enough to fight with the church. So they were forced to tolerate certain things.

There were clear signs of official impatience with the activist priests, some of whom received death threats while others were called in to the prosecutors and threatened with legal action. In December 1983, police searched an apartment that Fr. Popiełuszko owned. Upon entering, they went straight for a cache of weapons, which certainly suggested that they knew where it was: had they planted it there? Popiełuszko was jailed.[28] But when, in March 1984, the police came to take him to the prosecutor's office for interrogation, his parishioners would not allow them in the church. As word spread, workers from the Warsaw Steelworks came to his support.[29] In July, Fr. Popiełuszko was summoned to the prosecutor's office for the fourteenth time, where he was informed that he would soon be tried on the charge of abusing his priestly office for political ends.[30]

---

26. *UPNB*, no. 17, 2 September 1983, p. 12.

27. 'They Know What They Want', *UPNB*, no. 11, 8 June 1984, pp. 24–6; originally in *Tygodnik Mazowsze*, no. 83.

28. 'The Case of Fr. Jerzy Popiełuszko', *UPNB*, no. 5, 8 March 1984, pp. 14–15.

29. 'The Harassment of the Church, Priests and Churchgoers', *CSSR Reports*, no. 22, 5 March 1984, p. 29.

30. Calendarium', *UPNB*, no. 13, 5 July 1984, p. 4.

He was charged with possessing illegal publications, ammunition and explosives, but these charges were dropped in a broad amnesty on 21 July, Poland's Independence Day.

By autumn, an assault on the Church was becoming evident. Government spokesman Jerzy Urban, writing under a pen name in the official weekly *Tu i Teraz* ('Here and Now'), charged Fr. Popiełuszko with manipulating collective emotions.[31] Reports soon surfaced of an investigation of Fathers Popiełuszko and Jankowski, Wałęsa's priest, both said to be suspected of anti-state activity. Colonel Sucharski:

> There was a file on every move, every gesture, every word of 18–20 'feisty priests', as we called them. Still, we were attacked at every conference for not doing enough, since Popiełuszko and others like him were functioning. I was personally present at the conference where Kraszewski, the vice-minister, attacked our director for his inaction. So, then he would come and ask, 'Why can't you silence [Father] ___?' We tried to compromise them, make their lives unpleasant, but it didn't work.

Then, on 20 October, word came that Father Popiełuszko had been kidnapped by 'unknown perpetrators' the night before. The next day, the media broadcast descriptions of three men, including one dressed in a police uniform, described as the presumed kidnappers, all based on information provided by Popiełuszko's chauffeur, Waldemar Chróstowski, who had managed to escape.[32] Four days later, the suspects – three officers of the Interior Ministry – were found.[33] Their leader, Captain Grzegorz Piotrowski, said under interrogation that he had planned the kidnapping because the authorities were ineffective in the face of Father Popiełuszko's political activity.[34] Within days, the priest's body was found in a lake, bound and gagged, with a rope looped around his ankles and his throat. He had been beaten and then thrown into the water while he was still alive.[35]

The government sought frantically to cool the passions aroused by this murder. Government spokesman Jerzy Urban contended that the whole affair was a carefully timed provocation *against the authorities*.[36] He did not say who the

31. 'Government Press Spokesman on Father Popiełuszko, September 19, 1984', *UPNB*, no. 18, 20 September 1984.

32. There have been suggestions that Chróstowski may have co-operated in this plot. This charge has never been proven, but there is some circumstantial evidence of it. 'The Case of Father Popiełuszko, 1947–1984: Kidnap and Murder, Principal Developments: October 19–November 1, 1984', *UPNB*, no. 21, 1 November 1984, p. 9.

33. Ibid.

34. 'Kidnap and Murder, Principal Developments', p. 16.

35. 'Kidnap and Murder, Principal Developments', p. 20; 'Calendarium: Friday, November 2–Thursday, November 15', *UPNB*, no. 22, 15 November 1984, p. 4.

36. 'Kidnap and Murder, Principal Developments', p. 10.

provocateurs were: hard-liners who wanted more repression? Oppositionists?[37] The government had reason to be concerned. The murder had torn apart the surface calm that martial law and its aftermath had imposed on Polish society and significantly weakened any support the Party might have enjoyed. Jaruzelski and Kiszczak responded with a public trial of the accused, to which the Western press was invited, a virtually unprecedented action that indicated the desperation they must have felt as they saw the wave of social revulsion that this act created. They knew they would be blamed.[38] Years later, Rakowski insisted that the 'provocation' had been organised by Moscow or another power hostile to Jaruzelski's government:

> On 16 May 1981, Honecker [of East Germany] went to Moscow and he met with Brezhnev, Andropov, Gromyko and others. Honecker argued: the Polish Party leadership is very weak; they are not fighting counter-revolution. So, they should get rid of Jaruzelski. So, I think that this was a huge provocation against Jaruzelski's policy.

I suggested to Rakowski that the murder had undermined the legitimacy of the regime. He responded: 'I agree with you. Therefore, we reacted very strongly against this murder'. Jaruzelski called upon the Central Committee plenum to condemn 'this act of dangerous banditry that has so disturbed public opinion', and further appealed to all to oppose efforts by 'enemies of People's Poland' to destabilise the country, explicitly recognising the explosive character of the crime.[39] An article in *Trybuna Ludu* said Popiełuszko's murder was an attempt to 'discredit the party, its program and leadership, to create a conflict between State and Church, to render Poland's socialist system repugnant, to activate political opposition, to resume ideological subversion'.[40]

But these efforts to distance the regime from this repugnant act failed. The tide of outrage could not be contained, as mass public protests emerged. *Tygodnik Mazowsze* disputed the government's interpretation:

> The crime was aimed against its victims and so, against the clergy, against Solidarity and against all social opposition – not against the generals. Nevertheless, what it meant to Jaruzelski was the destruction of all... his efforts towards 'normalisation'.[41]

---

37. Ibid.
38. Kaufman 1989, pp. 158–9.
39. Kaufman 1989, p. 16.
40. 'Calendarium: Friday November 2–Thursday November 15', *UPNB*, no. 22, 15 November 1984, p. 8.
41. 'It Was Not a Political Provocation', *UPNB*, no. 2, 17 January 1985, p. 19.

There were widespread suspicions that the trial had not revealed the higher-ups who were presumed to be involved in the plot.

When I asked him about it, Colonel Sucharski discounted the notion that the murder was planned by the Party. However, he suggested that an atmosphere was created from above that demanded that *something* had to be done to silence the outspoken priests, without specifying what. Then, some people simply took it upon themselves to do it:

> There was both pressure from the top and the overzealousness of an idiot. We were regularly attacked because Popiełuszko and others like him continued to function. There was never a word about murder. Piotrowski, who was responsible for Popiełuszko, got from his direct superior: 'Why is Popiełuszko still speaking out?' I am convinced that it was Piotrowski's overzealousness under pressure from his superiors.

Popular reaction

Popiełuszko's murder, like the Bydgoszcz events, became another major turning-point in the struggle between Solidarity and the state. The immediate reaction among priests who were close to Solidarity was to be fearful that they might be next. In some cases, workers set up guard units to protect them.[42] But ultimately many priests became more outspoken. Maciej Mach recalled: 'It made priests more radical as if it inspired them with courage'. Father Zalewski said:

> The murder of Popiełuszko, and the investigation and trial, contributed to radicalising attitudes of the priests. Masses for the Homeland spread across the whole country; priests became more radical: in general, they were no longer afraid of speaking out in public.

> **Jan Ciesielski:** The Church introduced certain favourable changes towards Solidarity and opposition activities. They allowed us more freedom, more access to the premises. There emerged a group of priests who voiced their own opinions, calling things by their names, who until that time were over-shadowed by Popiełuszko.

This trend was confirmed by the Minister for Religious Affairs, Adam Łopatka, who spoke of an increasing number of 'anti-socialist clerics'. Łopatka stated that several churches had become pockets of unrest.[43]

More important was the response of the general public. Karol Miller recalled feeling that 'When Popiełuszko was murdered, my friends and I said to each

---

42. Wałęsa 1992, p. 82.
43. 'Calendarium: May 10–22', *UPNB*, no. 11, 2 May 1985, p. 8.

other that the last branch on which this political system was sitting had just been cut off'. The revulsion and anger at the murder of this popular priest created a significant movement that could not be ignored. Jan Lityński said:

> Not everyone identified with Solidarity, but everyone identified with Fr. Popiełuszko. It was the whole nation against the authorities. If there were any debate about whether or not to join Solidarity or a new trade union, or whether or not Solidarity should exist, from this moment there was no doubt.

> **Janusz Onyszkiewicz:** Popiełuszko's funeral was another occasion where people saw masses of people, so that gave them the sense that Solidarity still existed, at least in spirit.

> **Piotr Polmański:** After Father Popiełuszko's death, there was one huge national pilgrimage to his grave. We demanded freedom for political prisoners.

The trial of Popiełuszko's murderers, as Wałęsa noted:[44]

> exposed to a stunned public the moral degeneracy and contempt for the rule of law prevailing among civil servants in the Security Service. A detailed analysis of the crime, the motives of each of the defendants, the customs and morals peculiar to Department IV [the secret-police section that kept track of the Church], and generally the morality of its agents – whose job, theoretically, is to protect the citizens – cast a damning light on the socialist system. We all knew about it, of course, but it is another thing to see and hear, up close and first-hand, the spectacle of organised hatred.

Later, Jacek Kuroń contended that as a result of the killing, General Jaruzelski had to 'take notice of popular demands as never before since martial law, and in this sense he has partly undone the effects of his military coup'.[45] In Warsaw, a crowd of several thousand marched toward the Tomb of the Unknown Soldier carrying two wreaths. That same day, thousands marched through the streets calling for the release of Bogdan Lis, among others. Many Solidarity activists felt that the murder and the subsequent trial showed a weakened state apparatus:

> **Zbigniew Bujak:** The trial of the murderers of Fr. Popiełuszko meant that the authorities were divided. The fact that they couldn't keep the secret showed that the structure was weakening. Too many people knew that the police murdered Fr. Popiełuszko.

> **Bogdan Lis:** They had no concept of how to solve the situation. The curtain that covered the methods used by the Ministry of Internal Affairs was torn aside, revealing their lawlessness. That was a defeat.

---

44. Wałęsa 1992, p. 85.
45. Kuroń 1985, p. 21.

In its haste to distance itself from the crime, the government turned upon the secret police. Colonel Sucharski recalled a partial verification of the secret police soon after the trial. The murder, he said, 'had to be condemned':

> After the verification, 15 people in our province resigned, about 18–20 were moved from our services to the militia, and 8–10 were fired because they were 'unfit' for the security service. It brought about a lot of bitterness. From that point on, public disapproval hit all the security services: we got badly treated, regardless of what we did. Some of us were called 'murderers', even though we had nothing to do with it. Some people now refused to co-operate with us, so it did great, great harm to our work.

The secret police were aware of the damage that had been done, and many of them found it demoralising. Their difficulties mounted. Colonel Sucharski recalled that this event, and others, left the opposition with the high moral ground, and resulted in increasing problems for the secret police. Earlier there had been close co-operation between the criminal and the secret police, which Sucharski illustrated with the following story:

> In the old days, there was a great feeling of fraternity between our services. Once, my driver and I were riding, both drunk like pigs, and we crashed the car. The policeman fixed something in the car so that it could be claimed that the accident was caused by the car's mechanical condition. Not only did we not get in trouble, but we even got money back from the insurance. The co-operation between the police and our services was perfect.

But the years of political struggle undermined this closeness. Soon,

> There was no collective feeling, no fraternity, no solidarity to speak of, and distrust grew among us. The lack of trust and the bad atmosphere in the services was the beginning of the end of the services themselves. We became supervised by the police more and more, to the point where we had a separate boss: the second in command was our chief, and he made all the decisions; then, suddenly, the power was moved to his boss, to the chief of police. When our services sent out letters, papers, whatever, they stopped being signed by our direct superior; they had to be signed by the chief of police on the provincial level. Then, there were budget cuts and technical cuts, to the point where we were having troubles with cars and transportation. All of a sudden, it was all controlled by the police. We were told that it was all to camouflage our actions. We were aware of the fact that the importance of our services was declining, and we were being phasing out.

As a result, Sucharski said: 'People at my level started discussions about the future: what to do next? The opinion was that the apparatus as such would cease to exist; many of us understood that this situation could not continue'. One indication of the effect on morale was that the opposition won over even some of the secret police, and *they even began to get information from inside the secret police.* Sucharski reported:

> They had very good informers, and they wrote quite a bit of truth about actions taken by the police and our services. For example, we had a guy who was considered to be a hard *beton*; we all looked at him with contempt. It turned out that he was the main informer to the opposition. One guy who was supposedly so much against the clergy – it turned out that he was actually passing on information to the bishop. Another guy, a colonel who was chief of the Third Department persecuted really religious people. As soon as he retired, he had a ceremonial church wedding where he officially apologised to society for the wrongs he was responsible for.

The realisation that there were informers inside the secret police, said Sucharski, led to 'an internal investigation to find the source of the leak and we were all suspected'. They could not determine the source. As a result, 'They began to investigate our own people. They followed us, checked where the wife worked, if the kids went to religion classes or to church on Sundays'. It can easily be imagined how this distrust could affect the spirit in a department which was hated and feared by the rest of the society, and now, apparently, not trusted by their fellow officers. They had a sense of being pursued: 'We were specialists: when we walked into our house or our apartment, we knew if there was a bugging device or not'. It is not surprising that this new agency created what Sucharski called 'a strong feeling of embitterment and in fact even an opposition movement within the services'.

The changed atmosphere that brought problems for the secret-police opened new possibilities to the opposition, which it quickly seized. On 10 November, 22 people in Kraków announced the formation of the 'citizens' initiative for the defence of human rights and against the use of force, meant to be one of the Helsinki Commission groups to monitor human rights'.[46] They appealed for help in collecting and publicising information on illegal violence against citizens by the police or Security Service, and were soon joined by similar groups in Warsaw, Gdańsk, and several other cities.[47] They noted a number of other murders besides Popiełuszko's, as well as assaults and kidnapping. Janusz Onyszkiewicz:

> Until Popiełuszko's death it was felt that the authorities would not tolerate any independent, open activities, so everything was strictly underground. But

---

46. 'Calendarium', *UPNB*, no. 22, 15 November 1984, p. 9.
47. 'Calendarium', p. 10; 'KOPPs: Citizens' Committees Against Violence', *UPNB*, no. 22, 15 November 1984, p. 20.

after, there was no longer the fear that anything which came into the open would be immediately crushed by the authorities. We felt that if we set up some human-rights projects, it would be extremely difficult for the authorities to arrest these people. We created these committees immediately, and I must say that we were seen almost like kamikazes. But we thought that the risk was not that big, so we were not heroes; our judgement was simply different.

Onyszkiewicz argued that the creation of these *open* committees encouraged people to come forward who might have otherwise stayed silent:

It was very difficult for somebody who felt that he was badly treated to find out how to report something – but with our names, addresses, telephone numbers published, people could phone up and to say 'I was beaten by the police or my brother-in-law was killed in the police-station'.

This was the first group to emerge above ground since the declaration of martial law, and it heralded other efforts to emerge from the underground. Around this time, some of the Solidarity leaders who had been imprisoned, and who were no longer part of the underground, attempted to create a public presence. Władysław Frasyniuk recalled: 'At the end of 1984 and the beginning of 1985, all over the country, there was an attempt to organise legal, open Solidarity structures. It ended with our arrest in February 1985'. Andrzej Sokołowski remembered other ways in which things began to change:

People started to lead normal lives. The authorities were not so serious; they didn't tell you on television that you could be executed for not coming to work or for listening to Radio Free Europe broadcasts. People knew that they would not do it on a large scale, but nobody wanted to be an example.

A new youth movement: 'Freedom and Peace'

The level of repression the regime could muster was becoming less terrifying, especially to some youth who had been too young to participate in Solidarity. Lech Budrewicz thought that the new generation saw matters differently: '1984 was the end of the identification of young people with Solidarity in general. The new generation had a different point of view. The adults remembered Wałęsa from 1980, but the youth saw him as an *apparatchik*'.

In May 1984, Mirosław Zabłocki was charged with refusing to do his military service because he refused to take the military oath.[48] Shortly before Fr. Popiełuszko's murder, Marek Adamkiewicz, an activist in the Student Solidarity Committee, also refused to take the oath, although he was willing to serve

---

48. 'Calendarium: October 5–18', *UPNB*, no. 20, 18 October 1984, p. 8.

in the military. Adamkiewicz was sentenced to two and a half years. Then, in March 1985, 13 people from several locations in Poland began a hunger strike at a church near Warsaw to win Adamkiewicz's release.[49] These young people did not have an activist past, but they were joined by some Solidarity activists.

In discussions at the hunger strike, the participants decided that an open, above ground peace movement was possible in Poland. They sought the removal from the military oath of the pledge to support the 'fraternal alliance with the Soviet Army', and alternative service for conscientious objectors, with some form of alternative service.[50] Jan Rokita, one of the founders of the group, which called itself Freedom and Peace [*Wolność i Pokój* = WiP]: 'We decided to set up an institution that could defend people who refused to take the military oath and attack popular consciousness on this subject'. Jacek Czaputowicz explained the original goals of WiP:

> The oath spoke of defending peace with the alliance of the Soviet army and the Warsaw Pact, but they could not accept these words. The second point was that they say that they defend the fatherland, but with this government, they can't be sure of that, since the government used the army against Polish workers in '56, '70 and '81.

> **Jacek Szymanderski:** Military training in West Germany takes one year; in Poland it takes two years. Why? Are our soldiers stupider? They depend on brain-washing, on preparing the soldier to obey any order – *every* order. Remember that this army was used four times against our own population, and to defend the interests of the international Communist empire. Now, if you want to prepare a man to obey *any* order, first you have to prepare him to obey senseless orders. It must be brutal because your dignity, your common sense, should be completely crushed, and brutality is an important factor in this preparation. So, if we succeeded in getting alternative service, then if the army wanted to have people in it, it would have to be more attractive, more human.

In April and May, people in several cities signed the founding declaration of WiP.[51] Later, the group called for abolishing the death penalty.[52] Concern for ecology also became an important part of its concerns.

These people came together out of their experiences in the 1980s. Władysław Frasyniuk: 'I think that WiP came into being because there was a group of young

---

49. 'Calendarium: March 15–27', *UPNB*, no. 7, 27 March 1985, p. 3; Ruffin and Choroszucha 1989, p. 7.
50. Ruffin and Choroszucha 1989, p. 3.
51. Ruffin and Choroszucha 1989, p. 7.
52. Czaputowicz interview.

people who couldn't fit into Solidarity, and who wanted to be involved and who were convinced that legal open methods of activity were more effective here'. Jacek Czaputowicz, a student activist in the late 1970s and one of the founders of WiP in Warsaw said: 'We were not workers; we couldn't belong to a trade union'. Czaputowicz and Adamkiewicz had been interned together during martial law.[53] Czaputowicz remembered:

> We knew each other from '80–'81. Freedom and Peace is a movement of the new generation. Sometimes I compare the situation of the opposition to people who were active in the universities in '68: they knew everybody from their generation; they grew up and worked in different professions, and they organised KOR. The same process worked here. Also, we were not in Solidarity. While we did not have to take responsibility for a whole nation, people from Solidarity did. For us, small actions: a hunger strike or a demonstration was quite a success. For Solidarity it was not.

The movement differed from Solidarity in a number of ways, as Jacek Szymanderski explained: 'There is no formal membership or leadership. Centralisation is very, very weak'. This difference was appealing to some young people who despite being moved by Solidarity were also critical of it. Małgorzata Górczewska had been in high-school during 1980–1:

> I looked for an organisation which I could accept and which could accept me. I didn't want Solidarity. From the period of open Solidarity I saw some small elements of totalitarianism in some of the activists: the blind anti-communism, when people from Solidarity spoke of how they would get rid of all the communists. When I was 18, I rebelled against the Church as an institution, and Solidarity was always in prayer, and that annoyed me. That is why I looked for youth organisations other than Solidarity. In '85, people from WiP made contact with us. My friends were in prison for refusing to go into the army, so I felt that it was necessary for me to be in it and to be active. I also liked very much the way in which WiP operated as an alternative movement. In December '85, I signed the declaration of WiP. I came out from underground activity to open activity.

She was among those who founded WiP in Gdańsk. One of the things that defined the group was its insistence upon openness. When they began, it was unclear how dangerous such open activity would be. Jan Rokita:

> The clear-cut strategy of Solidarity as a union was one of survival: to wait out the bad times until a more favourable time came. We decided that it was

---

53. Ibid.

time to start doing something – that the philosophy of survival was no longer sufficient. We judged the conditions to be favourable enough for starting open political activity. The Solidarity leadership did not agree.

Apart from the Helsinki Commission, the Gdańsk WiP were the first to come out into the open, and unlike the former, they were the first openly to defy legality. But they remained a small group. Górczewska said that her group in Gdańsk had only ten to fifteen people for a good while:

> For the most part, Solidarity had kept its hands off the army, a posture which had ultimately proved fatal in December 1981. But for WiP, the army was the centre of attention. This stance was courageous because the army was still held in high regard by Poles, including many Solidarity activists, and because the government's ability to control the army was central to its grasp on power.

Jacek Szymanderski said: 'From the diplomatic service we sometimes heard that the Communists see us as a very dangerous part of the opposition because of the possible impact on the army'.

By September, WiP began a campaign to get men to send their military identity documents back to the Ministry of National Defence to protest the imprisonment of Adamkiewicz. Those who did so received three months in jail.[54] Jacek Szymanderski was arrested at the end of 1985. Early the next year, Czaputowicz and Piotr Niemczyk were charged with 'founding and directing an association [WiP] aimed at a crime', and 'collaborating with the western peace movements'.[55] But as Rokita noted: 'They spent a half year in prison, and then amnesty came'. In response to the Chernobyl nuclear disaster, WiP activists held unimpeded demonstrations in Wrocław and Kraków.[56] Lech Budrewicz: 'This was a very important moment. People in WiP started to believe that something was possible'.[57]

Exhaustion

Despite these promising developments, in June 1986 Zbigniew Bujak, the last of the prominent national Solidarity leaders, was captured. It was a demoralising blow to many people. Jan Lityński reported:

> Thanks to the capture of Zbyszek [Bujak], they managed to destroy his legend. It was the end of the old leadership of Solidarity and of the TKK. After the

---

54. Ibid.
55. Interview with Szymanderski; Ruffin and Choroszucha 1989, p. 9.
56. Ruffin and Choroszucha 1989, p. 10.
57. For a more extended discussion of the role of WiP in nurturing the re-emergence of the opposition in Poland, see Kenny 2001.

arrest of Zbyszek there was a tendency toward secret activity, without names – a conspiracy. The leadership didn't dare to have open activity. Then, the authorities could think that Solidarity was dead.

But even before his capture, many people were finding it hard to continue, as Bujak himself indicated in his last interview before his apprehension. The interviewer presented a picture of a movement in trouble:

> We are less optimistic. After five years of underground work, people are physically and mentally tired. Much of it is routine work, often no more than a rehash of pre-August [1980] techniques . . . Many are of the opinion that since de-legalisation we have been gradually losing all possibilities of defending workers' rights, that is, of doing what a union should be doing. There are no new ideas, and what radicalism there is takes the form of verbal clichés about independence, and so on. It may be . . . the beginning of the end.

Bujak agreed with this assessment. Yet he encouraged people to keep up their efforts, and he pointed to WiP as a hopeful sign.[58] Public opinion polls showed that while some eighty percent of those surveyed continued to support Solidarity, a deep sense of discouragement seemed to have settled in. More than half of those surveyed had a net income below the social minimum, while a quarter were living below the biological minimum.[59] A majority felt that the only way to improve their situation would be to work abroad.[60]

Bujak was captured while I was on my first visit to Poland. When I spoke with people in Warsaw, Kraków and Gdańsk at that time, virtually everyone was deeply discouraged and expected no change in their lifetime. Lech Budrewicz recalled of that time: 'The biggest success of the government was not that it arrested people and destroyed organisations, but that it killed hope'. Grażyna Staniszewska, who led Solidarity in Bielsko-Biała, recounted how the exhaustion persisted:[61]

> At the end of the '80s, as a matter of fact, there were just a few people involved in the opposition. We tried to create the impression that the opposition in the underground movement was still enormous, and yet they could be counted on the fingers of one hand.

The government perceived this trend, and a new amnesty, just months after Bujak's capture, eventually freed almost everyone. General Kiszczak explained

---

58. Bujak 1986, pp. 15–16.
59. 'Independent Public Opinion Research in Krakow', *UPNB*, no. 16, 19 August 1986, p. 23.
60. Ibid.
61. 'Communism's Negotiated Collapse: The Polish Round Table, Ten Years Later', A Conference Held at the University of Michigan, April 7–10 1999.

that public support for Solidarity was diminishing, which led the government to conclude that 'The fading away of illegal activities will gradually continue'.[62] Yet Solidarity did not disappear; in fact, the amnesty appears to have been the result not of an improving situation from the point of view of the authorities, but of one that was increasingly desperate, as the stalemate was not ending.[63]

In fact, most people felt that this amnesty marked a change. Jan Lityński: 'In the '84 amnesty, almost all the prisoners were released, but the authorities were expected to put them back into prison, and they did. But in '86, everybody knew they would not be put back into prison – because of Popiełuszko'. The murder had altered the complexion of events. In this new situation, the opposition could and did function more openly, as public regional and national leadership bodies of Solidarity were reconstituted.

Nonetheless, people were tired after carrying on for years. Janusz Pałubicki noted that with the 1986 amnesty, many people left the underground.

> **Jacek Kuroń:** Before, the struggle for the release of political prisoners had given the movement considerable impetus. The vitality of the underground owed much to the common admiration for its activists. This admiration has faded now as the activists do not face imprisonment any more but a fine of 50,000 zlotys instead.[64]

Some who left the underground ceased activity, but others emerged into open activity. A corner was being turned.

62. Kiszczak 1986a, pp. 14, 16.
63. Paczkowski 2003, pp. 485–6.
64. Kuroń 1987, p. 28.

Chapter Eighteen
Negotiating the End

In retrospect, it is clear that the government side was also becoming demoralised. A Party member, described as a 'hard-line professor', gave an anonymous interview to an underground paper in 1985 expressing his concern that his side had lost its direction.

> It is believed ... that one must not talk to adversaries; this really proves a lack of confidence in the strength of one's own argument. I am most worried about the internal state of the party. Our Secretary and others like him at all levels have banned discussion ... We are told that what is needed is discipline and the so-called 'closing of ranks' but the true reason ... is to make everybody shut up. Discipline understood as the obedient carrying out of all orders ... can be a disaster for the party. The party cannot go on being torn by the fear of reasoned argument on the one hand and of new desertions on the other.[1]

A member of the secret police who had recently transferred from the criminal police stated that the effectiveness of his new branch was 'nil. It can't be otherwise, with police methods you can harass the underground, but you can't destroy it'. When asked why not, he responded:

> You can't put them all in jail. There's only one effective means of intimidation: mass executions. Like in Hungary in 1956 ... The reaction of

---

1. 'Interview with a Hard-Line Professor', *UPNB*, no. 16, 19 August 1986, pp. 30–1.

society is unpredictable. Bloody riots could start and then no-one would be safe. The Party guys know they would be the first to hang on the lamp posts. That's why the Party shrinks from such a solution.

His concern was that a 'few years more and if people hold on as they do now and the Party goes on as stupidly as it does now, the Party will lose the grip'.[2] Colonel Sucharski said that members of the secret police had been hopeful when martial law was declared: 'Our perception was that perhaps we would go up again'. But over time, this outlook changed:

> As we watched martial law washing out, we realised that it was time to look for another job ... Ideological activity was dead. Before, meetings would be every two months in a factory; now, they weren't happening at all. People left our security services after 12 years, 10 years. They got no retirement, not a penny. (To get it, you had to work at least 15 years). They could not get a job. They were, in essence, blacklisted because they had worked for the secret-police.

Discontent with the economy grew even on the government side. Politburo member Janusz Reykowski said:[3]

> I noticed among the younger members of the Party apparatus, and also to a great extent among the government circles, a group of people who wanted reforms and agreements. I realised that they were frustrated to a great extent for economic reasons ... They looked at those living in the West, and they knew how much worse off they were. They knew that they could not realise their ambitions in that system.

In November 1987, the government tried once again to gain some support by posing a referendum: did the population favour significant economic and political reform – to be carried out, of course, by the government itself. The referendum was defeated, in a humiliating turn for its proponents. Perhaps because of this mood, around the same time Mieczysław Rakowski wrote of the 'new political constellation which is developing within the Socialist bloc',[4] referring to Gorbachev's policy of *perestroika*, Rakowski asked: 'Could it be that there are still people who hold on to the belief that when the explosion occurs we shall invoke the interest of the state and warn that someone could intervene in our internal affairs. But what if this someone ... shows himself unwilling to intervene?' Clearly, Rakowski was suggesting that a new situation was emerging:

---

2. 'Inteview with a Member of Security Services', *UPNB*, no. 16, 19 August 1986, pp. 34–5.
3. 'Communism's Negotiated Collapse: The Polish Round Table, Ten Years Later', A Conference Held at the University of Michigan, April 7–10 1999.
4. Rakowski 1988, p. 18.

When compared to the situation in the late 1970s the present opposition is far more powerful, both qualitatively and numerically. We should not forget that it was a small group of KOR activists that set fire to the entire Baltic Coast. Today the opposition's chief goal is to gain legal guarantees for its existence and activities. Is this simply wishful thinking, something never to come about? ... *De facto* we have already recognised the opposition as a permanent feature in Poland's political landscape.

He noted the leadership's growing isolation: 'Intellectual life outside the Party is nowadays far more interesting, far more lively than within ... we are unable to produce charismatic personalities. The Party apparatus is constantly eroded'.

In the fall of 1987, the Politburo produced and leaked a document that hinted at allowing the creation of 'new associations', such as political discussion clubs, where 'different interests, outlooks and opinions should be openly expressed'. It stated that 'The party does not want the right to monopoly in governing'.[5] Around the same time, a prominent Soviet historian, in an interview with *Polityka*, called for a truthful examination of history, including *Katyń* – a reference to the murder of some 15,000 Polish officers by the Soviets during World War II,[6] an event which the USSR had always attributed to the Germans and which had been forbidden territory for discussion, one of the so-called 'white spots' in Polish history. Openness about this issue showed that very real and significant changes were taking place.

By December, there had emerged a movement among Solidarity activists to create open Solidarity founding committees.[7] Then, at a time when Solidarity's field of activity was opening up, on 1 February 1988, the government once again raised food prices, hoping to be able to make them stick. At the time, in the midst of winter, workers remained quiet. But March saw a series of demonstrations in several urban centres on the twentieth anniversary of the 1968 student upheaval. Then, in late April, strikes began, first among Bydgoszcz transit workers. It was quickly settled with a large pay rise, but it was followed the next day by a strike of some 4,000 steelworkers in the *Nowa Huta* Steel Mill plant outside Kraków: the number of participants soon grew to 12,000. The workers demanded a 50 percent wage increase for themselves and 20 percent for all Poland's industrial and health workers, teachers and pensioners, as well as the reinstatement of Solidarity activists who had been fired. Increasing the pressure, a few days later they were joined by steelworkers at the Stalowa Wola mill, which produced for

---

5. 'Calendarium, Sept 30–Oct 14', *UPNB*, no. 20, 14 October 1987, pp. 3–4.
6. Ibid.
7. 'Attempts to Register Soidarity Factory Unions: Something is Beginning to Move', *UPNB*, no. 24, 1987, pp. 24–6.

the military.[8] At the same time, a growing number of job actions and founding committees of Solidarity were appearing, both in workplaces and in schools.[9] On May Day, there were demonstrations in support of the steelworkers in *Nowa Huta*.[10] The next day, some 3,000 workers in the Gdańsk Shipyard began an occupation strike, while in Wrocław workers in the *Pafawag* factory began a strike in solidarity with the steelworkers.[11] There were also short strikes at many other workplaces.

The government used its riot-control troops to crush the strike in the *Nowa Huta* on 5 May. People were beaten, while the symbols of the strike were savagely destroyed. Ewa Kyrzyżostanek, a worker in the mill:

> They came and told us to kneel and lie down. We were reluctant; one of them hit me on the head with a truncheon and we quickly kneeled down ... One of them hit my leg and said: 'So you don't want to work, you bitch!' and told us to run. I fell over – they were worse than the Germans.[12]

Five days later, facing a similar threat, workers in the Gdańsk Shipyard 'suspended' their strike. Although they had been offered pay rises, they refused to sign any agreement that did not provide for explicit recognition of Solidarity. Their statement said:

> We have failed to win the victory. But though we are not leaving the shipyard triumphant, we are leaving with our heads high, convinced of the necessity and justice of our protest against social conditions in Poland, and against all violations of our dignity ... Our strike is an important step toward the realization that we will need to struggle in order to prevail ... This strike ends without an agreement, and that's proof that Poland's political, social and economic paralysis will continue and worsen and that resolution still lies beyond our reach. We remain faithful to the slogan of our strike: 'No freedom without Solidarity'.[13]

Despite the government managing to settle the strike, the threat that the workers could resume the fight for Solidarity remained.

---

8. 'Calendarium, April 15–29', *UPNB*, no. 8, 29 April 1988, pp. 4–6.
9. 'Clandestine Factory Commission of Solidarity Formed at the Lubin Coal Mine Communique', 3 January 1988, 'Inter-School Committee of Solidarity Formed', Warsaw, 15 January 1988, 'Acts of Defiance', 'Other Acts of Defiance', *UPNB*, no. 8, 29 April 1988, pp. 9–11.
10. 'Calendarium: April 30–May 15', *UPNB*, no. 9, 16 May 1988, p. 2.
11. 'Calendarium: April 30–May 15', p. 3.
12. 'The Strike in the Gdańsk Shipyard', *UPNB*, no. 10, 27 May 1988, p. 6, based on reports in the underground press, primarily *Tygodnik Mazowsze*, no. 250, 11 May 1988.
13. Wałęsa 1992, p. 145.

These events changed the political atmosphere in Poland, and the change was evident everywhere. Bogdan Borusewicz argued that Solidarity had been *de facto* recognised in the Gdańsk Shipyard 'through the lack of repressions after the strike'. Moreover, he contended, 'Kiszczak has declared that he will be releasing political prisoners and he has been doing just that. This is not because the strike was weak and had no support'.[14] Two journalists who interviewed shipyard workers reported that the atmosphere in the shipyard had changed.[15] On the first day after the strike:

> The foremen who only yesterday shouted and threatened us became suddenly very careful. The director came to one of the departments and declared that there would be no blacklists. Those who did not join the strike now are ashamed and come up with excuses: pregnant wife, mother-in-law in hospital, etc.

I arrived in Poland to continue my interviews in early May 1988, before the strike in the Gdańsk Shipyard had ended. I found the atmosphere quite different from what I had seen in 1986. Far from suffering from a sense that nothing would change 'in my lifetime', I now found an enormous sense of optimism. Most people foresaw the end of the regime within five to ten years – a prediction that proved to be overly pessimistic! Another indication that things were changing took place in July, when the *Sejm* altered the draft system to allow young people the option of alternative service for conscientious objectors, thereby providing a victory to WiP.[16] By that time the Polish affiliate to the Helsinki Committee   a group formed to keep tabs on the human and civil rights situation in the Soviet bloc – now revealed its hitherto secret membership. It stated: 'We believe that at present new conditions make it possible to undertake ... wider initiatives aiming at curtailing the authorities' arbitrariness and the repressiveness of the legal system'.[17]

A key question at that time was the following: *should Solidarity negotiate*, meaning 'compromise', *with the government?* As Adam Michnik later put it,[18] 'How can one think about making a pact with an enemy? How can one think of compromise with someone who should be punished for what he had done?' And, as Michnik noted, there was a wing of the opposition that was not ready to compromise. As one person, who had joined a split-off of Solidarity called

---

14. Borusewicz 1988, pp. 12–13.
15. Moi and Hoffer 1988, p. 14.
16. 'Calendarium: June 24–July 7', *UPNB*, no. 13, 8 July 1988, p. 4; 'Calendarium: 8 July–29 July', *UPNB*, no. 14, 30 July 1988, pp. 3–4.
17. 'The Helsinki Committee in Poland Reveals Its Membership, 24 July 1988', *UPNB*, no. 18, 30 September 1988, p. 11.
18. 'Communism's Negotiated Collapse: The Polish Round Table, Ten Years Later', A Conference Held at the University of Michigan, April 7–10 1999.

Fighting Solidarity, put it to me: 'The government will pretend to reform without reforming anything. But in the political sphere, and especially in the military, the government will keep control, so they will stop real economic reforms which would make them lose control after some time'. Rather, he charged, with distrust: 'There is a group within the Solidarity leadership which wants to make a deal with the government at all costs'.

The strikes clearly affected the thinking of a segment of the authorities. Political commentator Dawid Warszawski (the pseudonym used by Konstanty Gebert) noted that at the August Party Plenum, General Czesław Staszak, the Head of the Security Service, 'saw in the strikes in April–May not a provocation of irresponsible extremists, but an alarm bell which the authorities have stupidly ignored'.[19]

Then, on 15 August, a new round of strikes broke out, starting with the mines in Upper Silesia. They quickly spread to other mines, sixteen in all. Within days, farmers announced that they were undertaking to help the strikers, as they had done in August 1980. Soon, the strikes began to spread. Szczecin port workers, the Cegielski factory in Poznań, the Railway Rolling-Stock Repair Yard in Wrocław, the Stalowa Wola Steelworks, the port of Świnoujście, bus depots and the port in Szczecin, more mines, and finally, on 22 August, the Gdańsk Shipyard joined. While all of these strikes had demanded the reinstatement of Solidarity, the Gdańsk Shipyard made that its only demand, and they called upon workers in other firms to join the strike.[20]

The shipyard was soon surrounded by ZOMO and its telephone links were cut. Despite this show of force, the strike grew: the Warsaw Steel Mill, more mines, another shipyard in Gdańsk. The result was, as Adam Michnik remarked, that it 'became clear that the strategy of martial law had failed . . . It was necessary to talk with Solidarity'.[21] This was so because it was now evident that there would be continuing rounds of disruption with no-one to bargain with to win social acceptance. Rakowski acknowledged that they had recognised that they could not resolve the crisis without negotiating with the opposition: 'How did the negotiations start? The leadership was losing hope that we could cope with the crisis without the opposition, and in 1988 that was a conviction which was more and more prevalent within . . . the central leadership of the Party'.

Apparently in recognition of this situation, on 26 August General Kiszczak appeared on television and raised the possibility of a roundtable meeting with 'representatives of various workers' and social groups', and notably without preconditions – meaning that the Solidarity leadership was free to participate.[22]

---

19. Warszawski 1988, p. 13.
20. Wałęsa 1992, p. 153.
21. 'Communism's Negotiated Collapse: The Polish Round Table, Ten Years Later', A Conference Held at the University of Michigan, April 7–10 1999.
22. Wałęsa 1992, p. 155.

Jaruzelski's advisor Jan Bisztyga asserted that the general's decision to act was based on three issues: (1) with the distribution of power that existed then, the economy could not be kept stable; (2) the Party could not continue to retain power; and (3) the Party could not wipe out Solidarity. Those who 'reject the constitutional order' would not be permitted to participate, and in particular the government did not want to allow Jacek Kuroń or Adam Michnik to be included in the talks, while previously they had ruled out Wałęsa and Bronisław Geremek, a key Solidarity advisor.[23]

But as the strikes persisted, the government began to broaden its offer. Government spokesman Jerzy Urban stated that the government was ready to talk with opposition representatives, including Wałęsa. The government resigned and a new one was formed, headed by Rakowski, by that time a proponent of *perestroika*. But even then, the Party leadership did not contemplate the far-reaching changes that this course of action would instigate.

> **Rakowski:** I don't think anyone from the Party saw the possibility on the horizon of us losing power. My belief was that we could arrange a political, social and economic situation that would allow us to retain power. Nobody dreamed we'd lose power.[24]

Professor Edmund Wnuk-Lipiński argued that the new team was 'trying to restore the power of the party by sharing responsibility but not power'.[25] If they had their way, Solidarity would broaden the base of support for the government without having any power itself.

For negotiations to proceed it was the position of the Solidarity leadership that the opposition had to be normalised, meaning, as Zbigniew Bujak noted:[26]

> First, freedom for political prisoners. The next dilemma was the problem of what to do with people who were in hiding. There was just no way that we could simply walk out of hiding and sit down at the table and talk. So, the next condition was that those people would not be arrested and would not go to prison before any talks could start. So, then an open above-ground leadership could be created.

On 31 August, the eighth anniversary of the Gdańsk Accords, the new government announced that it was ready for roundtable discussions with the opposition. Within a week, a Soviet spokesman made it clear that they supported such discussions. After the first round of preparatory discussions, Wałęsa called for an end to the strikes, because the government was now willing to discuss legalising

---

23. Wechsler 1989, p. 60.
24. Hayden 1994, p. 91.
25. Hayden 1994, p. 92.
26. 'Communism's Negotiated Collapse: The Polish Round Table, Ten Years Later', A Conference Held at the University of Michigan, April 7–10 1999.

Solidarity.[27] It was a controversial stance, since government spokesman Jerzy Urban still claimed that Solidarity did not exist, although he did acknowledge that its leaders could participate in the roundtable talks. Wałęsa had to convince many doubters within the opposition, while the Party leaders had to do the same with their partisans. That was particularly so as the government had still not accepted that Solidarity should be legalised, and that position remained unchanged well into the autumn. Kiszczak told Wałęsa that 'the army, police and party bureaucracy were afraid of the symbol Solidarity had become'.[28]

Alfred Miodowicz, the leader of the official unions, clearly felt threatened by the direction of events, and he called for a vote of no confidence in the government as these moves were taking place.[29] Miodowicz challenged Wałęsa to a televised debate, a move which provoked considerable speculation concerning its motive, although many feared it was a trap and that, in Adam Michnik's colourful words,[30] 'Miodowicz would eat Wałęsa'. When the debate took place, Wałęsa was felt to have won easily. One public opinion poll found that 78 percent of the public had watched the debate.[31] As an article in Solidarity's 'official' publication *Tygodnik Mazowsze* noted after the debate: 'Some offices of the official new unions were closed so that they would not have to receive their members' resignations . . . Many workplaces report that workers are joining Solidarity *en masse*'.[32] Shortly after the debate, at the December meeting of the Central Committee, almost half of the membership of the Politburo was replaced, indicating not only that there was considerable resistance to the direction the Party leadership was taking, but also that there was sufficient support to remove the opponents.[33]

There was resistance on both sides, which made the stances of Wałęsa and Jaruzelski crucial. As Michnik argued:

> These two were perhaps the only ones who had full credibility in their communities. Nobody would have gone for these negotiations without Wałęsa; on the other side, without Jaruzelski no move toward the Round Table discussions would have taken place.[34]

---

27. 'Calendarium: Strikes in Poland – Events 18 August–3 September 1988', *UPNB*, nos. 17–18 (double issue), 10 September 1988, p. 2.
28. 'The Third Wałęsa-Kiszczak Meeting, 16 September 1988', *UPNB*, no. 19, 30 September 1988, p. 7.
29. 'Calendarium: 4 September–30 September 1988', *UPNB*, no. 19, 30 September 1988, p. 3.
30. 'Communism's Negotiated Collapse: The Polish Round Table, Ten Years Later', A Conference Held at the University of Michigan, April 7–10 1999.
31. 'Calendarium: 29 November–30 December', *UPNB*, no. 24, 31 December 1988, p. 2.
32. 'After the Wałęsa-Miodowicz Debate', *UPNB*, no. 1, 14 January 1989, pp. 20–21; appeared originally in *Tygodnik Mazowsze*, no. 274.
33. Warszawski 1989a, p. 22.
34. 'Communism's Negotiated Collapse' conference.

But in fact each of them had some elements on their side, and others who distrusted them and who did not want the negotiations to proceed. Michnik: 'We got to see the conflict within the Party and the pushes and shoves from one side to another'. Each side feared that the forthcoming talks would help to legitimise the other. The Solidarity negotiators continued to insist that before the talks could take place, the union must be made legal. Adam Michnik: 'Solidarity's being legal became *the* issue. Lech Wałęsa did not agree to talk about any other points before that one was cleared'. On the other side, Bishop Orszulik, one of the Church leaders actively involved in the process, recalled that 'Many of the partners on the governmental side claimed that it would be difficult to re-legalise Solidarity because there would be hell from our "base", as Mr Ciosek put it'.[35]

Nonetheless, Prime Minister Rakowski acknowledged soon after Wałęsa's debate with Miodowicz:

> The man who won the approval from most Poles because of that debate is not the same Wałęsa who in the fall of 1981 spoke at Radom of 'violent confrontations'. This Lech Wałęsa has a different political profile. He came across as the partisan of entente and compromise.

Rakowski followed up this assessment in January 1989 at the Central Committee Plenum, when he proposed the legalisation of Solidarity. Although there was great resistance to the proposal – such that Jaruzelski, Kiszczak and Rakowski all threatened to resign if it were not accepted – they won their point.[36]

On 6 February, the Round Table talks opened in Warsaw, with no preconditions, between the jailors and those whom they had jailed. It was a meeting that evoked considerable apprehension on both sides. After opening statements, the participants broke up into smaller groups, each of which was responsible for an aspect of the coming transformation. The talks were punctuated by strikes of miners and steelworkers – often provoked by recalcitrant members of the *nomenklatura* who were opposed to the direction in which they were being taken by the Party leadership[37] – despite the efforts of their local leaders to persuade them to pull back while the roundtable negotiations proceeded. In fact, on the day the talks began, Miodowicz's union called a strike in a coal mine. So, Wałęsa was forced personally to beseech the workers to postpone their action while the negotiations proceeded. Some bitterly resisted his entreaties.

The results of the Round Table were startling to all on both sides. At first, the Party sought to bring in but not empower Solidarity. In the early discussions, before the Round Table talks began, Janusz Onyszkiewicz recounted:[38]

---

35. Ibid.
36. Wechsler 1989, p. 62.
37. Ibid.
38. Onyszkiewicz 1989, pp. 16–17.

> The Party and government side was inclined to cede some forty percent of
> seats to constructive opposition, leaving sixty percent for the Communists and
> the allied parties ... It was suggested to us that the *Sejm* seats should be filled
> not through open and free democratic elections, but through bargaining and
> by decision reached prior to the elections.

Ultimately, it turned out that the seats in the *Sejm* were to be determined by bargaining after all: Solidarity got the chance to compete for only 35 percent of the
seats in the *Sejm*. However, in return, all 100 seats in the newly-created Senate
were up for grabs (electorally). Janusz Rejkowski, one of the Round Table negotiators, recalled: 'I do not believe anyone at that table had an awareness that we
were negotiating the end of the system because if they did, it would have been
much harder if not impossible'. As Aleksander Hall, leader of the Young Poland
opposition group, put it:[39] 'The results of the Round Table were startling for both
sides'. By mid-April, the Solidarity union was once again officially registered by
the Warsaw Provincial Court, and a few days later so was Rural Solidarity.[40]

It soon came out that part of the deal was that 46 high-level officials would
run unopposed for seats that opposition candidates were not allowed to contest,
although they still had to garner over fifty percent of the vote.[41] In June, the elections took place and their results shocked everyone: Solidarity won every *Sejm*
seat that it contested, as well as 99 of the 100 Senate seats. Moreover, of the 46
'safe' candidates, almost all failed to achieve the requisite majority of the elector-
ate and were both humiliated and eliminated. Rakowski said that he and other
Party leaders had had no idea what the results of the election would be: 'It wasn't
only the reason of being prisoners of the past tradition of un-free elections, and
the fact that the end of the Round Table talks looked good, but there was also the
fact that the opposition told us that they were not interested in power'.

Professor Jerzy Wiatr, a Jaruzelski advisor, thought that the Party leaders
'became victims of their own wishful thinking ... they underestimated the people
they were negotiating with'. The Solidarity negotiators were equally surprised at
the outcome. If the Communist negotiators had not realised what they had done,
neither did those from Solidarity's side. Adam Michnik recalled: 'We ... won on
such a scale that it simply frightened us. We did not expect it in our wildest
dreams ... The Communist system was simply and thoroughly rejected by the
Polish population'.[42]

---

39. 'Communism's Negotiated Collapse: The Polish Round Table, Ten Years Later', A
Conference Held at the University of Michigan, April 7–10 1999.

40. *UPNB*, no. 7, 1 May 1989, pp. 3–4.

41. Warszawski 1989b, p. 11.

42. 'Communism's Negotiated Collapse' conference.

Apparently, there were some highly-placed officials who were not disposed to accept the results of the election. Janusz Rejkowski stated:[43]

> There was a time between the 6th and the 8th of June, when people who thought along those lines mobilised and demanded that the election results be annulled. They came to the Politburo with that demand, and they prepared a report saying that annulling the elections was the only solution, and there was a dramatic struggle caused by that report and an effort to neutralise that kind of thinking.

Solidarity's sweeping victory was a herald of the future elections to come, when there would be no seats reserved for the Communist Party or its coalition partners.

It forced the Solidarity leaders to rethink their strategy. Their intent on entering the negotiations had not been to take power immediately; they had expected to constitute the opposition in parliament. However, the scale of their victory brought about popular demands that they constitute a government. In July, Adam Michnik, who was then the editor of what had become the most important newspaper in Poland, *Gazeta Wyborcza*, wrote an editorial for the paper entitled 'Your President, Our Prime Minister', in which he proposed that while the newly-created post of president could be taken by the Polish United Workers' Party, the day-to-day governing could be done by a Solidarity-led coalition. That is what happened, as the Communist Party's former coalition partners, the Peasant Party and the Democratic Party joined the Solidarity-led coalition, which gave it a clear majority in parliament. These parties could clearly see the handwriting on the wall: if they didn't go where the voters had clearly gone, what would happen to them during the next election?

There was an important caveat to this arrangement: two generals, both members of the Politburo, were put in control of the police and the military – in other words, the instruments of repression. That was a potential danger that, fortunately, was never realised. A little over a year later, that arrangement ended, as Wałęsa became president and the political transition was complete. The economic transformation would take longer – the first couple of years were difficult (that is another story). But a decade later, it was well advanced.

Poland's freedom was facilitated – and, fundamentally, made possible – by the programme of Mikhail Gorbachev as the leader of the Soviet Union. His refusal to continue to impose the will of the Soviet Union on its satellites in Europe enabled Poland, and the rest of the Soviet bloc, to go their own way. The Soviet empire came to an end. Before long, so did the Soviet Union, as the world's last great empire fell to pieces.

---

43. Ibid.

Conclusion

Despite the civil war, the fight with the peasantry over land, and the battle with the Church, the insurrection in Poznań in 1956 was a shock to Poland's rulers.[1] Those events established that the working class had a real role in shaping the nation's policies and in removing if not choosing the nation's rulers. It was a role that the rulers regularly ignored – much to their eventual regret. But over time it became the way Poles intervened – it was the only way left open, as every other effort proved to be fruitless. In 1956, they were quite successful in improving conditions for many – they removed direct control by the Soviet Union, the Church regained a certain level of autonomy from the state, the secret-police powers were reduced, there was more freedom, and the standard of living improved.

Despite its significant successes, within a few years the workers' council movement was rendered toothless and its activists dispersed. Its lessons were not widely disseminated. Into the 1960s, life returned to a new normal: not nearly as oppressive as it had been, but with a gradual tightening of the apparatus and the loss of control from below. By the end of the 1960s, the gains made in popular control from 1956 were gone, and the consumer economy stagnated as more and more production went into war material and heavy industry. Opportunity became increasingly constricted. Over time, discontent grew.

---

1. Torańska 1987, pp. 58–9.

Then, the student and worker disruptions of 1968 and 1970 discredited the authorities among the new post-war generation that would be of central importance to the nation's future: it became the generation that made Solidarity (just as the baby boomers became central to the Civil Rights movement in the United States). These events certainly taught lessons of various stripes. The students felt isolated and defeated. The brutality exercised against the demonstrators, including the use of deadly force in 1970, terrified people and drove them deep underground or into apathy. But discontent remained, even if it was softened by the increase in living standards that accompanied the end of the Gomułka era. There were efforts at self-organisation, but it was not until the worker uprisings of 1976 – when the government carried through on its promise not to repeat its use of deadly force (even though it still severely repressed those who dared to challenge its dominance) – that organisation grew apace.

KOR emerged at that time, and its activists publicly identified themselves and provided their contact information. Workers (and students) began coming together. In this period, the lessons of 1970 and 1976 were widely discussed: workers should not go into the streets, because doing so offered great opportunities for provocateurs, or for people who had different plans from those of the demonstration organisers. In several places, public lectures were given and underground literature published where these issues and many others were discussed. One lesson became paramount: they should stick together and support one another. While these lessons were most developed and internalised on the Baltic Coast, they were also assimilated much more broadly in the working class around the country. This period of intellectual enrichment for people who were becoming activists prepared the basis for the emergence of Solidarity.

The trigger of sudden significant price rises, especially for food, in the context of growing hostility toward the Soviet Union and a general lowering of the standard of living, once again precipitated strikes, which this time, thanks to a new determination showed by the workers, demanded an independent union with the right to strike. Once those strikes began, the degree of organisation and the extent to which people had learned the lessons of their past became manifest, as what were, in reality, general strikes broke out in the port cities and before long spread to other key cities and workplaces.

By this time, the ability of the state to control the political opportunity structure of the oppositionists had significantly diminished, as soon became evident first in the negotiations on the ports when workers simply refused to accept the terms they were being offered and insisted on a variety of conditions, as well as their demands. These conditions included the right to communicate among each other – not simply within a city or region, but between them. Workers in Szczecin made a condition of further negotiations that they have a team in Gdansk who could report to them, as did the copper miners in Lower Silesia. When it was becoming evident that the government was not bargaining in good faith, as little progress was made, the strikes swiftly spread way beyond the ports. This act made it plain to Poland's rulers that they would have to make historic concessions, such as none of their predecessors in the Soviet bloc had ever had to grant before. Thus, they reluctantly agreed to accept an independent union with the right to strike, and as a result Solidarity was born.

The birth of the union did not end the conflict, but instead took it to a higher level. The union organised itself not by trades or by companies, but by *region*. This meant that the union's actions and sights would inevitably develop politically, and that it constituted a real base of alternate power. It was a real threat to Communist and therefore Soviet domination; they knew that Solidarity was such a threat and felt endangered by it.

The authorities tried in various ways to limit the movement – for example, by trying to refuse the right to form such a union in areas that had not gone on strike; by trying to keep it under the control of the Polish United Workers' Party; by using police tactics to limit its autonomy; by using the secret police to intimidate people; by seeking to co-opt Solidarity leaders with privileges. These measures were all various ways to fight the union, as all elements who benefited from the *nomenklatura* system tried to push back. But all of these efforts failed. Workers fought back effectively, and in the course of doing so they often expanded their own power and increasingly constrained the government's. They succeeded in limiting the government's options and thereby effectively narrowed the state's own political opportunity structure.

They were aided in this effort by the fact that the ruling political party was itself deeply split, with a significant segment of the Party supporting Solidarity and the reform movement that it represented and encouraged. This deep intra-Party split prevented the hard-liners from being able to give their full attention to defeating the opposition movement that Solidarity led and nurtured. They were forced to turn inward before they could fully concentrate on their main concern: the opposition. The reform movement within the Party existed because of the social vitality of Solidarity; it drew its strength from Solidarity and, for a time, it protected Solidarity. But in the end, even the two together could not prevail, at least in the short-term.

While the government was unable for some time to focus solely on its opposition, it certainly paid the opposition significant attention, and its agents continually made efforts to limit Solidarity's reach and its gains. Several of these efforts were defeated, and through these contests the opposition's authority and power grew. This was the case until the confrontation between Solidarity and the government that was precipitated by an apparent provocation in Bydgoszcz.

That incident led the union to the brink of a national general strike, which if carried out had revolutionary potential. For that reason, it was quite dangerous, since it raised the possibility of a Soviet intervention. The probability of such an intervention was considerably diminished by the problems encountered by the Soviets from their invasion of Afghanistan. But the improbability of such an invasion was not really grasped by any of the collective actors in Poland at the time.

The strike was called off in a manner that brought about a feeling that the unions had been defeated. That sense of defeat felt by Solidarity activists widened the divisions within the union and set sections of it against one another, and it limited the options that activists felt were available to them. In particular, they felt that they no longer had in their arsenal the threat of a general strike. And indeed, although there was talk of it, especially during martial law, there was never again a credible threat of such an action. Instead, there was a general feeling that activists within the union were perhaps incurably divided – and that sense weakened the union.

By the autumn of 1981, the first (and last, until after the fall of Communism in Poland) national conference of Solidarity met. At that time, strikes were occurring with increasing frequency, as workers responded to frequent provocations, or, even when the strikes were not provoked, the authorities often simply refused to settle with them. Strikes at enterprises that made consumer goods were particularly ignored and allowed to persist, such that the public found itself increasingly deprived of goods and services that they felt they needed. The government simply blamed Solidarity. These actions were perceived by the Solidarity activists as intentional, to drive wedges between the union and the Polish population. As shortages appeared everywhere in stores – shortages that certainly appeared to be deliberately brought about – this sense of conspiracy was intensified. By late autumn of 1981, the lack of goods available in the shops had become increasingly evident, provoking a sense of desperation and anger in the population. The Solidarity leadership responded to this growing sense by talking tough, but also by advancing reasonable proposals, which the government ignored. So, Solidarity's leaders were unable to produce an effective programme to change the direction of events. Even as times worsened, the feeling of desperation grew stronger, which provided an opening for the military *coup d'état* on 12–13 December 1981.

That night, the government took the movement by surprise and rounded up some 10,000 Solidarity activists and their supporters. In a number of places, workers sought to resist by using their collective power. Most of their successes were very limited, as within days the military and the police were able to gain control – with the exception of Upper Silesia. In Upper Silesia, coal miners engaged in strikes or other work actions, including going underground, where the military could not reach them. Those strikes were heroic; they deeply affected the workers who participated in them, and they signalled that there was substantial resistance despite the mass detentions. But they could not tip the balance of power.

With such a mass round-up, inevitably the government was not able to apprehend everyone. Some people escaped because they were outside the country when the round-up took place. Seweryn Blumsztajn was in Paris at that time; he immediately became a source of information for interested foreigners and a fundraiser for the movement in Poland. Key leaders in Warsaw, Kraków, Katowice, Wrocław, Gdańsk and elsewhere were able to avoid arrest and then to begin to rebuild the opposition. Over time many of them were also caught, but not before they had been able to begin to organise an underground resistance. Some managed to avoid capture by the police for years.

Gradually, opposition activity again began to cohere. The government's apparent hope that with most of the Solidarity leaders and activists in prison, life would go back to 'normal' – that is, to what it had been before the 1980 strikes – was dashed. People who were detained would be released, and then when they had gone back into active opposition, they were once again arrested. This process persisted over some years. By the time of Bujak's capture in 1986, the scandal of the murder of the opposition-supporting priest Father Popiełuszko had long before become widely known, and the opposition was revitalised. It was clear that open dissent was not going away, and that it still had substantial support throughout much of the society. And it was evident that following the amnesty that freed Bujak and others, they would not be returning to prison.

But it was not yet certain what the effect of the opposition would be. At the time of Bujak's capture, the people with whom I spoke anticipated years of opposition before they could hope for change. They were sometimes prepared to make deals with the 'reds' to get them off their backs. This atmosphere remained until the strikes in the summer of 1988, two years later. These strikes in April, May, and again in August, which once again demanded recognition of Solidarity, made it clear that support for the opposition remained.

Suddenly, because of the demonstrated inability of the government to legitimate itself or to improve the economy, and the insistence of another new generation of workers on their allegiance to Solidarity – and, tellingly, because of the rise to power of the reformists in the Soviet Union, led by Mikhail Gorbachev, which made acceding to that demand more feasible – Rakowski's administration began to discuss Poland's future with the Solidarity leadership. It appeared that Gorbachev was prepared to relax Soviet control over its satellite. The Polish government had considerably greater room for manoeuvre in developing a *rapprochement* with the resurgent opposition. While the manoeuvrings concerning the conditions required for such discussions to take place delayed the process for a period, inevitably (if negotiations were to be held) they led to an agreement that Solidarity would be granted legal status and that the activists who were still in hiding would be allowed to re-enter society without fear of arrest. Wałęsa's non-status as the head of a supposedly 'non-existent' organisation ceased to be a barrier to the talks. The Solidarity activists demanded all this before any further negotiations could take place.

Through a lengthy process, those discussions led to elections. The elections were supposed to be 'fixed', with the expectation that Communist rule would continue and that the Solidarity-supported members of parliament would be a constitutional opposition. Once the elections took place – the first free elections in Poland for decades – the Polish people made it clear that they were unwilling to accept the arrangement. Solidarity won virtually every seat it contested, including 99 of the 100 seats available in the Senate. Seeing these results, the Communist's erstwhile allies for virtually the entire post-war period, the Peasant Party and the Democratic Party moved to support the Solidarity-endorsed deputies, thereby creating a Solidarity-led government and ending Communist rule in a most unexpected fashion. Even before Wałęsa's succession to the presidency, which finished that process in Poland, the entire Soviet empire imploded and ceased to exist, as all the nations under Soviet domination since World War II went their own way. A watershed had been passed, and Poland was now writing its own history for the first time in a very long time.

Who done it?

It should be clear from the evidence presented here that this is a story of the organised working class, certainly aided by KOR and by Catholic priests and the Polish Pope, having carried out a lengthy struggle that finally ended Soviet domination and Communist rule in Poland. Arguably, they also played a major role in ending the Soviet empire in eastern Europe, and in bringing down the Soviet Union itself – the last of the great empires in the world. The workers struck and they demanded and created Solidarity. They did so after many of them had built their own independent organisations, and after a national network had begun to develop as workers from one region became acquainted with those from another. It was Solidarity that won the right for farmers, students and others to organise themselves independently; and Solidarity fought to expand the rights and standing of the Church. KOR recognised the central importance of these developments when, at the Solidarity Congress, it announced that it was dissolving itself because Solidarity had taken over the tasks for which KOR had been originally created.

Both KOR and the Church provided significant aid to this effort. KOR had connections with the international press, which in turn brought news back into the country. It became a crucial source of information for the international press – including the BBC, Radio Free Europe, the Voice of America and other broadcasters. These sources then broadcasted the material they received from KOR, which was often how Poles got it. It provided advisors and helped workers to connect with already-existing dissidents and with one another. By publicising their names and contact information, they helped to break the barrier of fear that the government had created throughout the society. KOR helped to nourish and encourage the opposition; it did not will it into being, nor did KOR lead the workers around – although they were happy to listen to the advice of its members.

The Church was also a major supporter of Solidarity. On his first trip back to his homeland, before Solidarity existed, Pope John Paul II encouraged people to think and act independently and morally. Once Solidarity was created, he supported it; when he came to Poland, he met openly with Wałęsa. While the attitude of the hierarchy in the country was more ambiguous, there were many priests who openly encouraged the opposition. After martial law was declared, the Church was often the only place where people could meet, discuss and organise. The Church collected money to aid prisoners and their families.

But all of this activity on the part of these two organisations does not obviate the fact that the workers were their own agents, that they created their own groups and built their own underground organisations before Solidarity was created, made their own decisions concerning the choices that the government offered in the negotiations during August 1980 and thereafter. Not all of their choices were perhaps the wisest, especially in the latter part of 1981 when the union was under great stress and rank-and-file workers were more likely to strike and to make more extreme demands than their leaders wished. But there is no reason to think that others – independent intellectuals or church-based – would necessarily have made better decisions. And we know that in 1980 the suggestions from both the Church and KOR – to be more moderate, to settle before they had won the right to have an independent union with the right to strike – were not the right decisions, which the workers themselves actually made.

Of course, we have to reckon that as Solidarity represented almost the whole of the society through its members and their families, many others were involved in what it was doing and helped the union movement to make its decisions through families and friends, as well as in other more formal ways. But the workers themselves were central to what happened, both the creation of Solidarity and the turns it made during its existence. The examination, here, of how the strikes began that established negotiations with the government and eventually won the right to create Solidarity makes that clear – in Gdańsk, Gdynia, Szczecin, Warsaw, Kraków, Wrocław, Katowice and Jastrzębie. So too does the development of the conflict between Solidarity and the government both before and after martial law was declared.

It is also quite evident that the workers' struggles for a decent standard of living, control over their lives, the economy, and their working conditions, were inextricably intertwined with their national subjection by the Soviet Union. The Soviets had imposed their system upon Poles, together with the rest of Eastern Europe. There was no way to remove it save by ending Soviet control. So workers, acting as a class, played the central role in resolving the issue of national oppression.

Political opportunity structure

The experience of Solidarity in Poland makes very clear the crucial role of the interaction of collective actors in social movements. There is no way to understand what happened in this social movement, or any other for that matter, without grasping that none of the collective protagonists was able to determine events on their own. Both Solidarity and the Party/state it confronted sought to expand their opportunities for action and to limit those opportunities available to their opponents. The actions each side took toward the other engendered differences about how to respond *within* each group. Thus, both the ruling party and Solidarity had significant factional differences. Within the Polish United Workers' Party, the reformers were sympathetic and tied to Solidarity, and dependent upon the union for its successes, while it played a major role in preventing the Party from acting freely against the opposition. (There was also another faction, based on the *nomenklatura* and the apparatchiks, who feared losing their benefits). Although Solidarity had no significant tendency within it that was an agent of the Party, it was riven by factional differences between those who sought to avoid constant conflict with the authorities – who were seen as 'moderates' – and those who were more radical, and these differences made the union's choices of action more difficult. In both cases, the factional differences within both Solidarity and the Communist Party seriously affected the ability of each of them to respond to the moves of the other in a forceful way.

While scholars of social movements are used to examining these calculations with respect to social movements that challenge the state, there has been much less effort to place the same consideration on the state itself. One of the lessons of this study is that it is sometimes as important to focus on the political opportunity structure in which the *state* has to operate and make choices of action, as it is to do so with respect to social movements.

Eventually, after having resolved the factional dispute within the ruling Party, the Polish government was able to get to where it wanted to go. However, despite all the pressure it exerted, despite martial law, the detention of 10,000 activists overnight, and the outlawing of the union, public support for Solidarity could not ultimately be crushed. The union movement survived for years underground until the regime was forced once again to negotiate, this time for free elections that ended Communist rule. Had the Party been unified, it would much sooner and much more easily have been able to oppose and possibly cripple the movement that produced Solidarity. But the huge social upheaval that had won and sustained Solidarity had clearly influenced the entire society, including the make-up of the Party and its policies, during the period that Solidarity was legally active. It is difficult to see how, given Solidarity's vast social support, such an outcome could have been avoided. For a lengthy period, Party leaders were inundated by the flood of Solidarity-influenced policies and members; it was not easy for them to turn things around, and ultimately they could not do so. By the end of the decade, they had to come to terms with Solidarity's demands, although they did not recognise at the time that they were literally negotiating an end to their rule. So, it is evident that the popular movement that Solidarity represented and furthered deeply affected what options the government had as it sought to deal with a challenge more powerful and sustained than confronted any other state in the Soviet empire.

Heretofore, political opportunity structure has generally been considered with respect mainly to the possibilities for action available to social movements. But we should also be aware that governments may be faced with the same considerations. In studies of social movements, analysts should be aware of the interaction between social movements and the state, at least in circumstances where the social movement has a significant social impact. These circumstances make the analysis more complex, but more in tune with reality.

The transition from Communism

The story of the transition in Poland is not necessarily a happy one. If a movement that was based upon the working class succeeded in resolving Poland's *national* oppression, its effect on class issues is much less clear. I spent the academic year 1990–1 in Warsaw, as part of the exchange programme between Indiana University and Warsaw University. While there, I witnessed the latter stages of the presidential campaign that saw Wałęsa elected president. It was a terribly difficult time. Jobs were disappearing as businesses, factories and mines closed down. Many of the large factories that were the base of Solidarity's strength ceased to exist: the Gdańsk Shipyard, the *Nowa Huta* Steel Mill outside of Kraków, many mines and other workplaces. On a structural level, the loss of these places meant both that the most important bases of Solidarity were disappearing, and with them its power. On a *personal* level, many of the workers were left without what had been relatively well-paying jobs. This loss of jobs continued for a few years after the transition, until 1992, and unemployment has become a permanent part of the social landscape since.

Class conditions deteriorated as the government plunged into a market economy. Under Communism, there was relative equality among most of the population; people were poor, but they had decent clothes; if you had to ride the overcrowded trams, so did almost everyone else. Now, differentiation was rapidly taking place, and desperation appeared alongside it. It was exacerbated by the huge inflation of almost 300 percent that struck the country as it began its transition away from the command economy to a market economy.[2] People lost jobs and income; national production declined by 8 percent, real wages by 25 percent, and unemployment soared to 6 percent.[3]

Solidarity had created a community that integrated disparate people under these circumstances. Now, that trend disappeared; nastiness replaced it. For example, in Warsaw a poverty-stricken old woman came into a shop and asked to buy one egg because that was all that she could afford. The clerk yelled at her, claiming that they only sold five or ten eggs at a time, and if she could not afford that then she should get out of line. My wife, who witnessed this encounter, bought the woman ten eggs. But the woman was not alone. Homelessness began to appear; dumpster-diving became more common. In some small mining towns, the mines closed because they were unprofitable. There was no other employment available for the men in Upper Silesia, and there had always been a shortage of jobs for women, beyond teaching, nursing (if a hospital were available), and clerking – and there were only so many such jobs. As a result, a whole family could be bereft. And because of the severe shortage of housing, moving to where employment might be more obtainable was often not an option. Some families committed suicide together, unable to envision an alternative for themselves; there were cases where they would shut the windows and turn on the gas. People on pensions because of old age or illness found that what they received did not provide them the ability to live; they were short on money for housing, food, medical expenses.

While Polish farmers had prevented their land from being collectivised – unique in this regard amid the Soviet bloc – there were strict limitations placed on their ability to sell it and on how much land they could own. As a result, their standard of living was low and they had a hard time competing with the high-tech competition from Western Europe. Far too many still farmed tiny plots of land, and these farms would have to be consolidated. For the young, this transformation was a real opportunity. But this was not the case for many of those who were older.

---

2. Wałęsa 1992, p. 244.
3. Paczkowski 2003, pp. 511–12.

It was a very difficult period. Within a short time, the social ethic changed from social solidarity to dog-eat-dog, with each person having to fend for himself or herself. As Poland's economy became integrated into the West, there was no broad support for a powerful union such as Solidarity had been. It certainly would have inhibited new investment. The new market economy that the government quickly jumped into opened up opportunities for many, especially in the cities, where there is lots of evidence of new wealth. But it has also meant poverty, as the safety nets and social supports were taken away and people were left on their own. The weak and the vulnerable suffered, even as others prospered. For those left out of the new system, Communism may still appear enticing. But it is gone for good.

Researching the Polish Revolution

In 1986, I came to Poland almost accidentally to observe the changes Solidarity had wrought. I was not an expert on Eastern Europe and I had not expected to do any research there. However, my field of concentration is social movements. I had been inspired by the emergence of Solidarity while I was working on another book, and I was aware that Poland had a history of social upheaval. So when I learned that my application to participate in the exchange programme between Indiana University and Warsaw University had been accepted, meaning that I would be going to Poland for around five weeks in the summer of 1986, I decided to see if I could learn about Solidarity and the significant social movements that had characterised Communist Poland.

I began asking around to see if anyone I knew was acquainted with somebody who knew someone there. In this manner, David Finkel, a friend of mine, connected me to Jane Dobija, a Polish-American woman who had been moved by Solidarity to go to Poland, where she became for a time the Polish correspondent for National Public Radio. Jane kindly provided me with letters of introduction to two independent journalists in Warsaw and Krakow. Each of them gave me connections that opened up the world of the opposition. In Krakow, Krzysztof Kasprzyk brought me to the *Misztrzejowice* church in the suburb of *Nowa Huta* (which was a centre of opposition) on a Thursday evening, when the weekly 'Mass for the Fatherland' was held. This was a political 'Mass' – really a community meeting – at which I recorded some of what was going on and took some photographs.

When it was over I felt I should tell the priest, Father Jancarz, that I was not a KGB agent. 'I don't give interviews', he responded. I assured him that I was not asking for an interview. He assented, and I said that I had just finished writing a book about the US Civil Rights movement, that what I had seen that night reminded me of it, and that I was moved by it. 'Now you may have an interview', he said.

We sat and talked, and after a while he invited me to speak at his Christian workers' university in lieu of the scheduled speaker Stefan Bratkowski (who had led the Journalist Union during the Solidarity period, had been expelled from the ruling Party, and had become a leading opponent of the regime). Bratkowski had heart trouble and could not appear on the scheduled date, so I was to be his replacement. I said that I would be pleased to come, but this was Poland: what could I offer him? 'Tell us about the Civil Rights movement and the anti-Vietnam War movement in the States', he said. No problem.

On the way to the church on Saturday, we stopped to pick up Maciek Szumowski. He had been editor of the Krakow Party paper, *Gazeta Krakowska*, during the Solidarity days, and by all accounts had made it into the best paper in Poland. Later, when I interviewed him, he told me what he had done with the paper as its editor: he had run competing points of view in the paper and had editorialised against Party policy, forcing the Party leadership to send letters to its own paper that expressed their disagreement with his editorials. When martial law was declared, he was fired and expelled from the Party. Now he was working with the church. He had returned to his professional roots and was making television documentaries that were being distributed through what amounted to an underground television network played on VCRs throughout the country.

Kasprzyk introduced me to Szumowski not as an academic, but as an American leftist. Without skipping a beat, Szumowski immediately asked me how I felt about working with the church. I told him that in my view, you work with whomever you can agree with and do not try to draw lines between yourself and others. I did not know it at the time, but Szumowski was testing me for sectarianism – and I had passed a gatekeeper. In part, that was why, when I returned in 1988, he was willing to help me.

At the church, Szumowski began the discussion that followed from my comments, and I learned a great deal from what he said:

> We are privileged to have among us someone who actually saw these events [referring to the Civil Rights movement] and can tell us what happened. Many of us heard these things on the radio or on television, but we did not believe what we heard.

Szumowski's remark first revealed to me the magnitude of the gulf that existed between the regime and the population: in Communist Poland, people's natural tendency was to disbelieve *everything* they were told from official sources. If the communists said something was white, people assumed it must be black. One of my interviewees, Kazimierz Graca, a coal miner with whom I later spoke, confirmed that insight when he told me: 'If the Party was in favour of something, we were opposed to it; on the other hand, if the Party opposed something, we were in favour of it'. Since the standard of truth for many people was that whatever the government told them must be false, in this odd way, the regime still defined truth for many people.

A few days later, I interviewed Szumowski and asked him with what conscience he had stayed in the Party during the repression of student protests of 1968 and the worker protests of 1970 and 1976. He became agitated and insisted that he had acted decently and responded:

> I must admit that very soon after I joined, it was evident what the Party was and what was possible. But there was always in my mind a will to do something to justify staying within the Party. There were already many who were ashamed of being in the Party. Having this complex, many people were eagerly looking for the possibility to express their honesty, their private truth, their own morality. Without this complex, I would not have behaved in Solidarity as I did. I was simply ashamed at having had this party-card and at any price I wanted to show that I was a good and honest man, even against the daily practice of party life, which we knew was terrible. There was always the illusion, the hope, that something could be done, and if you left the Party you lost that chance. If I had left the Party earlier, which former Chief Editor of *Gazeta Krakowska* would you be talking to now? Then, during the Solidarity period, there would have been no-one. Without the help of some fragment of the Party in '56 or '70 or '80, the political opposition would not have gained at least its passive support.

Kasprzyk and Szumowski were the first of several former members of Poland's Communist Party with whom I spoke. They provided me a window of understanding into the functioning of the Party and the motivations of some of the people in it. Later, their willingness to speak with me enabled me to get to know an important segment of the reform movement within the Party, and therefore to have some understanding of the inner-life of the Party and the conflicts it contained.

After the discussion, Father Jancarz took me up to his quarters, offered me tea and cake, and informed me that I was not yet finished: within an hour I would be speaking to another group. Around 6pm on Saturday night, some 75 workers and students showed up at the church. I spoke, they asked questions. It went on for three hours. On Saturday night! Knowing that such a meeting simply would not take place in America, this experience was quite an eye-opener to me as to the intense political atmosphere in Poland.

Afterwards Jancarz told me that the next morning he was going to Gdańsk and offered to take me with him and to introduce me to Lech Wałęsa. I already had plans to go to Gdańsk that next day and I accepted his offer to meet Wałęsa. Sure enough, on Monday I was ushered into an audience with the Nobel Prize winner, where I and a journalist from *The Washington Post* took turns asking him questions.[1]

The next day, a woman whom Adamiecki had asked to show me around Gdańsk brought me to the Dominican Church in the city centre – an important gathering place for the opposition – to speak to a group of journalists, all of whom had lost their jobs when martial law was declared in 1981. I was asked to speak to them about the Civil Rights movement, which I did. I then asked if anyone would be willing to meet privately with me and tell me of his or her own experiences. Two who spoke English volunteered, and I met with them subsequently. In addition, some of them appreciated what I had told them and decided I should meet some acquaintances of theirs, Andrzej Gwiazda and Joanna Duda-Gwiazda. They were among the original organisers of opposition in Gdansk, and Andrzej had contested Wałęsa for the presidency of Solidarity. I met and spoke with them and some of their co-workers for two afternoons.

One thing had become apparent to me from my discussions with people: there was a deep pessimism about anything happening to change the status quo at any time in the near future. They felt little hope for the future.

By the time I left Poland after five weeks, I realised that I had developed good enough connections to speak with anyone I wished in the Polish opposition. The opportunity to have a fairly extensive array of in-depth interviews with a variety of activists scattered geographically and politically, with different occupations and educations, belonging to different social strata, and with a broad range of experiences, had virtually dropped into my lap. I could certainly not walk away from it, even though I had never personally imagined I would undertake research in Eastern Europe.

My five-week stay had made me aware of the intense political atmosphere in Poland, which I found fascinating. (My Polish friends said that I was catching

---

1. I did not realise what a coup this was until I read Jan Kurski's *Lech Walesa, Democrat or Dictator?* Kurski was Wałęsa's press secretary from October 1989 through to July 1990. He notes that at least during his tenure, it was very difficult to get an interview with Wałęsa. They were booked several weeks in advance. I was able to get in because Father Jancarz, one of the leading opposition priests, had the connection.

the 'Polish disease' – which referred to how the heat of Polish politics attracted people). I had never seen anything like it since my graduate student days at Berkeley in the 1960s. Solidarity had long impressed me with the depth of social feeling it had tapped and for its ability to confront a government in the Soviet bloc with such success. Now I had the opportunity and the time to try to understand it. Such a study was especially alluring because it offered me the chance to examine a major social movement in a very different political, economic and social system than that with which I had been familiar. (For example, in 1986 and 1988, when I left Poland, I took the then-apparently-customary-but-unnerving route of giving all my notes and tapes to the American embassy. They, in turn, took them out of the country in their diplomatic pouch and then mailed them to me. In that way, I avoided the possibility that my materials might be taken from me at the border. But from the time I surrendered my precious and hard-gained tapes and notes until I received them in the mail, I was uneasy). I did not realise at the time the burden I was undertaking: to familiarise myself with Polish culture and history. That was why I decided to try to stay in people's homes where I travelled. I saw it as a way to familiarise myself with the ethnography of Poland: to learn what Polish life was like.

In the summer of 1987, I took an intensive course in Polish and then continued my studies during the year. I convinced the Indiana University committee that ran the exchange programme to select me a second time – something unprecedented – based on my project proposal to interview the oppositionists. (My status of not being a Poland scholar actually helped me here because I had nothing to lose if the government reacted negatively to my work, whereas established Polish scholars told me it was difficult for them to do what I proposed because they might be denied permission to return to the country).

As I prepared to begin the research in earnest, change became evident: just days before I was to return to Poland, in 1988, strikes broke out in several parts of the country. They continued into early May and completely changed the atmosphere. Then, in the summer of 1988, I returned. When I arrived, it was apparent that people's tune had changed: now they expected an end to the Communist regime within ten years – no, five! (It turned out they were all too pessimistic, as the end came within a mere 15 months).

That summer, I spent three and a half months interviewing Solidarity leaders, leaders of the intellectual opposition, leaders of the movement to reform the Party, journalists and some people affiliated with the Church. For this purpose, I visited four cities, each of which was a major centre of opposition: Warsaw, Kraków, Wrocław and Gdańsk. For the most part, these interviews were conducted in Polish and translated for me on the spot. That was important even for the few who spoke English because I wanted them to be comfortable in their language and to be able to express themselves most fully. I didn't realise it then, but my timing was perfect. I was able to get lengthy interviews with many people because with the regime still in power, they had lots of free time. Later, it became somewhat more difficult.

In the fall of 1989, I was on sabbatical when a new non-Communist government took power, so I decided to return to see what had happened and to continue my research. I financed this trip myself; I spent another three-and-a-half months there, and besides returning to the cities I had already visited, I spent several weeks in Upper Silesia, dividing my time between the major city there, Katowice, and the coal mining region of Jastrzębie, which had played a crucial role both in the August strikes that established Solidarity and in the response to the government's declaration of martial law – Upper Silesia was the only region that offered serious sustained resistance, including one prolonged strike underground.

Because of the change in regime, I now felt that I could apply for the position of Indiana University Exchange Professor, which would send me to Warsaw University for a year-long exchange. Under the Communist government, I had worried that doing my research in that position might have been injurious to one or the other university. So, I spent the academic year 1990–1 teaching and doing research in Poland, mostly in Warsaw. In 1997, I decided that I needed to return one more time, and I won a small grant from the Russian and East European Institute at Indiana University for that purpose. I spent six weeks there in the summer interviewing key participants, mostly in the western city of Poznań, where important events had taken place in the first post-war upheaval in Poland in 1956.

On this last trip, I made a breakthrough in the sociological character of my respondents. I managed to have a lengthy interview with a former colonel in the secret-police who, after some time, opened up to me and told me a great deal from his point of view. He referred me to a colonel in the Ministry of the Interior. I then approached Mieczysław Rakowski, the last leader of the Polish United Workers' Party, and of the Polish government. He gave me several hours of interviews. As a result, I managed to obtain a representative perspective from the government as well.

In each city I visited, I was able to meet with the opposition leadership thanks to the connections I had already established, and they guided me to key people. Because I was vetted, they were quite willing to talk with me. That others chose the people was fine with me because they knew who I needed to speak with much better than I did. I was not looking for a random or statistically representative sample, but rather to speak primarily with the leaders, who were not limited to those who held offices or positions, but included those people recognised as having played a leadership role and those who were key activists. My intention, about which I informed my respondents, was always to use their names, and I have done so, except in the few cases where I was asked to withhold the name.

In 1998 and 1999, I supplemented these interviews by contacting people who had been in the Solidarity leadership and who were in exile in the United States and Canada. I interviewed people in Sacramento, California, New York City, Chicago and Toronto. These included interviews with people who played key roles in Solidarity and were in exile because the Polish Communist government wanted to punish them.

All in all, I interviewed 150 people. They included not only the Solidarity leaders and activists I have already mentioned, but leading intellectuals, including several in and associated with KOR, priests and others affiliated with the Church, journalists and academics and leaders of the reform movement within the Communist Party during the 1980s.

There were very few occasions when I had to talk someone into granting me an interview. In one of these, in the coal-mining region of Jastrzębie, there was an important activist who felt he had been badly treated by Solidarity, then newly-empowered. I spent quite a while arguing to him that he should speak with me because otherwise no-one would hear his story. Eventually, he relented and we talked for over six hours. On another occasion, one of the interviewees in Toronto was giving me the brush-off: he told me he had little time and he went through his experience with so little detail and so quickly that I was learning little. I stopped him after about twenty minutes and told him so. Apparently, he had encountered journalists previously who were just looking for a juicy quote before promptly leaving. I told him that I needed lots of details and follow-up questions, and that if he didn't have the time perhaps we should just not continue. He looked at me, surprised – astonished really – and began again. Although he had originally said he only had two hours to spare, we spent eight hours together.

People were extraordinarily generous with their time, and they worked hard to try to remember the events in which they had participated, concerned to get the sequences correct, and to recall not only how they judged things when we spoke, but how they had felt at the time. I was frequently asked if my question referred to how they saw things then or at the time they were occurring. Accuracy was almost an obsession with most people. I sometimes asked people who had spent several hours, even days, talking to me why they were willing to give me so much time. (These interviews sometimes went on for so long that they were uncomfortable and exhausting, for me and for them). Almost invariably, they answered that they felt it was important for their story to get out. On one occasion, I told one interviewee that my sympathies were with the opposition movement. He responded that he did not care who I supported so long as I got the story straight and told the truth. I walked away with a sense of great responsibility. If they were willing to expend so much time and effort with me, then I had an obligation to make the time they spent worth their while by telling their stories.

When someone complained about my detailed questions, I explained that the only way I and my readers could really understand what had happened was on the basis of the specifics of individual lives and experiences. I used as a motto something the German poet Heinrich Heine said: 'Theory is grey, but the tree of life is green'. This was the perspective that informed the research itself and the book. That tree had its branches and twigs, its leaves and roots and rootlets, and it was those I probed. I was as detailed as possible in asking people to take me into meeting rooms and demonstrations, and to allow me to observe their conversations, to the degree that they were able to reconstruct them. When possible I sought more than one account of an event.

I decided to approach the interviews whenever possible by taking life histories, which usually took several hours, and in some cases several days. I felt that the key to my study was C. Wright Mills's insight that great historical events are reflected in people's lives in specific ways. The particularities are unique, but individually they reflect – and collectively they constitute – the broad course of history. Mills put it this way:

> The facts of contemporary history are also facts about the success and the failure of individual men and women. When a society is industrialized, a peasant becomes a worker; a feudal lord is liquidated or becomes a businessman. When the rate of investment goes up or down, a man is employed or unemployed. When wars happen, an insurance salesman becomes a rocket launcher; a store clerk, a radar man; a wife lives alone; a child grows up without a father. Neither the life of an individual nor the history of a society can be understood without understanding both.[2]

Therefore, what better way to understand historical events than to probe how they were manifested through people's lives and their understanding of those lives, and conversely, how those lives and those understandings affected and shaped the events? My hope was to come to know the oppositionists, to see the individual paths they followed as they became a significant collective opposition, which culminated in the Solidarity movement. And then what did they do?

I did not use an interview form; rather, each interview was tailored to the specifics of the life and life experiences of the person with whom I was speaking. I approached these interviews by beginning with the broadest formulation of a

2. Mills 2000, p. 3.

question, which then served in a certain sense as a Rorschach test: my subjects could interpret the question as they wished and answer it in ways I might not have anticipated. Gradually, I would sharpen and specify my questions in search of what I sought. I probed the lives of my subjects in detail to learn how they had intersected historical events. One answer suggested another question. Someone who was in the army during, say, December 1970, when there were major demonstrations and severe repression on the Baltic coast, could tell me the official line he heard concerning these events, how his fellow soldiers reacted, how officers and enlisted men differed in their reactions, how the government got its line across to them, in what way they got information other than the official line, and how they felt about these things. Even peripheral relationships to such events could yield revealing information.

I never knew what turns in an individual's life might give me some insight or information from a unique point of view. I went through their lives chronologically, seeking the intersections between the broad sweep of history and their own experiences and awareness. I would generally begin each interview by asking them for about a five minute overview of their activity, which then provided the broad framework for me to ask questions.

With this approach, I was able to acquire many details of people's lives to give meaning to the historical generalities. I felt that the only way I could really understand what had happened was on the basis of the specifics of individual lives and experiences. One beneficial result of this approach was that people were less likely to fall back on canned, pre-digested perspectives, and could instead speak from their experience. It also turned out to be a good way of disarming my informants. For example, when I began an interview with a former colonel of the secret police, his initial distrust in answering considerably diminished as we followed the trajectory of his life, rather than just approaching the difficult questions. As a result, he was very open and provided me with a window into the government's efforts in response to its opposition. The interview took place over the period of a week.

Of course, when doing oral history of this character, there is always a question of truth: were my respondents remembering correctly? Were they remembering truthfully, or were they trying to shade their answers to reflect well on themselves? I had various ways to check on these matters of concern. There was, firstly, the known history against which I could check their statements. Sometimes I would say that such-and-such a statement conflicted with that history, and they would then have to rethink what they said. When I interviewed multiple persons about the same events, I would check the perceptions of one against the other. Once again, sometimes I would point out that someone else had said something that contradicted what they were saying. Sometimes, both they and

I would forget to follow up on something and then we would remember it later and come back to it. So, the interviews were not simply linear progressions.

I found people to be very careful in answering my questions. It was not uncommon – as I was inquiring about events that had taken place years, or in some cases decades, earlier – for a respondent to ask if I wanted to know what he or she thought at the time the event was taking place, or at the time of the interview, so as to be sure of what question I was asking and how to answer it properly.

One thing I had not anticipated when I began the interviews was how articulate and even eloquent my informants would be. As a result, as I read them over it became clear to me that their words should see the light of day, that as much as possible, I should let them speak because their words make much clearer what happened and how and why it happened, and because they are able to bring readers much closer to the actual events than I ever could. The richness of these interviews deepens our understanding of the history.

One note of caution: these interviews are not presented exactly as they were spoken. They are the speakers' words, but they have been edited to remove repetitive statements; there were times when issues were discussed more than once, or when an issue that I or the interviewee had forgotten to cover at first was recalled and returned to later. Some of these discussions have been aggregated for the purpose of coherence. Often, my questions have been edited out, to put in place a coherent statement of the person's views. In all cases, care has been taken to record not just the person's words, but his or her meaning as well.

I have had the good fortune to examine and become involved with the Civil Rights movement in the United States, and Solidarity in Poland – two of the most important social movements of the twentieth century. Each of them necessitated significant transformation of the political and social systems of which they were a part; each required and allowed the activists and leaders to stretch their abilities and to grow. Sometimes these were wrenching tasks that occasioned deep turmoil within the individuals who were involved and within their communities. I was aware of the importance of such changes from my research into the civil rights movement and because of my own experience participating in social movements in the 1960s.

There is more than one way to reach such changes. In my research on the civil rights movement, I was frequently able to make use of written sources: interviews, memoirs, autobiographies and biographies. That was not really an option for me with regard to Solidarity, not only because there was very little in the way of similar published sources in Poland, but also because my Polish did not permit me to mine what was available. So, as I contemplated how I would go about my research in Poland, I decided that gathering such interviews would both open up opportunities for me and would also create a body of scholarly material that might be of use to other researchers.

My work on each of these movements aided me in understanding the other. For instance, during my first trip to Poland, when I met Fr. Jancarz, what led him to invite me to speak to his students at his underground Christian workers' university was my knowledge of the Civil Rights movement in the USA. Similarly, after travelling around Poland and having spent hundreds of hours in people's homes, and speaking with them about their experiences in the opposition movement, I felt that I had participated in an intense seminar in which the learning curve was very high. As I thought about this experience, I wondered if there was some way I could bring it to my students. Obviously, I could not bring them to Poland, nor could I expect them to sit through the many (and sometimes tedious) hours of translated interviews. So, I developed a course that brought activists in the Civil Rights movement into my class and interviewed them about their lives.[3] They were able to show my students what their lives had been like before the movement, why they became involved, what choices they had made, and how those choices affected history. Every time I taught this course, the students enthusiastically received it.

---

3. See Bloom 1982.

Glossary of Interviewees

Adamowicz, Paweł: (Gdańsk), law student at University of Gdańsk; was a leader of a student strike in 1988.

Adamiecki, Wojciech: (Warsaw) in his early years, he was a member of the Communist Party. He quit the Party in the 1960s. He worked with Jacek Kuroń and other dissidents through the 1970s and 1980s. During that period, he was an independent journalist.

Banasiak, Aleksandra: A nurse in Poznań who spent the day trying to save lives during the siege of the secret-police headquarters. She was honoured decades later for her role.

Blumsztajn, Seweryn: (Warsaw) Had dissident roots going back to his childhood; friend of Adam Michnik, Jacek Kuroń, Jan Lityński and other activists. Was one of the organisers of the student demonstrations in 1968; active in Solidarity. During the period of martial law, he was in exile in Paris, where he organised outside support for Solidarity.

Bogacz, Zbigniew: (Upper Silesia) a mining engineer, Bogacz supported the Solidarity strike in his mine. He served as Secretary for the Jastrzębie inter-factory workers' committee, established after the strike. He was also a member of the National Miners' Commission in Solidarity, a post that put him in the national leadership. After martial law was declared, he was one of the leaders of an underground strike for two weeks.

Borusewicz, Bogdan: (Gdańsk) a student activist in 1968, he spent three years in jail for that activity. He became an activist with a group in a while at the Catholic University of Lublin. Borusewicz joined KOR and worked with the opposition in Gdańsk during the later 1970s. He was one of the organisers of the strike in the Gdańsk shipyard that created Solidarity. He continued an active role during the 16 months of legal Solidarity and later became active in the underground.

Brzuzy, Ryszard: a miner in the brown coal fields and a Solidarity activist there; participant of the Round Table talks; later became a Solidarity representative to parliament in 1989.

Budrewicz, Lech: (Wrocław) a student activist in the SKS, Budrewicz became a lawyer and worked with Solidarity. He became an adviser to Władysław Frasyniuk, the leader of the union in Wrocław.

Bujak, Zbigniew: (Ursus) organiser of the union in the Ursus tractor factory, outside of Warsaw. Bujak became one of the leading members of the union. He was the regional union leader and on the Solidarity national committee. During martial law, he evaded arrest and went underground. He was the longest-serving member of the Solidarity leadership underground. He was caught in 1986. Later, he became a Solidarity member of parliament and a leader of the non-communist left within the parliament.

Celejewska, Małgorzata: (Gdańsk) worked as an accountant in one of the smaller shipyards in Gdańsk. She became the Gdańsk regional treasurer.

Ciesielski, Jan: (Kraków) one of the leaders of Solidarity in the steel mill in the suburb of Nowa Huta. By virtue of that position, Ciesielski was one of the leaders of Solidarity in the Kraków region.

Dębski, Adam: (Kraków) An engineer in a factory in Kraków. Dębski organised the Solidarity union in his factory and became one of the leaders of the regional Solidarity union. From martial law, he was one of the organisers of underground Solidarity.

Frasyniuk, Władysław: (Wrocław) a bus driver, Frasyniuk became the leader of the regional Solidarity union in Wrocław and a member of the Solidarity national committee. He led the underground in Wrocław until he was detained in December, 1982 and was one of the founding members of the underground Interim Coordinating Committee of Solidarity.

Gil, Mieczysław: (Kraków) a party member until the period of legal Solidarity, Gil became one of the leaders of the union in the huge Lenin Steel Mill in the Kraków suburb of Nowa Huta. He was also one of the leaders of the Kraków region.

Gurecki, Winicjusz: (Szczecin) Served on the National Tourist Workers Commission; organised underground publishing of *Jedność* ['Unity'] to keep alive previously legal newspaper of the West Seashore Region of Solidarity; arrested May 1982; carried out longest hunger strike in prison.

Górczewska, Małgorzata: (Gdańsk) worked on an underground paper during martial law. Went to university in Gdańsk and there became involved with a group of anarchists, later with a group called Wolność I Pokój [Freedom and Peace], which opposed the draft and which helped people subject to it, and helped soldiers who did not wish to continue in the army. Theirs was probably the first group to emerge in the open from the underground after the declaration of martial law.

Goździk, Lechosław: (Warsaw) organised the workers' council in the FSO automobile plant in Warsaw in 1956. The council movement spread and became a major player in the Party factional struggles that followed the 1956 uprising in Poznań that year.

Grabus, Jerzy: (Poznań) actively participated in the siege at the secret police headquarters in Poznań in 1956. Had previously had connections with partisans who fought the Communists in the early years after World War II.

Graca, Kazimierz: (Upper Silesia) participated in the two-week-long underground strike in his mine after martial law was declared.

Handzlik, Stanisław: (Kraków) One of the leaders of the union in the Lenin Steel Mill in the suburb of Nowa Huta, and in the Kraków region.

Jarmakowski, Andrzej: (Gdańsk) a student activist, Jarmakowski became active in the Young Poland group. Young Poland was a group of young conservative activists. They differentiated themselves from KOR by virtue of being to the right, but they worked with KOR. Jarmakowski was responsible for helping to organise and prepare the program for the Solidarity Congress in October, 1981.

Jaworski, Seweryn: (Warsaw) began the 1980 Solidarity strike in the Warsaw Steel Mill. Jaworski served as vice-chair of the Warsaw inter-factory Solidarity during the period of legal Solidarity, and at the Solidarity Congress he was voted on to the National Commission. Under martial law, he gained the reputation as being one of the most solid opponents of the regime.

Jedynak, Tadeusz (Upper Silesia): worked in the July Manifesto Mine in Jastrzębie-Zdrój, one of the strike organisers there; later one of the members of the strike committee; vice-chair of the Interfactory Strike Committee; leader of Solidarity in Upper Silesia; served on Solidarity's national commission interned after marshal law, active in the underground after release; elected to *Sejm* from the Solidarity list after the Round Table agreements.

Jerschina, Jan: (Kraków) A professor of sociology at one of the oldest universities in Europe Jagiellonian University. Jerschina was one of the dissident party members who actively fought for a line of co-operation with Solidarity.

Jerzy: (Warsaw) A Solidarity activist, drafted into the military after martial law; a member of the self-governing councils.

Kaczyński, Lech: (Gdańsk) became active in 1977, first working with Borusewicz, and (KOR) Bureau of Intervention in Warsaw. In 1978, he became active in the

Committee for Free Trade Unions. He served as an adviser to Lech Wałęsa, and as a member of the Regional Coordinating Committee, and of the Solidarity National Commission. In 2005, he was elected President of Poland, a reign that lasted until 2010, when he died in a tragic plane crash en route to a memorial for the Polish officers who had been murdered on Stalin's orders, in the Soviet Union in Katyń during World War II.

Kasprzyk, Krzysztof: (Kraków) a member of the Party, Kasprzyk was one of the people in charge of arrangements for the world press during Pope John Paul II's first trip to Poland in 1979. Kasprzyk became one of the leaders of the "renewed Journalist's Union." It was not actually part of Solidarity, but had been taken over by rebellious members. He left the party upon declaration of martial law.

Kozłowski, Maciej: (Kraków) was a journalist, working for *Tygodnik Powszechny* [*The Catholic Weekly*]

Krystosiak, Aleksander: (Szczecin) A secondary leader of the 1970 strike in Szczecin. Krystosiak led a group that became the organisers of the 1980 strike in their shipyard. He was one of the leaders of the strike committee during their negotiations with the government. Later, he was vice-chair of the Szczecin regional Solidarity.

Krzaklewski, Marian: became Wałęsa's successor as head of the Solidarity union in the nineties.

Kubiak, Hieronim: (Kraków) a liberal Party member, Kubiak was never in the opposition. He was elevated to the Politburo during the Extraordinary Party Congress of 1981 to represent the reformers and remained there until the end of the Communist regime in 1989.

Kupka, Ginter: a miner, leader of a mineworkers union in Gliwice, Upper-Silesia.

Kuroń, Jacek: (Warsaw) a member of the Communist Party, twice expelled. Kuroń and Karol Modzelewski were imprisoned in 1964 for their Open Letter to the Party (which was never published in Poland, just circulated.) The letter analysed the Polish Communist system in Marxist terms, called it a class society, ruled by a ruling class, the *nomenklatura*, and requiring a working class revolution to overthrow it. Kuroń was also actively supporting the student upheaval of 1968, having gotten out of prison shortly before it. He was one of the founders of KOR, and was always among those who intended it to take a more political direction. Kuroń was continually seeking ways to change Polish society. During the Solidarity period, he was one of the leading advisers to Solidarity. In the 1980s, he continued to write about the subject. He was elected to parliament in 1989, and served for a while as a cabinet member. In this position, he was one of the most popular members of the government.

Lipski, Jan Józef: (Warsaw) A member of the Socialist Party before and during World War II, he remained in when that party was forced into a merger with the Communist Party. Lipski played a prominent role as a public dissident on important occasions. He was one of the founders of KOR.

Lis, Bogdan: (Gdańsk) a member of the party, Lis became active in the Committee for Free Trade Unions and worked closely with Andrzej Gwiazda, Borusewicz, Walentynowicz, Wałęsa and others. He organised his factory and others to come out quickly in support of the demands of the Gdańsk shipyard workers. He became a member of the Solidarity national committee.

Lityński, Jan: (Warsaw) An activist from his youth, Lityński was one of Kuroń's protégés. He was one of the organisers of the 1968 demonstrations in Warsaw. Early on, he became active with KOR, though he was not one of the founders. He was elected to parliament in 1989 and worked closely with Jacek Kuroń.

Łuczywo, Helena: (Warsaw) An activist in 1968, Łuczywo dropped out of any activity until 1976. Then, encouraged by Jacek Kuroń, she became a translator for journalists seeking to interview workers in the Ursus tractor factory. From there, she became the editor of *Robotnik*. During the martial law period, she evaded capture and edited the Solidarity underground paper, *Tygodnik Mazowsze*. She also created the whole system of safe houses for the Warsaw underground. With the end of Communism, she became the managing editor of *Gazeta Wyborcza*, the Solidarity-backed daily newspaper that became the most widely read paper in Poland.

Machnicki, Stanisław: Machinist who travelled to Warsaw as part of the delegation from the Cegielski complex in Poznań in 1956 to discuss the workers' grievances with the central leadership.

Majewski, Sławomir: (Gdańsk) Participated as a youth in the 1970 strike in Gdańsk, where he was shocked at the violence of the government. In 1976, though he was a member of the youth wing of the Party in his factory, he publicly opposed the repressions against the workers and quit the Party. In 1980, he was active in the strike and later in Solidarity.

Maleszka, Leszek: (Kraków) A member of the student counterculture, he joined the Student Solidarity Committee in 1977 and worked with KOR. Later, he worked in the Solidarity structure from its beginning. In 1981, I started working for the official organ of Solidarity in the Małopolska (Kraków) Region. Toward the end of Solidarity he was deputy editor-in-chief of this publication. In Jan, 1982, he was interned. After his release, Maleszka wrote articles for some ten underground publications in the Małopolska Region and in Warsaw.

Matuszewska, Alicja: (Gdańsk) was the leader of the civilian workers who worked for the military; later became the Solidarity National Treasurer.

Miller, Karol: Served in the Ministry of the Interior with a concentration on the Church. His name is a pseudonym, which was the condition of his talking to me.

Młodzik, Krzysztof: (Upper Silesia) played a leading role after martial law was declared in organising an underground strike in his mine.

Modzelewski, Karol: (Wrocław) A leading intellectual oppositionist, he co-wrote with Jacek Kuroń the *'Open Letter to the Party'* that sent them both to jail. In 1956, he was a student at Warsaw University. There, he participated in the movement of renewal, helping to organise a national organisation of young people, students and workers. During this time, he made contact with the workers at the Żerań automobile factory in Warsaw who were leading the national movement for workers' councils. In 1968, he worked with the student protestors. During the Solidarity period, he was the union's first leading national spokesman. He quit after feeling that the leadership had betrayed democracy during the Bydgoszcz crisis. Situated at Wrocław University, he was a respected voice in the nation and worked with dissidents in the region. Muszyński, Marek: A Wrocław activist in the Polytechnik; helped build and was active in the underground for years, starting with martial law.

Muskat, Mariusz: a Kraków activist in the student upheaval of 1968; worked with KOR; active in Solidarity; was a leader of underground Solidarity in the period of martial law and thereafter.

Nowak, Edward: (Kraków) An engineer in the Nowa Huta Steel plant, he became a leader of Solidarity there. He was one of the active members in the movement of economic renewal in 1981.

Onyszkiewicz, Janusz: (Warsaw) A mathematician at Warsaw University, he became a leader of Solidarity on the campus, and joined the Solidarity national leadership, where he later became its national spokesman. When Solidarity was in power, he served as Minister of Defence.

Pałubicki, Janusz: (Poznań) one of the leaders of Solidarity in Poznań, he became the regional leader under martial law, and continued through the '90s in this position.

Pinior, Józef: (Wrocław) Became the Solidarity treasurer for the Wrocław region. Pinior learned of the impending government coup in December, 1981 and withdrew all the union funds from the bank about 10 days before. He hid the money and used it during the period of martial law to help finance opposition efforts.

He played a leading role in the underground, succeeding Frasyniuk as its leader until he, too, was captured.

Płatek, Stanisław: (Upper Silesia) joined the party in 1978; joined Solidarity in 1980; stayed in the party at the request of Solidarity; left the party in 1981, after Bydgoszcz. Was a Solidarity member in the Wujek Mine. Helped organise a strike there in response to martial law. Was a witness to the shooting in that mine in December, 1981.

Pławiński, Tadeusz: (Gdynia) President of the Solidarity union in the Paris Commune Shipyard in Gdynia.

Pleszak, Józef: (Upper Silesia) one of the organisers the Solidarity strike in the July Manifesto Mine. Served on the factory committee of Solidarity; later served on the Interfactory Commission. Was one of the organisers of the Solidarity underground in 1982.

Polmański, Piotr: (Upper Silesia) A coal miner, he got active in Solidarity.

Potocki, Andrzej: (Kraków) Chair of Klub Inteligencki Katolickiej in Kraków.

Rakowski, Mieczysław: Prime Minister of Poland during the 1989 Round table negotiations. From the Solidarity era he was Deputy Prime Minister in charge of relations with the trade unions and the mass media, as well as science, education and culture. He was a parliamentary deputy from 1972 89, as well as a member of the CP since 1948 and on the Central Committee from 1964–90. From 1958–81, he was editor of *Polityka*, which was and remains Poland's leading socio-political weekly. He not only crafted what was the most critical newspaper in Poland and Eastern Europe, but he was also editor and a special on German affairs in establishing a detente between Poland and Germany in 1970. He has been head of the Polish Journalists' Association. He has been awarded the Golden Cross of Merit and the White Eagle for his journalistic achievements.

Regucki, Zbigniew: (Kraków) High Communist Party official. Before Solidarity he was the editor-in-chief of the Communist Party paper *Gazeta Krakowska*. In the Solidarity period, he became chief of staff to Stanisław Kania, the Party Secretary.

Rozpłochowski, Andrzej: (Katowice) Led the Solidarity union in the Katowice steel mill; was the head of the regional Solidarity union and served on the Solidarity national committee.

Rybak, Józef: Participated in the assault on police stations in Poznań in 1956.

Sawicki, Ryszard: (Lower Silesia) was chair of the Solidarity union for the copper mining region in Lubin and was a member of the Solidarity National Commission.

Skwira, Adam: (Upper Silesia) Participated in Solidarity. Was one of the strikers in the Wujek Mine after the declaration of martial law. Participated in the battle there.

Śliwiński, Paweł: (Gdańsk) A high school student when martial law was invoked, he became an underground activist.

Stawski, Grzegorz: (Upper Silesia) was active in the Solidarity union in the July Manifesto Mine; Became a leader of the union there and in the regional Solidarity.

Stelmachowski, Andrzej: (Warsaw) A leader of KIK, a close adviser to the church, he became an adviser to the workers in Gdańsk. Played a role in the negotiations to establish the union in 1980, and often intervened thereafter. Was called in to mediate during a strike at the Nowa Huta steel mill in May, 1988.

Stępniewski, Jan: Professor of accounting at the University of Paris when I interviewed him, Stępniewski was active in Solidarity in Wrocław, where he used to be on the faculty of the University of Wrocław.

Sucharski, Adam: pseudonym for a colonel in the secret police who granted me a lengthy interview and was quite open, on condition that I not reveal his identity.

Strzelec, Mirosława: (Katowice) was a nurse at the Katowice Steel Mill. She was one of the first activists in the union there, a leader of the union. She played a crucial role in the resistance that was organised there during martial law, and stayed underground for the whole of that period. When I interviewed her in 1989, she was dying of cancer and impoverished.

Surdy, Grzegorz: (Kraków) Was an activist in the Student Solidarity Committee; participated in the resistance when martial law was declared; worked in the underground; detained – while in prison, he participated in hunger strikes; was an activist in Freedom and Peace (WiP).

Szablewski, Alojzy: (Gdańsk) Active in the Home Army, he took part in the Warsaw uprising of 1944. He was made a German prisoner of war. When he returned home, he remained in the army until purged. He became a worker in the Gdańsk shipyard and played a leading role in the strike there in 1980. He was the local leader of the Solidarity union in the Gdańsk shipyard, a role he reprised in a strike in May, 1988.

Szumowski, Maciej: (Kraków) was a television journalist. During the Solidarity period, he was made the chief editor of the Kraków Party newspaper, *Gazeta Krakowska*. He made the paper a model of journalistic excellence. During his administration, the paper was recognized within Poland as the best paper in the country. Szumowski was a part of the pro-Solidarity tendency within the Party. He was purged after martial law was declared.

Terakowska, Dorota: (Kraków) A leading political journalist for *Gazeta Krakowska*. After martial law, she became a leading writer of children's books.

Tomaszewski, Tadeusz: (Upper Silesia) A worker in the Kazimierz Juliusz Mine at the time the workers went on strike there in 1951.

Waszkiewicz, Jan: (Wrocław) A professor at Wrocław University, he lost his job after signing a public statement in support of the workers facing repression in 1976. He became part of the KOR network and edited the *Bulletin of Lower Silesia*, which was directed to workers. During the Solidarity period, Waszkiewicz became the spokesperson for Solidarity.

Wilk, Mariusz: (Gdańsk) former student at Wrocław University, Wilk joined the shipyard strikers in Gdańsk in 1980 and became the editor of their daily newsletter. After the strike, Wilk worked for the union as a journalist. During the period of martial law, Wilk and others produced an underground volume of interviews with leaders of the underground, called *Konspira*. See the bibliography for the English language translation.

Wróblewski, Andrzej Krzysztof: (Warsaw) For many years a journalist for the liberal weekly *Polityka*, Wróblewski was one of the few working journalists who did not belong to the Polish United Workers' Party. He resigned his position after martial law was declared and only returned after the Communist regime ended.

References

Abbott, Andrew 1997, 'On the Concept of Turning Point', *Comparative Social Research*, 16: 85–105.

Alton, Thad 1955, *The Polish Post-War Economy*, New York: Columbia University Press.

Anasz, Marian and Włodzimierz Wesołowski 1974, 'Changes in Social Structure of People's Poland', in *Transformations of Social Structure in the USSR and Poland*, edited by M.N. Rutkevitch, W. Wesołowski, V.S. Semyonov, M. Jarosińska and V.V. Kolbansky, Warsaw: Institute of Philosophy and Sociology.

Anderson, Benedict 1991, *Imagined Communities*, London: Verso.

Anonymous 1980, 'Solidarity and KOR: An Interview With Gdańsk Leaders', *Labour Focus on Eastern Europe*: 13–15.

Anoshkin, Viktor Ivanovich 1998, 'The Anoshkin Notebook on the Polish Crisis', translated and annotated by Mark Kramer, *Cold War International History Project Bulletin*, 11(Winter): 17–31.

Ascherson, Neal 1982, *The Polish August*, New York: Penguin.

Bakuniak, Grzegorz and Krzysztof Nowak 1987, 'The Creation of a Collective Identity in a Social Movement: The case of Solidarność in Poland', *Theory and Society*, 16: 401–29.

Banas, Joseph 1979, *The Scapegoats: The Exodus of the Remnants of Polish Jewry*, London: Weidenfeld and Nicolson.

Bardach, Juliusz, Bogusław Leśnodorski and Michał Pietrzak 1985, *Historia Panstwa i Prawa Polskiego*, Warsaw: Państwowe Wydawnictwo Naukowe.

Barker, Colin 1990, 'The Frying Pan and the Fire', unpublished paper.

Barker, Colin and Kara Weber 1982, 'Solidarność: From Gdańsk to Military Repression', *International Socialism*, 15.

Barker, Ewa 1980, 'Unpublished Interview with Anna Walentynowicz', personal communication.

Barker, Ewa 1981, 'Interview with Two Gdynia Workers', in *The Polish August: Documents from the Beginnings of the Polish Workers' Rebellion, Gdańsk, August, 1980*, edited by O. MacDonald, San Francisco, CA: Ztangi Press.

Barnes, Samuel H. and Max Kaase 1979, *Political Action*, Beverly Hills, CA: Sage.

Bauman, Janina 1988, *A Dream of Belonging*, London: Virago Press.

Bernhard, Michael 1987, 'The Strikes of June 1976 in Poland', *Eastern European Politics and Societies*, 1(3): 363–92.

—— 1991, 'Reinterpreting Solidarity', *Studies in Comparative Communism*, 24(3): 313–30.

—— 1993, *The Origins of Democratization in Poland: Workers, Intellectuals, and Oppositional Politics, 1976–1980*, New York: Columbia University Press.

Bernstein, Carl and Marco Politi 1996, *His Holiness: John Paul II and the Hidden History of Our Time*, New York: Doubleday.

Bielasiak, Jack 1983, 'The Party: Permanent Crisis', in *Poland: Genesis of a Revolution*, edited by A. Brumberg, New York: Vintage Books.

Bielasiak, Jack and Maurice D. Simon (eds) 1984, *Polish Politics: Edge of the Abyss*, New York: Praeger.

Blazynski, George 1979, *Flashpoint Poland*, New York: Pergamon Press.

Bloom, Jack M. 1987, *Class, Race and the Civil Rights Movement*, Bloomington, IN: Indiana University Press.

Borusewicz, Bogdan 1983a, 'Solidarity Underground in Gdansk Region', *Uncensored Poland News Bulletin*, 4: 12–13.

—— 1983b, 'August Today: Extracts from an Interview with Bogdan Borusewicz', *Uncensored Poland News Bulletin*, 20: 37–8.

—— 1988, 'An Interview with Bogdan Borusewicz', *Uncensored Poland News Bulletin*, 11: 12–13.

Bratkowski, Stefan 1982, 'Bratkowski's Letter to Members of the Polish Union of Journalists, Warsaw March 20', *Uncensored Poland News Bulletin*, 7: 23–4.

Bromke, Adam 1969, 'The Party and Poland's Political Crisis', *The World Today*, 25(3): 117–26.

—— 1971, 'Beyond the Gomułka Era', *Foreign Affairs*, 49(3): 480–92.

—— 1978, 'Czechoslovakia 1968 – Poland 1978: A Dilemma for Moscow', *International Journal*, 23(4): 740–62.

—— 1981a, 'Poland and Hungary in 1956', in *Poland: The Last Decade*, Ontario: Mosaic Press.

—— 1981b, 'Poland Under Gierek: A New Political Style', in *Poland: The Last Decade*, Ontario: Mosaic Press.

—— 1983, *Poland: The Protracted Crisis*, Ontario: Mosaic Press.

Bromke, Adam and John W. Strong (eds) 1973, *Gierek's Poland*, New York: Praeger Publishers.

Broue, Pierre 1972, *Pologne, 24 Janvier, 1971: Gierek face aux grevistes de Szczecin*, Paris: Societe d'Edition, Librairie, Informations Ouvrieres.

Brumberg, Abraham 1983, *Poland: Genesis of a Revolution*, New York: Vintage.

Brus, Włodzimierz 1988, 'The Political Economy of Reform', in *Creditworthiness and Reform in Poland: Western and Polish Perspectives*, edited by P. Marer and W. Siwiński, Bloomington, IN: Indiana University Press.

Bujak, Zbignew 1982, 'Balance Sheet for the Year', *Uncensored Poland News Bulletin*, 23: 38–48.

—— 1983, 'Interview on the Forthcoming Papal Visit', *Uncensored Poland News Bulletin*, 12: 13–17.

—— 1986, 'The Last Interview with Zbigniew Bujak', *Uncensored Poland News Bulletin*, 16: 14–18.

Cave, Jane 1982a, 'The Martial Law Decree of December 13, 1981', *Poland Watch*, 1: 1–8.

—— 1982b, 'Worker Response to Martial Law: The December Strikes', *Poland Watch*, 1: 8–18.

—— 1982c, 'Internees Detained without Trial', *Poland Watch*, 1: 18–23.

—— 1982–83, 'The Banning of Solidarity', *Poland Watch*, 2: 46–52.

—— 1983, 'The Legacy of Martial Law', *Poland Watch*, 4: 1–20.

Cave, Jane and Maya Latynski 1982–83, 'Solidarity in Łódź: An Interview with Witold Sułkowski', *Poland Watch*, 2: 53–69.

Cave, Jane and Marsha Sosnowska 1982, 'Protest and Resistance', *Poland Watch*, 1: 63–74.

Checinski, Michael 1982, *Poland: Communism, Nationalism and Anti-Semitism*, New York: Karz-Cohl Publishing.

Civic, Christopher 1983, 'The Church', in *Poland: Genesis of a Revolution*, edited by A. Brumberg, New York: Vintage Publishers.

Clarke, Roger A. (ed.) 1989, *Poland: The Economy in the 1980s*, Essex: Longman.

Crane, Keith 1988, 'The Economy Five Years After Martial Law', in *Creditworthiness and Reform in Poland: Western and Polish Perspectives*, edited by P. Marer and W. Siwiński, Bloomington, IN: Indiana University Press.

Czabanski, Krzysztof 1983, 'Privileges', in *Poland: Genesis of a Revolution*, edited by A. Brumberg, New York: Vintage Publishers.

Davies, Norman 1982, *God's Playground: A History of Poland*, (Volume II: 1795 to the Present), New York: Columbia University Press.

Dawson, Andrew 1989, 'Resources, Region and Reform: Plans and Prospects for the Polish Economy', in *Poland: The Economy in the 1980s*, edited by R.A. Clarke, London: Longman.

Drewnowski, Jan (ed.) 1982, *Crisis in the East European Economy: The Spread of the Polish Disease*, New York: St. Martin's Press.

Drzycimski, Andrzej 1982, 'Growing', in *The Solidarity Sourcebook*, edited by S. Persky and H. Flam, Vancouver: New Star Books.

Dziewanowski, M.K. 1977, *Poland in the Twentieth Century*, New York: Columbia University Press.

Dziurok, Adam 2001, 'Too Little German, Too Little Polish', *IPN Bulletin*, 9 (October).

Eisenstadt, Shmuel Noah and René Lemarchand 1981, *Political Clientelism, Patronage and Development*, Beverly Hills, CA: Sage.

Ekiert, Grzegorz 1991, 'The State against Society: The Aftermath of Political Crises in Hungary 1956–1963, Czechoslovakia 1968–1970, and Poland 1981–1989', unpublished doctoral dissertation, Harvard University.

Eysymontt, Jerzy 1989, 'Reform in the Polish Economy', in *Poland: The Economy in the 1980s*, edited by R.A. Clarke, Essex: Longman.

Fallenbuchl, Zbigniew M. 1973, 'The Strategy of Development and Gierek's Economic Manoeuvre', in *Gierek's Poland*, edited by A. Bromke and J.W. Strong, New York: Praeger.

Feiwel, George R. 1971, *Poland's Industrialization Policy: A Current Analysis: Sources of Economic Growth and Retrogression*, (Volume 1), New York: Praeger.

Flan, Helena (ed.) 1994, *States and Anti-Nuclear Movements*, Edinburgh: Edinburgh University Press.

Frasyniuk, Władysław 1982, 'Interview with W. Frasyniuk, Head of Solidarity's Lower Silesia or Wrocław Region', *Uncensored Poland News Bulletin*, 11: 14–18.

Frederickson, George 1995, *Black Liberation: A Comparative History of Black Ideologies in the United States and South Africa*, Oxford: Oxford University Press.

Garton Ash, Timothy 1985, *The Polish Revolution: Solidarity*, New York: Vintage.

—— 1990, *The Magic Lantern*, New York: Random House.

Gawronski, Jas 1993, 'False Idol', *In These Times*, 18(2): 18–19.

Glemp, Cardinal 1983, 'Cardinal Glemp's Interview for Brazilian Paper, March 2, 1984', *Uncensored Poland News Bulletin*, 5: 9–12.

—— 1984, 'Cardinal Glemp's Interview with Hans-Jakob Stehle', *Uncensored Poland News Bulletin*, 6: 12–16.

Goodwyn, Lawrence 1991, *Breaking the Barrier: The Rise of Solidarity in Poland*, Oxford: Oxford University Press.

Green, Peter 1977, 'The Third Round in Poland', *New Left Review*, I/101–2: 69–108.

Gross, Jan Tomasz 1983, 'In Search of History', in *Poland: Genesis of a Revolution*, edited by A. Brumberg, New York: Vintage Publishers.

Grudzinska-Gross, Irena 1982, 'The Image of Solidarity in the Mass Media', *Poland Watch*, 1: 50–53.

Grzybowski, Kazimierz 1956, 'Social and Economic Roots of the Workers' Uprising in Poznan', *Highlights of Current Legislation and Activities in Mid-Europe*, 4(11): 379–94.

Gyda, Jan 1982, 'August, 1980 as I Saw It', *Sisyphus, Sociological Studies* (Volume III: Crisis and Conflicts. The Case of Poland, 1980–81), Warsaw: Polish Scientific Publishers.

Haggin, Joseph 1992, 'Polish-American Effort may be Model for Pollution Control', *Chemical and Engineering News*, 70(51): 17–21.

Hahn, Werner 1987, *Democracy in a Communist Party: Poland's Experience Since 1980*, New York: Columbia University Press.

Hall, Aleksander 1984, 'A Well-Known Oppositionist Withdraws from Solidarity, Remains Underground: Aleksander Hall's Credo, 7 January, 1984', *Uncensored Poland News Bulletin*, 5: 22–5.

Hauser, Ewa 1982–3, 'Solidarity's Response to the Ban', *Poland Watch*, 2: 11–21.

Hayden, Jacqueline 1994, *Poles Apart: Solidarity and the New Poland*, Portland, OR: Irish Academic Press.

Hughes, Everett Cherrington 1945, 'Dilemmas and Contradictions of Status', *American Journal of Sociology*, 50: 353–9.

Hundley, Tom 2007, 'Tortured Priest's Tenacity Exposes Betrayal in Church', *Chicago Tribune* (26 February 2007).

Information Centre for Polish Affairs 1988, 'On Cooperation between Solidarity and Rural Solidarity, part of an interview from the underground *Słowo i czyn* (Word and Action)', *Uncensored Poland News Bulletin*, 4: 13–14.

Jain, Ajit (ed.) 1983, *The Origins and Implications of Polish Trade Unions*, Baton Rouge, LA: Oracle Press.

Jakowczyk, Zbigniew 1982, 'Voices from Poland', *Social Text*, 5(Spring): 3–21.

Janicka, Krystyna 1986, 'Changes in Social Structure and in How it is Popularly Perceived', in *Social Stratification in Poland, Eight Empirical Studies*, edited by K.M. Słomczyński and T.K. Krauze, New York: M.E. Sharpe, Inc.

Jarosińska, Maria and Jolanta Kulpińska 1974, 'Transformation of the Working Class in People's Poland', in *Transformations of Social Structure in the USSR and Poland*, edited by M.N. Rutkevitch et al., Warsaw: Institute of Philosophy and Sociology.

Jarosz, Tomasz 1982–3, 'The Everyday Reality of Martial Law', *Poland Watch*, 2: 114–18.

Jaruzelski, Wojciech 1998, 'Commentary', *Cold War International History Project Bulletin*, 11: 32–9.

Jedynak, Tadeusz 1984, 'Interview with Tadeusz Jedynak', *Uncensored Poland News Bulletin*, 1: 17–19.

Kalabinski, Jacek 1984, 'Media War in Poland: The Government vs. the Underground', *Poland Watch*, 5: 63–82.

Kantorski, Father Leon 1983, 'The Truth is My Ministry, My Duty, and My Right: Reverent Kantorski's Dialogue with the Authorities', *Committee in Support of Solidarity Reports*, 15: 3–7.

Kaufman, Michael 1989, *Mad Dreams, Saving Graces, Poland: A Nation in Conspiracy*, New York: Random House.

Keane, John H. (ed.), 1988, *Civil Society and the State*, London: Verso.

Kemp-Welch, Anthony 1983, *The Birth of Solidarity: The Gdańsk Negotiations, 1980*, New York: St. Martin's Press.

Kennedy, Michael 1991, *Professionals, Power and Solidarity in Poland: A Critical Sociology of Soviet-Type Society*, New York: Cambridge University Press.

Kenney, Padraig 2001, 'Framing, Political Opportunities and Civil Mobilization in the East European Revolutions: A Case Study of Poland's Freedom and Peace Movement', *Mobilization*, 6(2): 193–210.

Khrushchev, Nikita 1970, *Khrushchev Remembers*, translated and edited by S. Talbott, Boston, MA: Little, Brown & Company.

Kiszczak, Czesław 1986a, 'Interior Minister on Martial Law, Solidarity and Opposition', *Uncensored Poland News Bulletin*, 12: 34–42.

—— 1986b, 'Extensive Excerpts from the Interior Minister's Statement, Sept. 11, 1986', *Uncensored Poland News Bulletin*, 18: 13–17.

Kołakowski, Leszek 1983, 'The Intelligentsia', in *Poland: Genesis of a Revolution*, edited by A. Brumberg, New York: Vintage.

Kolankiewicz, George 1973, 'The Working Class', in *Social Groups in Polish Society*, edited by D. Lane and G. Kolankiewicz, New York: Columbia University Press.

—— 1981, 'Renewal, Reform or Retreat: The Polish Communist Party after the Extraordinary Ninth Congress', *The World Today*, 37(10).

Kolankiewicz, George and Paul Lewis 1988, *Poland: Politics, Economics and Society*, London: Pinter Publishers.

Koralewicz, Jadwiga 1987, 'Changes in Polish Social Consciousness during the 1970s and 1980s: Opportunism and Identity', in *Crisis and Transition: Polish Society in the 1980s*, edited by J. Koralewicz, I. Bielecki and M. Watson, Oxford: Berg Publishers.

Koralewicz-Zębik, Jadwiga 1984, 'The Perception of Inequality in Poland, 1956–1980', *Sociology*, 18(2): 225–62.

Korbonski, Andrzej 1983, 'Dissent in Poland', in *Dissent in Eastern Europe*, edited by J. Leftwich Curry, New York: Praeger.

Kowalik, Tadeusz 1983, 'Experts and the Working Group', in *The Birth of Solidarity: The Gdańsk Negotiations, 1980*, edited by A. Kemp-Welch, New York: St. Martin's Press.

Kowalski, Andrzej 1983, 'Prisoners of Conscience', *Uncensored Poland News Bulletin*, 7: 16–19.

Kozłowski, Maciej 1988, 'Regulation No. 42', *Uncensored Poland News Bulletin*, 24: 15–18.

Kramer, Mark 1998, 'Jaruzelski, the Soviet Union and the Imposition of Martial Law in Poland: New Light on the Mystery of December, 1981', *Cold War International History Project Bulletin*, 11: 5–14.

Kriesi, Hanspeter, Ruud Koopmans, Jan Willem Duyvendak and Marco G. Giugni (eds) 1995, *New Social Movements in Western Europe: A Comparative Analysis*, Minneapolis: University of Minnesota Press.

Kubik, Jan 1994a, *The Power of Symbols Against the Symbols of Power*, University Park, PA: Pennsylvania State University Press.

—— 1994b, 'Who Done It: Workers, Intellectuals, or Someone Else? Controversy over Solidarity's Origins and Social Composition', *Theory and Society*, 23: 441–66.

Kuczma, Jozef 1982, 'August, 1980 as I Remember It', in *Sisyphus, Sociological Studies*, (Volume III: Crisis and Conflicts: The Case of Poland, 1980–81), Warsaw: Polish Scientific Publishers.

Kuczyński, Paweł and Krzysztof Nowak 1988, 'The Solidarity Movement in Relation to Society and the State: Communication as an Issue of Social Movements', *Research in Social Movements, Conflict and Change*, 10: 127–45.

Kulerski, Wiktor 1983, 'Are We Going to Survive? A Conversation with Wiktor Kulerski', *Uncensored Poland News Bulletin*, 20: 34–7.

Kuroń, Jacek 1977, 'Reflections on a Program of Action', *The Polish Review*, 22: 51–69.

—— 1982a, 'Propositions on Solving an Insoluble Situation', *Uncensored Poland News Bulletin*, 7: 7–13.

—— 1982b, 'Underground Debate on the Future of Solidarity: Kuroń's Open Letter', *Uncensored Poland News Bulletin*, 11: 10.

—— 1985, 'Jacek Kuroń on the Popieluszko Affair: Crime and Politics', *Uncensored Poland News Bulletin*, 1: 17–22.

—— 1987, 'Jacek Kuroń: Patience and Perseverance Will Not Suffice', *Uncensored Poland News Bulletin*, 1: 27–30.

—— 1990, *Wiara i Wina: Do i Od Komunizmu* [Faith and Guilt: To and From Communism], Warsaw: Biblioteka Kwartalnika Krytyka.

Kuroń, Jacek and Karol Modzelewski 1967, 'A Revolutionary Socialist Manifesto', London: Pluto Press.

Kusmierek, Józef 1983, 'Things I Have Known', in *Poland: Genesis of a Revolution*, edited by A. Brumberg, New York: Vintage.

Kwitny, Jonathan 1997, *Man of the Century: The Life and Times of Pope John Paul II*, New York: Henry Holt and Company.

L. Jan 1983 'The First Anniversary of Civil Resistance Groups/KOS', UPBN, 4 (February 25): 15–18.

Laba, Roman 1986, 'Worker Roots of Solidarity', *Problems of Communism*, July–August: 47–67.

—— 1991, *Worker Roots of Solidarity: A Political Sociology of Poland's Working Class Democratization*, Princeton, NJ: Princeton University Press.

Labedz, Leopold (ed.) 1980, *Survey: A Journal of East and West Studies*, 25(1): 3–18.

Lamentowicz, Wojciech 1982, 'Swedish TV Interview with Professor Wojciech Lamentowicz', *Uncensored Poland News Bulletin*, 6: 23–5.

Lane, David 1973, 'The Role of Social Groups', in *Social Groups in Polish Society*, edited by D. Lane and G., New York: Columbia University Press.

Latynski, Maja 1984, 'The Church: Between State and Society', *Poland Watch*, 5: 12–23.

Lechowicz, Leszek 1982, 'The Mass Media Under Martial Law', *Poland Watch*, 1: 41–50.

Lepak, Keith John 1988, *Prelude to Solidarity: Poland and the Politics of the Gierek Régime*, New York: Columbia University Press.

Leslie, R.F. (ed.) 1980, *The History of Poland Since 1863*, New York: Cambridge University Press.

Lewis, Flora 1958, *A Case History of Hope*, Garden City, NY: Doubleday.

Lipski, Jan Jozef 1985a, 'Interview with Dr. Jan Jozef Lipski on KOPPs', *Uncensored Poland News Bulletin*, 2: 30–1.

—— 1985b, *KOR: A History of the Workers' Defense Committee in Poland, 1976–1981*, translated by O. Amsterdamska and G.M. Moore, Berkeley: University of California Press.

Lis, Bogdan 1982a, 'Bogdan Lis's Speech in Gdansk, 31 August, 1982', *Uncensored Poland News Bulletin*, 17: 4–6.

—— 1982b, 'Is Another August Possible?' [Interview with Bodan Lis], *Committee of Solidarity Reports*, 6: 17–19.

—— 1984, 'Interview with Bogdan Lis for *Free Labor World*', *Uncensored Poland News Bulletin*, 12: 24–8.

Lopinski, Maciej, Marcin Moskit and Mariusz Wilk 1990, *Konspira: Solidarity Underground*, Berkeley, CA: University of California Press.

Machcewicz, Pawel 1996, 'Ostatnie Powstanie', in *Poznański Czerwiec w Świadomosci i Historii*, edited by Andrzej Borny, Poznań: Wydawnictwo WiS.

Maciejewski, Jarosław 1981, 'Po Dwudziestu Pieciu Latach', in *Poznański Czerwiec 1956*, edited by J. Maciejewski and Z. Tojanowicz, Poznań: Wydawnictwo Poznańskie.

Maciejewski, Jarosław and Zofia Trojanowicz (eds.) 1981, *Poznański Czerwiec 1956*, Poznań: Wydawnictwo Poznańskie.

MacDonald, Oliver 1981, *The Polish August: Documents from the Beginnings of the Polish Workers' Rebellion, Gdańsk, August, 1980*, San Francisco, CA: Ztangi Press.

—— 1983, 'The Polish Vortex: Solidarity and Socialism', *New Left Review*, 139: 5–48.

MacShane, Denis 1981, *Solidarity: Poland's Independent Trade Union*, Nottingham: Spokesman Press.

Majkowski, Władysław 1985, *People's Poland*, Westport, CT: Greenwood Press.

Malara, Jean and Lucien Rey 1952, *Poland: From One Occupation to the Other*, Paris: Editions du Fuseau.

Malinowski, Jan 1984, 'Polish Workers', *International Journal of Sociology*, XIV(Fall): 1–117.

Marer, Paul and Włodzimierz Siwiński (eds) 1988, *Creditworthiness and Reform in Poland: Western and Polish Perspectives*, Bloomington, IN: Indiana University Press.

Markiewicz, Władysław 1974, 'The Evolution of Social and Occupational Status of Intelligentsia in People's Poland', in *Transformations of Social Structure in the USSR and Poland*, edited by M.N. Rutkevitch et al., Warsaw: Institute of Philosophy and Sociology.

Marx, Karl 1960, *The German Ideology*, New York: International Publishers.

Mason, David 1985, *Public Opinion and Political Change in Poland, 1980–1982*, New York: Cambridge University Press.

Matejko, Alexander 1971, 'The Executive in Present Day Poland', *The Polish Review*, XVI(3): 32–58.

—— 1972, 'From Peasant to Worker in Poland', *East Europe*, 21(6).

—— 1973, 'The Industrial Workers', in *Gierek's Poland*, edited by A. Bromke and J.W. Strong, New York: Praeger.

—— 1982, 'The Structural Roots of Polish Opposition', *The Polish Review*, 27: 112–40.

Matyja, Stanisław 1981, 'Działaliśmy Jawnie I Głośno', in *Poznański Czerwiec 1956*, edited by J. Maciejewski and Z. Tojanowicz, Poznań: Wydawnictwo Poznańskie.

McAdam, Doug 1986, *Freedom Summer*, Oxford: Oxford University Press.

McAdam, Doug, John D. McCarthy, Mayer N. Zald 1988, 'Social Movements', in *Handbook of Sociology*, edited by N. Smelser, Beverly Hills, CA: Sage.

—— (eds) 1996, *Comparative Perspectives on Social Movements*, Cambridge: Cambridge University Press.

Michalski, Francis 1986, 'The Rise of a Political Opposition in Poland', *Poland Watch*, 8: 94–5.

Michnik, Adam 1993, *The Church and the Left*, edited and translated by D. Ost, Chicago, IL: University of Chicago Press.

—— 1982, 'The Polish War', *Poland Watch*, 1: 92–101.

Mieczkowski, Bogdan 1975, *Personal and Social Consumption in Eastern Europe: Poland, Hungary and East Germany*, New York: Praeger.

Mihalyi, Peter 1988, 'Common Patterns and Particularities in Eastern European Business Cycles', *Soviet Studies*, XL(3): 444–59.

Mills, Charles Wright 2000, *The Sociological Imagination*, Oxford: Oxford University Press.

Misztal, Barbara and Bronisław Misztal 1984, 'The Transformation of Political Elites', in *Polish Politics: Edge of the Abyss*, edited by J. Bielasiak and M.D. Simon, New York: Praeger.

Moi, Anna and Paweł Hoffer 1988, 'Gdansk and the Shipyard after the Strike', *Uncensored Poland News Bulletin*, 11: 14.

Morris, Aldon 1984, *The Origins of the Civil Rights Movement*, New York: The Free Press.

Mur, Jan date unknown *Dziennik Internowanego*, reprinted in Wałęsa 1987.

Najduchowska, Halina 1972, 'Polish Workers and Party Leaders Confrontation', *New Left Review*, I/73: 35–53.

Nanowski, Jarosław 1984, 'Rural Solidarity: An Interview with Jarosław Nanowski', *Poland Watch*, 5.

Niklewicz, Piotr 1983, 'Political Trials Since the Suspension of Martial Law', *Poland Watch*, 3: 11–19.

Norr, Henry 1985, 'Solidarity and Self-Management, May–July, 1981', *Poland Watch*, 7: 97–122.

Nowak, Edward 1985, 'An Interview on Krakow KOPP (Citizen's Initiative Against Violence)', *Uncensored Poland News Bulletin*, 8: 14–16.

Nowak, Stefan 1981, 'Values and Attitudes of the Polish People', *Scientific American*, 245(1): 45–53.

Nuti, Domenico Mario 1982, 'The Polish Crisis: Economic Factors and Constraints', in *Crisis in the East European Economy: The Spread of the Polish Disease*, edited by J. Drewnowski, New York: St. Martin's Press.

Oberschall, Anthony 1973, *Social Conflict and Social Movements*, Englewood Cliffs, NJ: Prentice-Hall.

Olson, Mancur 1977, *The Logic of Collective Action: Public Goods and the Theory of Groups*, Cambridge, MA: Harvard University Press.

Onyszkiewicz, Janusz 1989, '*Konfrontacje's* Interview with Janusz Onyszkiewicz', *Uncensored Poland News Bulletin*, 2: 16–18.

Orum, Anthony 1972, *Black Students in Protest*, Washington, DC: American Sociological Association.

Orwell, George 1952, *Homage to Catalonia*, New York: Harcourt.

Osa, Maryjane 1997, 'Creating Solidarity: The Religious Foundations of the Polish Social Movement', *East European Politics and Societies*, 11(2): 339–65.

Ost, David 1982–3, 'November 1982: Opposition at a Turning Point', *Poland Watch*, 2: 70–84.

—— 1990, *Solidarity and the Politics of Anti-Politics: Opposition and Reform in Poland Since 1968*, Philadelphia, PA: Temple University Press.

—— 2006, *The Defeat of Solidarity: Anger and Politics in Postcommunist Europe*, Ithaca, NY: Cornell University Press.

Paczkowski, Andrzej 2003, *The Spring Will Be Ours: Poland and the Poles From Occupation to Freedom*, University Park, PA: Pennsylvania State University Press.

Paczkowski, Andrzej and Malcolm Byrne 2007, *From Solidarity to Martial Law: The Polish Crisis of 1980–1981, A Documentary History*, New York: CEU Press.

Pawełczyńska, Anna and Stefan Nowak 1962, 'Social Opinions of Students in the Period of Stabilization', *Polish Perspectives*, 5: 38–50.

Pawelec, W. 1981, 'Seventeen Hot Days', *Sisyphus Sociological Studies*, (Volume III: Crisis and Conflicts: The Case of Poland, 1980–81), Warsaw: Polish Scientific Publishers.

Pelczynski, Zbigniew A. 1973, 'The Downfall of Gomułka', in *Gierek's Poland*, edited by A. Bromke and J.W. Strong, New York: Praeger.

—— 1980a, 'The October Turning Point', in *The History of Poland since 1863*, edited by R.F. Leslie, Cambridge: Cambridge University Press.

—— 1980b, 'The Little Stabilization', in *The History of Poland since 1863*, edited by R.F. Leslie, New York: Cambridge University Press.

—— 1980c, 'The Rise and Ebb of Stalinism', in *The History of Poland since 1863*, edited by R.F. Leslie, Cambridge: Cambridge University Press.

—— 1988, 'Solidarity and the Rebirth of Civil Society', in *Civil Society and the State*, edited by J.H. Keane, London: Verso.

Perlez, Jane 1997, 'Warsaw Journal: Old Cold War Enemies Exhume One Battlefield', *New York Times*, 11 November.

Persky, Stan 1981, *At the Lenin Shipyard: Poland and the Rise of the Solidarity Trade Union*, Vancouver: New Star Books.

Persky, Stan and Henry Flam (eds) 1982, *The Solidarity Sourcebook*, Vancouver: New Star Books.

Poland Watch Center 1982a, 'Notes from an Internment Camp', *Poland Watch*, 1: 24–8.

—— 1982b, 'Loyalty Declarations', *Poland Watch*, 1: 88–91.

—— 1982c, 'The Everyday Reality of Martial Law', *Poland Watch*, 2: 114–18.

Polish Helsinki Watch Committee 1981, *Prologue to Gdansk: A Report on Human*

Rights by the Polish Helsinki Watch Committee.

Popiełuszko, Father Jerzy 1983, 'Father Jerzy Popiełuszko's Sermon, August 28, 1983', *Uncensored Poland News Bulletin*, 20: 30–1.

Potel, Jean-Yves 1981, *The Promise of Solidarity*, New York: Praeger.

—— 1982a, *The Summer before the Frost: Solidarność in Poland*, translated by Phil Markham, London: Pluto Press.

—— 1982b, *Polish Dissident Publications: An Annotated Bibliography*, New York: Praeger.

Powiorski, Jan 1983, 'The Poles of '81: Public Opinion on the Eve of Martial Law', *Poland Watch*, 3: 109–132.

Pravda, Alex 1983, 'The Workers', in *Poland: Genesis of a Revolution*, edited by A. Brumberg, New York: Vintage.

Press, Eyal 1998, 'The Archive Eaters: A New Generation of Scholars Sinks its Teeth into the Cold War's Leftovers', *Lingua Franca*, 8(3): 59–67.

Raina, Peter 1978, *Political Opposition in Poland, 1954–1977*, London: Poets' and Painters' Press.

—— 1980, 'Solidarity and KOR: An Interview With Gdańsk Leaders', *Labour Focus on Eastern Europe*, London: 13–15

—— 1980, 'Report on the State of the Republic', *Survey: A Journal of East and West Studies*, 25: 3–18.

—— 1981, *Independent Social Movements in Poland*, London: Poets' and Painters' Press.

—— 1982, "Who Has Made Agreement Possible?" in *Uncensored Poland*, no. 1, 1982, 9.

—— 1982, "Solidarity Underground: Secret Factory Commissions" in *Uncensored Poland News Bulletin* no. 18, October 1: 12–13.

Rakowski, Mieczysław F. 1988, 'Mieczysław Rakowski's Candid Thoughts', *Uncensored Poland News Bulletin*, 10: 17–18.

—— 1973, 'December, 1970: The Turning Point', in *Gierek's Poland*, edited by A. Bromke and J.W. Strong, New York: Praeger.

—— 'Why Was it Poland?', unpublished manuscript.

Rex, John (ed.) 1987, *Crisis and Transition: Polish Society in the 1980s*, New York: Berg Publishers Limited.

Reynolds, Jaime 1978, 'Communists, Socialists and Workers: Poland, 1944–1948', in *Soviet Studies*, 30(4): 516–30.

'Rocznik Statistyczyny 1990, Warsaw: Central Statistical Office.

Rolicki, Janusz 1990, *Edward Gierek, Przerwana Dekada*, Warsaw: Wydawnictwo FAKT.

Romaszewski, Zbigniew 1982a, 'Get Ready for General Strike', *Uncensored Poland News Bulletin*, 13: 11–14.

—— 1982b, 'August, 1980, December, 1982: What Next? PART I', *Uncensored Poland News Bulletin*, 12: 21–31.

Roos, Hans 1966, *A History of Modern Poland*, New York: Alfred A. Knopf.

Rosenberg, Tina 1993, 'Meet the New Boss, Same as the Old Boss', *Harper's*, 286: 47–53.

Ruffin, Holt and Lech Choroszucha (eds.) 1989, *Wolność i Pokój (WiP): Documents of Poland's 'Freedom and Peace' Movement*, Seattle, WA: World Without War Council.

Rulewski, Jan 1984, 'Interview with Jan Rulewski, One of Solidarity Eleven', *Uncensored Poland News Bulletin*, 19: 18–21.

Rupnik, Jacques 1979, 'Dissent in Poland, 1968–78: The End of Revisionism and the Rebirth of Civil Society', in *Opposition in Eastern Europe*, edited by R.L. Tolkes, Baltimore, MD: John Hopkins University Press.

Rutkevitch, M.N., W. Wesołowski, V.S. Semyonov, M. Jarosińska, V.V. Kolbansky (eds.) 1974, *Transformations of Social Structure in the USSR and Poland*, Warsaw: Institute of Philosophy and Sociology, Polish Academy of Sciences.

Sakwa, George 1977, 'The Polish "October": A Re-appraisal through Historiography', *The Polish Review*, 23(3): 62–78.

Sanford, George 1983, *Polish Communism in Crisis*, New York: St. Martin's Press.

—— 1986, *Military Rule in Poland: The Rebuilding of Communist Power, 1981–1983*, New York: St. Martin's Press.

Sierpiński, Zdzisław 1982, 'Journalist Explains Why He Will Not Submit to Verification', *Uncensored Poland News Bulletin*, 6: 14–16.

Simon, Maurice D. and Roger E. Kanet (eds.) 1981, *Background to Crisis: Policy and Politics in Gierek's Poland*, Boulder, CO: Westview Press.

Singer, Daniel 1981, *The Road to Gdansk: Poland and the USSR*, New York: Monthly Review Press.

Siwiński, Włodzimierz 1988, 'Why Poland Lost its Creditworthiness', in *Creditworthiness and Reform in Poland: Western and Polish Perspectives*, edited by P. Marer and W. Siwiński, Bloomington, IN: Indiana University Press.

Słomczyński, Kazimierz M. and Tadeusz K. Krauze 1986, 'Introduction: The Background of Recent Polish Research on Social Stratification', in *Social Stratification in Poland: Eight Empirical Studies*, New York: M.E. Sharpe, Inc.

—— 1986, *Social Stratification in Poland: Eight Empirical Studies*, New York: M.E. Sharpe, Inc.

Słomczyński, Kazimierz M. and Wlodzimierz Wesołowski 1977, 'Transformations of Social Structure and its Perceptions', paper presented at the Congress of the Polish Sociological Association, Krakow.

Smelser, Neil J. 2010, *Reflections on the University of California: From the Free Speech Movement to the Global University*, Berkeley, CA: University of California Press.

Smith, Craig S. 2007a, 'In Poland, New Wave of Charges Against Clerics', *New York Times*, 10 January.

—— 2007b, 'New Warsaw Archbishop Resigns Over Communist Collaboration', *New York Times*, 8 January.

Smolar, Aleksander 1983, 'The Rich and the Powerful', in *Poland: Genesis of a Revolution*, edited by A. Brumberg, New York: Vintage.

Staniszkis, Jadwiga 1983, 'The Self-Limiting Revolution: An Interview with Jadwiga Staniszkis', *Poland Watch*, 3: 85–94.

—— 1984, *Poland's Self-Limiting Revolution*, edited by J.T. Gross, Princeton, NJ: Princeton University Press.

Stefancic, David R. 1992, *Robotnik: A Short History of the Struggle for Worker Self-Management and Free Trade Unions in Poland, 1944–1981*, New York: Columbia University Press.

Stefanowski, Roman 1976, 'Mechanization in Agriculture', *Radio Free Europe Research*, RAD Background Report/127, 4 June.

Stelmachowski, Andrzej 1988, 'A Turning Point? An Interview with Professor Stelmachowski', *Uncensored Poland News Bulletin*, 18: 13–16.

Sulek, Antoni 1990, 'The Polish United Workers' Party: From Mobilisation to Non-Representation', *Soviet Studies*, 42(3): 499–511.

Syrop, Konrad 1976, *Spring in October: The Story of the Polish Revolution, 1956*, Westport, CT: Greenwood Press.

Szajkowski, Bogdan 1983, *Next to God... Poland: Politics and Religion in Contemporary Poland*, New York: St. Martin's Press.

Szczęsiak, Edmund 1982, 'Notes on Biography', in *The Book of Lech Wałęsa*, London: Allen Lane.

Szczypiorski, Andrzej 1982, *The Polish Ordeal: The View from Within*, London: Droom Helm.

Szejnert, Małgorzata and Tomasz Zalewski 1986, *Szczecin, Grudzień-Sierpień-Grudzień*, London: Aneks.

Szelenyi, Ivan 1978, 'Social Inequalities in State Socialist Redistributive Economies', *International Journal of Comparative Sociology*, 19(1–2): 64–82.

Szulc, Tad 1995, *Pope John Paul II: The Biography*, New York: Scribner.

Talbott, Strobe (ed.) 1971, *Khrushchev Remembers*, New York: Bantam Books, Inc.

Tarkowski, Jacek 1981, 'Patrons and Clients in a Planned Economy', in *Political Clientelism, Patronage and Development*, edited by S.N. Eisenstadt and René Lemarchand, Beverly Hills, CA: Sage.

—— 1983, 'Patronage in a Centralized Socialist System: The Case of Poland', *International Political Science Review*, 4(4): 495–518.

Tarrow, Sidney 1993, *Power in Movement: Social Movements and Contentious Politics*, (2nd edition), Cambridge: Cambridge University Press.

Terlecki, Marian 1983, 'Days in the Underground Life of a Wanted Man', *Poland Watch*, 4: 83–96.

Terry, Sarah Meikeljohn 1981, 'The Sejm as Symbol: Recent Polish Attitudes Toward Political Participation', in *Background to Crisis: Policy and Politics in Gierek's Poland*, edited by M.D. Simon and R.E. Kanet, Boulder, CO: Westview Press.

Terry, Sarah 1988, 'External Debt and the Polish Leadership', in *Creditworthiness and Reform in Poland: Western and Pol-*

ish Perspectives, edited by P. Marer and W. Siwiński, Bloomington, IN: Indiana University Press.

Tilly, Charles 1999, 'Conclusion: From Interactions to Outcomes in Social Movements', in *How Social Movements Matter*, edited by M.G. Giugni, D. McAdam and C. Tilly, Minneapolis, MN: University of Minnesota Press.

Tolkes, Rudolph L. 1979, *Opposition in Eastern Europe*, Baltimore, MD: John Hopkins University Press.

Torańska, Teresa 1987, *Them: Stalin's Polish Puppets*, New York: Harper and Row.

Touraine, Alain, Francois Dubet, Michel Wieviorka and Jan Strzelecki 1983, *Solidarity: The Analysis of a Social Movement, Poland 1980–1981*, New York: Cambridge University Press.

Tymowski, Andrzej 1982, 'The Underground Debate on Strategy and Tactics', *Poland Watch*, 1: 75–87.

—— 1983, 'Solidarity or a Political Program?', *Poland Watch*, 3: 95–108.

—— 1991, 'Workers vs. Intellectuals in Solidarnosc', *Telos*, 90: 157–75.

Von Eschen, Donald, Jerome Kirk and Maurice Pinard 1971, 'The Organizational Substructure of Disorderly Politics', *Social Forces*, 49: 529–44.

Walendowski, Tadeusz 1982, 'The Polish Church Under Martial Law', *Poland Watch*, 1: 54–63.

Wałęsa, Lech 1987, *A Way of Hope: An Autobiography*, New York: Henry Holt and Company.

—— 1992, *The Struggle and the Triumph*, New York: Arcade Publishing.

—— 2007, 'Forward: From Romanticism to Realism: Our Struggle in the Years 1980–1982', in *From Solidarity to Martial Law: The Polish Crisis of 1980–1981, A Documentary History*, edited by A. Paczkowski and M. Byrne, New York: CEU Press.

Waliszewski, Leszek 1983, 'Solidarity in Silesia: An Interview with Leszek Waliszewski', *Poland Watch*, 4: 46.

Warecki, Stanisław 1982–3, 'The Landscape After the Battle', *Poland Watch*, 2: 118–24.

Warszawski, David [Konstanty Gebert] 1984, 'The Strategy of Provocation', *Uncensored Poland News Bulletin*, 2: 20–2.

—— 1988, 'The August Party Plenum', *Uncensored Poland News Bulletin*, 18: 12–13.

—— 1989a, 'The Party: Which Way Now?', *Uncensored Poland News Bulletin*, 1: 22–3.

—— 1989b, 'Who Is and Who Is Not on the "National List?"', *Uncensored Poland News Bulletin*, 9: 11.

Wasilewska, Anita 1982, 'War and Justice', *Poland Watch*, 1: 29–40.

Wasilewski, Jacek and Edmund Wnuk-Lipiński 1995, 'Poland: Winding Road from the Communist to the Post-Solidarity Elite', *Theory and Society*, 24(5): 669–96.

Wechsler, Lawrence 1989, 'A Grand Experiment', *The New Yorker*, 13 November: 59–104.

Weigel, George 1999, *Witness to Hope: The Biography of Pope John Paul II*, New York: Harper Collins.

Weydenthal, Jan B. de 1971, *The Dynamics of Leadership in the Polish United Workers' Party 1967–1968: A Case Study*, unpublished doctoral dissertation, Notre Dame, IN: University of Notre Dame.

—— 1981, 'Poland: Workers and Politics', in *Blue-collar workers in Eastern Europe*, edited by J.F. Triska and C. Gati, London: George Allen & Unwin.

White, George S. 1982–3, 'Political Trials Under Martial Law', *Poland Watch*, 2: 22–31.

Wilczyński, Józef 1984, 'The Economic Situation in Poland: From Reasonable Past Performance to Stagnation, and Hardships Ahead in a Naturally Well-Endowed Economy', in *Poland in the 80s: Social Revolution Against 'Real Socialism'*, edited by R.F. Miller, occasional paper, Department of Political Science, Research School of Social Science, Australian National University.

Wiślicki, Colonel 1982, 'The Commissar's Counsel', *Committee in Support of Solidarity Reports*, 3: 7–11.

Woźniczka, Zygmunt 2010, *Represje na Górnym Śląsku po 1945 roku*, Katowice: Śląsk.

Wujec, Henryk 1985, 'An Interview with Henryk Wujec', *Uncensored Poland News Bulletin*, 4: 34–8.

Wyszyński, Cardinal 1980, 'Sermon at Jasna Góra Following the Outbreak of Strikes', in *From Solidarity to Martial Law: The Polish Crisis of 1980–1981, A Documentary History*, edited by A. Paczkowski and M. Byrne, New York: CEU Press.

Yakowicz, Joseph 1979, *Poland's Postwar Recovery*, Hicksville, NY: Exposition Press.

Zaborowski, Wojciech 1986, 'Dichotomous Class Images and Worker Radicalism', in *Social Stratification in Poland: Eight Empirical Studies*, edited by K.M. Słomczyński and T.K. Krauze, New York: M.E. Sharpe, Inc.

Zagórski, Krzysztof 1974, 'Changes in Social Structure and Social Mobility in Poland', in *Transformations of Social Structure in the USSR and Poland*, edited by M.N. Rutkevitch et al., Warsaw: Institute of Philosophy and Sociology.

Zagozda, Andrzej 1982, 'Letter from Prison', *Uncensored Poland News Bulletin*, 10: 19–25.

Zald, Mayer N. and Bert Useem 1987, 'Movement and Countermovement Interaction: Mobilization, Tactics and State Involvement', in *Social Movements in an Organizational Society*, edited by M.N. Zald and J.D. McCarthy, New Brunswick, NJ: Transaction Books.

Zielinski, Janusz Z. 1973, *Economic Reforms in Polish Industry*, Oxford: Oxford University Press.

Ziemkowski, Aleksander 1981, 'Próba Chronolognicznej Rekonstrukcji Wydarzeń', in *Poznański Czerwiec 1956*, edited by J. Maciejewski and Z. Tojanowicz, Poznań: Wydawnictwo Poznańskie.

Index

www.ingramcontent.com/pod-product-compliance
Lightning Source LLC
Chambersburg PA
CBHW060019030426

42334CB00019B/2096